I0824164

HISTORIC PHOTOS OF
THE HUDSON LINE

TEXT AND CAPTIONS BY HENRY JOHN STEINER

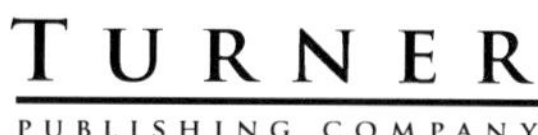

A steam locomotive makes its way up the east bank of the Harlem River en route toward Spuyten Duyvil. The Washington Bridge beneath which the train passes opened on December 1, 1888. Today, the area under the right arch is mainly occupied by the Major Deagan Expressway—Interstate 87.

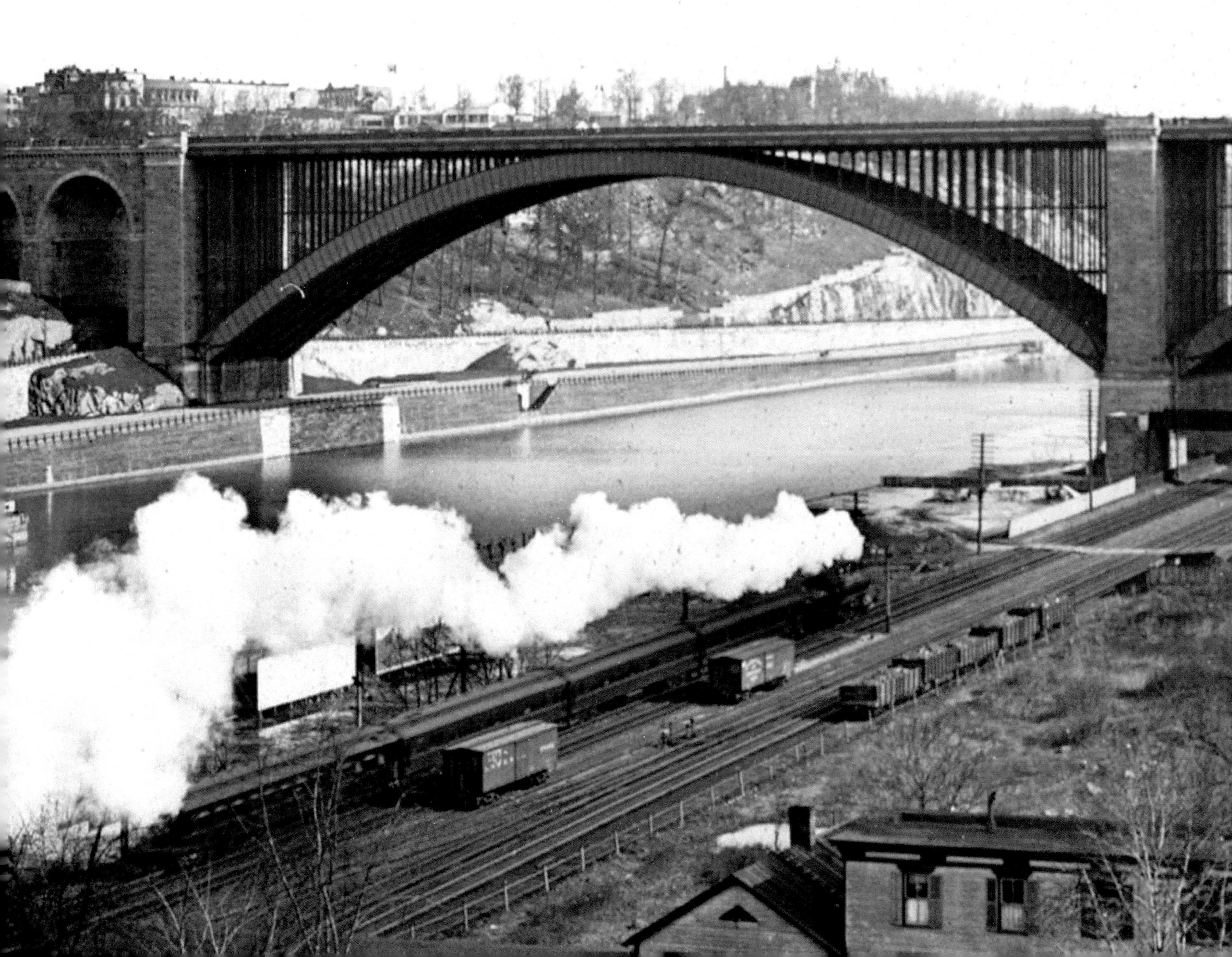

HISTORIC PHOTOS OF
THE HUDSON LINE

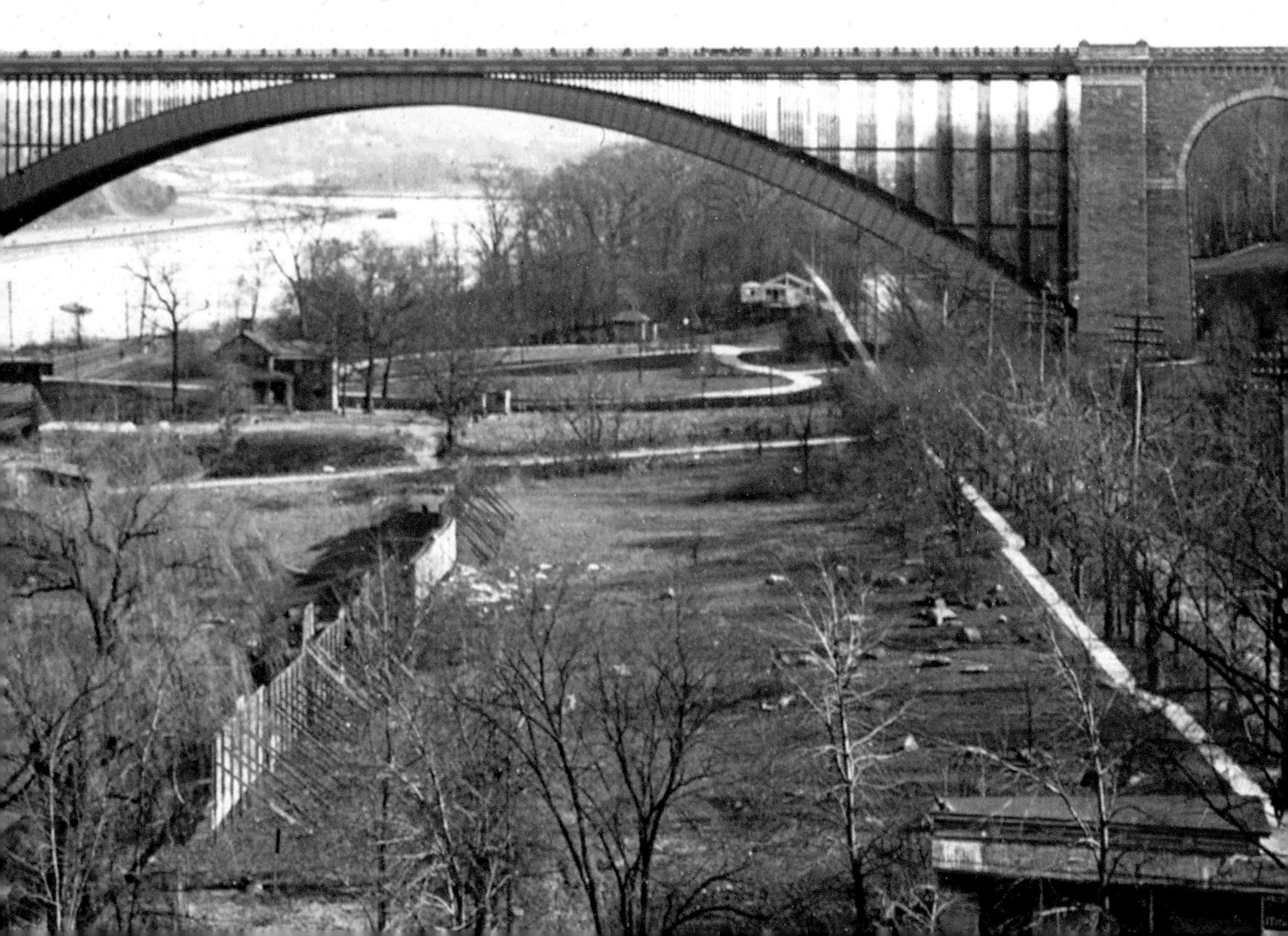

Turner Publishing Company
200 4th Avenue North • Suite 950
Nashville, Tennessee 37219
(615) 255-2665

www.turnerpublishing.com

Historic Photos of the Hudson Line

Library of Congress Control Number: 2009922655

ISBN: 978-1-59652-543-6

Printed in the United States of America

09 10 11 12 13 14—0 9 8 7 6 5 4 3 2 1

Contents

Acknowledgments vii

Preface viii

Lost Tranquillity and a Changing Shoreline (1853–1899) 1

Civic Pride and Civic Projects (1900–1920) 49

Through Roaring Times and Ruined (1921–1940) 117

The War Years and Postwar Era (1941–1960s) 165

Notes on the Photographs 199

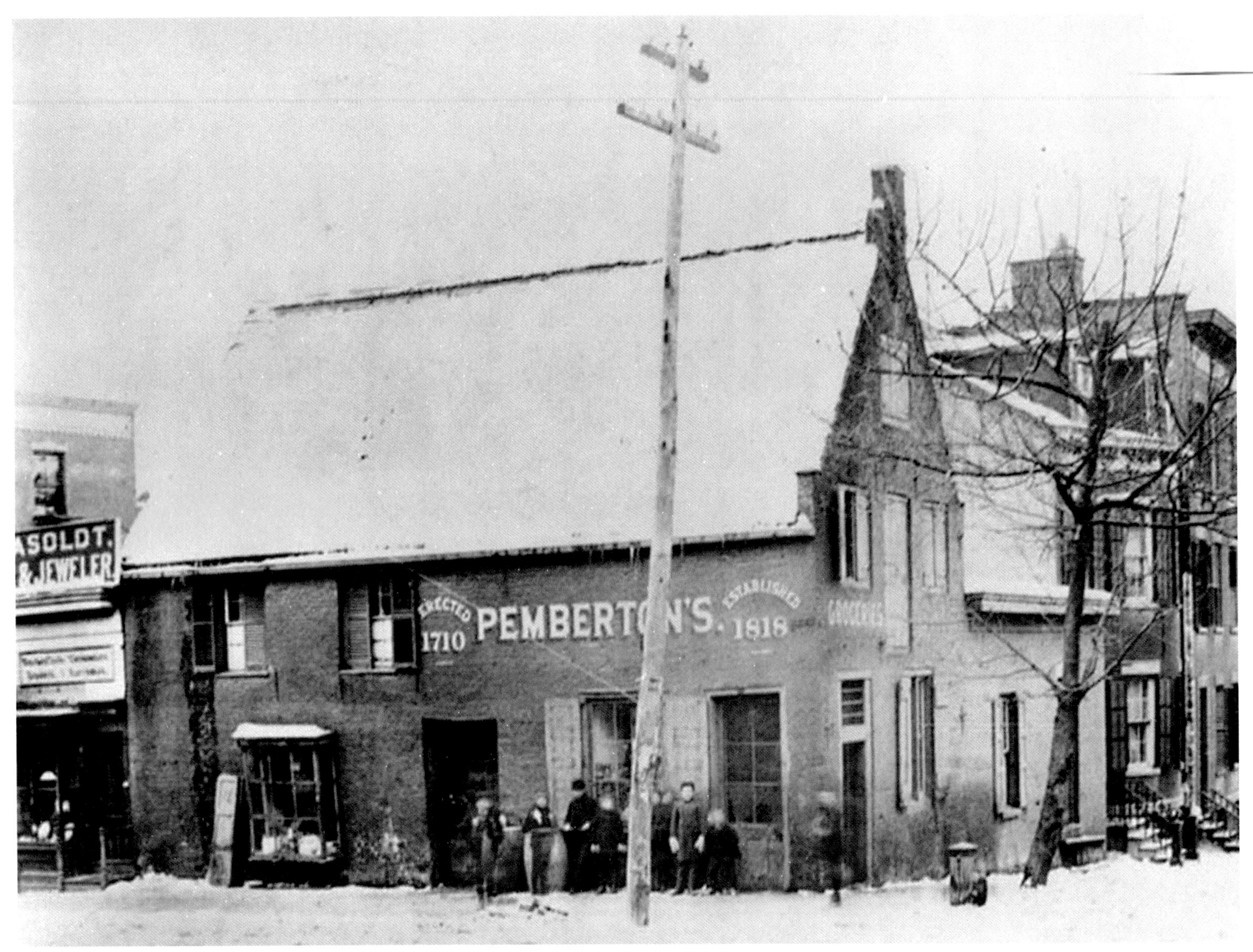

The Lansing-Pemberton House on North Pearl and Columbia streets in Albany. Erected in 1710, the structure survived into the early twentieth century, when it was demolished. The Hudson Line linked Albany in the north and New York City to the south with towns and communities situated beside the Hudson River and its vicinity, through which the line passed.

Acknowledgments

This volume, *Historic Photos of the Hudson Line,* is the result of the cooperation and efforts of many individuals and organizations. It is with great thanks that we acknowledge the valuable contribution of the following for their generous support:

The Library of Congress
The New York Public Library
The New York State Archives

Historic Photos of the Hudson Line would not have been possible without the collective efforts of many photographers, collectors, librarians, and curators, most of them anonymous. With respect to the text of this volume, particularly to be acknowledged are the contributions of Lucie Rohan Steiner, who assisted with research and provided the selections dealing with aviator Glenn Hammond Curtiss. Darla Kohler made valuable contributions and suggestions regarding the text. Andrew Arpey of the New York State Archives gave very helpful assistance interpreting some of the historic scenes of Albany. Former Westchester County legislator, John P. O'Leary, kindly shared useful information about his hometown of Yonkers. Staci Swedeen and Jim Capossela gave valuable advice in the planning stages of the project. The author's photo was taken by Donna Cris Caivano.

Preface

The photographs presented here document not only the Hudson River's timeless beauty, but also the progress of the communities that grew up beside the river. Between 1850 and 1970, the years represented here, the Hudson Valley was greatly changed by the Industrial Revolution. The region's products and influence were dispersed throughout the United States. In the twentieth century, America continued to move steadily toward world industrial and political ascendancy, and New York City, its grand emporium, became the financial center of the world.

The communities of the Hudson River Line have long been influenced by two main factors, their proximity to the great river and their connection to the great city—the commercial and cultural center of Manhattan. The river and the city have shaped those river towns from colonial times, when they were almost nameless rural destinations. Once, they were the precincts of the Native American, the fur-trader, the plantation owner, and the tenant farmer, but circumstances marked them for rapid change.

In short time, the early Hudson River landings grew into commercial, manufacturing, and political centers of their own. The communities became part of the interwoven fabric of the Hudson Valley, and the primary connecting cord was the river itself. In this way, communities on opposite sides of the river, in some cases miles distant, could be more closely connected than neighboring towns and villages inland.

Washington Irving wrote half seriously, in 1835, of the changes he saw coming: "The country is suddenly to be deluged with wealth. The late simple farmers are to become bank directors, and drink claret and champagne; and their wives and daughters to figure in French hats and feathers; for French wines and French fashions commonly keep pace with paper money." In Irving's commentary is a note of national pride for America's rising fortunes and perhaps a smile of regret for a quieter, more bucolic life.

The Hudson River sloop, a mute messenger, linking the river communities with Manhattan, brought farm-grown harvests to the city's workers and shopkeepers; on the sloop's return, it carried marvelous comforts, tools, and fashions to villagers and farmers. The quiet of the Hudson River was shattered, first by the steamboat, and then by the even louder percussion of the steam locomotive. In the mid nineteenth century, the people of Albany and New York City found themselves separated by only about four hours, rather than an uncertain number of days, as in the time of the sloops.

The Hudson River Line tied the river communities closer, like beads on a string, but it is arguable that the blistering pace of the train tied them closer in spirit to Manhattan than to each other. With economic growth came opportunity, and opportunity brought people. Wave after wave of immigration and migration brought new groups of people to the Hudson Valley, from the Irish and Italians, whose hands actually built the Hudson River Line, to African-Americans and immigrants from all lands.

The twentieth century and the age of the automobile saw new roads and new routes between urban and suburban centers and faster ways for the people of Hudson River communities to travel to and interact with one another. Many of the influences that shaped these communities are still imprinted on their twenty-first-century characters. The developments of the modern age have shifted the focus away from the Hudson as a key highway and industrial center. Today, people along the river are considering new ideas of what their communities might become.

—Henry John Steiner

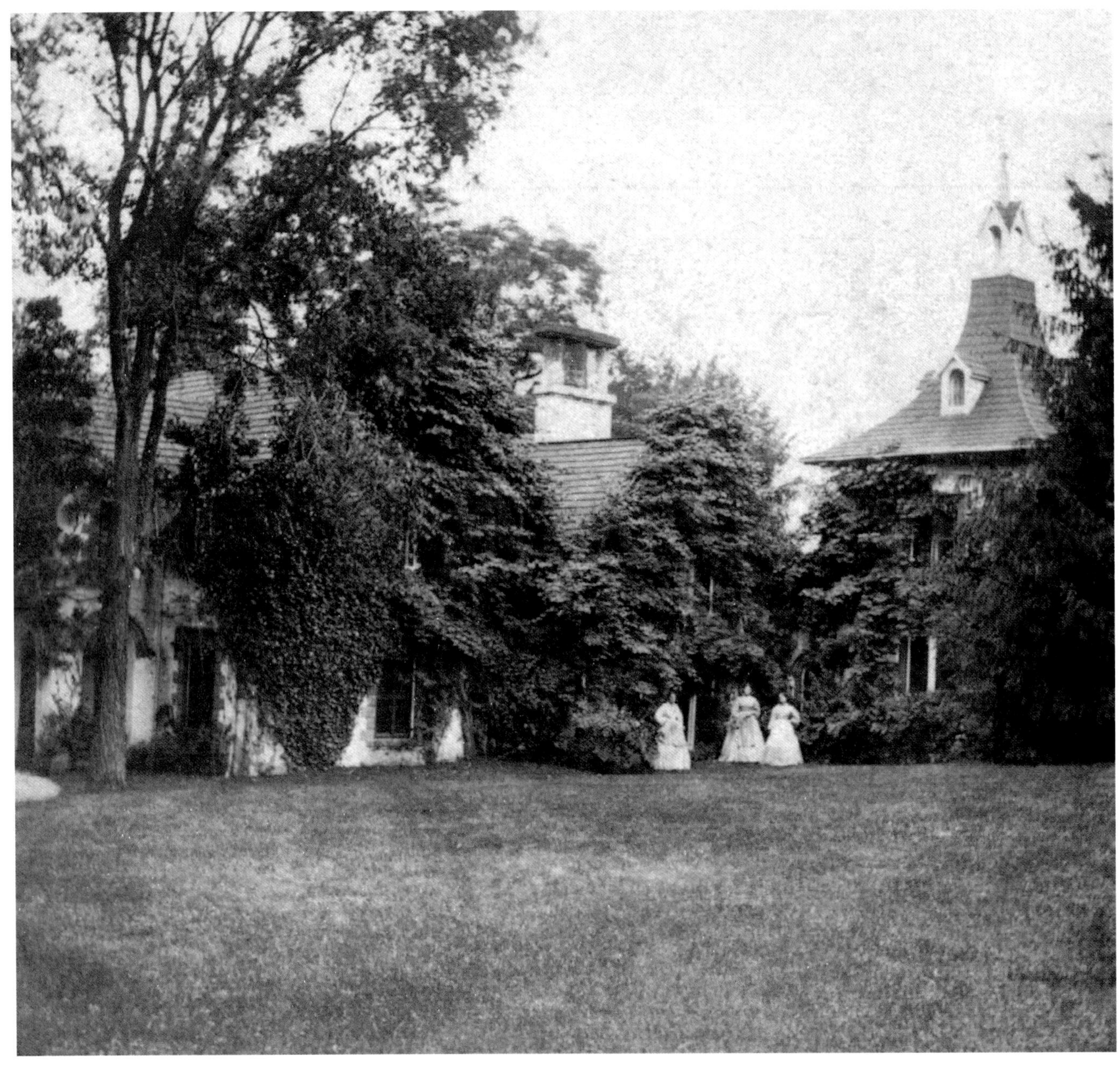

Sunnyside was the small, Hudson River estate of American literary great Washington Irving (1783–1859). The house, at Tarrytown, was built upon an old tenant farmhouse that Irving bought in 1835. His "Wolfert's Roost" is Irving's quasi-historic account of its genesis. Sunnyside is one of the most famous historic houses in America, with its wisteria-covered entry and "Spanish tower." Irving, a bachelor, left the house to his nieces, who continued to reside there after his death.

LOST TRANQUILLITY AND A CHANGING SHORELINE

(1853–1899)

Even as the Hudson River School of artists began to capture the natural beauty of the Hudson Valley, the landscape was on the brink of significant change. The photographer was called upon to document what followed. The train and the steamboat were nearly concurrent inventions of the Industrial Age. Chronologically, the steamboat had the edge—it required no road, and it was not much encumbered by private ownership of land along its route. The Hudson River railroad line, unlike many of the railroads leading west, sought to utilize relatively level shoreline. This choice was to stimulate and accelerate commerce and growth along the Hudson's riverfront communities. Access to Manhattan made for cross-pollination in the arts, engineering, politics, education, business, and architecture. There was an intensifying flow of goods, services, and wealth emanating from Manhattan. The tides of immigration were felt in each river town.

Jessie Benton Fremont was an early, satisfied customer of the Hudson River Line. She and her husband, John C. Fremont, the first Republican candidate for President, had just settled on a Hudson River estate at Sleepy Hollow. "My visiting list for the summer is just twenty-five miles long for the Hudson is a great street and people dine and visit by rail when they are past driving limits." Earlier, Washington Irving was at first very disturbed at how the trains shattered the tranquillity of his waterfront home at Tarrytown. But when the railroad ordered its trains to stop especially for him, the convenience of the railroad soon counterbalanced the noise.

Commodore Cornelius Vanderbilt became the controlling shareholder of the Hudson River Railroad in 1864, the year he decided to forgo steamships for trains. In 1870, the Hudson River Railroad was to become a key part of one of the first great corporations in American history, the New York Central and Hudson River Railroad. Vanderbilt had obtained control of the New York and Harlem, with its Park Avenue route down the center of Manhattan, in 1863. The merger meant that the Hudson River Line could utilize the Harlem Line route into Manhattan by redirecting most of its trains along the Harlem River and finally into Grand Central Depot. This route to Grand Central Terminal is still used today.

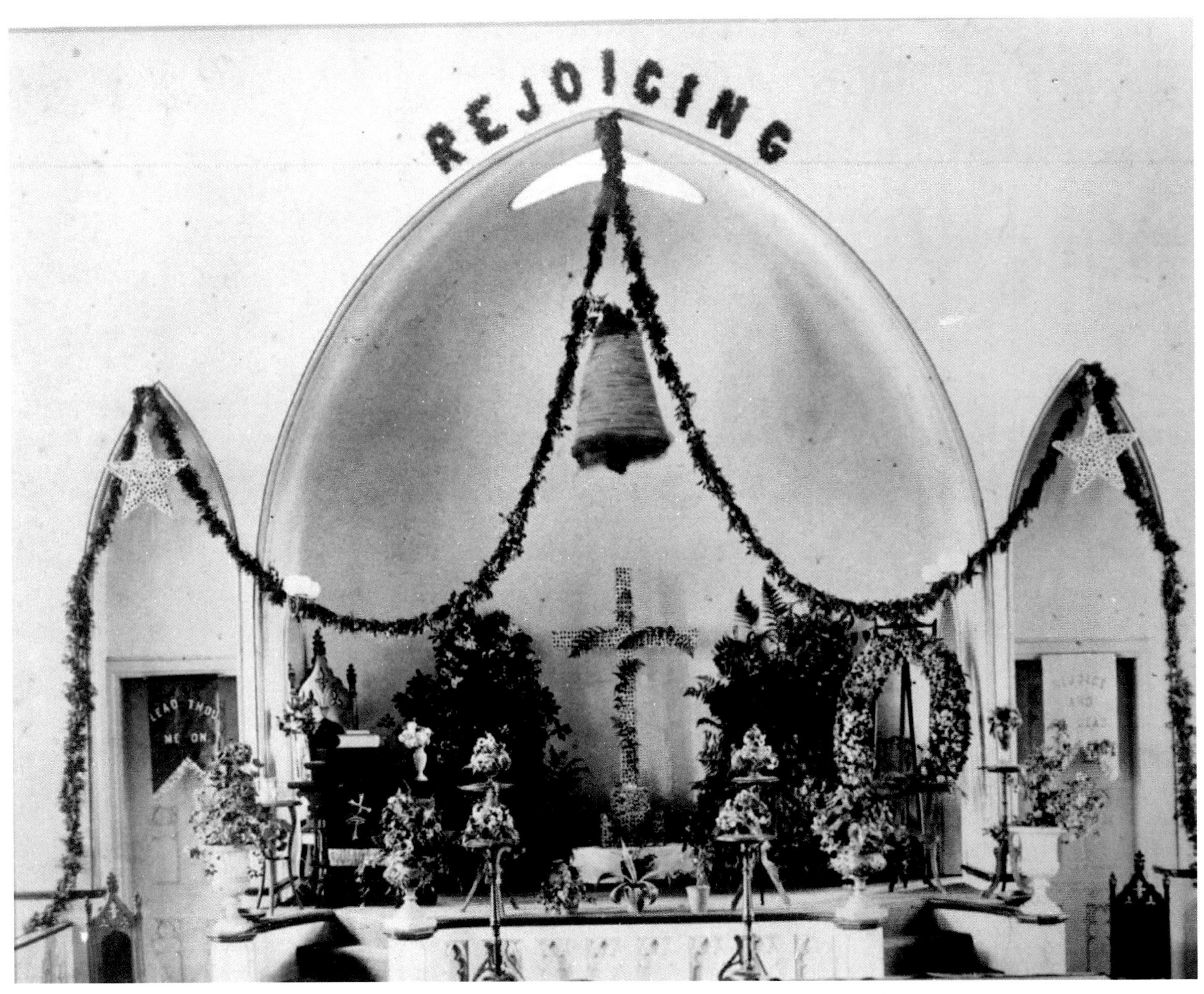

The apse of the Second Reformed Church in Kingston is decorated for Easter Sunday in 1853. Construction on the Gothic Revival structure began in 1850. The church was designed by Thomas Thomas (1817–1888) known as "the first national architect of Wales;" he designed more than 1,000 chapels. The British Army burned Kingston, the first capital of New York State, in 1777, during the Revolutionary War.

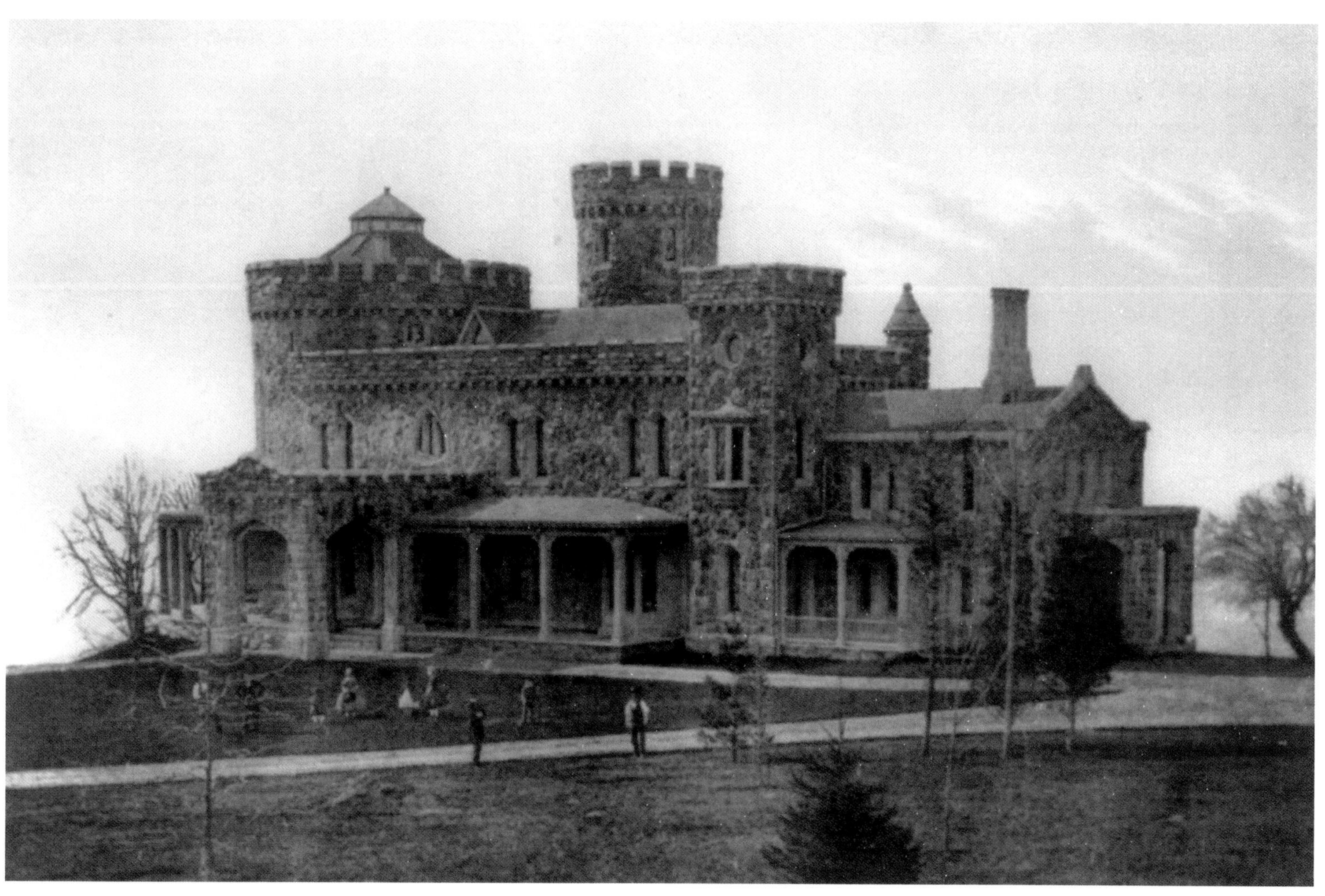

Herrick's Castle in Tarrytown was also known by the name of Herrick's Folly. It is shown here about 1860, in a photolithograph by A. A. Turner. John J. Herrick (d. 1881) was a steamship executive and had the mansion erected between 1854 and 1856. Many Tarrytown locals considered the construction costs a prodigal expense. The residence, also known as Ericstan, later became Miss Mason's Castle School, located near the future site of Marymount College. Herrick's Castle was razed in 1944.

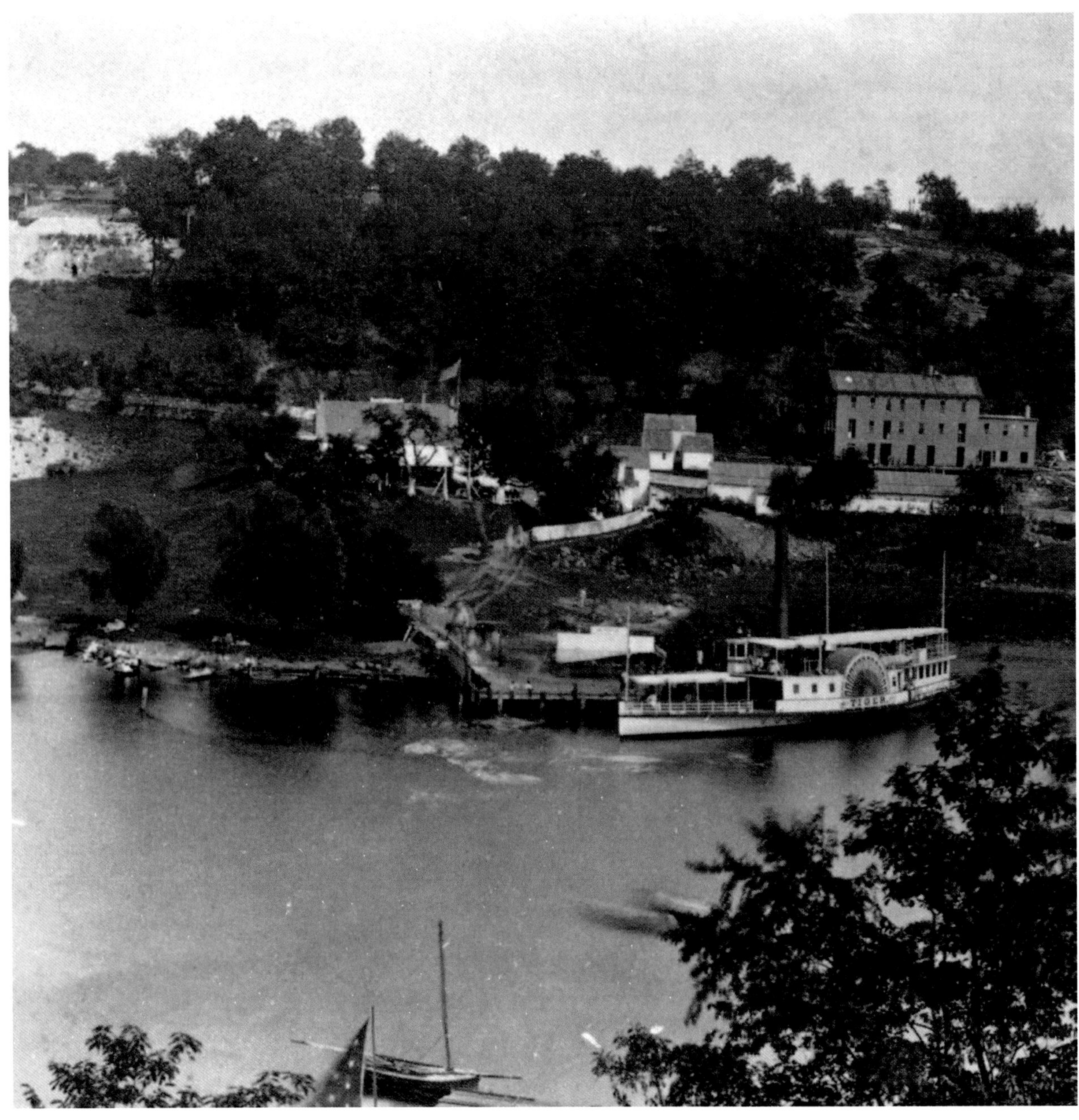

This shot by photography pioneer Charles Wager Hull (d. 1865) shows a steamboat at the north end of Manhattan, around 1862. In that day, elegant hotels were appearing on both sides of the Harlem River to serve weekend tourists up from lower Manhattan. Boathouses also were making an appearance, a sign of the rising popularity of rowing as a sport and pastime.

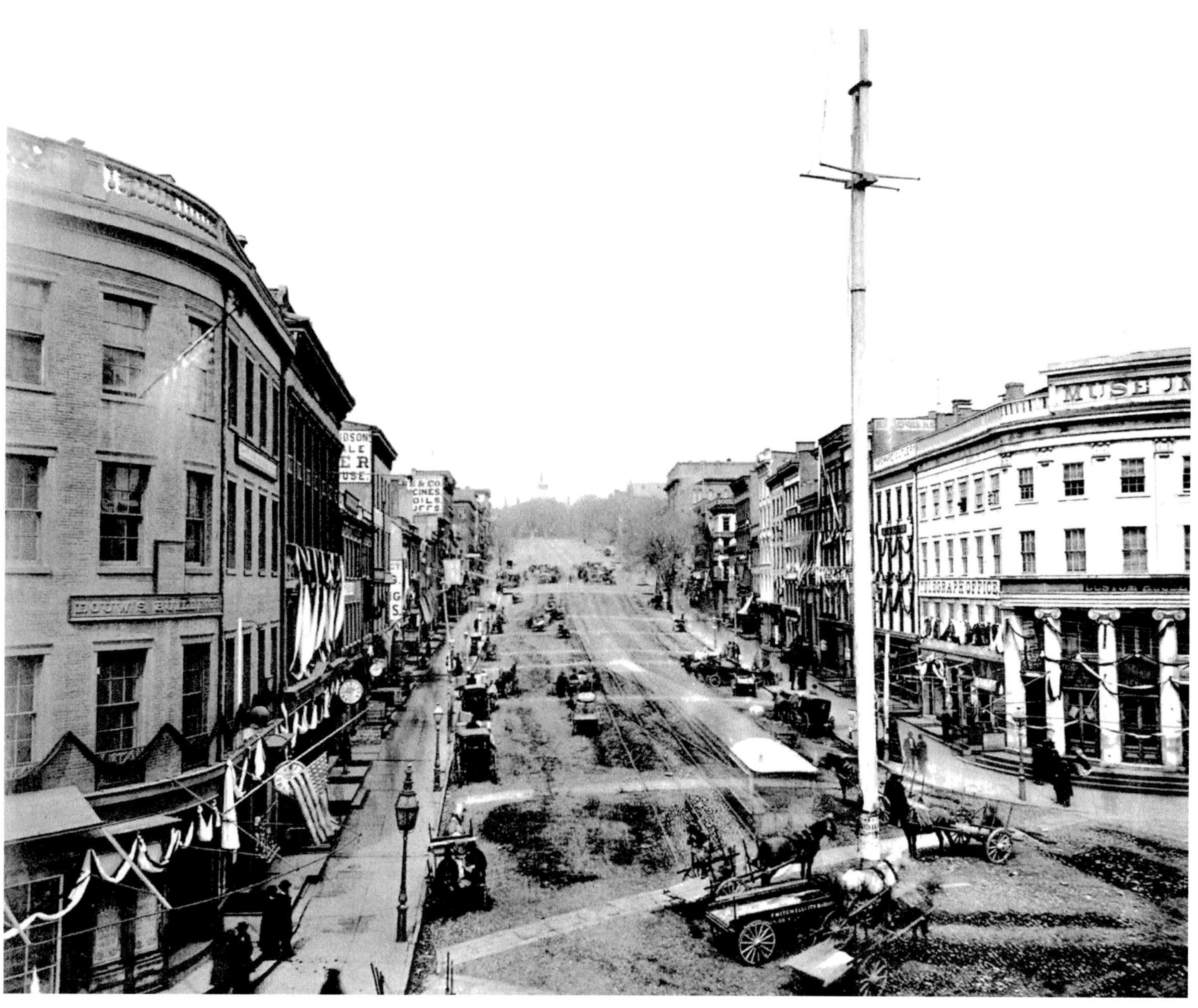

State Street in Albany is draped in mourning for the funeral cortege of President Abraham Lincoln. The Stars and Stripes flies at half-mast to the left of the trolley tracks, which end abruptly at the bottom of the hill. On April 26, 1865, throngs of Albany mourners waited until 1:15 A.M. to view the president's remains in the assembly chamber. The last mourner passed the casket 12 hours later. That afternoon the "Lincoln Special" steamed west.

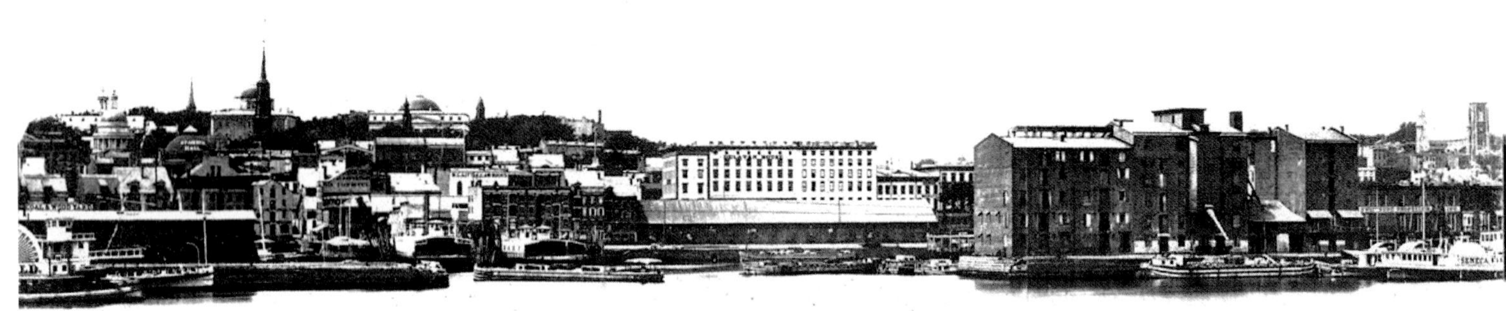

Featured at center is the Delavan House, one of America's first temperance hotels. The building was the project of Edward C. Delavan (1793–1871), a wealthy Albany-based temperance reformer and real estate investor. Fire destroyed the building on December 30, 1894, and by 1900, Union Station had been constructed on the site to serve the traveling public at Albany, the Hudson Line's northern terminus. C. S. Rabineau, a professional photographer later associated with the Eastman Kodak Company, recorded this Albany waterfront panorama in 1869.

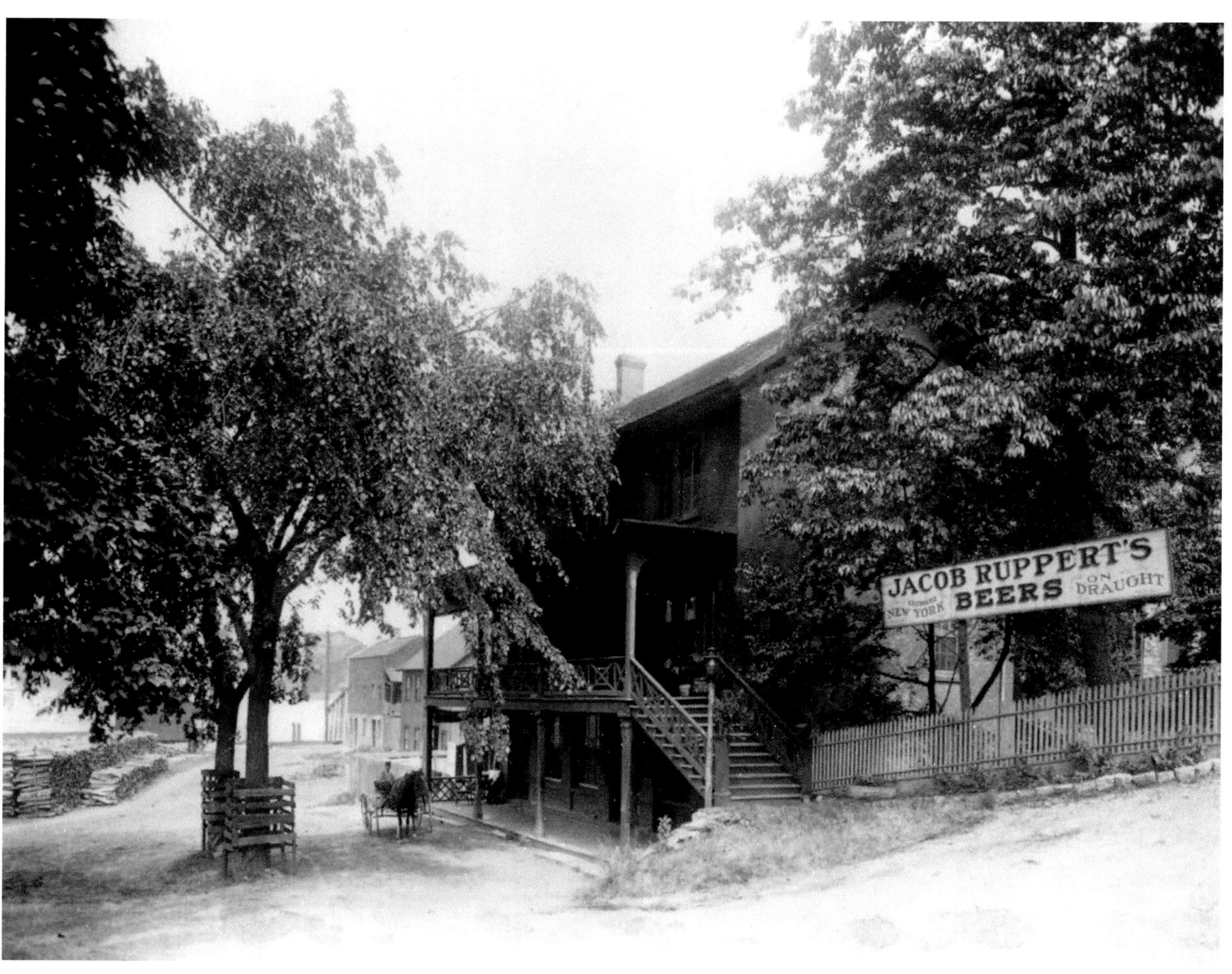

The Garrison Hotel in Garrison, New York, located directly across the Hudson River from West Point, is shown here in the latter half of the nineteenth century. Benedict Arnold lived in Garrison at the time of his treason in 1780. As commander of West Point, General Arnold was rowed daily across the Hudson River to his post at the American fortress. Jacob Ruppert, a leading New York City brewer, advertises his product on the banner at right.

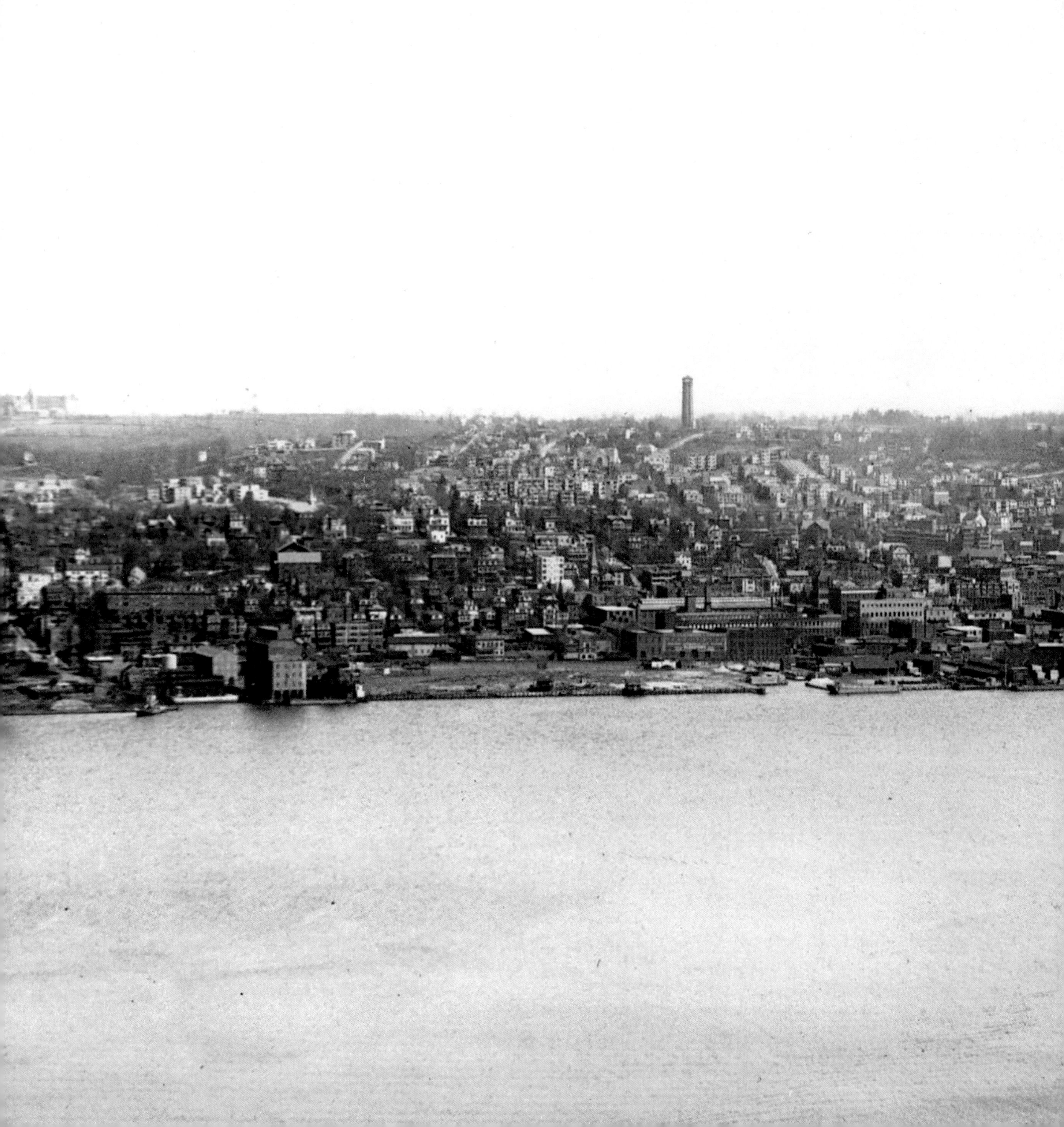

The City of Yonkers grew up from a Dutch plantation of the mid-1600s, situated at the junction of the Saw Mill River and the Hudson. By the late 1800s it was a prosperous industrial center, styled "the city of gracious living." Among its leading manufacturing plants were Otis Elevator Company and Alexander Smith and Sons Carpet Company. This panorama was recorded about midday from the opposite shore of the Hudson.

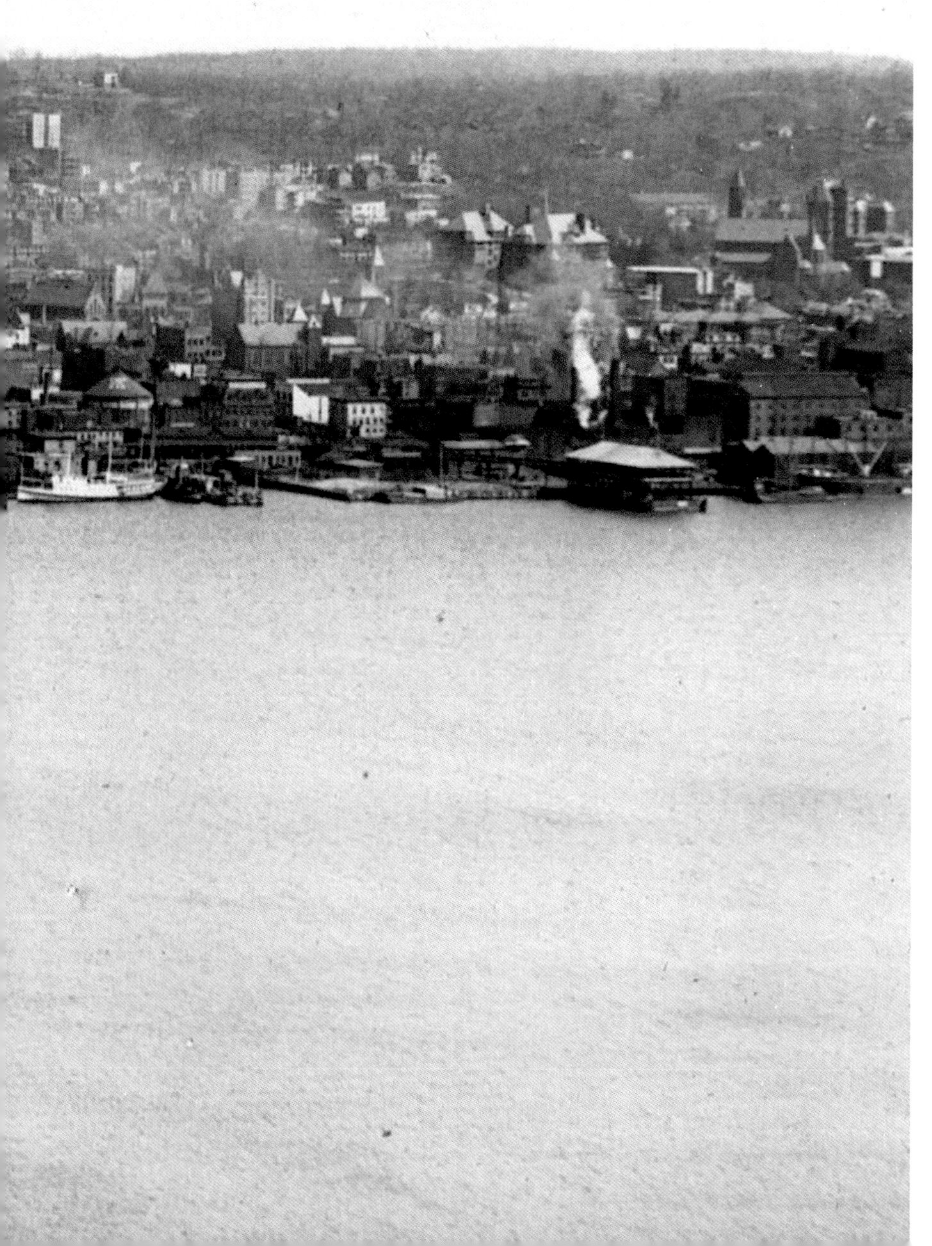

New York City's original Grand Central Depot opened in 1871 at the order of controlling shareholder Cornelius Vanderbilt, becoming the Hudson Line's southern terminus. Architect John B. Snook (1815–1901) designed the depot, and Robert G. Hatfield (1815–1879) designed the train shed pictured here. This structure was built of glass and steel and was modeled on Saint Pancras Station in London. The train shed was demolished in 1903 when construction began on the new Grand Central Terminal.

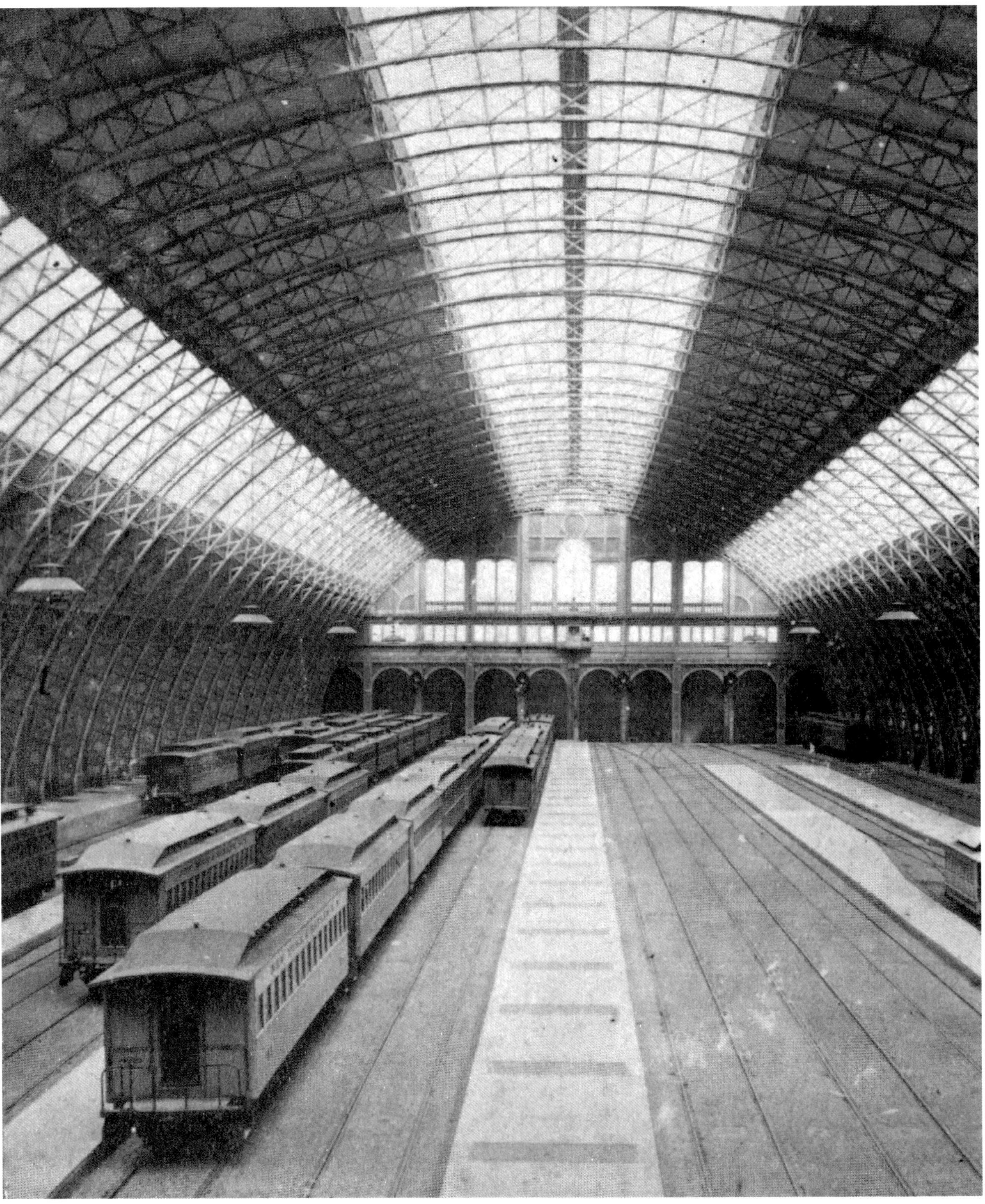

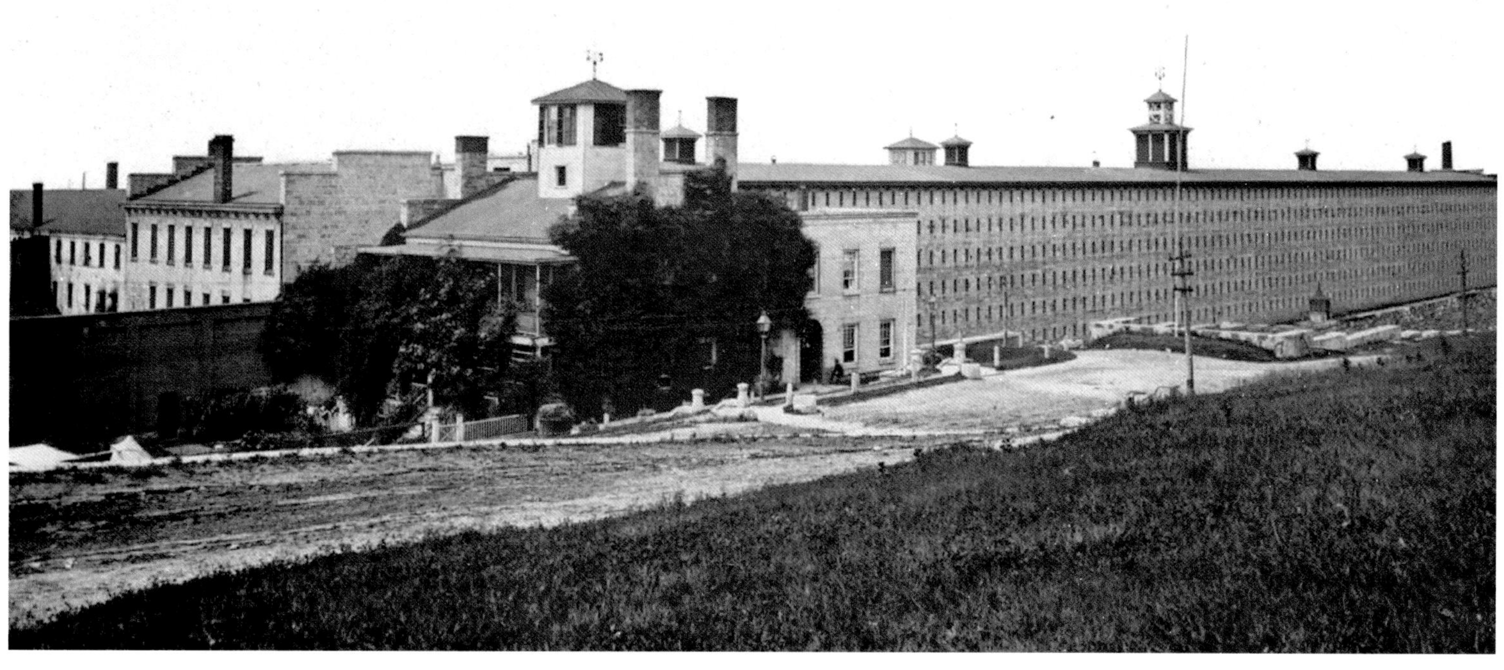

Sing Sing Prison in Ossining is one of the oldest correctional facilities in New York State. The Town of Ossining was previously named Sing Sing, after a Native American tribe, Sint Sinck, living there in the 1600s. The earliest portion of the prison dates from 1825 and was constructed by prisoner labor using the rich local stone quarries. In popular usage, to be sent to Sing Sing was to be sent "up the river" or to the "big house."

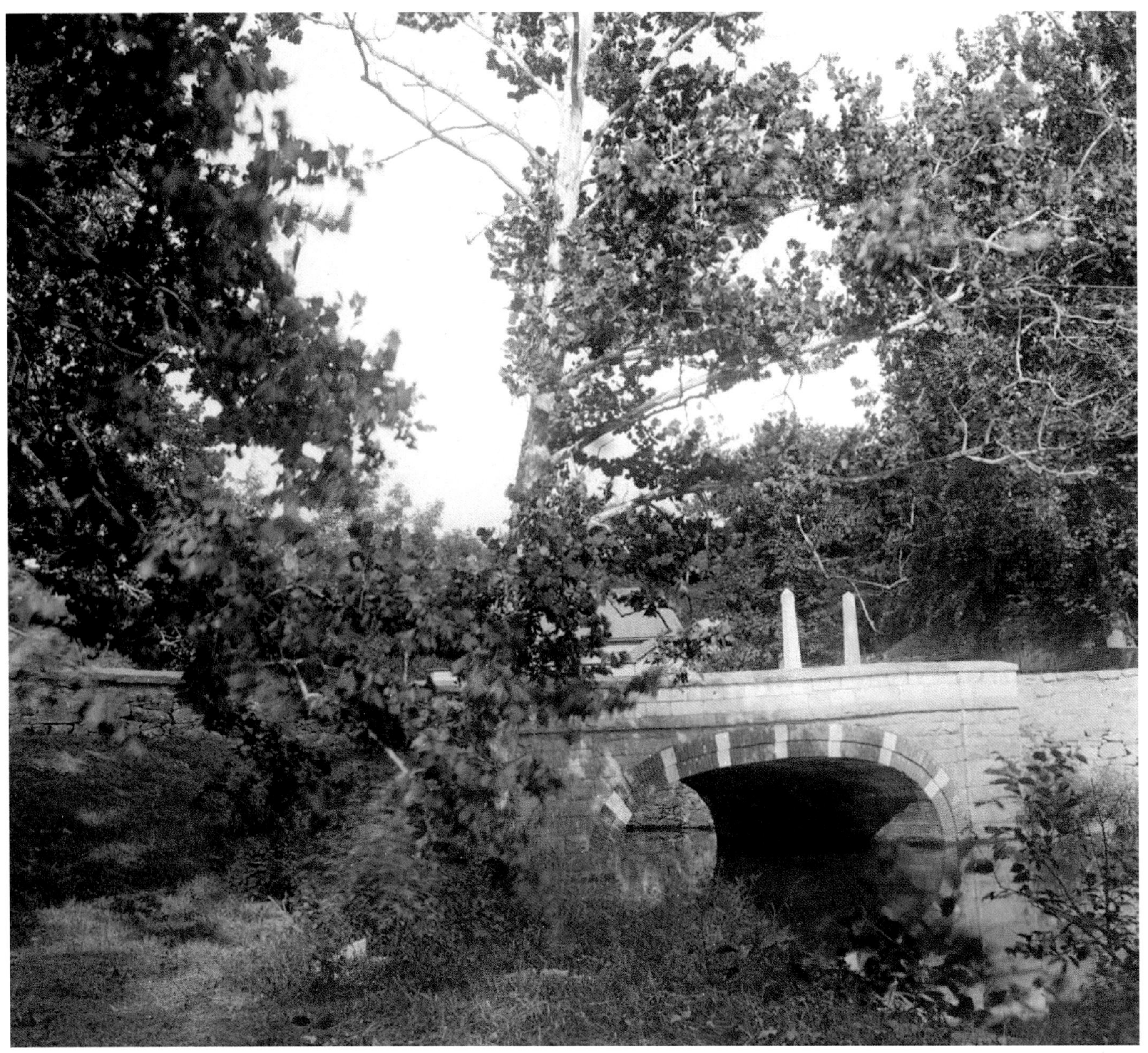

There has been a succession of bridges bearing the name Sleepy Hollow Bridge, all at roughly the same location in the Village of Sleepy Hollow near Tarrytown. They all crossed the Pocantico River along Broadway, also called the Albany Post Road. This is where, in Washington Irving's "The Legend of Sleepy Hollow," schoolteacher Ichabod Crane is unhorsed by the Headless Horseman. The stone bridge pictured here stood from approximately 1872 to 1912.

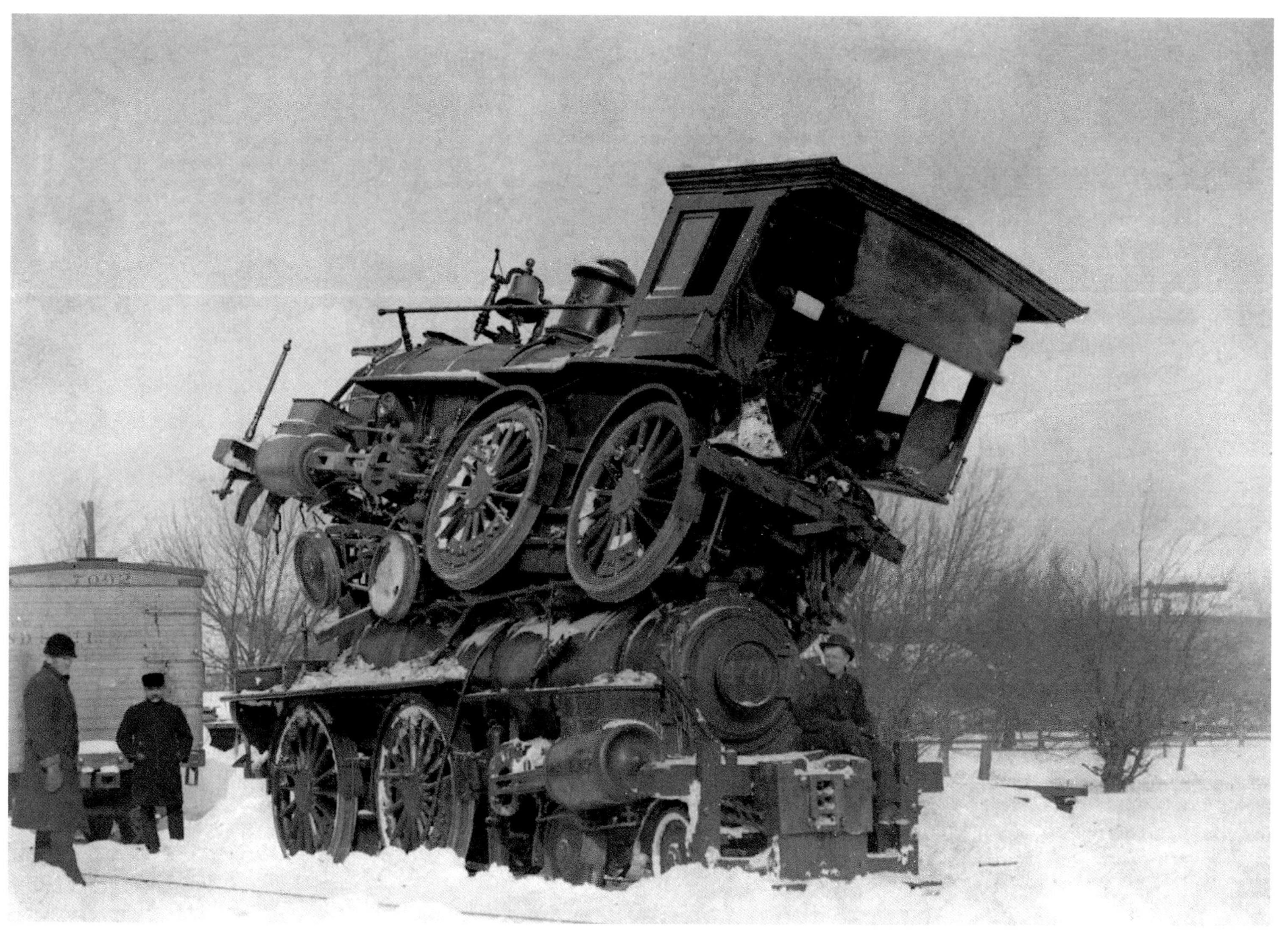

The pileup at Batavia was one of the more dramatic mishaps in an age of frequent railroad accidents. It occurred on February 18, 1885, during a blizzard. Among only four passengers, there were no fatalities, but the small city of Batavia, otherwise known for the manufacture of agricultural equipment, became legendary for the wreck. This image was recorded by photographer William Henry Jackson.

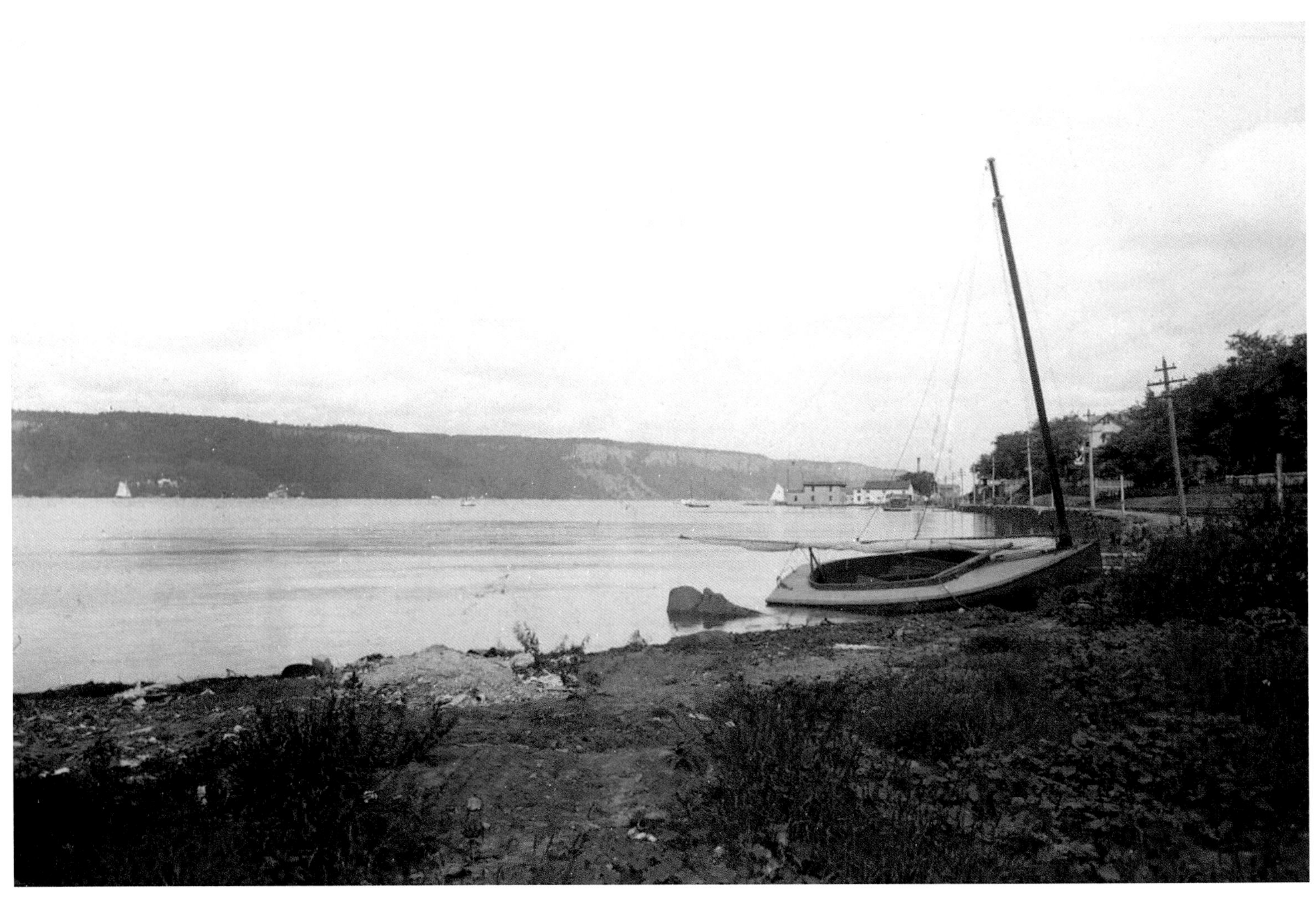

This view of the Hudson River shore shows "Chip Rock Reach," a name not in use today. In this picture the camera looks to the northwest at the Palisades. "Reach" refers to the several reaches by which sailing ships calculated their progress on the Hudson. The "Chip Rock Reach" is that segment which parallels the Palisades between Weehawken and Piermont. The rails of the Hudson Line follow the eastern shoreline on the right.

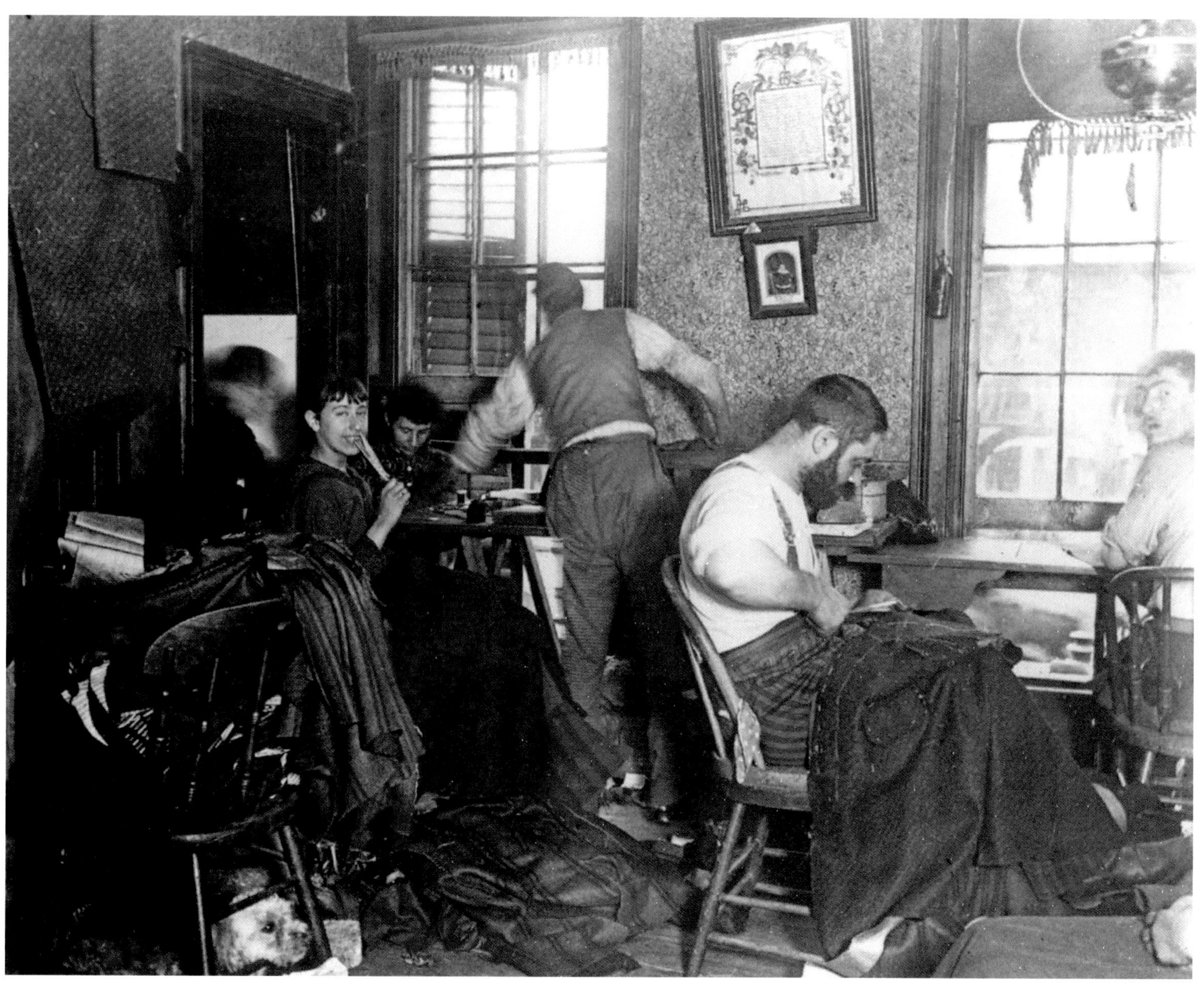

This 1889 photograph of a New York City "sweat shop" was taken by the famed social reformer Jacob Riis (1849–1914) and was included in his landmark book, *How the Other Half Lives.* These Ludlow Street workers in Manhattan are crafting new pants at the rate of 45 cents a dozen. The Danish-born Riis decried the Industrial Revolution's inhumane exploitation of disadvantaged people, which he experienced first-hand as a young man.

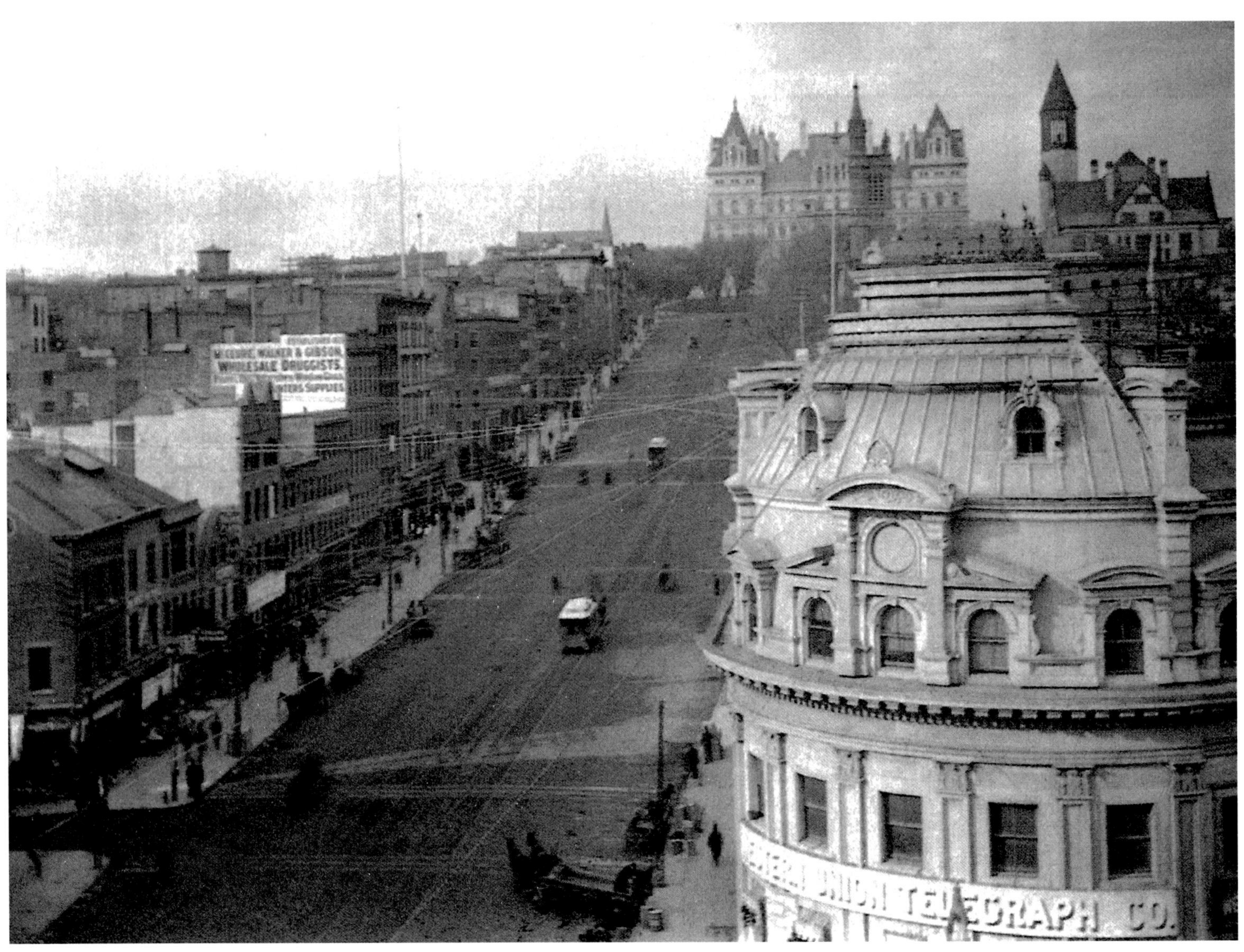

Albany's Museum Building, built by Thorp and Sprague, was also known as the Marble Column Building. It stood at State Street and Broadway until 1904. The building was the last home of the Albany Museum, founded in 1797 at Beaver and Greene streets. In the distance is seen a billboard for Walker and Gibson Wholesale Druggists. The partners, Charles Gibson and William J. Walker, were successful businessmen with splendid neighboring townhomes on State Street, now part of the Nelson Rockefeller Institute of Government.

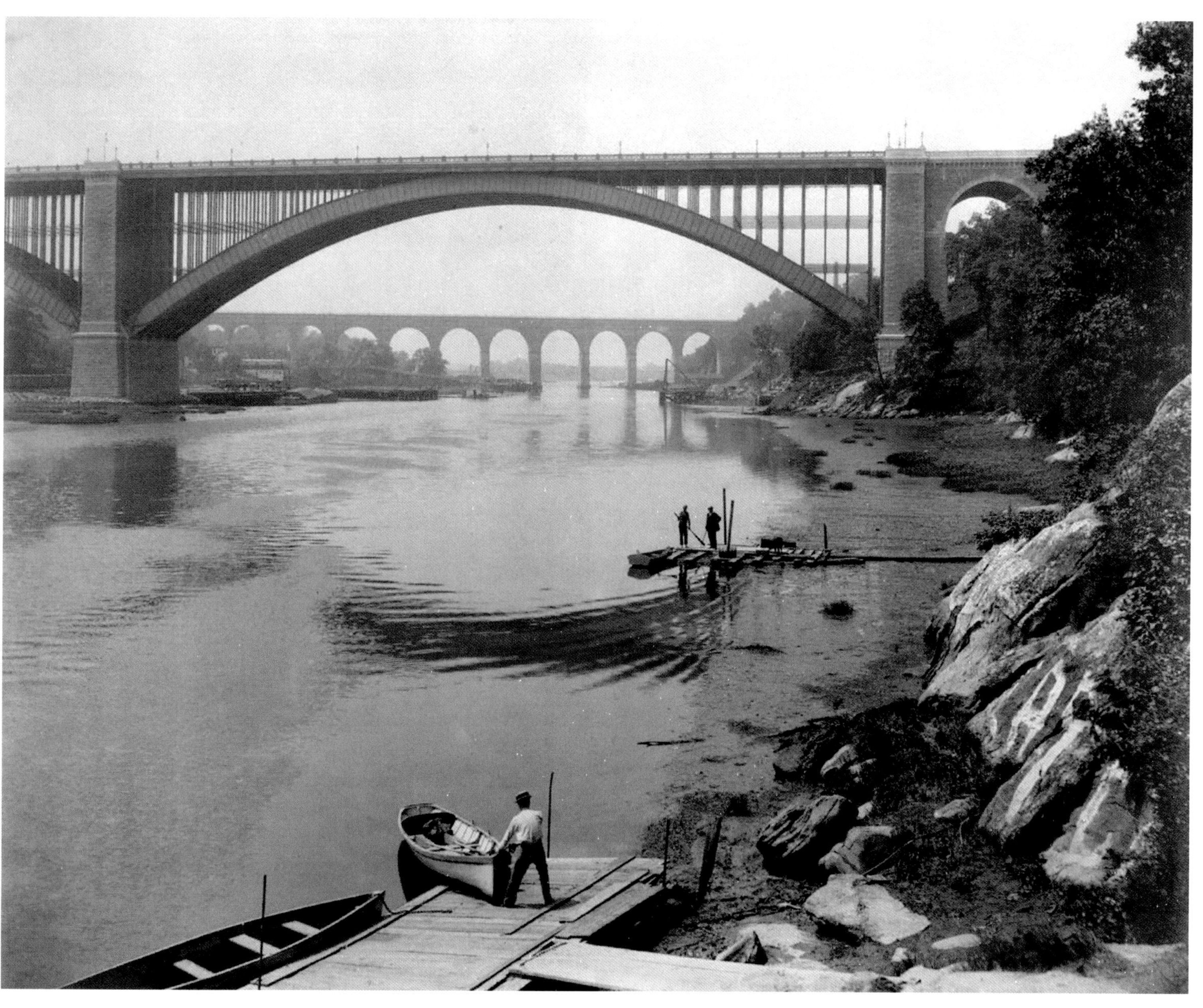

Taken in 1890 from Manhattan, this photograph depicts morning tranquillity on the Harlem River. High Bridge can be seen to the south under an arch of the Washington Bridge.

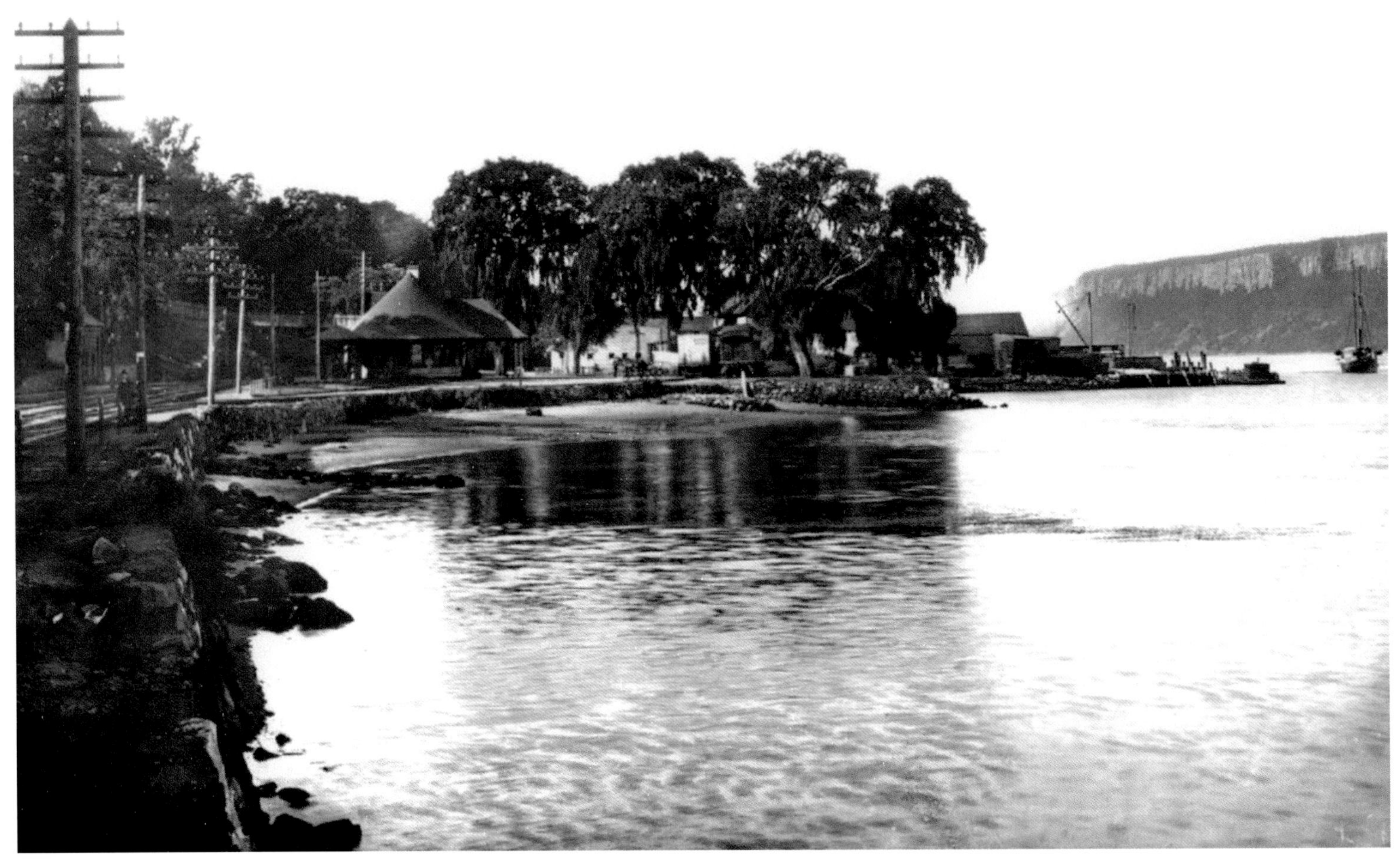

The colonial crossing of the Hudson at Dobbs Ferry figured prominently in the Revolutionary War, particularly when Washington's Headquarters was located across the river at Tappan, New York. This late-nineteenth-century view shows the Palisades across the river and to the south. The photographer, William Henry Jackson (1843–1942), was well known for his paintings and photographs of America's western landmarks. Jackson's work is displayed on several pages in this book.

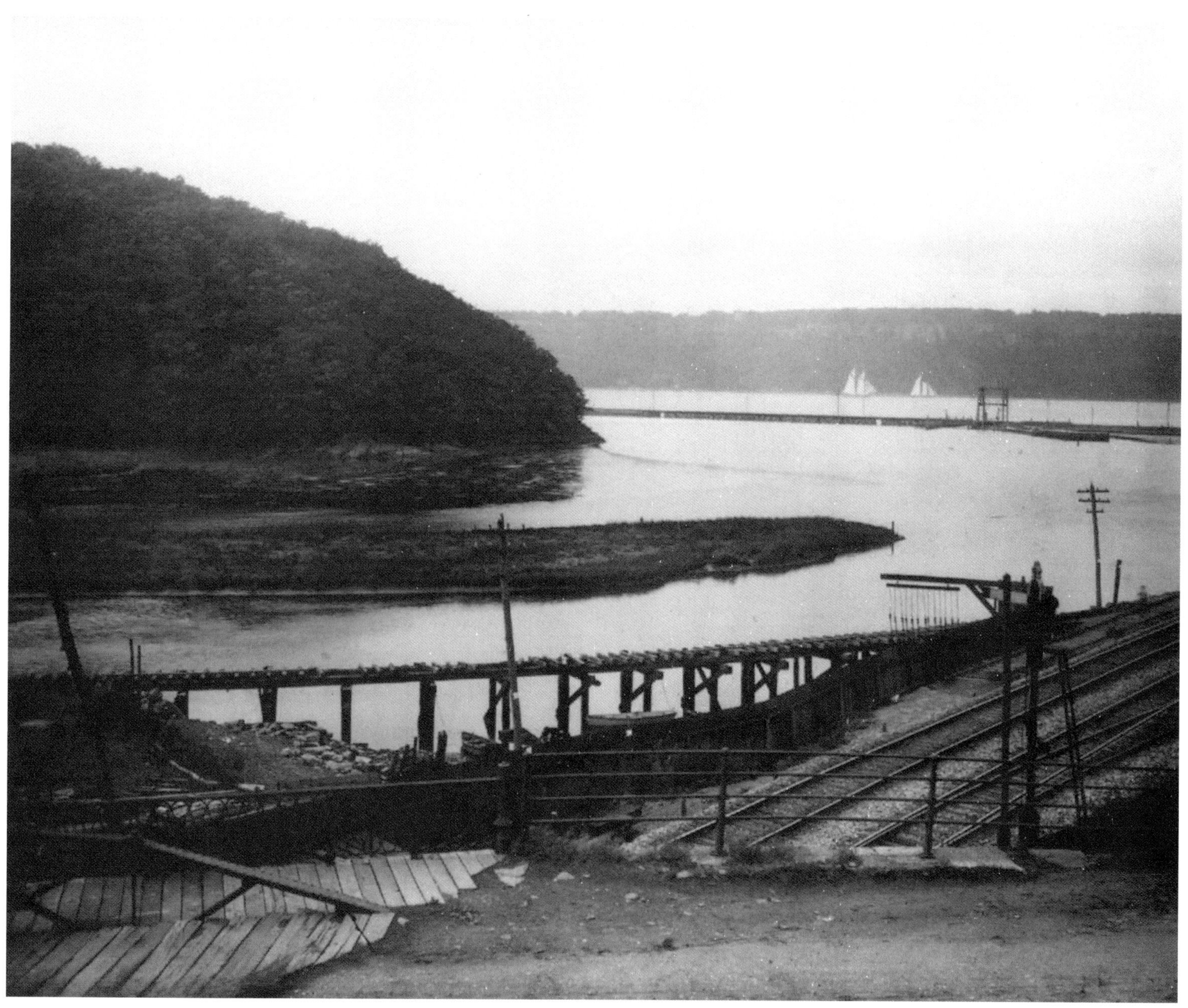

The name Spuyten Duyvil refers to the junction of the Hudson River and the Harlem River. There is debate about the exact meaning of the name, but the words are frequently translated "in spite of the devil." After the 1871 opening of Grand Central Depot, most train travelers from Manhattan caught their first glimpse of the Hudson River here.

Following Spread: This view of Peekskill Bay was captured by William Henry Jackson about 1890. The shadow of Bear Mountain is visible in the distance beyond Jones Point on the left. An American garrison at Peekskill guarded the approach to the Hudson Highlands during the Revolutionary War, until a much more formidable fortress was built to the north at West Point.

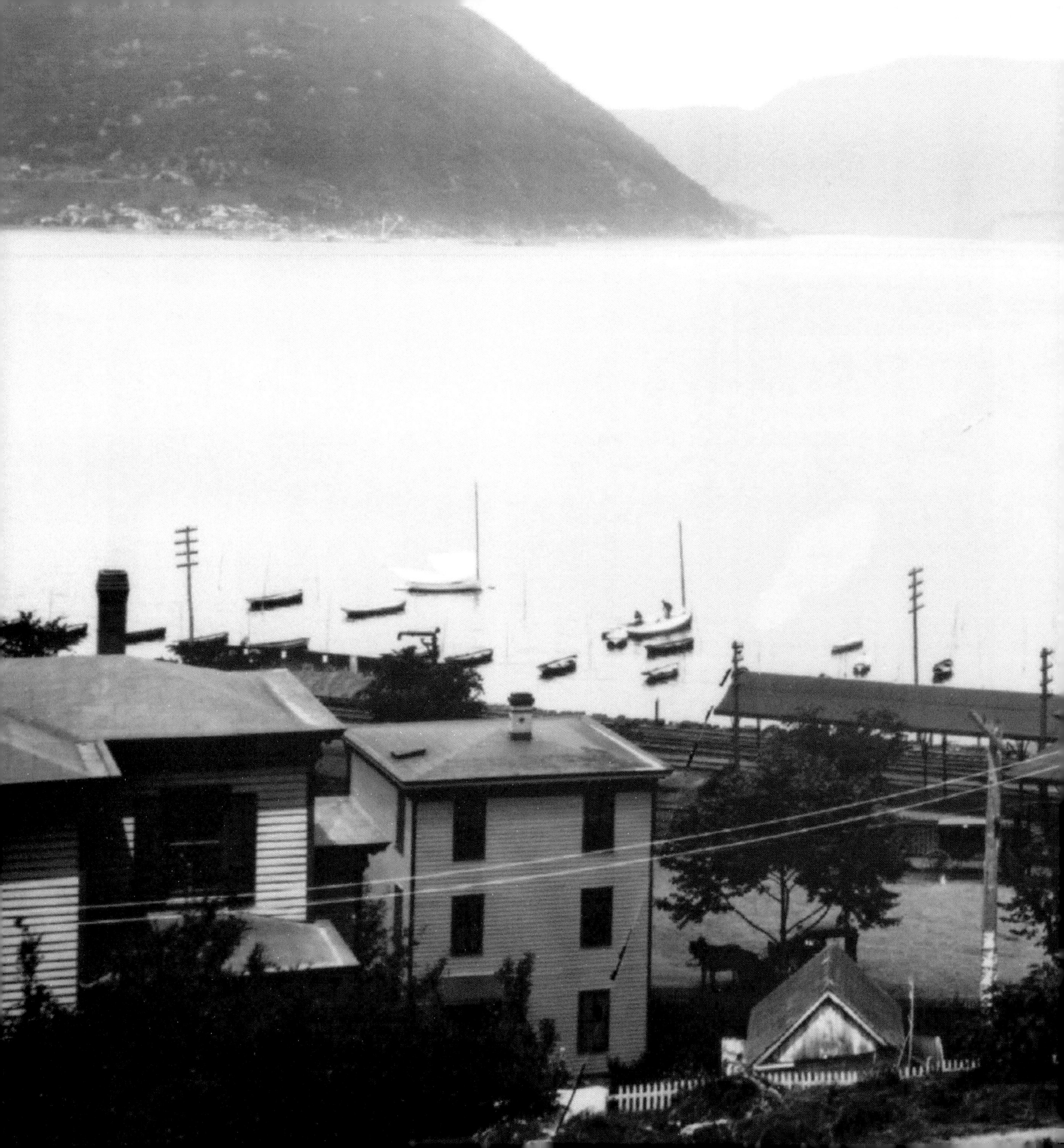

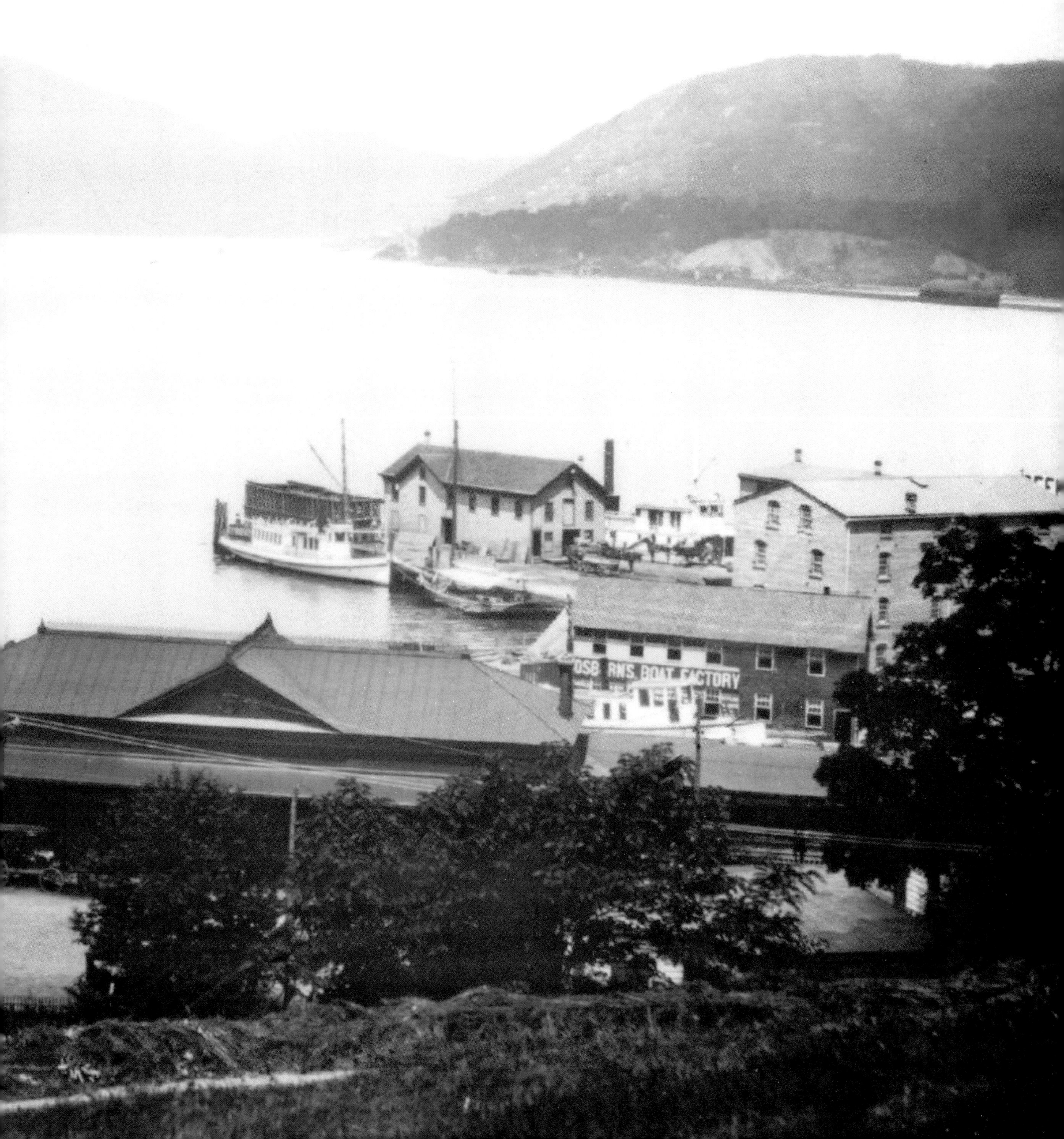
OSB RN'S BOAT FACTORY

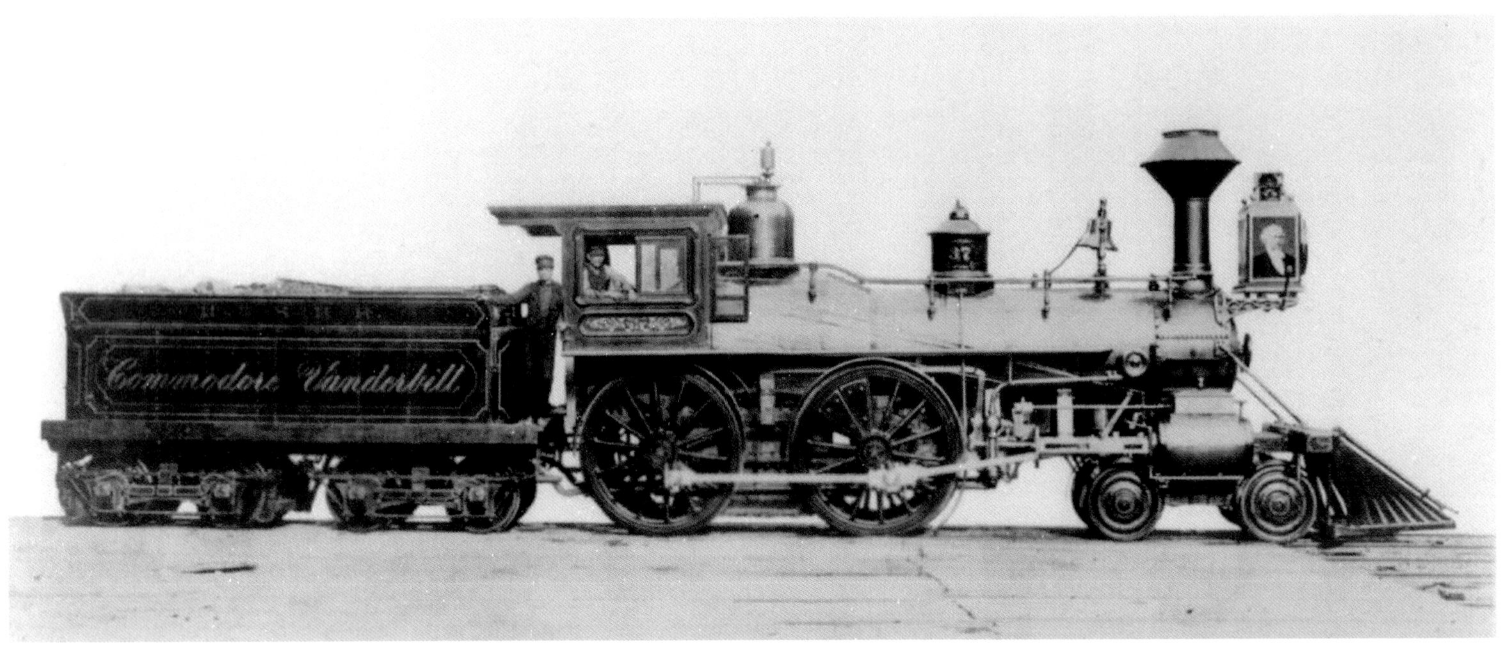

The *Commodore Vanderbilt* was made in 1870 by the American Locomotive Company and featured a portrait of magnate Cornelius Vanderbilt on the lightbox at front. An example of the "American Standard" for locomotive design, it featured a four-wheeled truck at front able to negotiate curves independent of the drive wheels, a large cowcatcher, and a large, spark-suppressing smokestack. It was built for service on the Hudson Line.

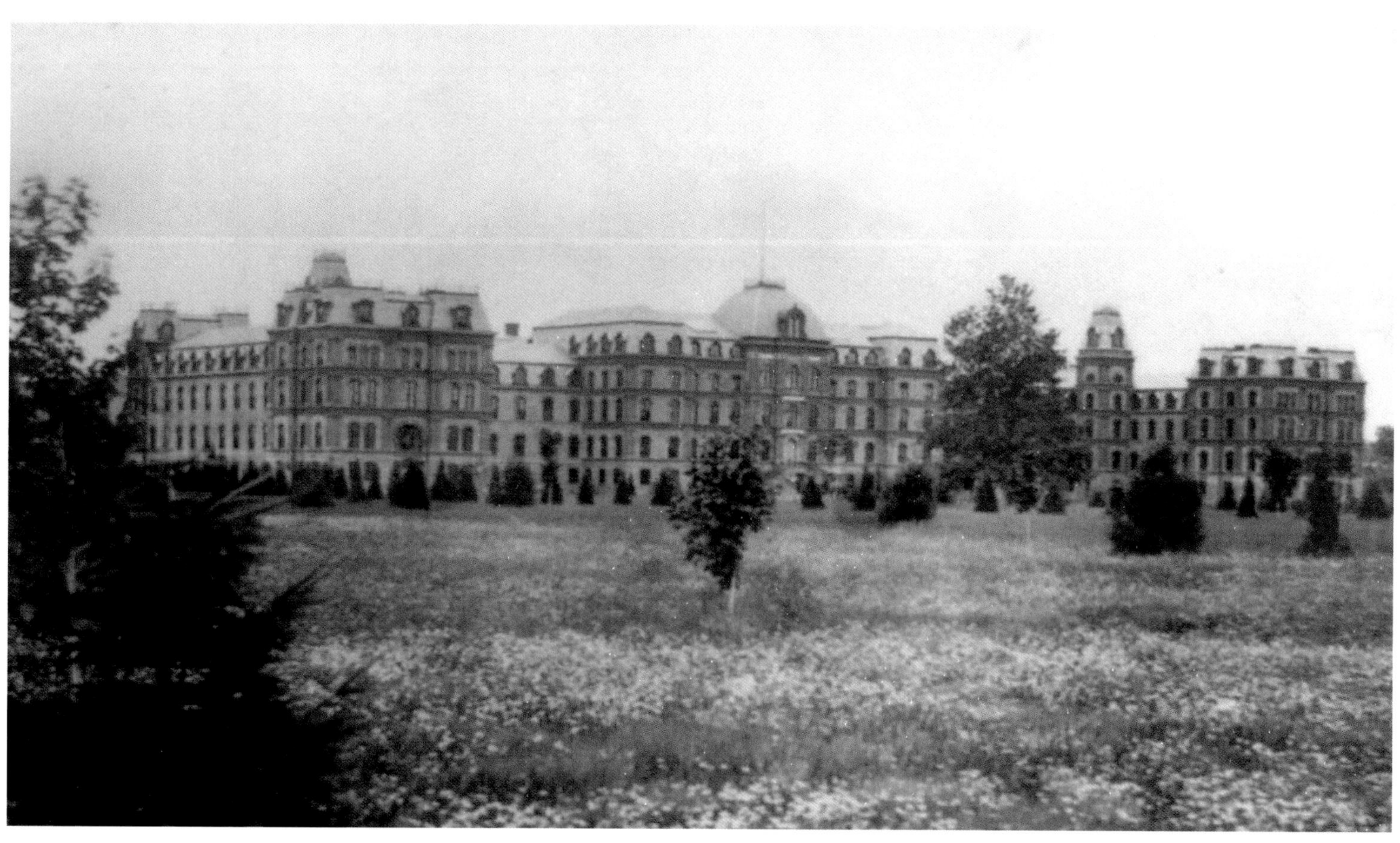

Matthew Vassar, a wealthy Poughkeepsie brewer, founded Vassar College in 1861. In its early years, the women's college consisted of only the main building, pictured here about 1892. "Main" was designed by James Renwick, Jr. (1818–1895), and it housed the dinning hall, library, classrooms, offices, museum, and quarters for faculty and students. Renwick also designed St. Patrick's Cathedral in New York City. The much-expanded women's college at Poughkeepsie became co-educational in 1969.

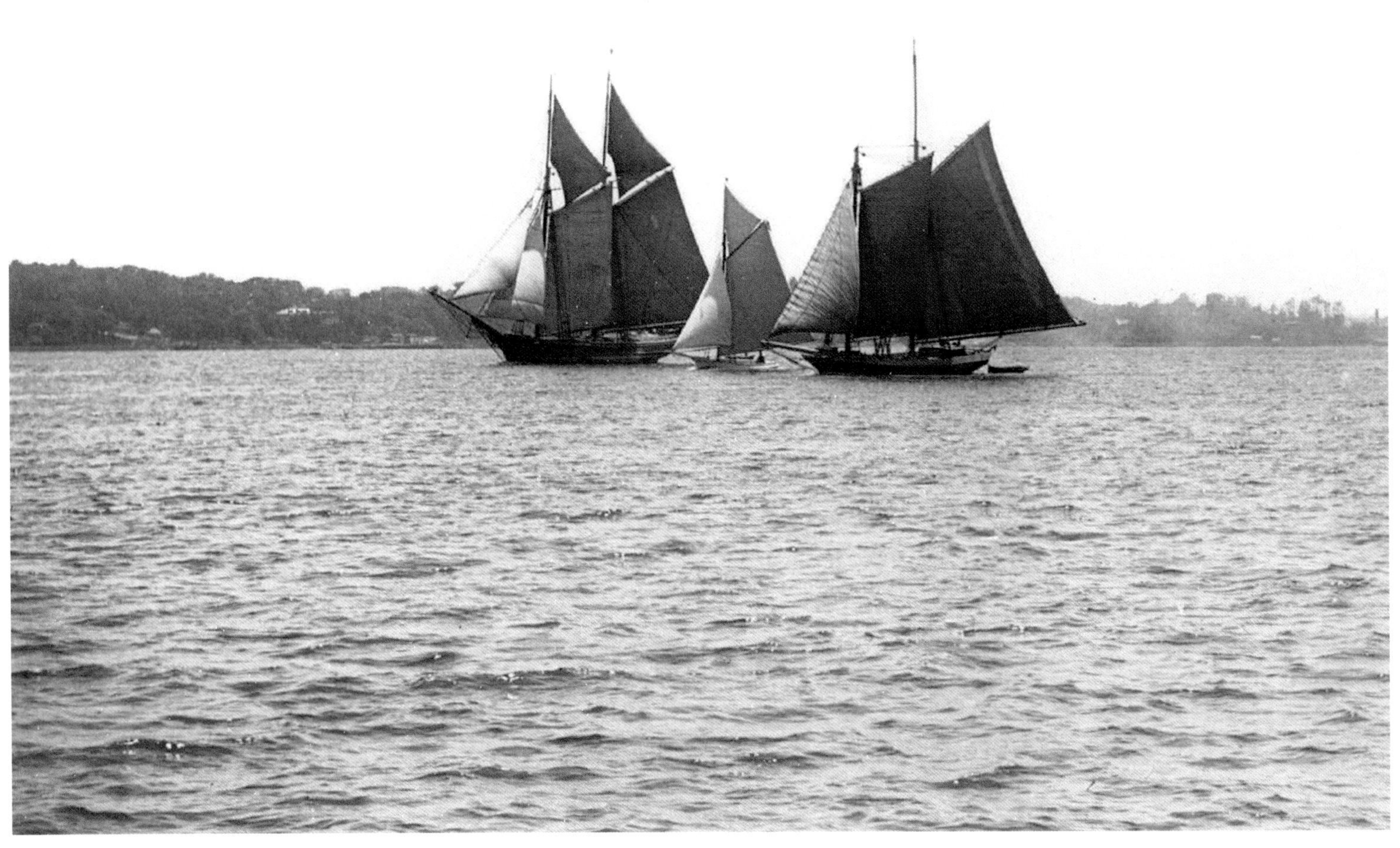

Market sloops and sailboats like these were the primary mode of travel on the Hudson before the advent of the steamboat. Manhattan is seen in the background, just below Spuyten Duyvil on the Hudson River. According to a Gilded Age historian of New York, Reginald Pelham Bolton, Spuyten Duyvil means "sprouting meadow."

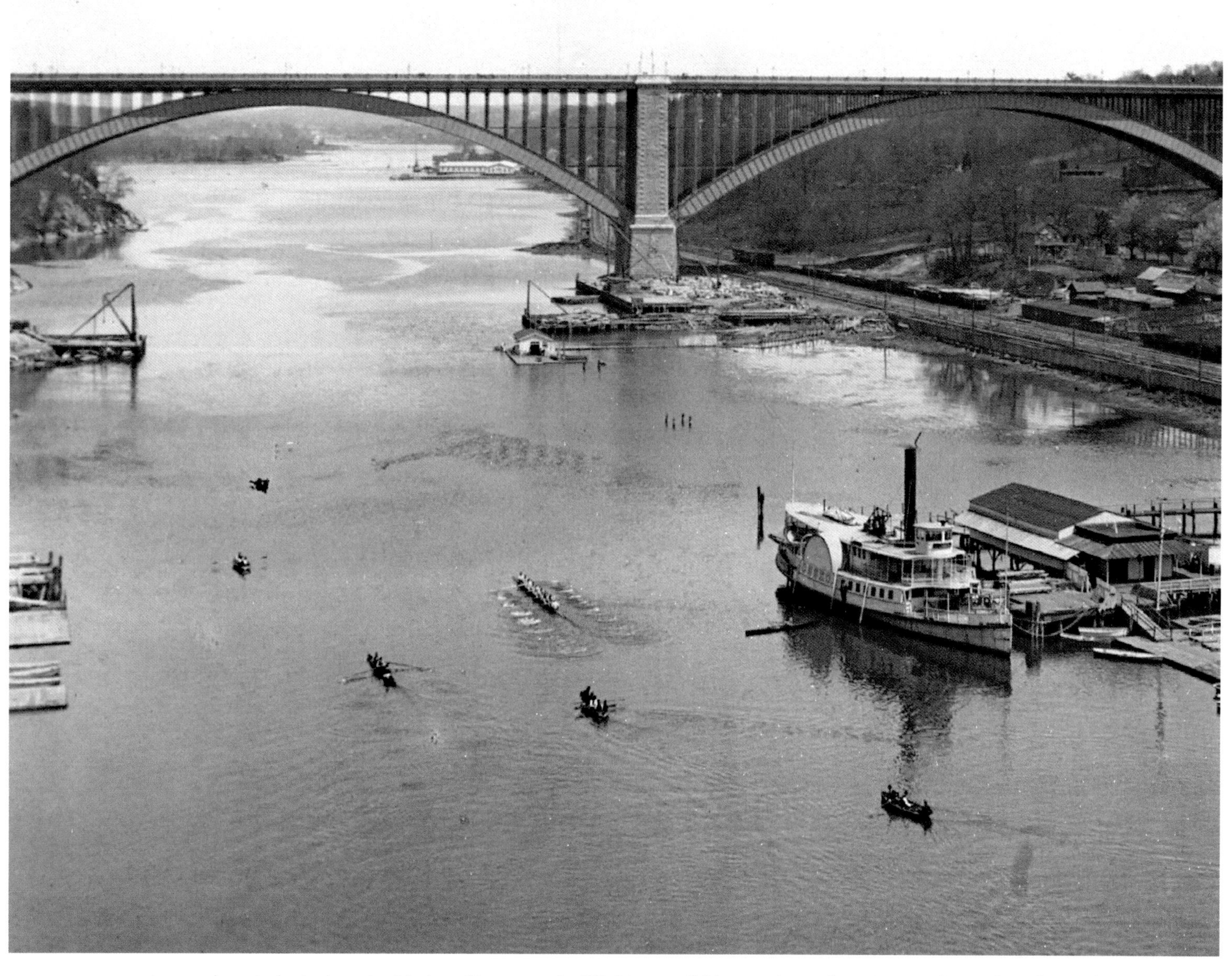

A steamboat is docked on the Harlem River near the Washington Bridge, as six small rowing vessels pass by. The Harlem River was a traditional rowing course. The Hudson Railroad line passes under the east span of the bridge on the Bronx side.

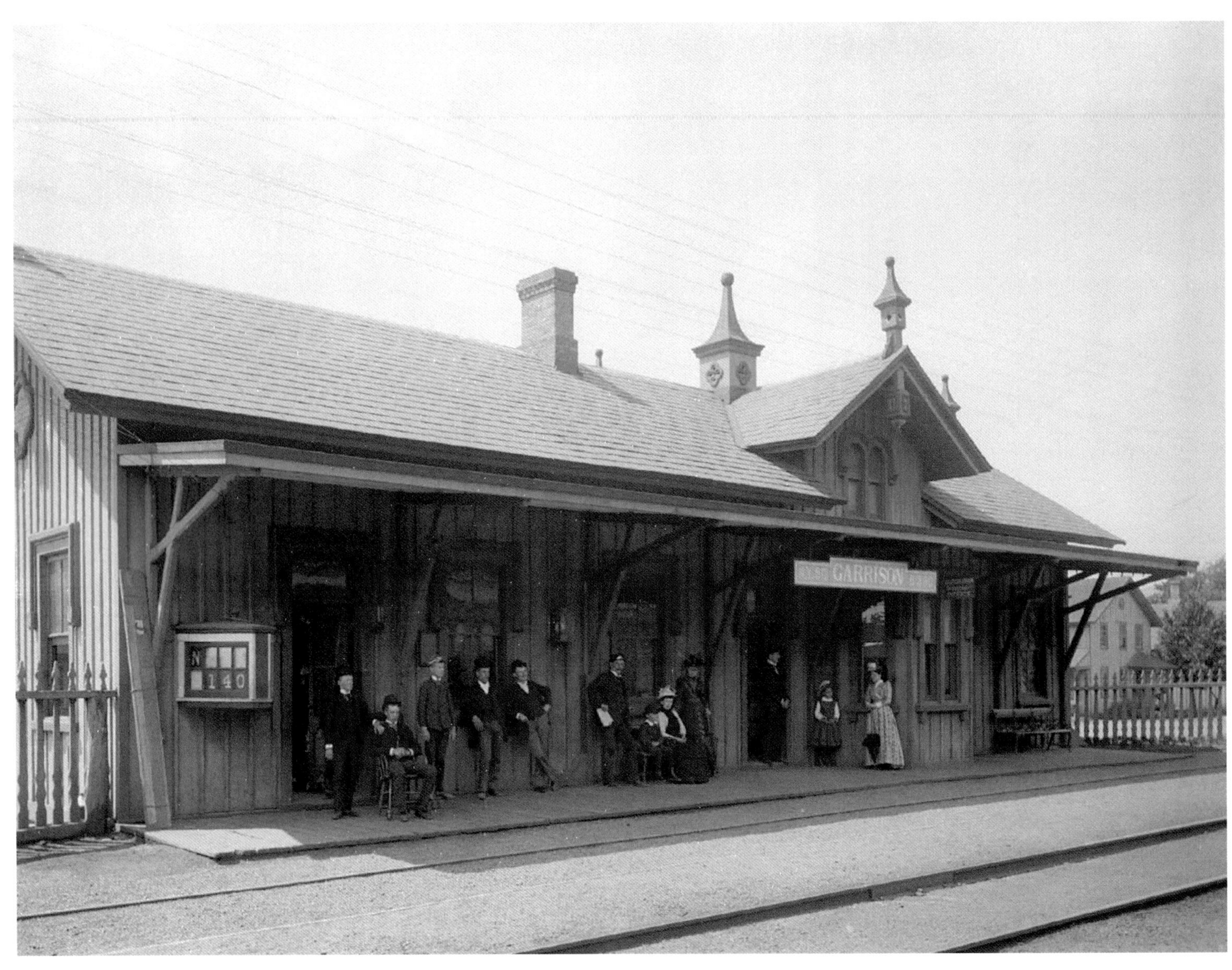

Citizens await the train at the Garrison, New York, railroad terminal sometime in the late nineteenth century. In 1897, Garrison would become the scene of a Hudson Line train wreck that took the lives of 20 people.

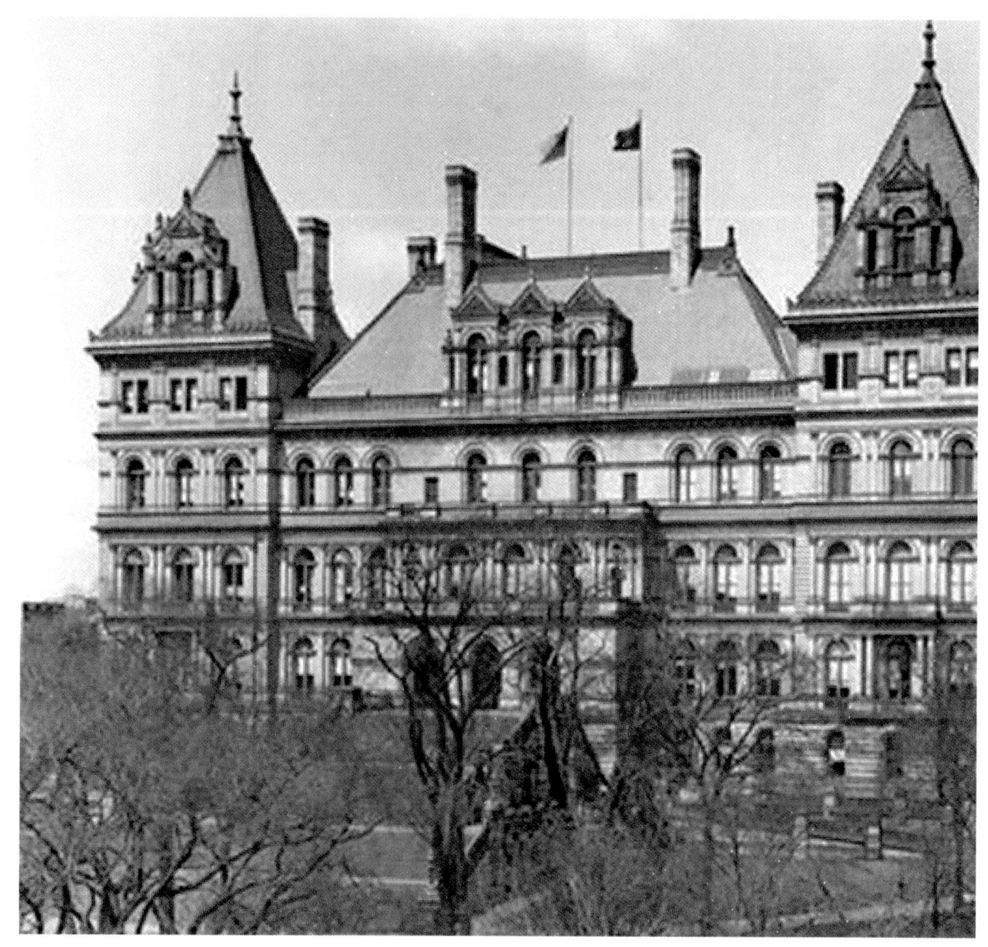

The New York State Capitol in Albany.

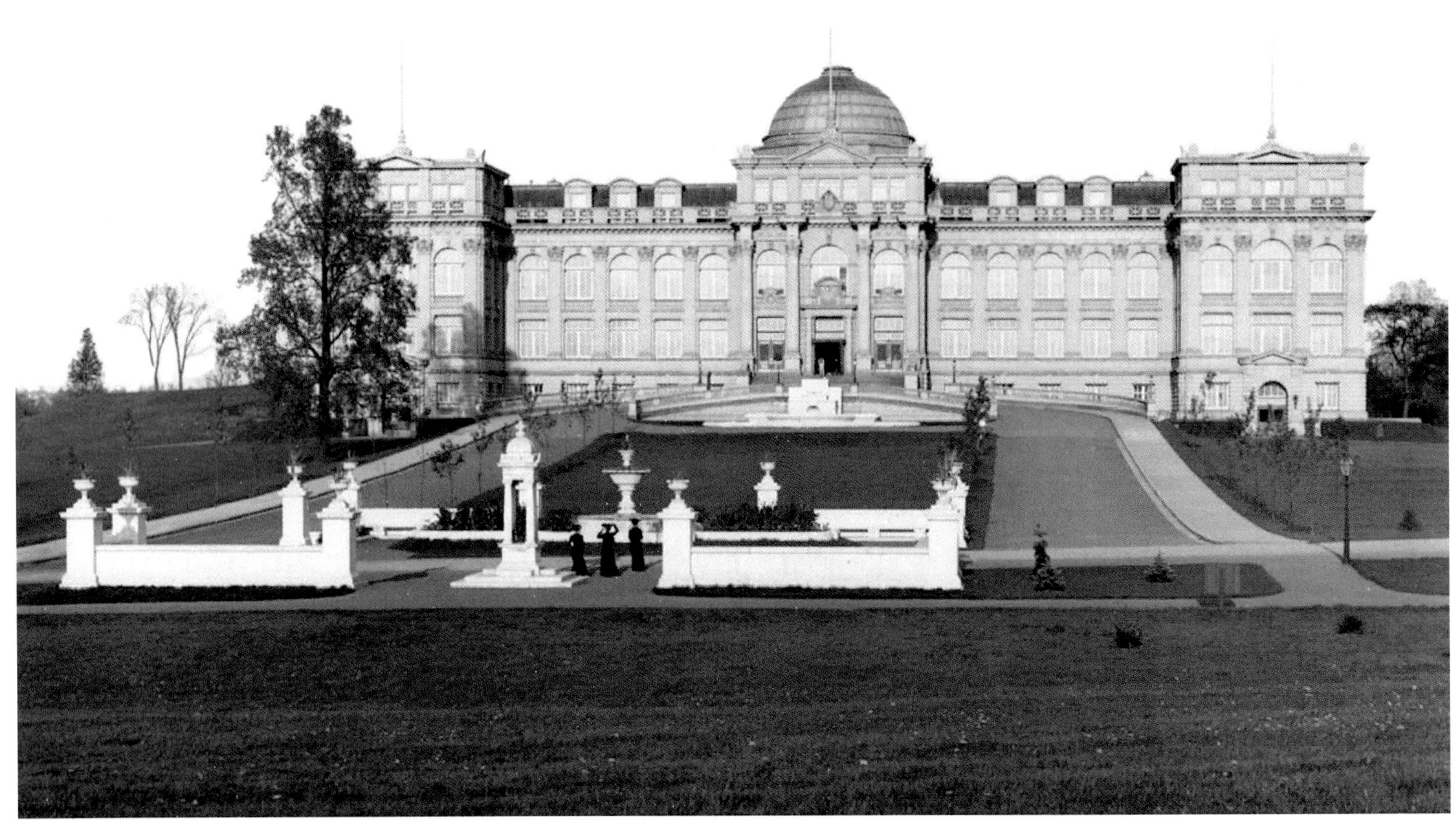

The Bronx was named after an early-seventeenth-century settler of the area, Jonas Bronck (1600–1643), a Swedish sea captain. The Bronx Park and Botanical Garden, modeled after the Royal Botanical Garden in Kew, England, was built on 250 acres there in 1891.

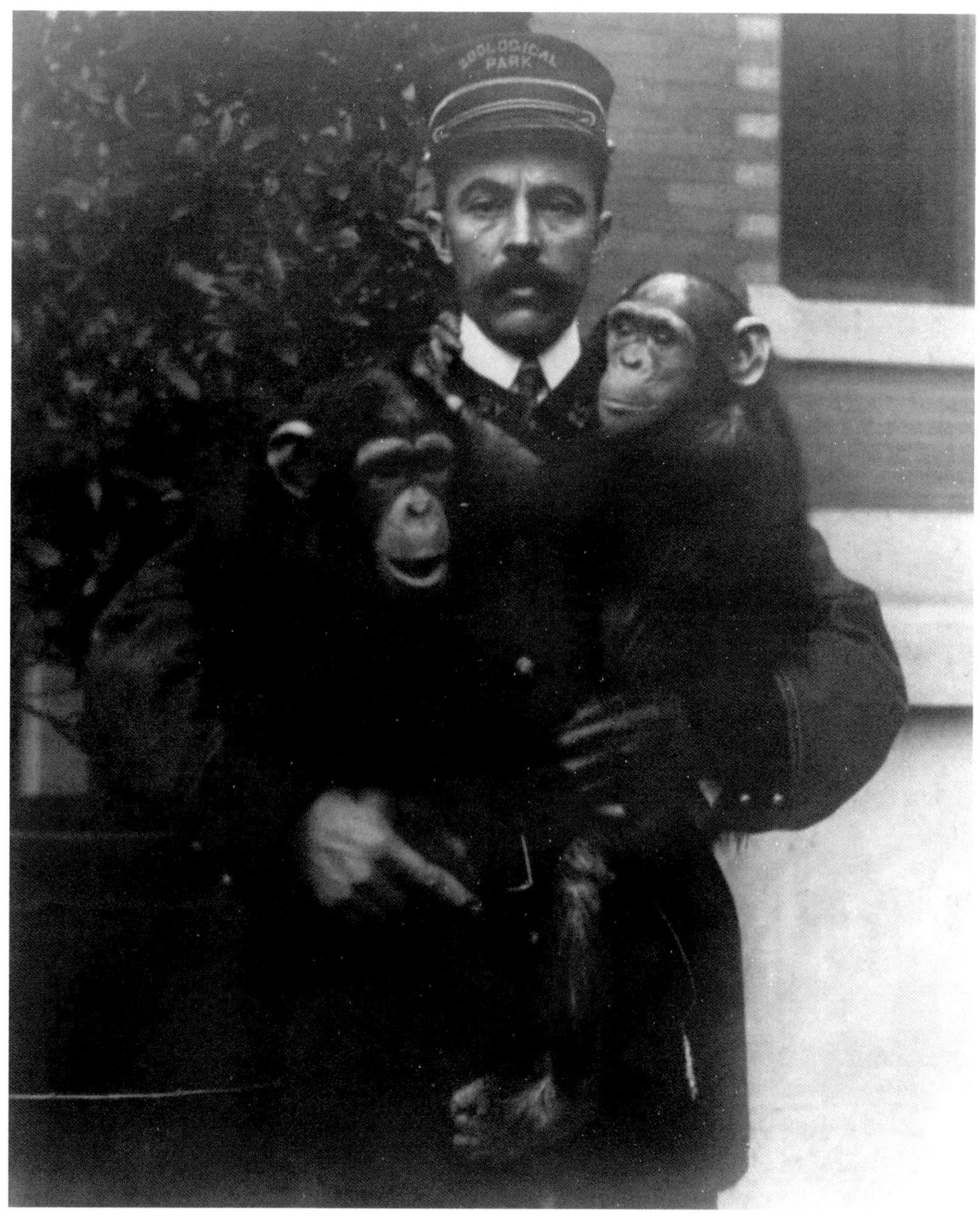

The Bronx Zoo opened with 843 animals in 22 exhibits in 1899, near the Bronx Botanical Garden. It was designed by Heins and Lafarge, the architectural firm that also designed the Cathedral of St. John the Divine in upper Manhattan.

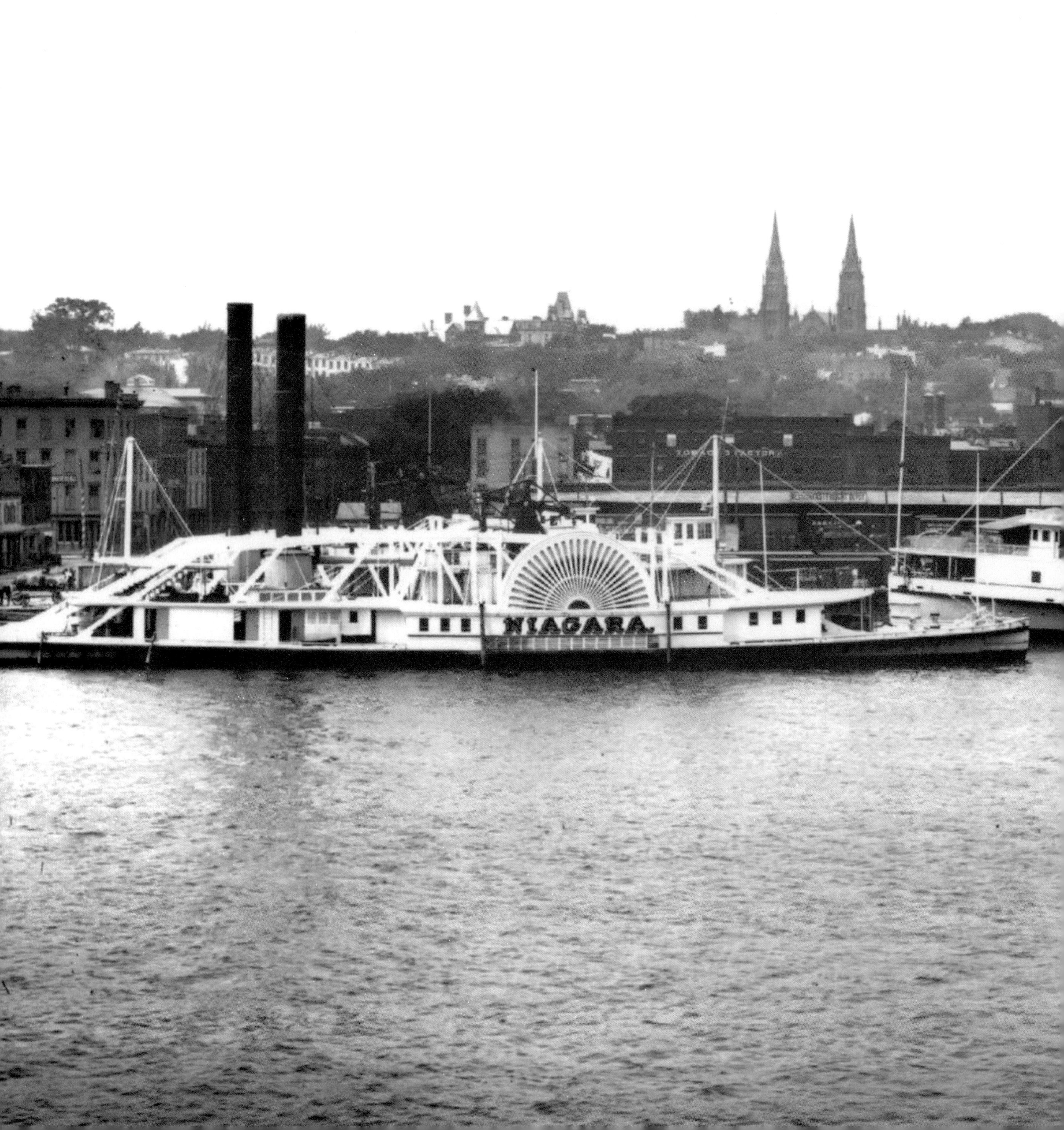
NIAGARA.

Recorded about 1890, this stereograph of the Albany waterfront shows the *Niagara* and *Dean Richmond* steamboats at anchor.

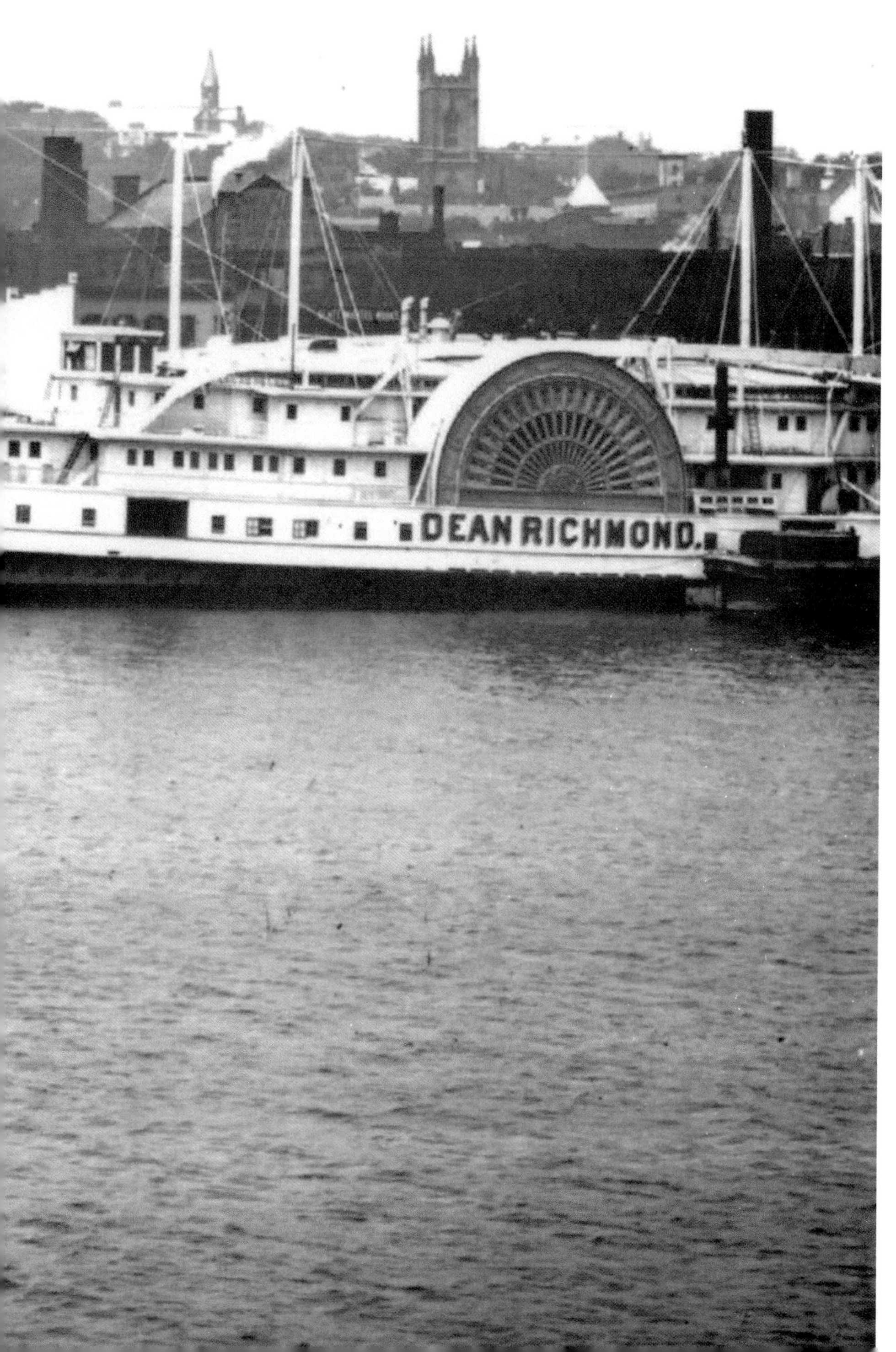

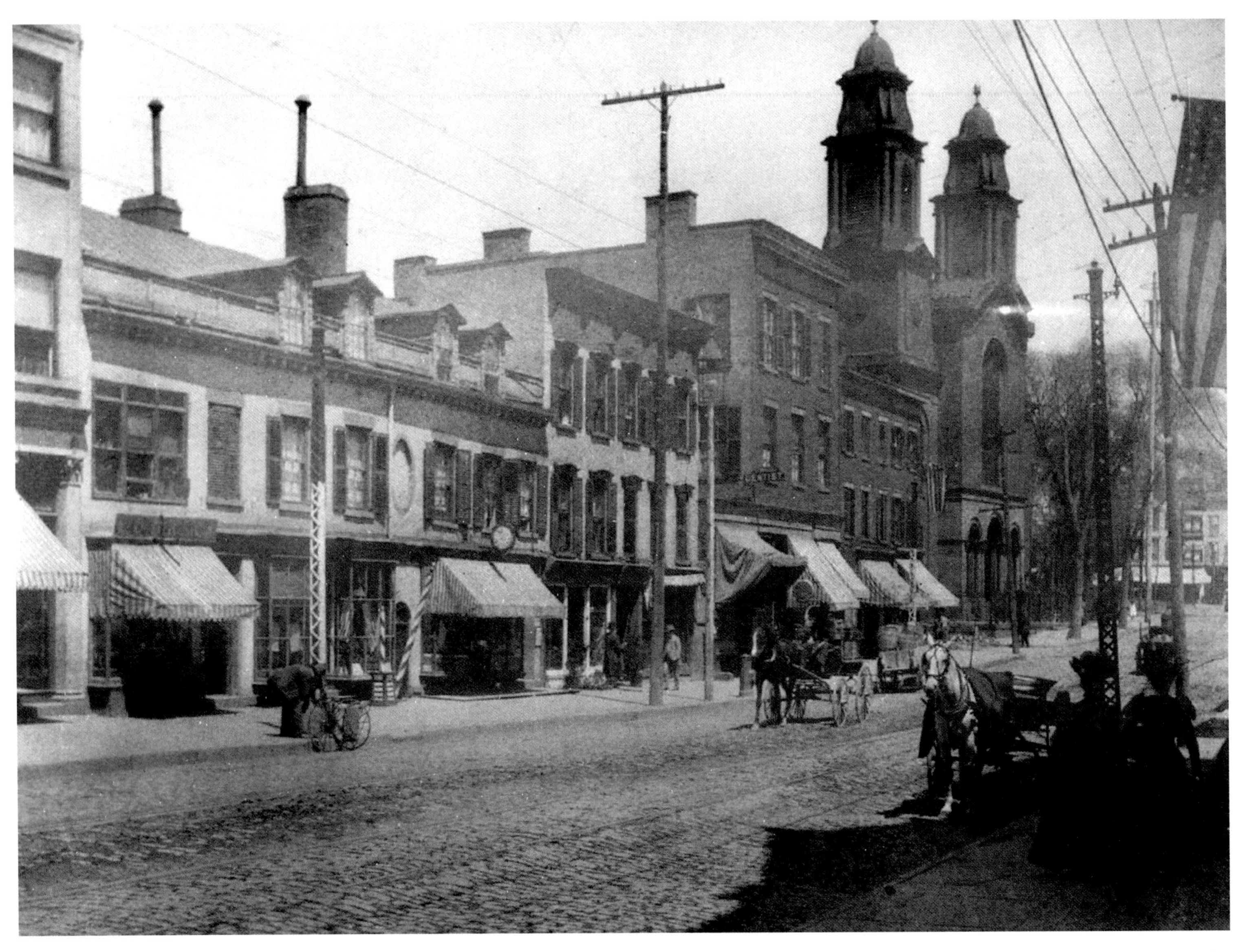

A day in the life of Albany, near the William Visscher Building at 100-102 North Pearl Street. Pedestrians and horse-drawn vehicles traverse the pavement around 1895.

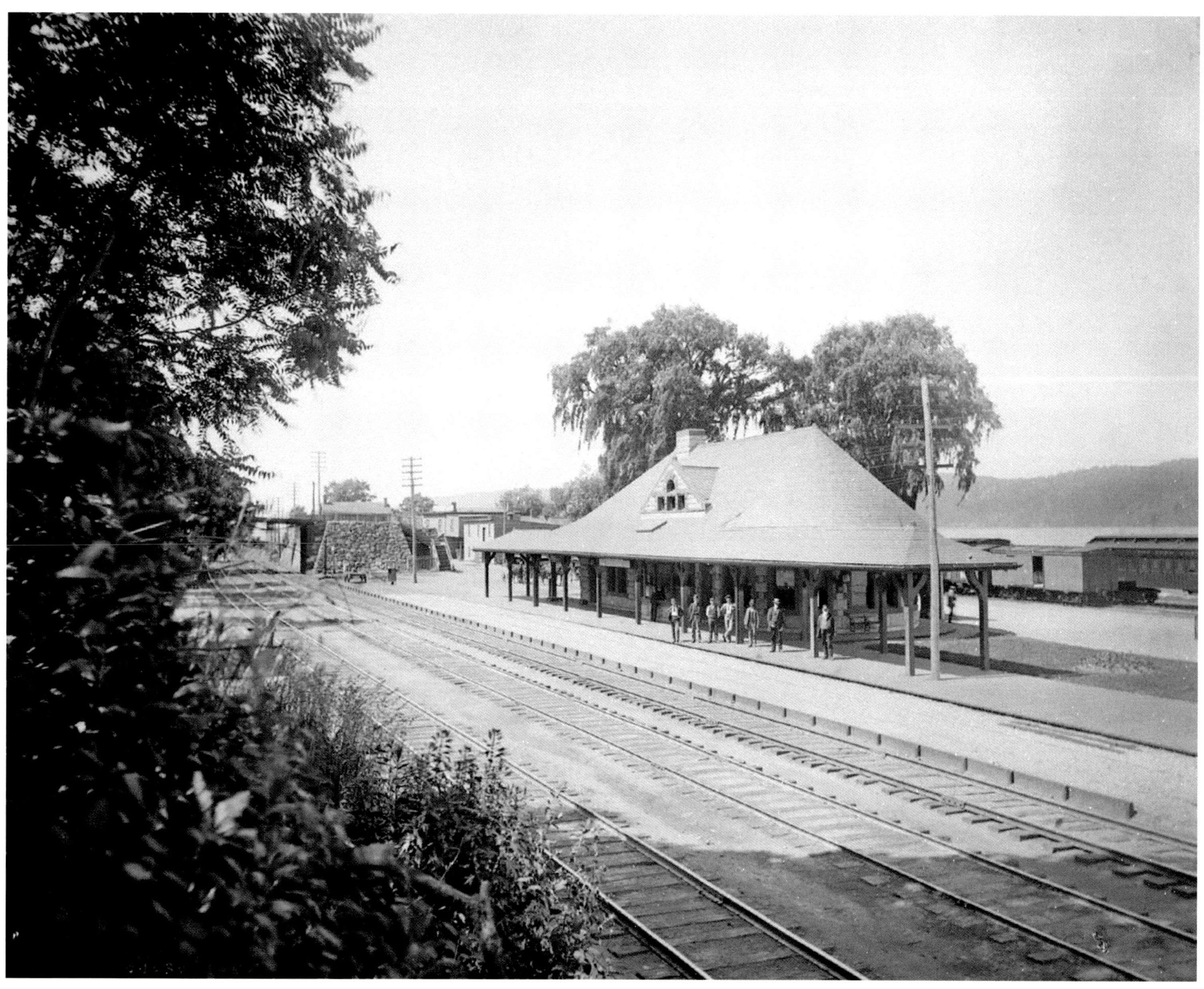

Locals await the train at the Dobbs Ferry railroad station, in Westchester County, on a day in the late nineteenth century.

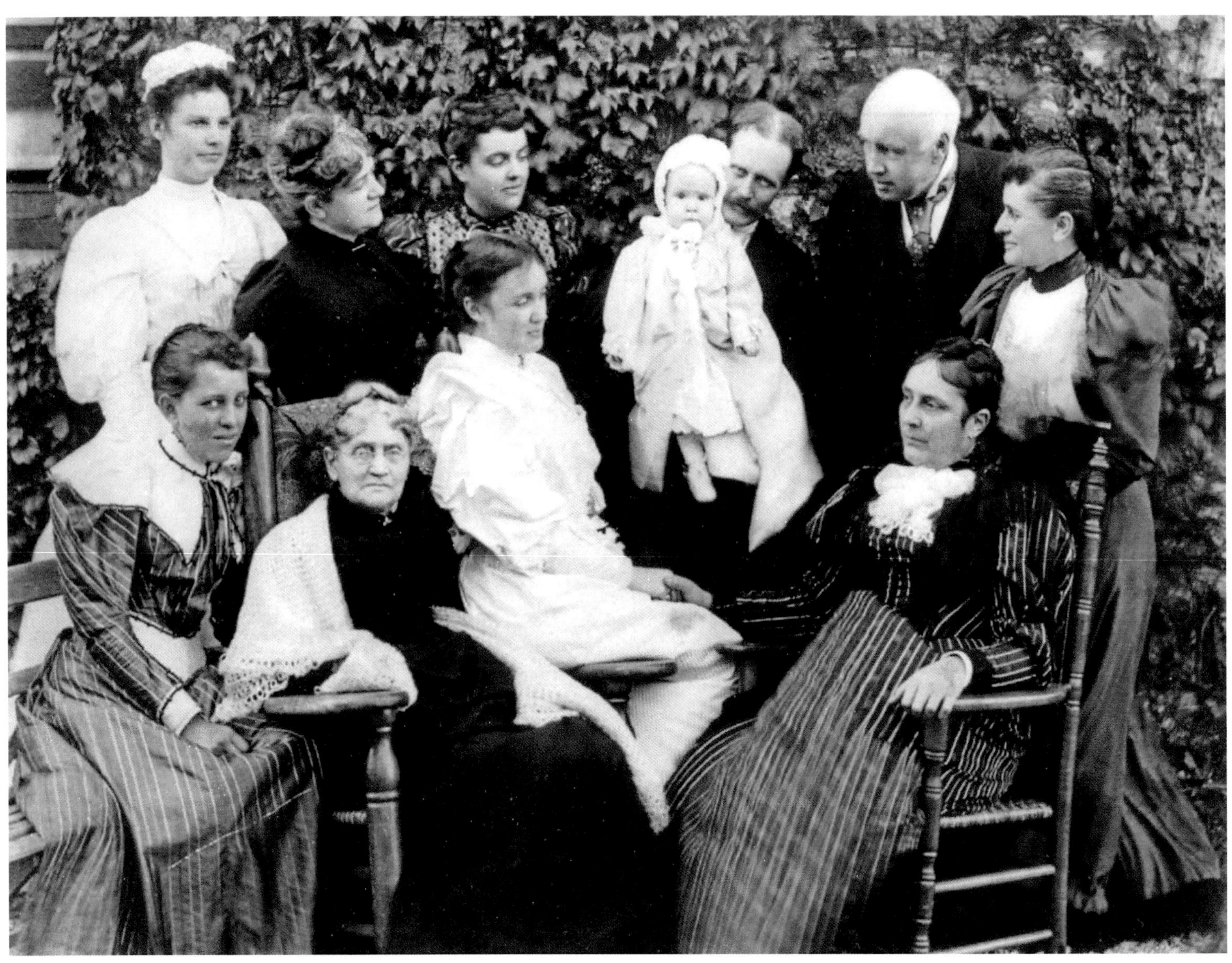

Colonel Robert Green Ingersoll (1833–1899) was a Union Civil War cavalry commander at the Battle of Shiloh, an attorney, and a noted spokesman for agnosticism and free thought. He is shown here, late in life, with his family at "Walston," the Dobbs Ferry residence of his son-in-law, Walston H. Brown. On the Hudson in Westchester County, Dobbs Ferry figured prominently in the Revolutionary War when General Washington's forces camped there in 1781.

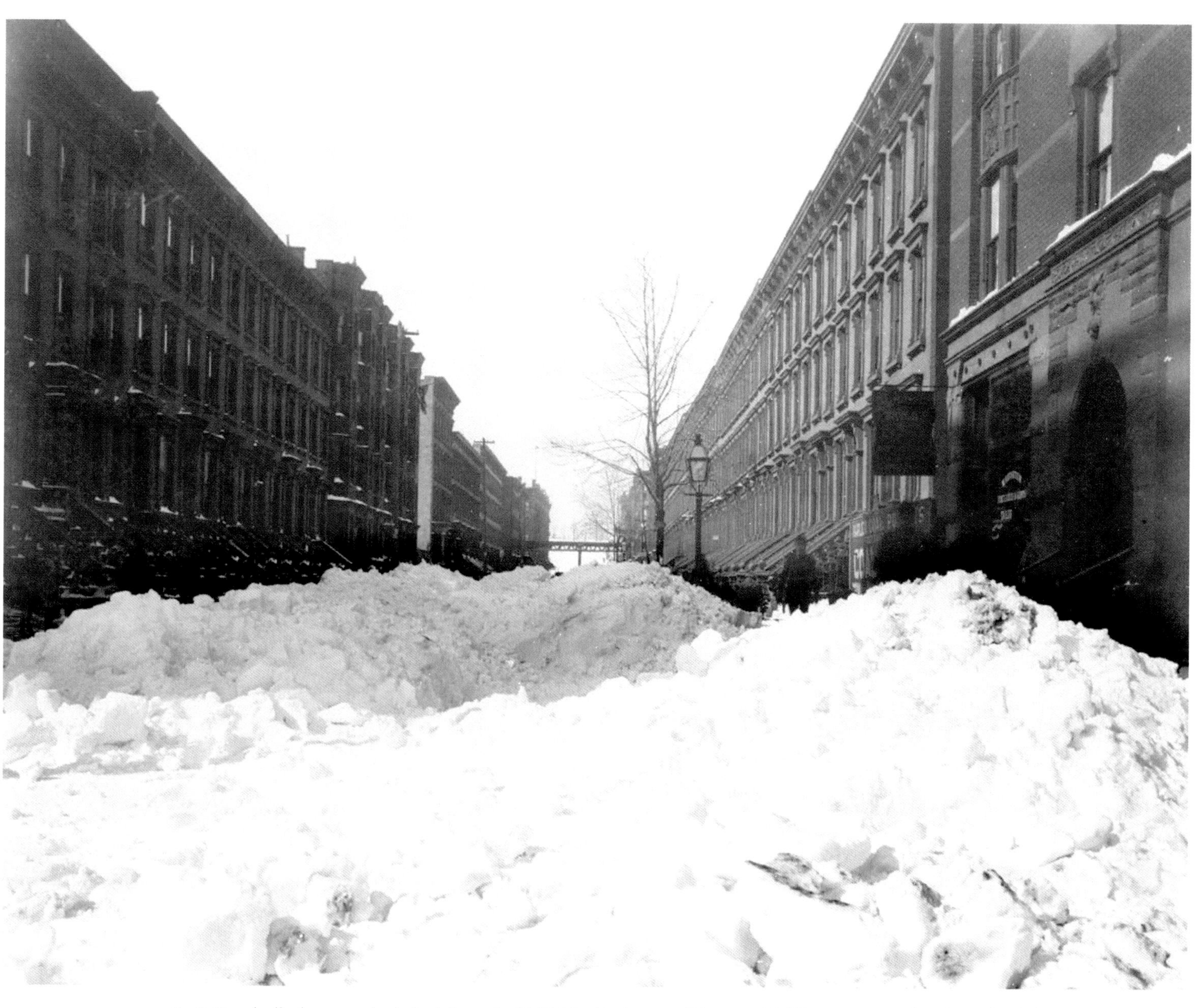

R. F. Turnbull photographed the blizzard of 1899 in Harlem on February 13. The storm paralyzed much of the eastern U.S. and led to record-setting cold temperatures.

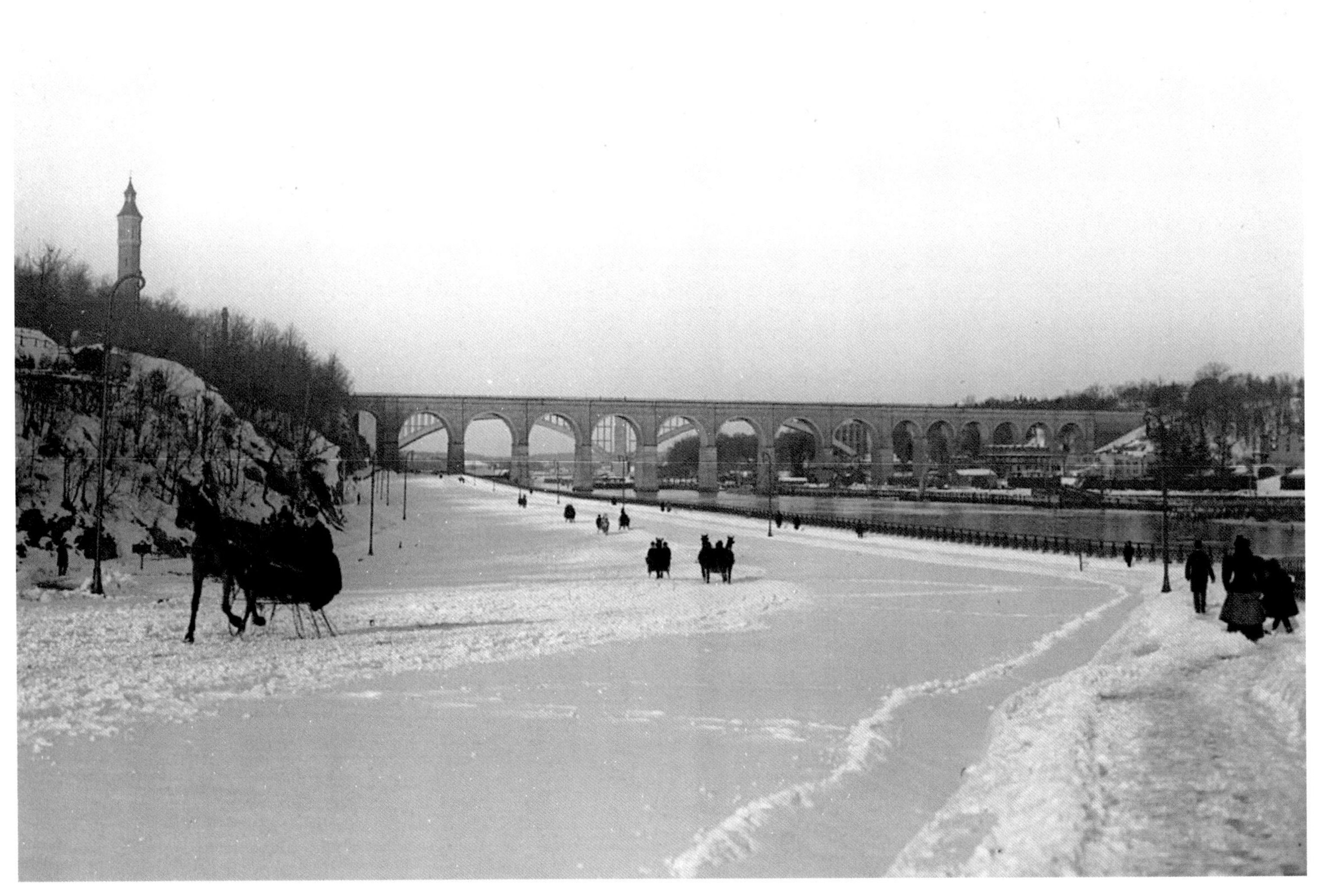

The Harlem River Speedway opened July 2, 1898, after five years of construction and nearly four million dollars. It was located on the west bank of the Harlem River, between 150th Street and Dyckman Street, and was intended for the use of horse-drawn vehicles. Here horse-drawn sleighs make their way in the snow south of High Bridge, as pedestrians stroll on the partly cleared walkway.

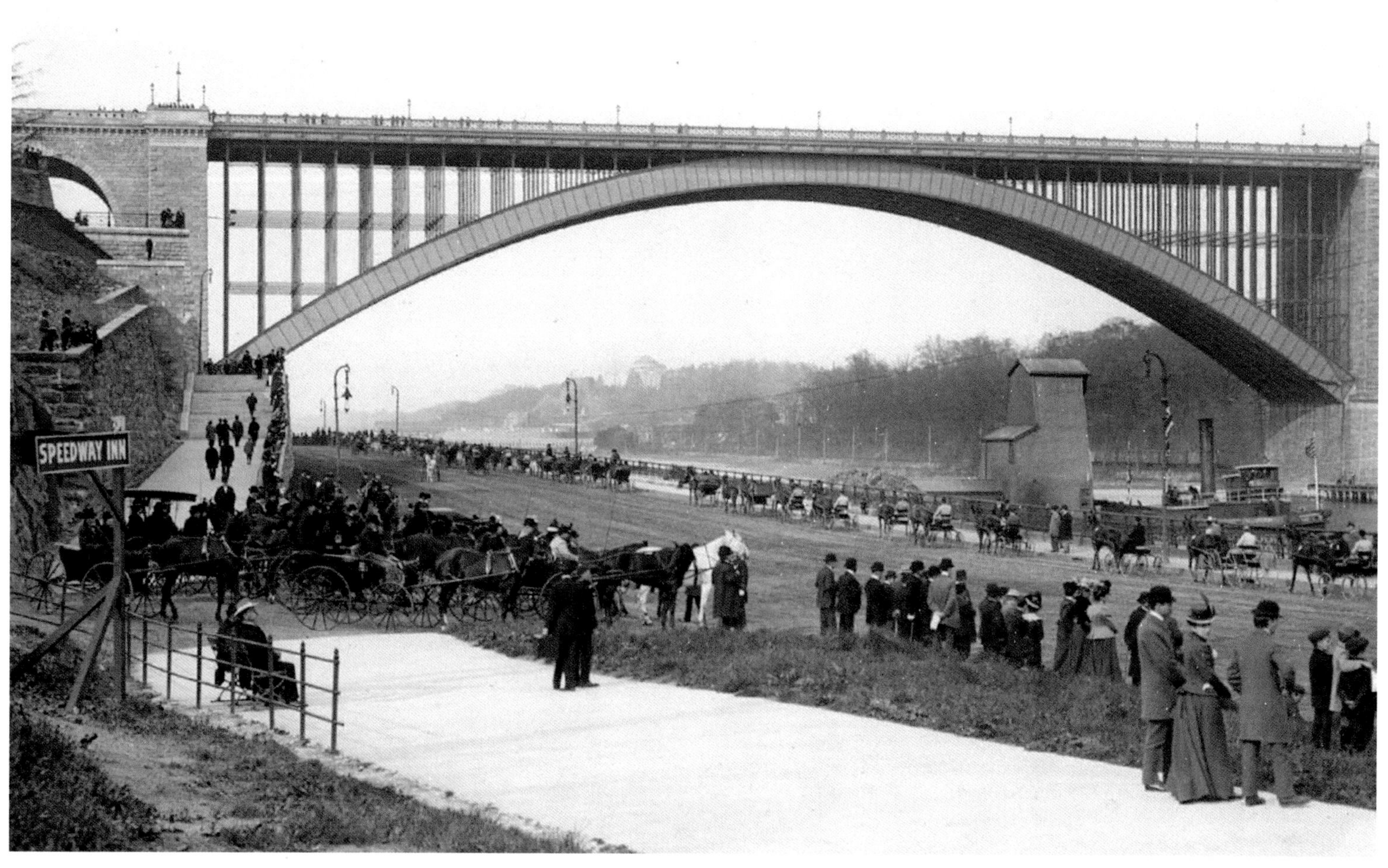

Spectators edge forward from the paved sidewalk to watch light, horse-drawn carts race along the Harlem River Speedway. The Speedway Inn, advertised at left, must have done a lively business the day of the race. Opened to cars in 1919, the speedway became the Harlem River drive in 1922, and was expanded into today's Franklin Delano Roosevelt Drive later in the twentieth century.

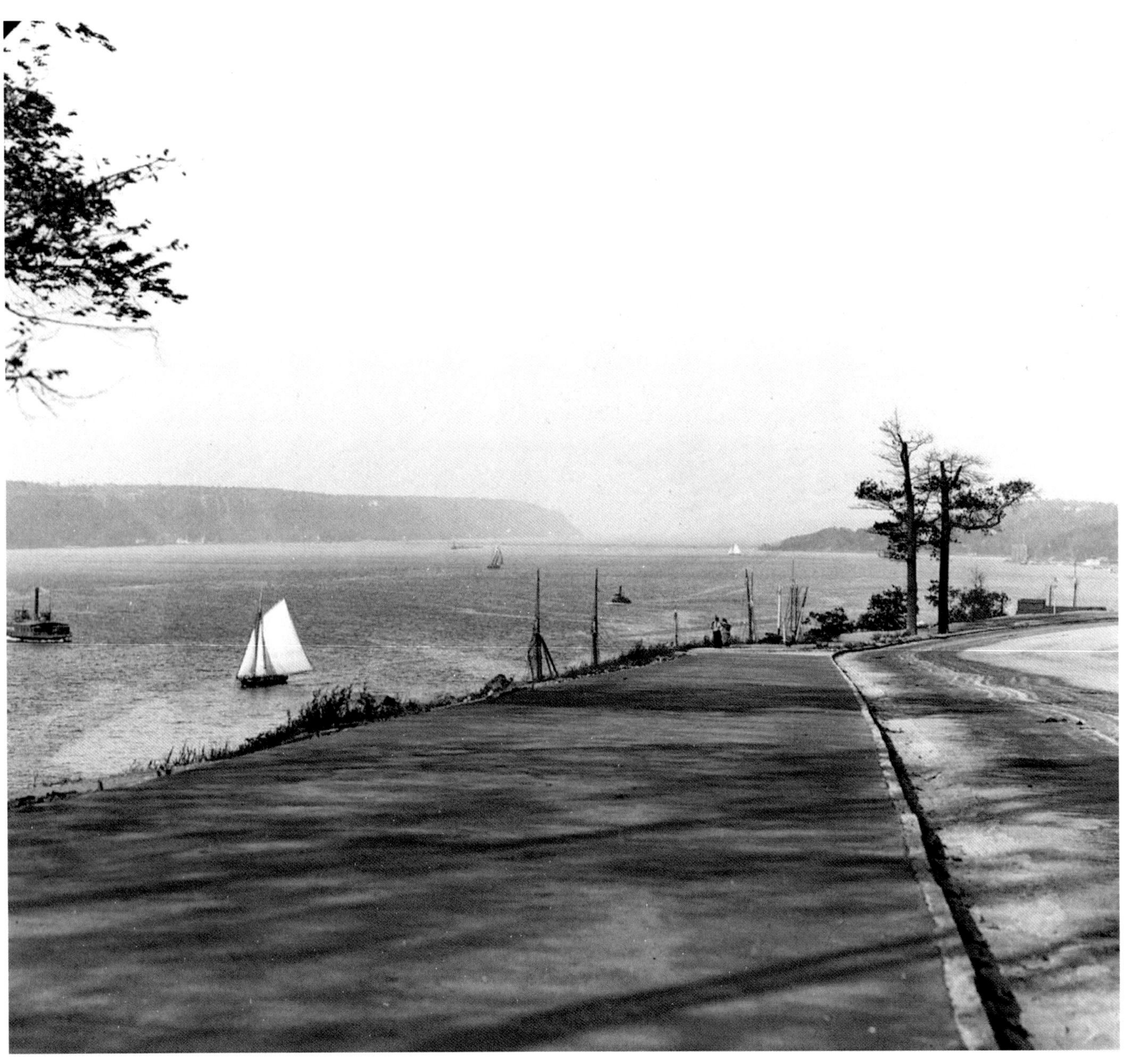

This photograph was taken shortly after the completion of Grant's Tomb in 1897. The camera looks north from the tomb in Morningside Heights toward the future location of the George Washington Bridge, between Washington Heights and Fort Lee, New Jersey.

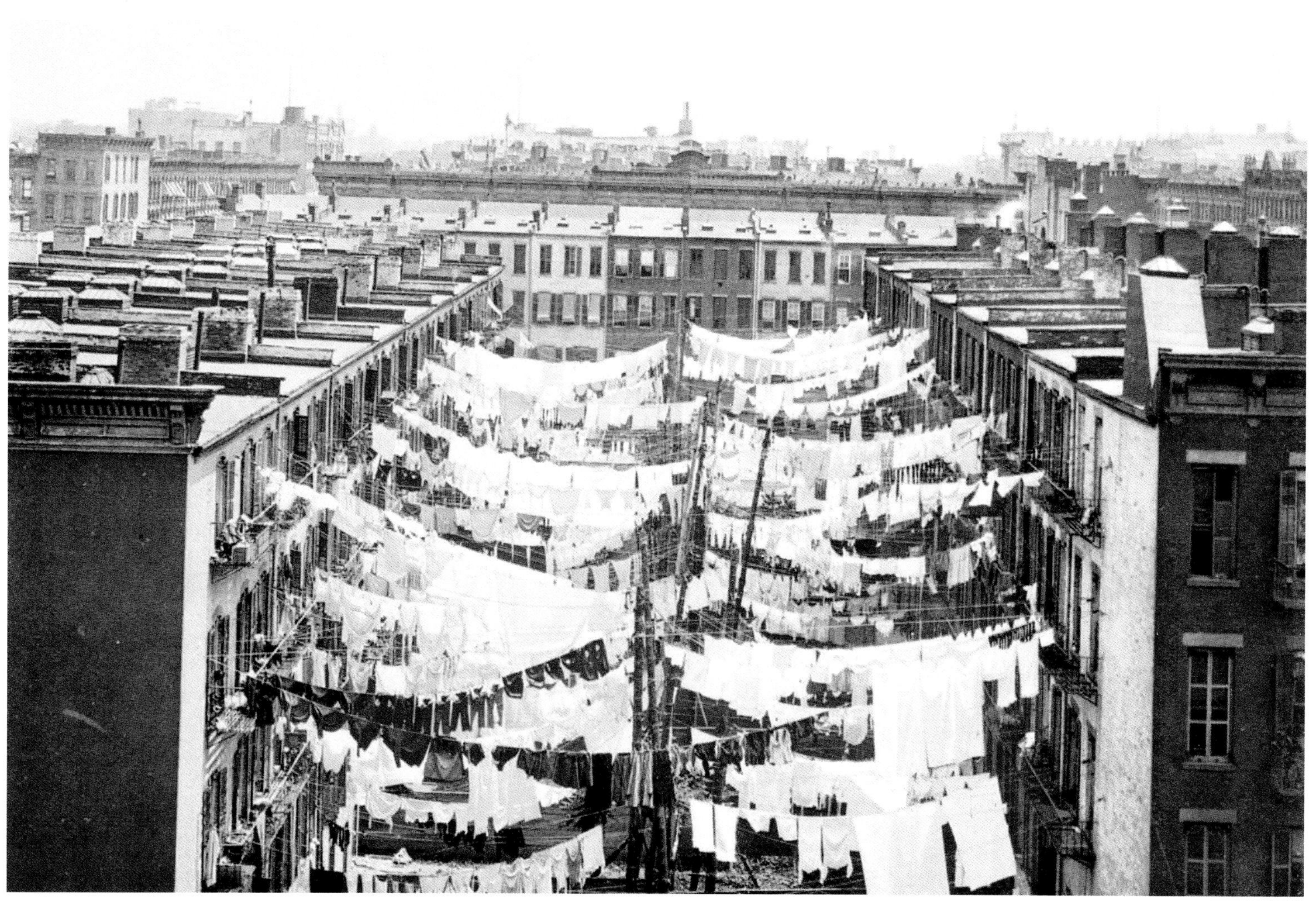

This is 107th Street between Park Avenue and Fifth Avenue in New York City. The New York clothesline, wrote Jacob Riis, is "poverty's honest badge."

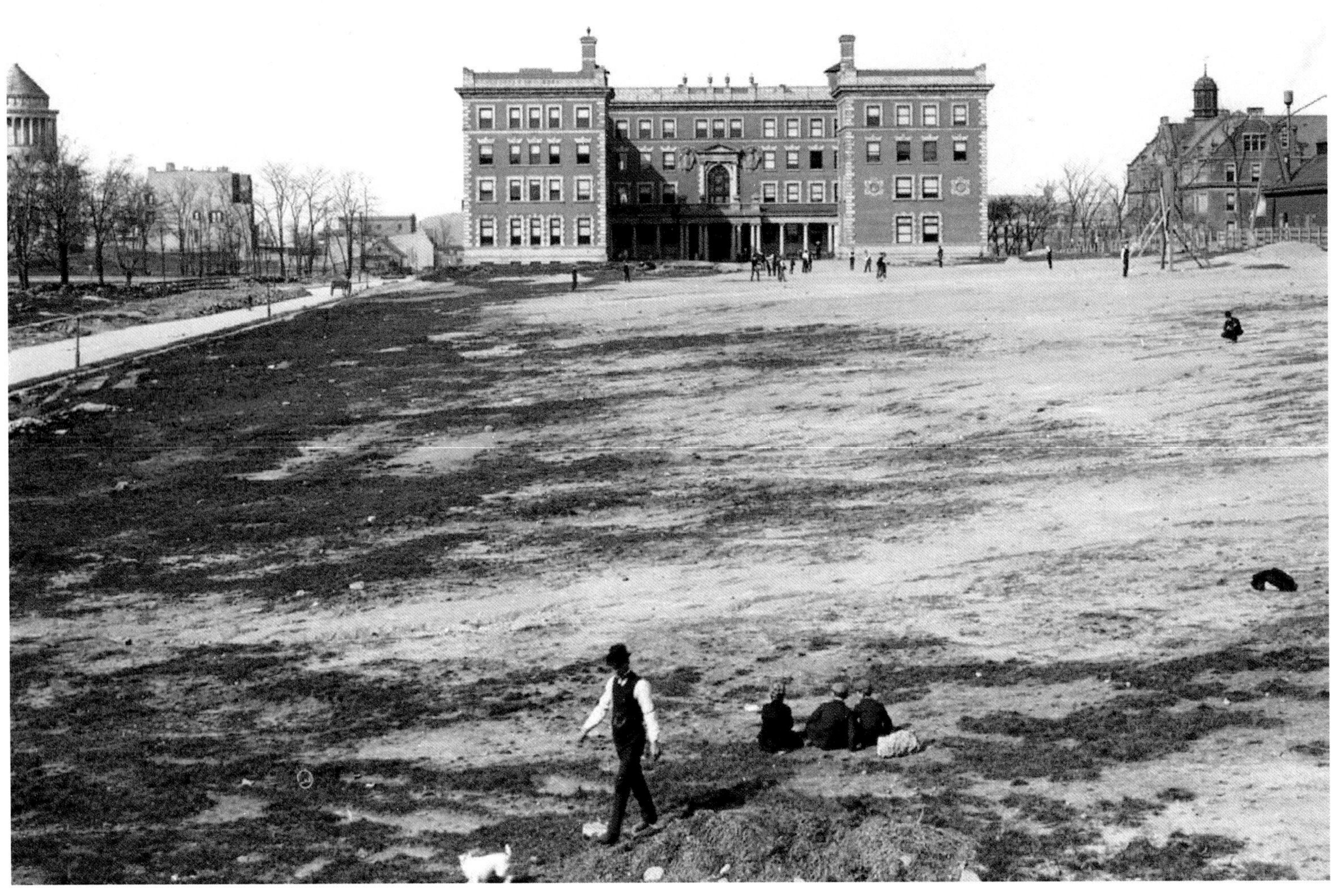

The Battle of Harlem Heights, September 16, 1776, gave new confidence to the Continental Army after Washington's defeat at the Battle of Long Island on August 27. It is said that the advanced American and British forces met in a buckwheat field that once lay at Barnard College on Morningside Heights. The women's college moved into this building in 1897, the year that Grant's Tomb (visible at left) was completed.

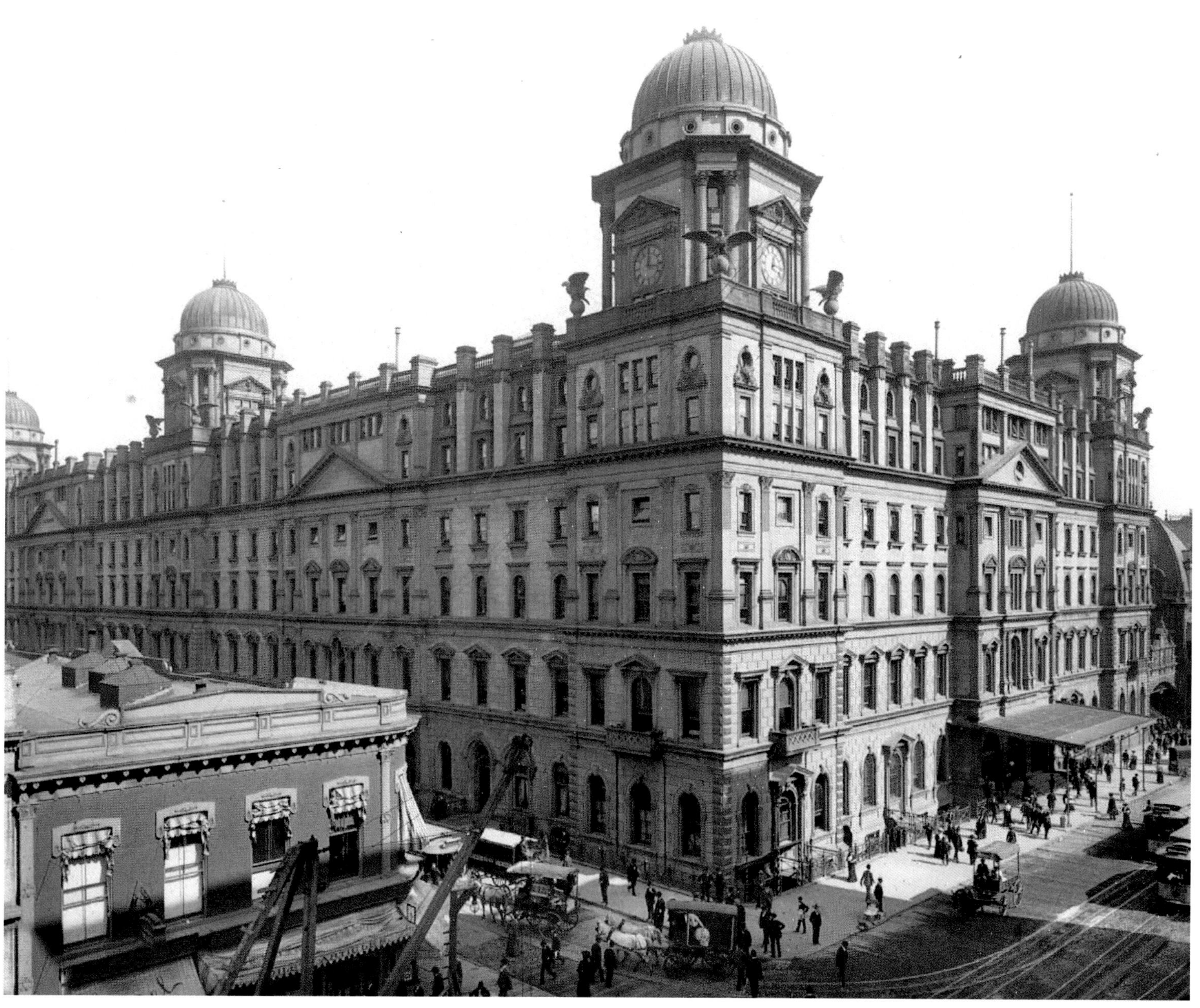

The old Grand Central Depot opened in October 1871. Its train shed featured convenient platforms that were the same height as the passenger cars. The building is shown here after its expansion between 1899 and 1900, and after receiving the new name of Grand Central Station. Tracks that earlier had continued south past 42nd Street now ended at the station. It would be replaced with Grand Central Terminal, completed in 1913.

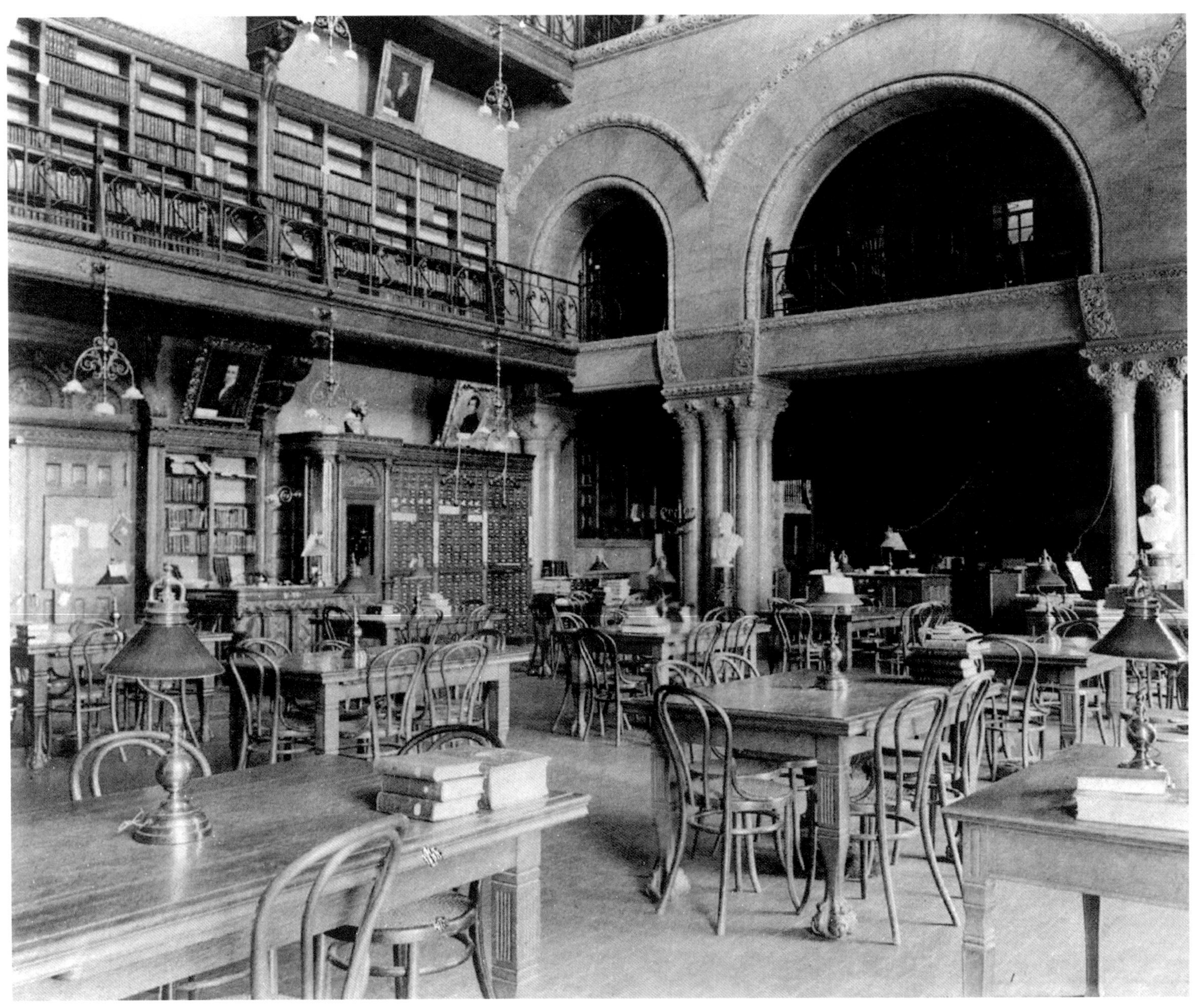

The old New York State Library was once located in the New York State Capitol at Albany, until a 1911 fire severely damaged it, destroying a large portion of its collection. During construction of the capitol and its library, a succession of architects supervised the project, with Henry Hobson Richardson (1838–1886) chiefly responsible for the Richardsonian Romanesque details notable throughout. Construction began in 1867 and was not completed until 1899, a model of government inefficiency that cost twice as much as the nation's capitol in Washington, D.C.

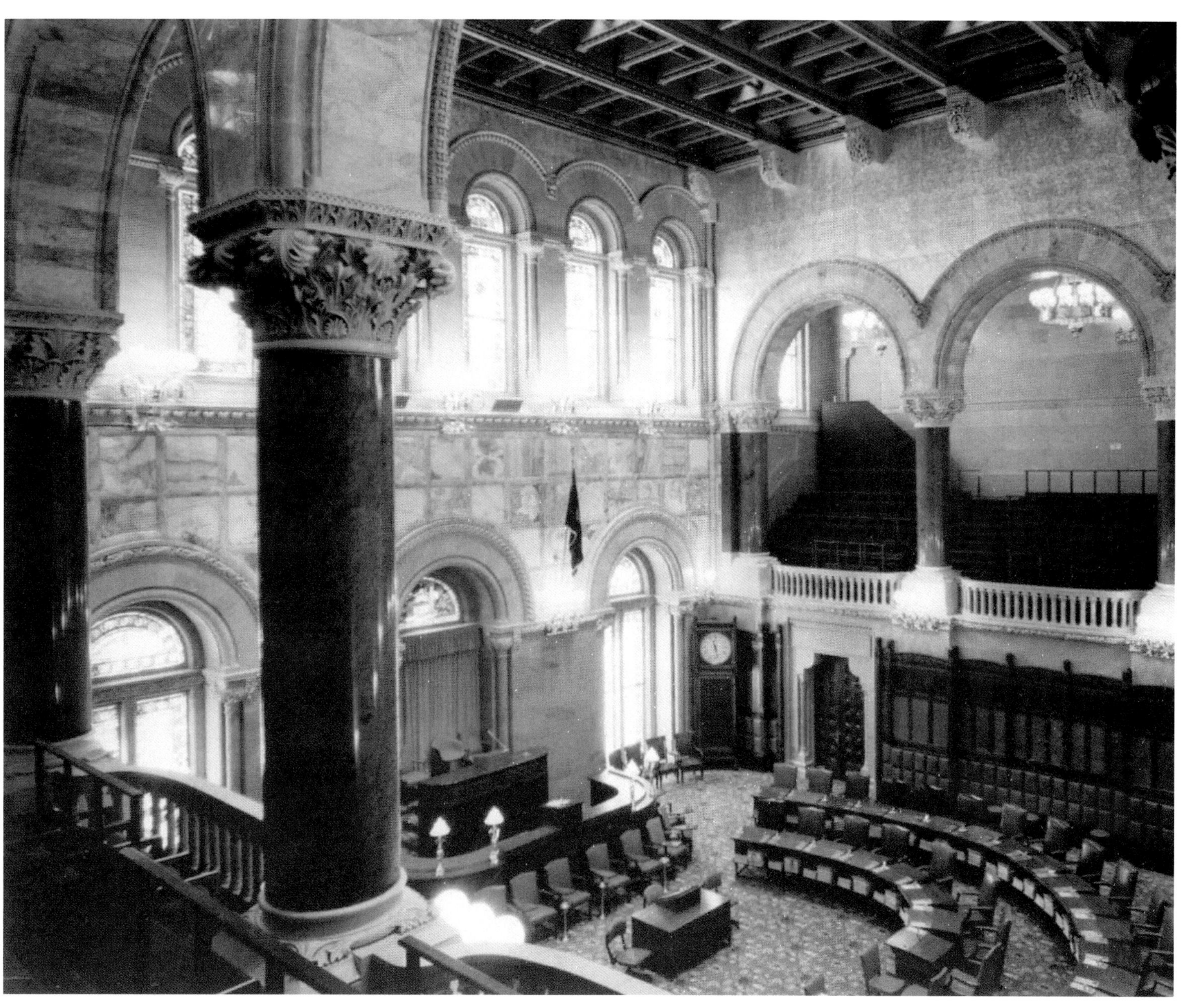

The Senate Chamber of the New York State Capitol in Albany.

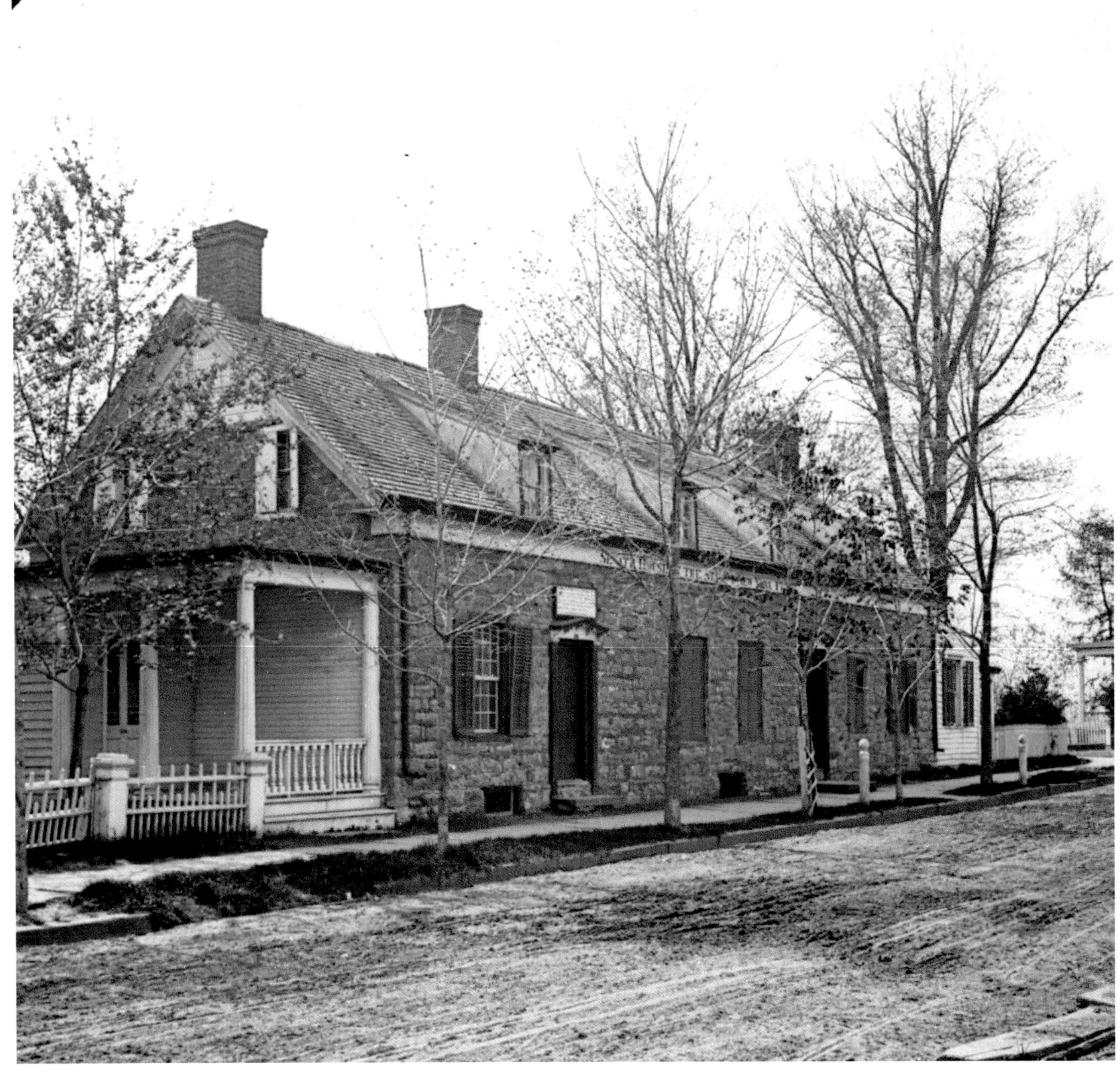

Kingston was the first capital of New York State. This picture of the Old State House is presented here at wintertime near the turn of the century. The British set fire to the building, and the rest of Kingston, on a raid up the Hudson River in 1777.

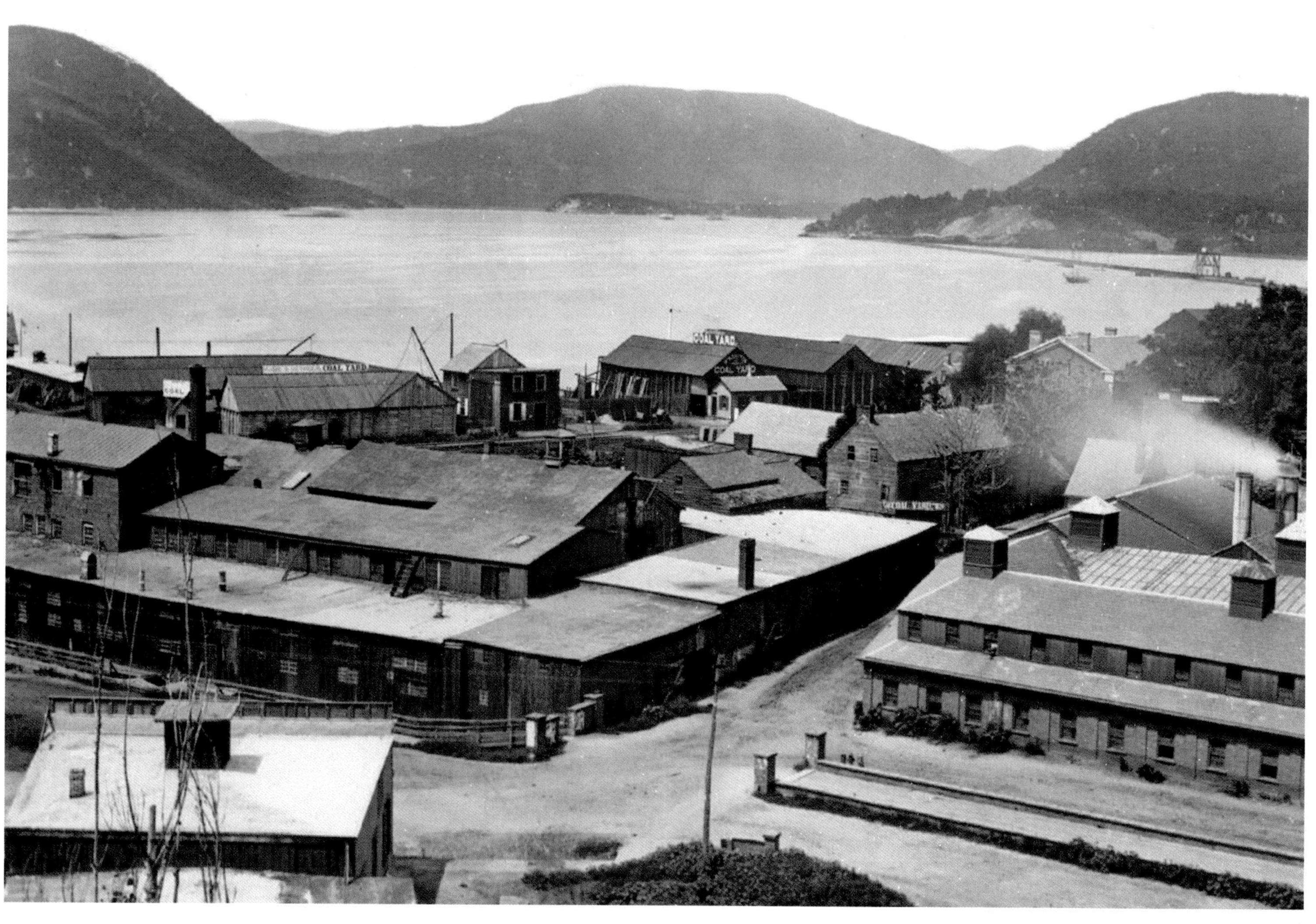

In the mid-1600s, Jan Peeck was an early European to have dealings with the native inhabitants at Peekskill. During the Revolutionary War, Peekskill helped supply Continental soldiers with gunpowder and provisions. In the nineteenth century, the place evolved into a waterfront factory town, manufacturing stoves and other iron products.

A steamer drops down the river below Anthony's Nose and telegraph poles mark the western shoreline in this photograph taken at the close of the century. The name "Anthony's Nose" dates from the 1600s, and the mountain constitutes the "South Gate" of the Hudson Highlands.

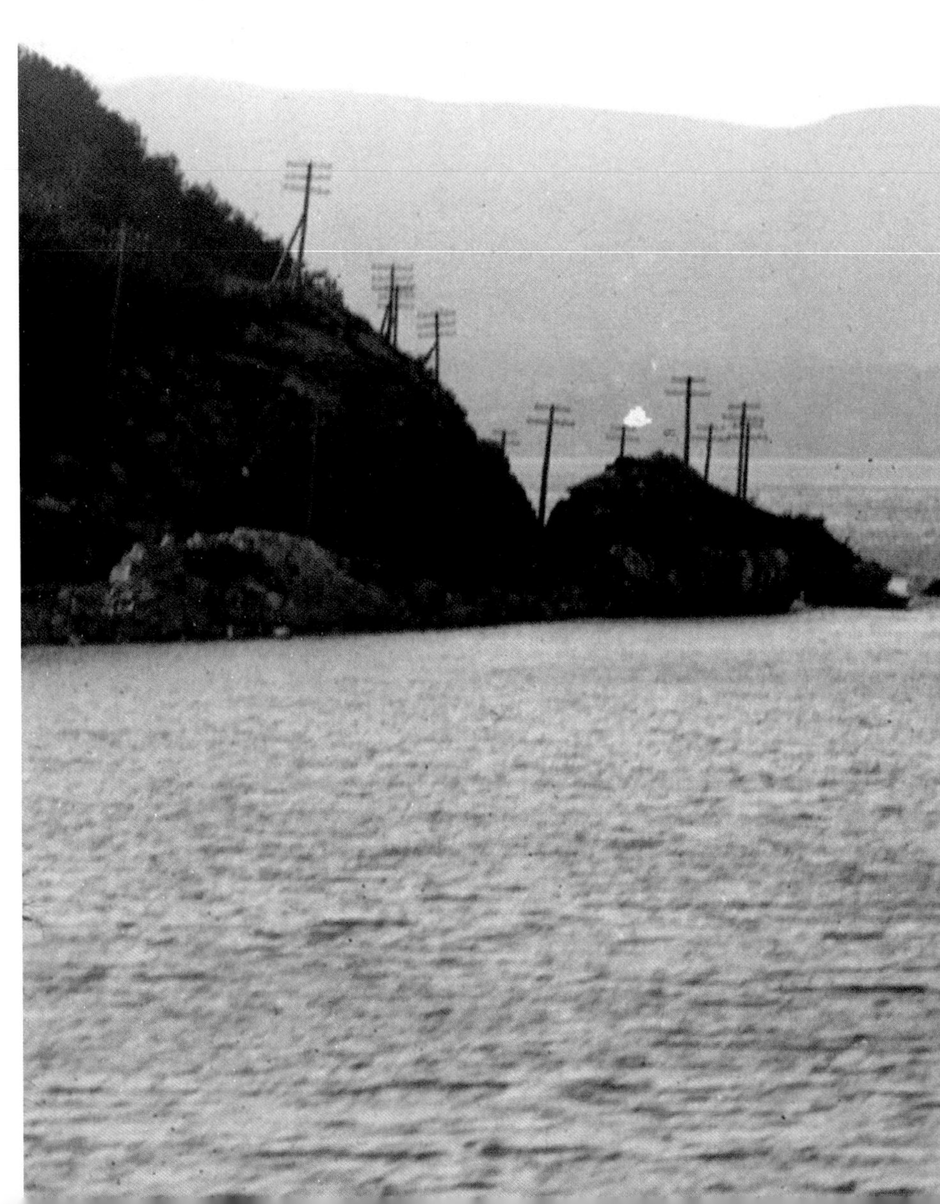

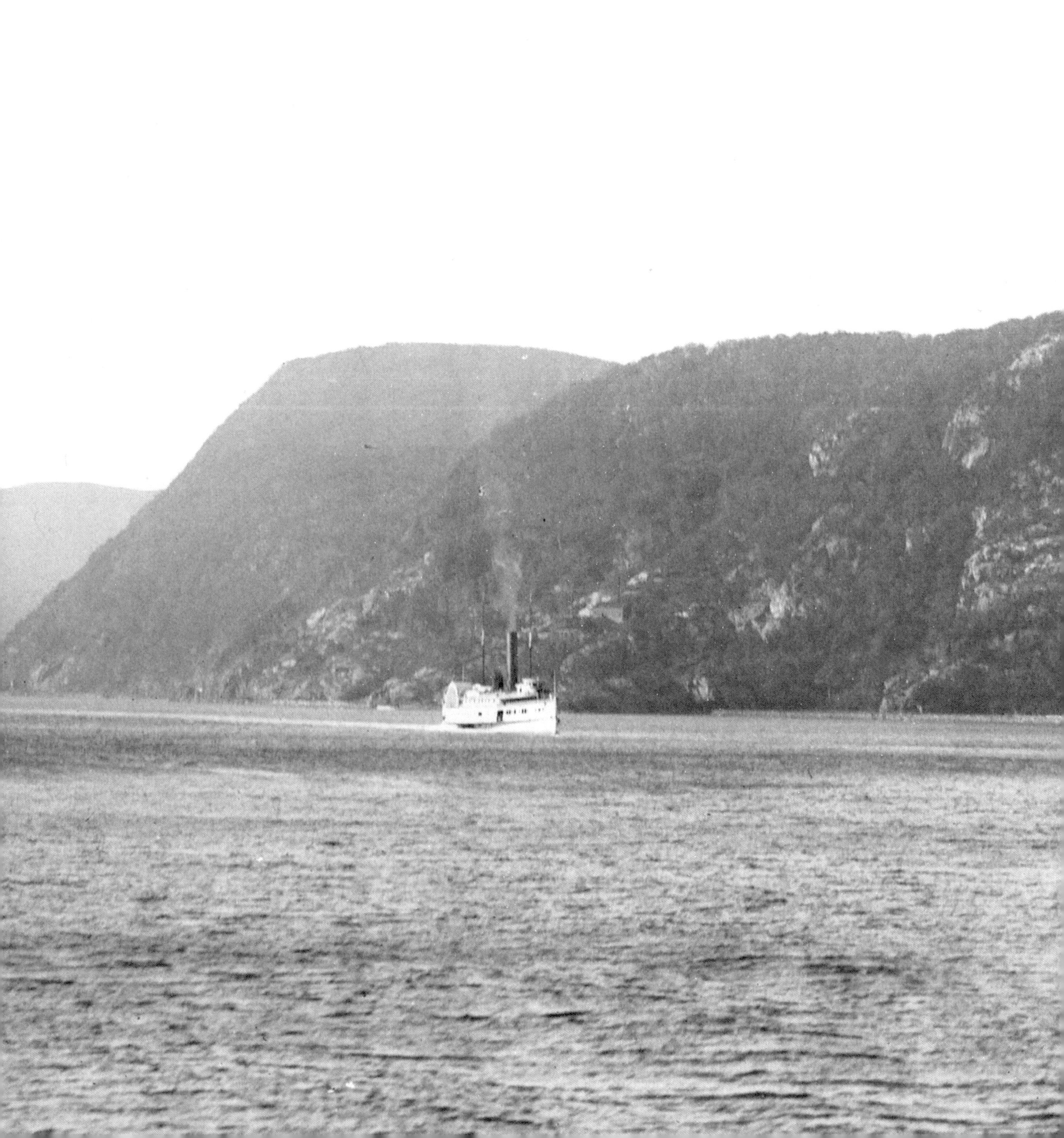

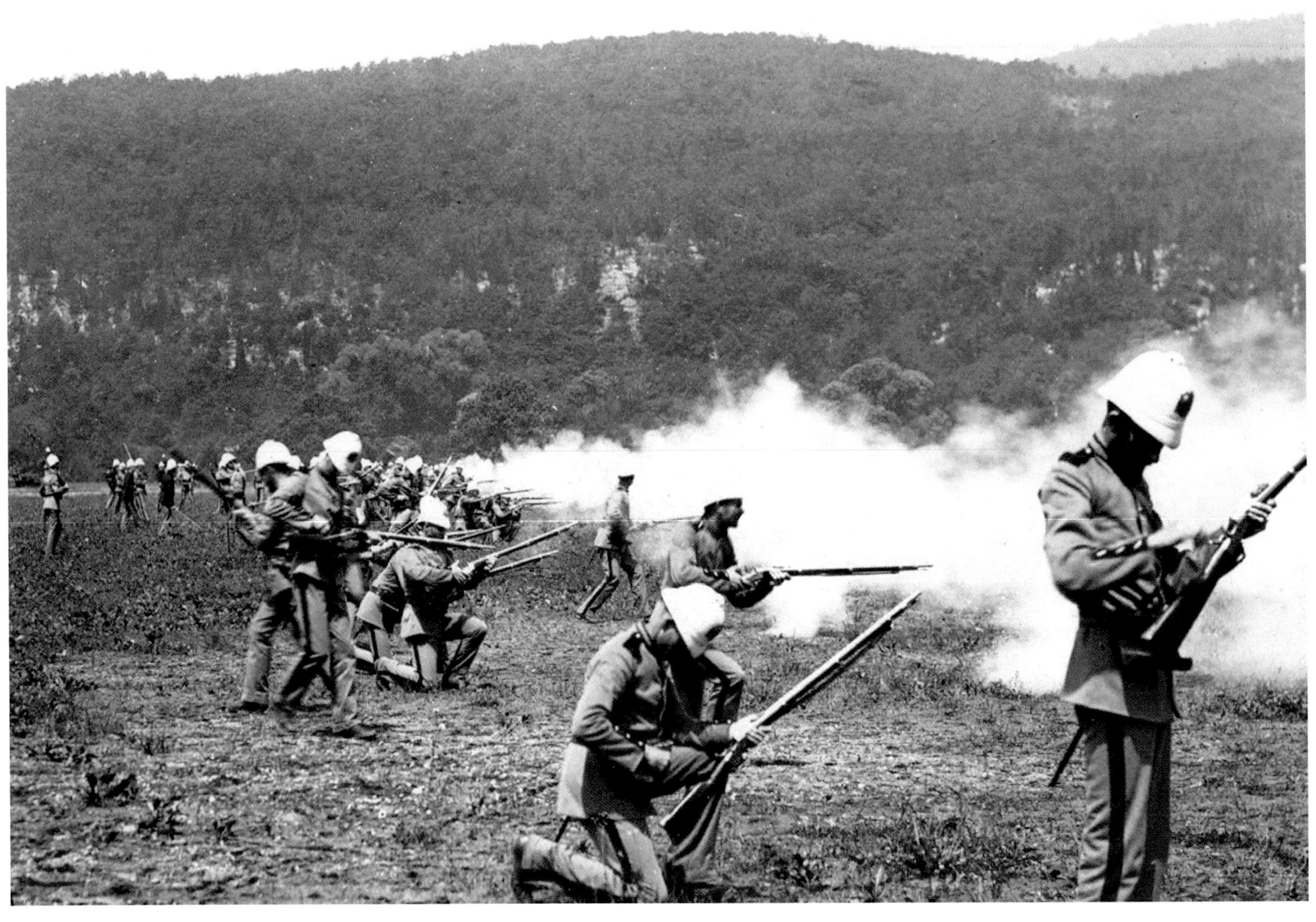

Peekskill State Camp, seen here in the late nineteenth century, is now Camp Smith, named after former New York governor Al Smith. In 1882, the original camp included roughly 100 acres and lay east of the Hudson, at the foot of the well-known peak Anthony's Nose. The summer militia encampments held there focused on marksmanship and drill. The camp is now designated a CTA, or Collective Training Area, by the National Guard Bureau.

Civic Pride and Civic Projects

(1900–1920)

In the closing decades of the nineteenth century, Hudson River villages had ceased to be mere hamlets. No longer dots on a map, they assumed a new status as village corporations, larger entities with boundaries and populations and taxes to be levied for services provided. The ambition and vigor with which these incorporation designs were pressed forward would determine how each river town evolved in the twentieth century.

Much of the land along the Hudson had turned from forest, to farm, to estate; the next step would be residential development. The "captains and kings" of industry had already made homes on the banks of the Hudson; now it was the turn of the manager and the successful small business owner. The first upper-middle-class, suburban, residential developments began to appear in the first decade of the twentieth century.

The waterfronts and centers of towns continued their commercial and industrial growth. Yet now, homegrown manufacturing of shoes, pottery, buttons, fertilizer, boats, and bricks was giving way to the production of rock drills, automobiles, and furnaces. With the fruits of these ventures came civic improvements: paved roads, electric streetlamps, new libraries, and improved water supplies to meet rising demand. Hudson Line communities took pride in current innovations and embraced them—the automobile among them. There was growth in the number of churches, schools, municipal buildings, and civic organizations, which reflected the vitality and civic pride of the river towns.

New York City was expanding too, but on a larger scale, yet similar changes are notable in New York City itself. In the "consolidation" of 1898, the great city became a metropolis, incorporating the four surrounding boroughs and vastly increasing its resources and influence. The change ensured the city its workforce, its tax base, its political sway, and, ultimately, its power to dictate its own destiny. The Bronx Parks, past which the Hudson Line railroad ran on its way north, were a reflection of civic identity as well as a practical release from the pressures of too much municipal success. The respite in the greenery of the Bronx was to be short-lived. Soon New Yorkers would have to travel farther to escape the urban giant they were creating.

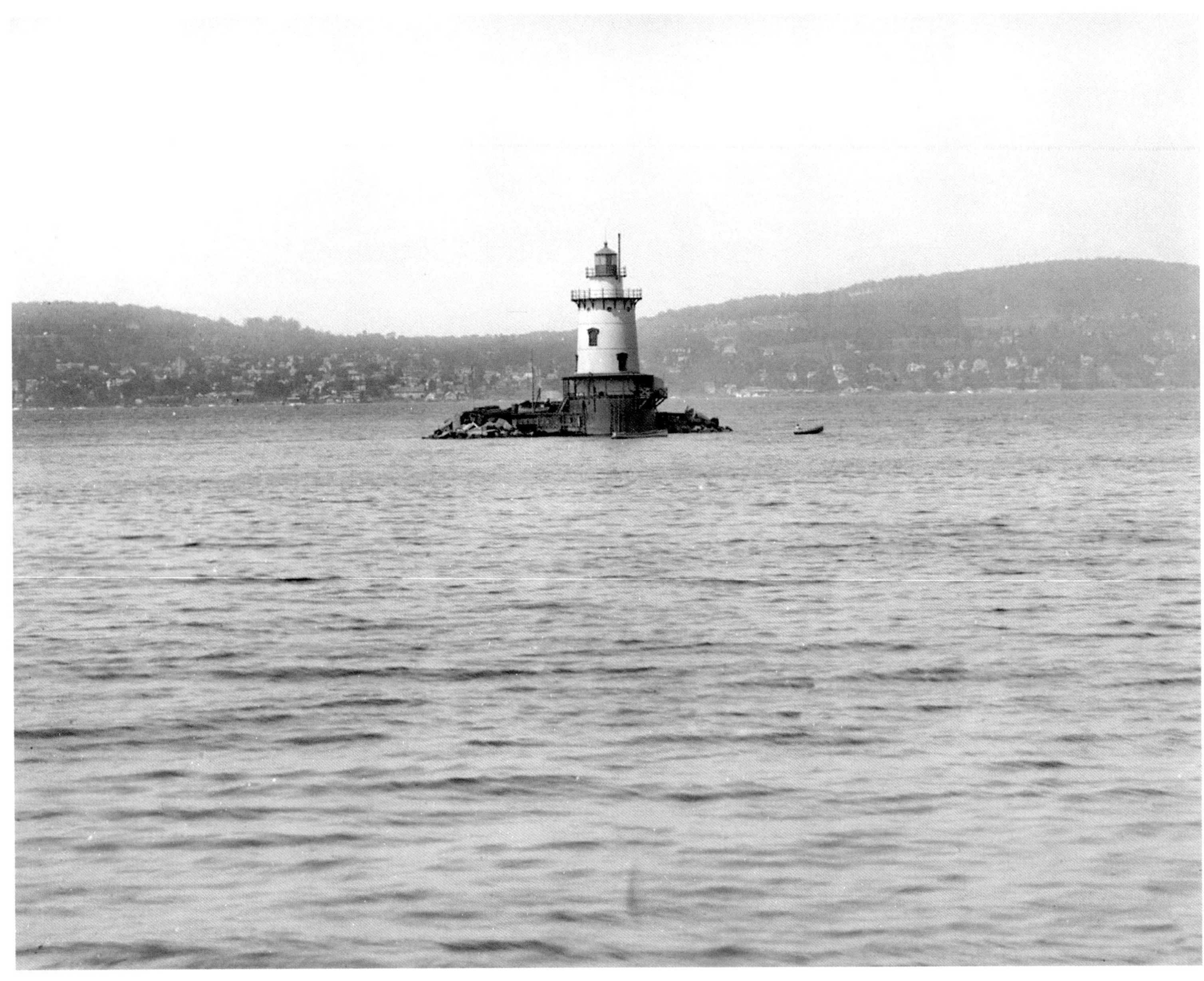

The cast-iron caisson Sleepy Hollow Lighthouse stands in Sleepy Hollow, but has been known in years past as the Tarrytown Lighthouse. It was built in 1883, and this photograph was taken in the early twentieth century, before the General Motors landfill operations brought the shoreline almost out to the lighthouse itself. For decades the car plant obscured the view of the light from shore. The structure was decommissioned in 1965.

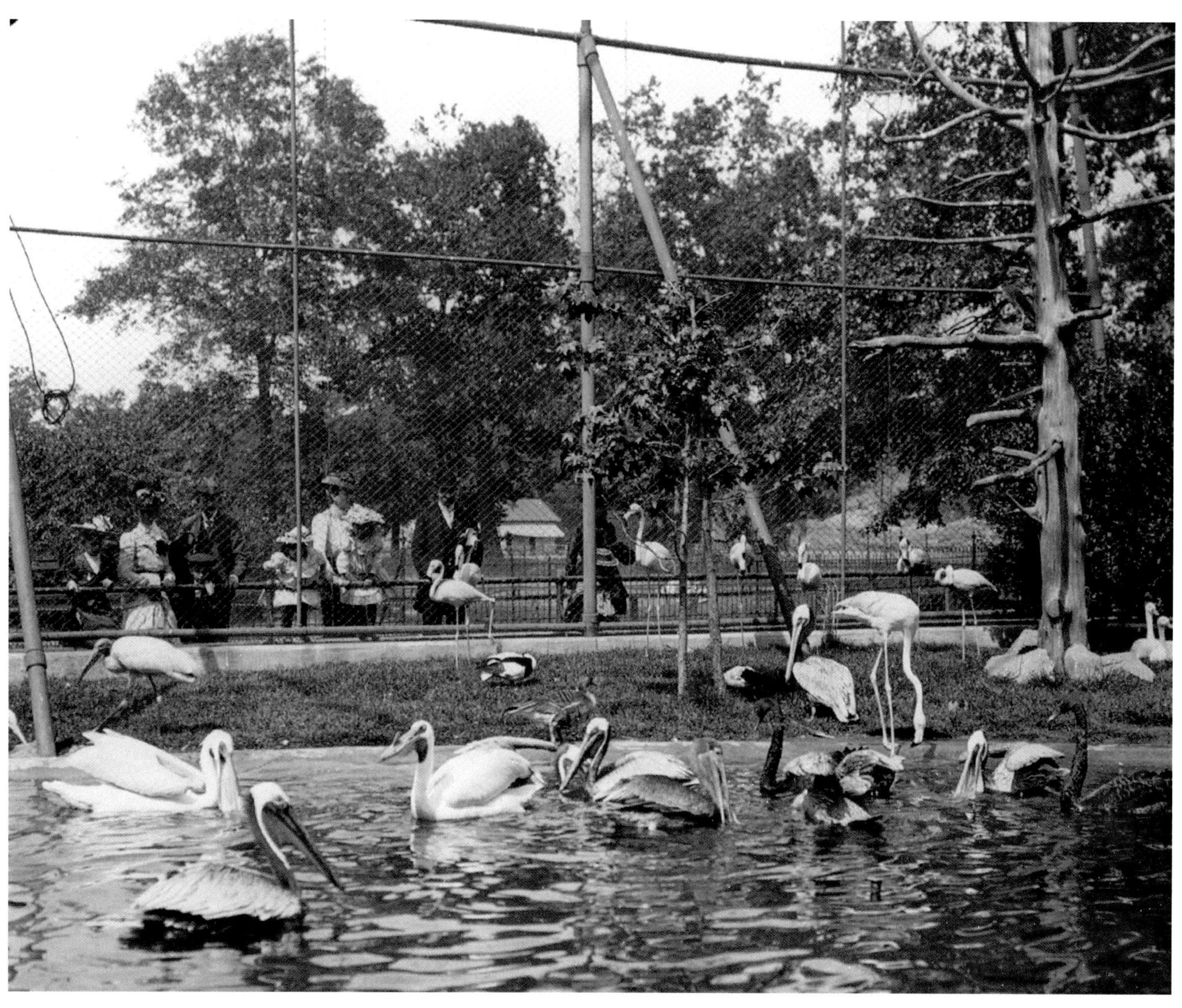

Opened in 1899 on 285 acres of the Bronx, the Bronx Zoo was originally called New York Zoological Park. Visitors in view here watch flamingos at an aviary pool in the early twentieth century. In 1995, a snowstorm collapsed the Victorian iron aviary enclosure, releasing more than 30 exotic birds to harsh weather conditions.

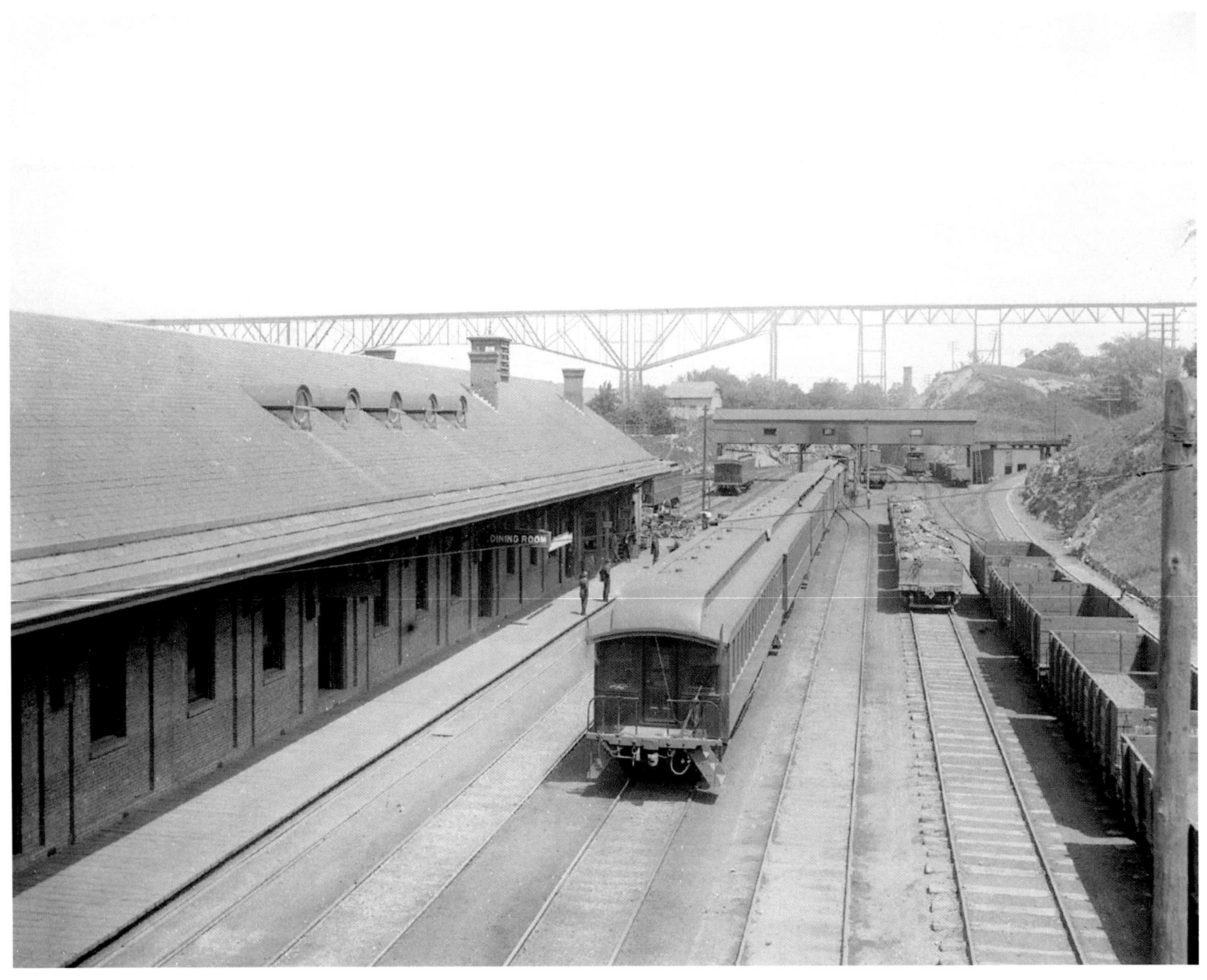

Passenger cars and freight cars idle on the tracks in this view recorded at the Poughkeepsie station. In the distance, the Poughkeepsie-Highland Railroad Bridge, built in 1889, spans the Hudson River, linking Poughkeepsie on the east bank with Highland on the west. The bridge was slated to reopen in 2009 as a pedestrian bridge for the local state park that today covers the area.

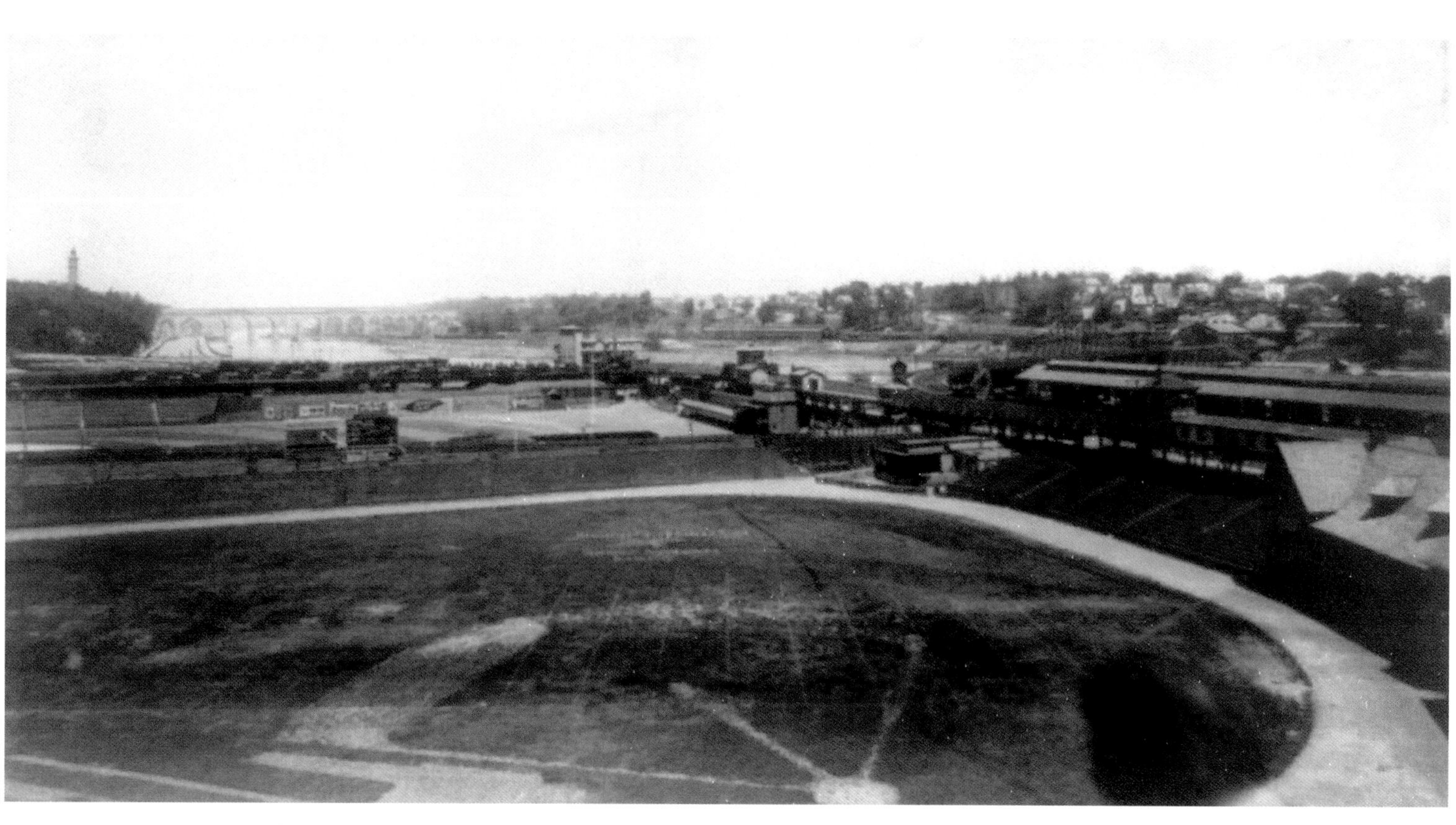

This photograph, by Irving Underhill (1872–1960), was taken about 1901. The Polo Grounds were located at 155th Street and Frederick Douglass Boulevard, just across the Harlem River from the future site of Yankee Stadium.

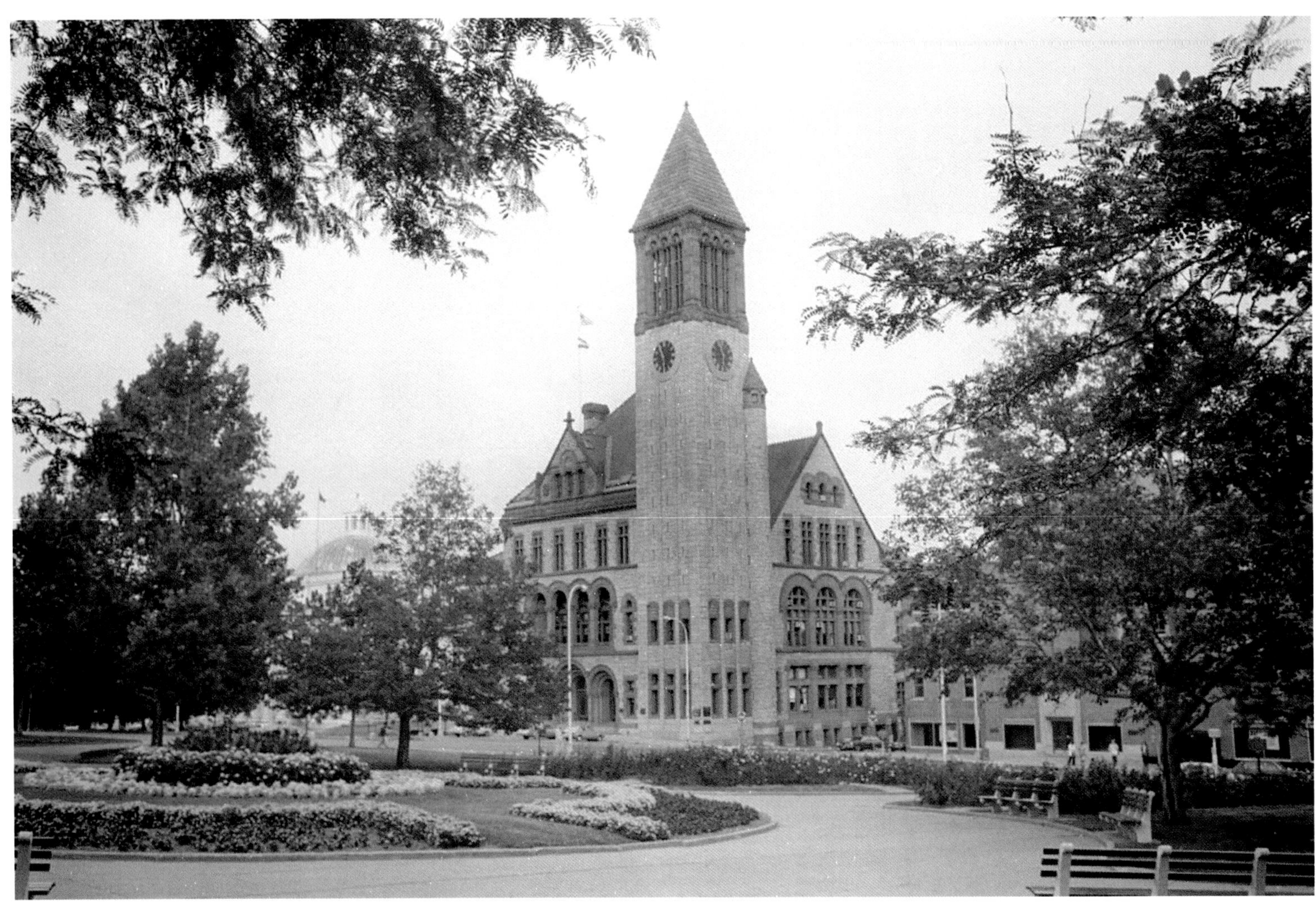

Architect Henry Hobson Richardson designed Albany City Hall before he was assigned to continue the work in progress on the New York State Capitol. The city hall was completed in 1883 and built of granite, in the Romanesque style. One of its most prominent features is the 60-bell carillon in its clock tower.

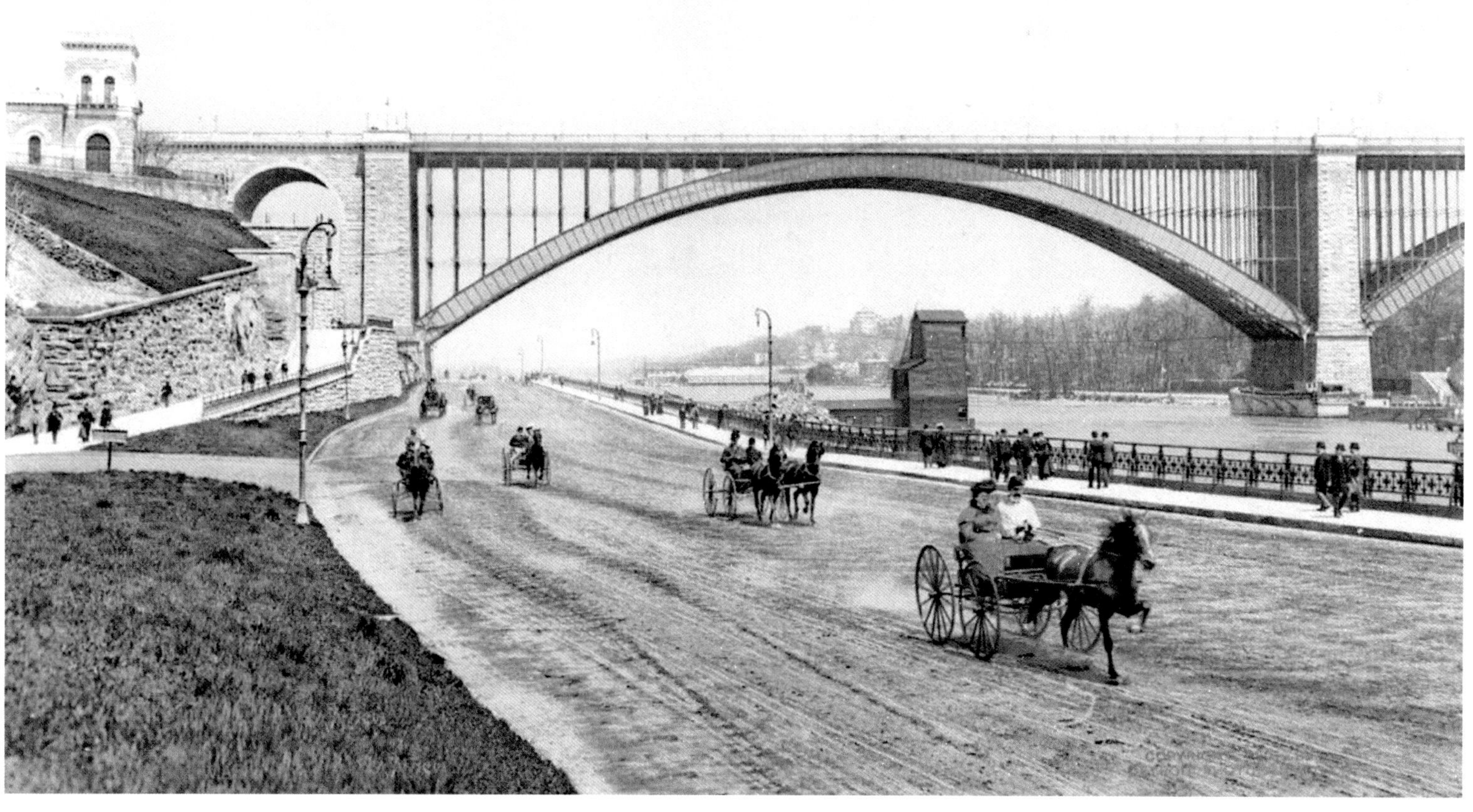

Here is a section of the Harlem River Speedway, just south of the Washington Bridge, illuminated at night with incandescent streetlamps. Equestrians, bike riders, sulkies, and all two-wheeled vehicles were restricted from use, but surreys and runabouts could be taken down the course at full speed. Pedestrians were able to cross from side to side through the speedway's three tunnels.

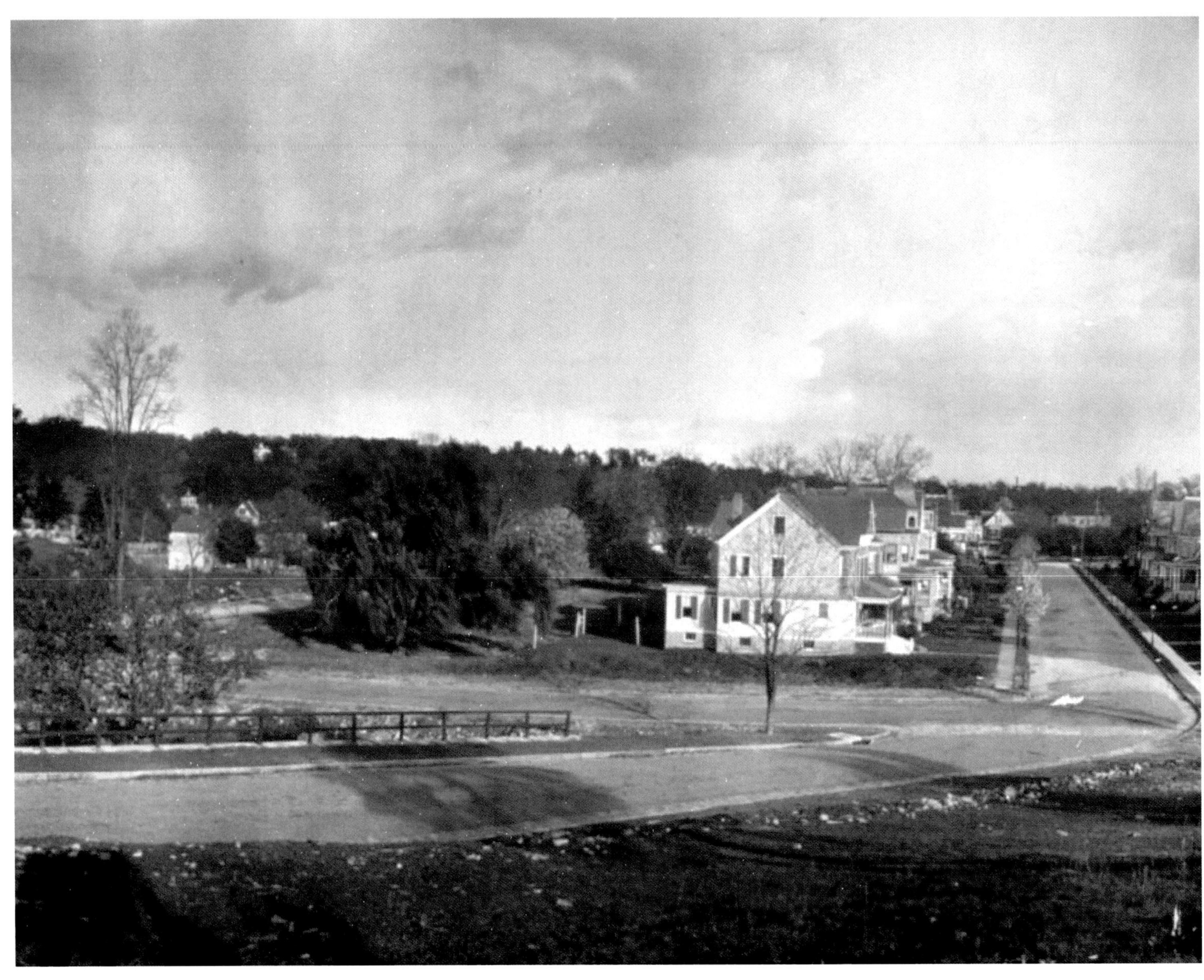

In 1888, the American Real Estate Company constructed a luxury suburban neighborhood named Park Hill, shown here around 1902. The development was built in southwest Yonkers on a wooded plateau. The homes were designed in a variety of styles including Tudor, Arts and Crafts, Queen Anne, Victorian, Gothic Revival, and, later, Mediterranean.

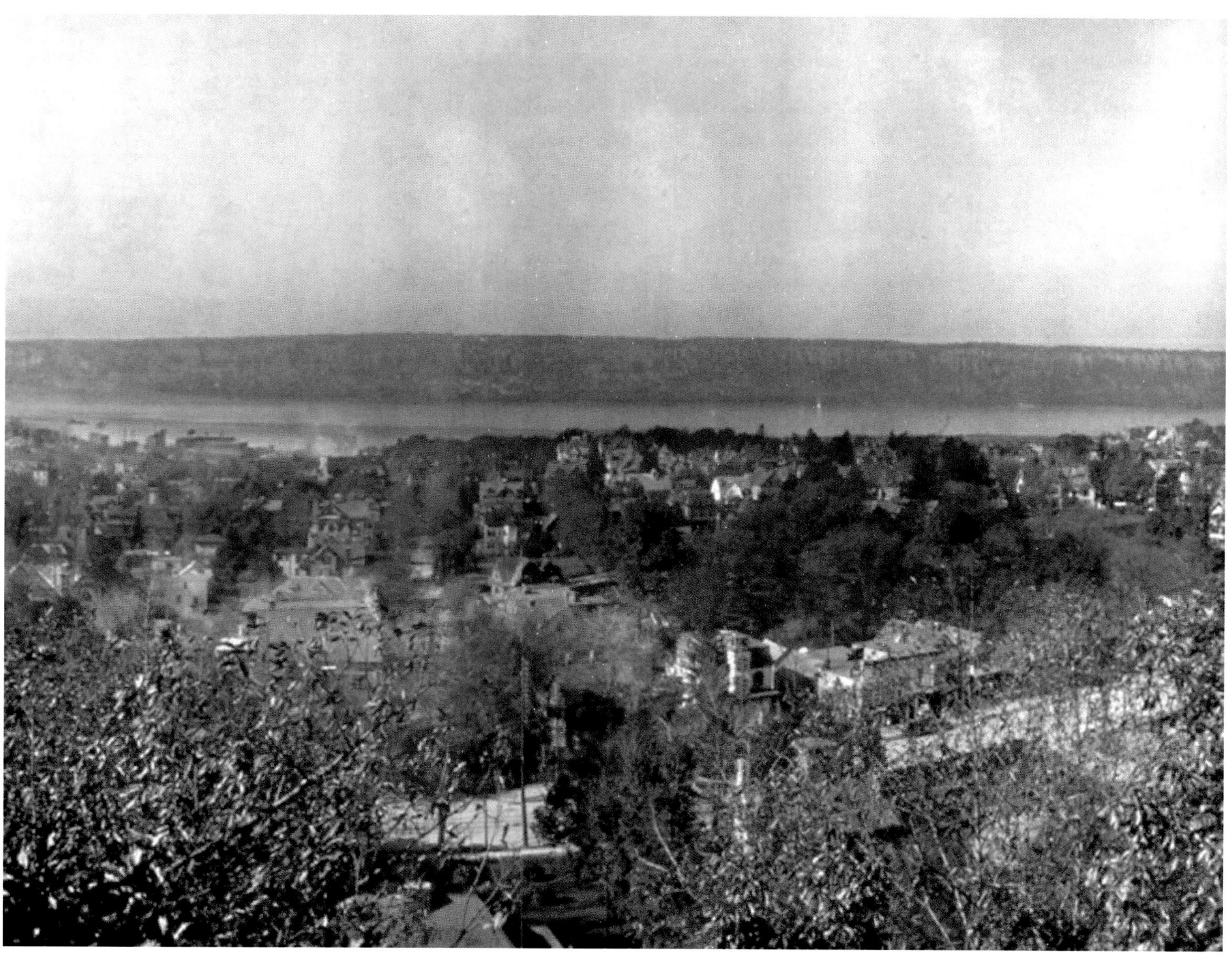

Visible from Park Hill in 1902, downtown Yonkers stretches out in the distance, below and to the right, with Riverdale to the left. Across the Hudson River are the Palisades. Park Hill itself rises about 300 feet above sea level.

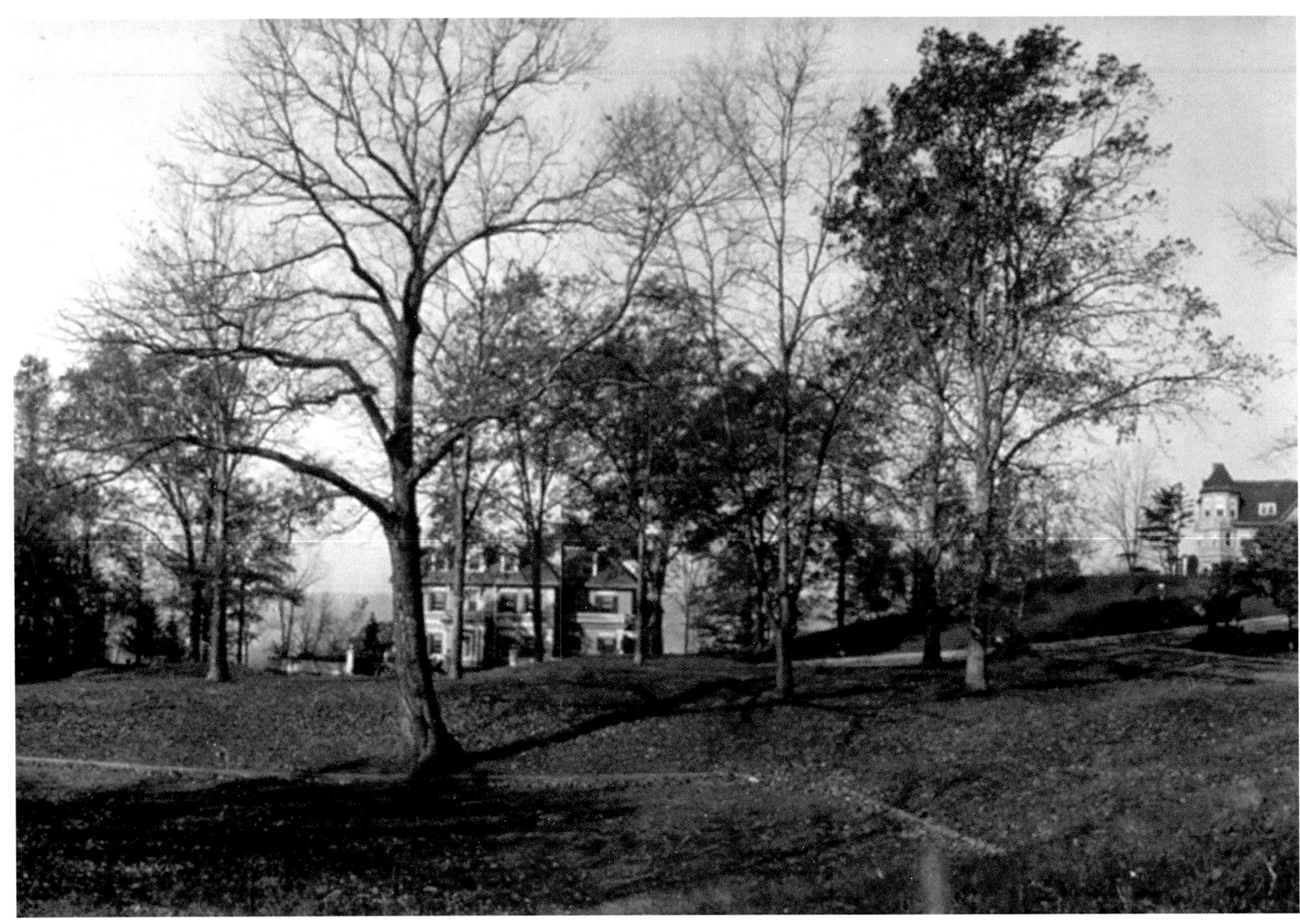

In 1902, there were already 150 homes in Park Hill.

Between 1837 and 1842, the Old Croton Aqueduct was constructed from the Croton River to Manhattan. It was a massive project for its day, supervised by engineer John B. Jervis, and built mainly with Irish and Italian immigrant labor. In the city, pollution, epidemics, and fires demanded that fresh water be brought to Manhattan. The aqueduct crossed the Harlem River at High Bridge and continued to the Receiving Reservoir, located where Central Park's Great Lawn lies today.

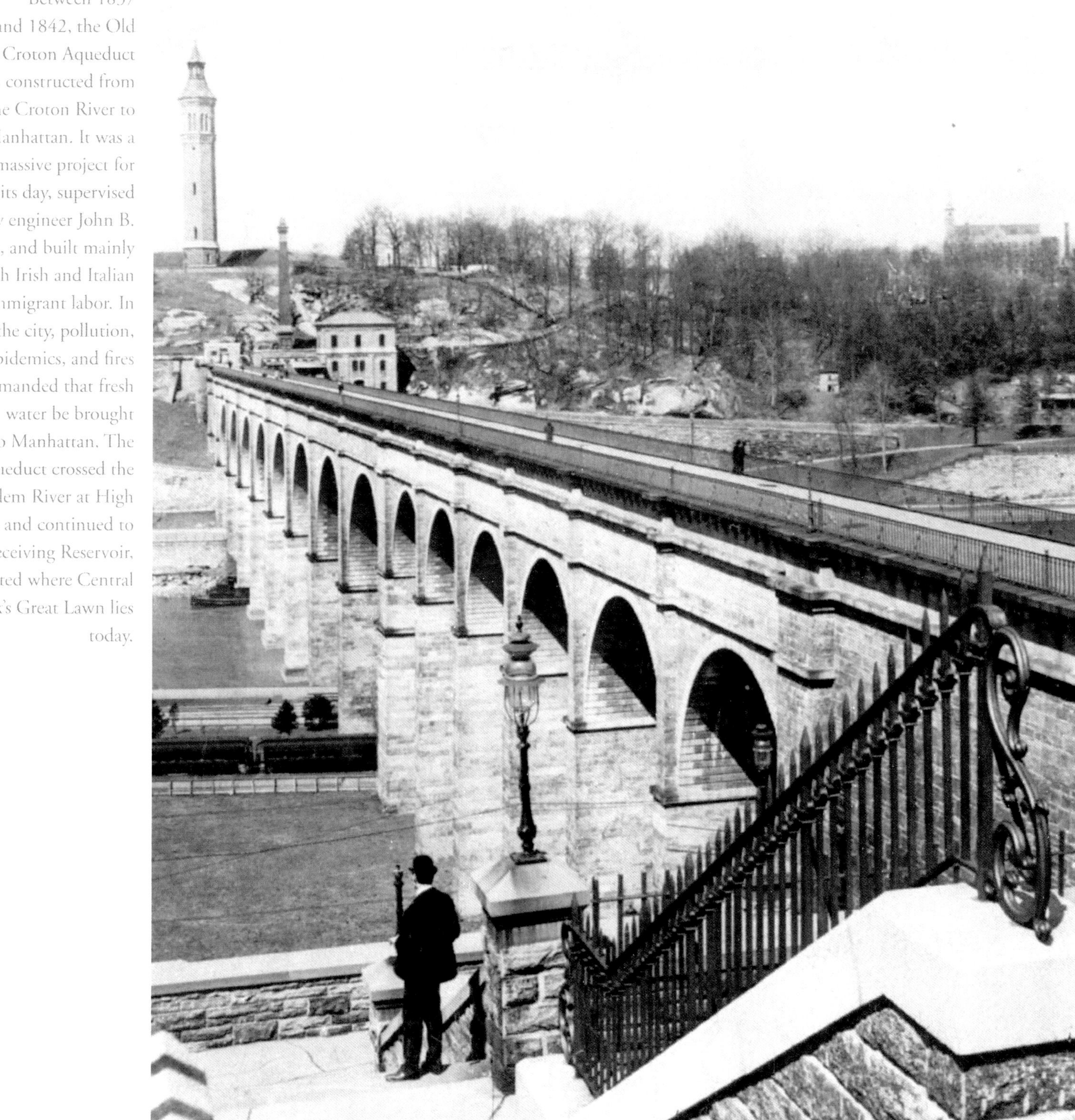

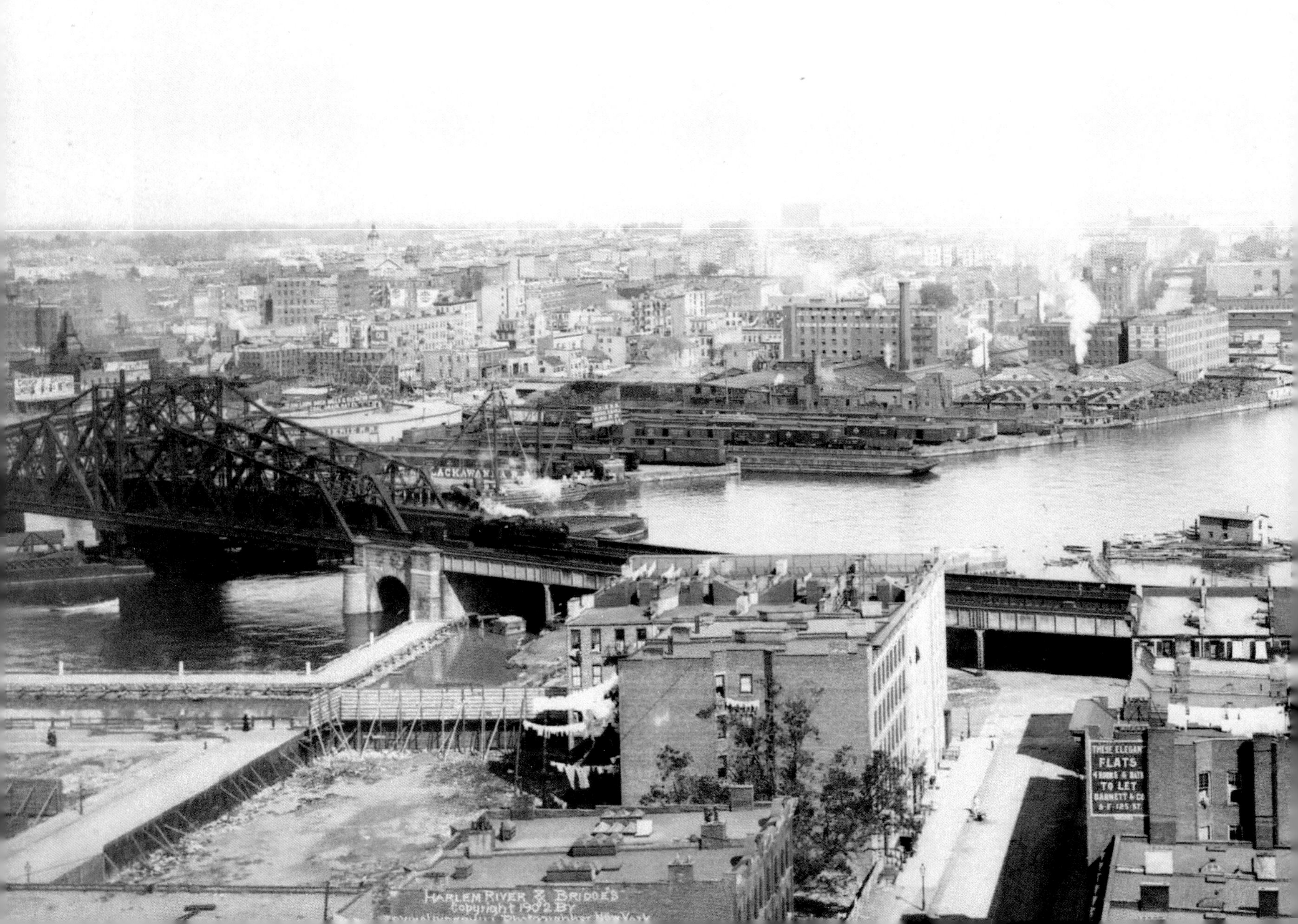
HARLEM RIVER & BRIDGES
Copyright 1902 By
FLATS
TO LET

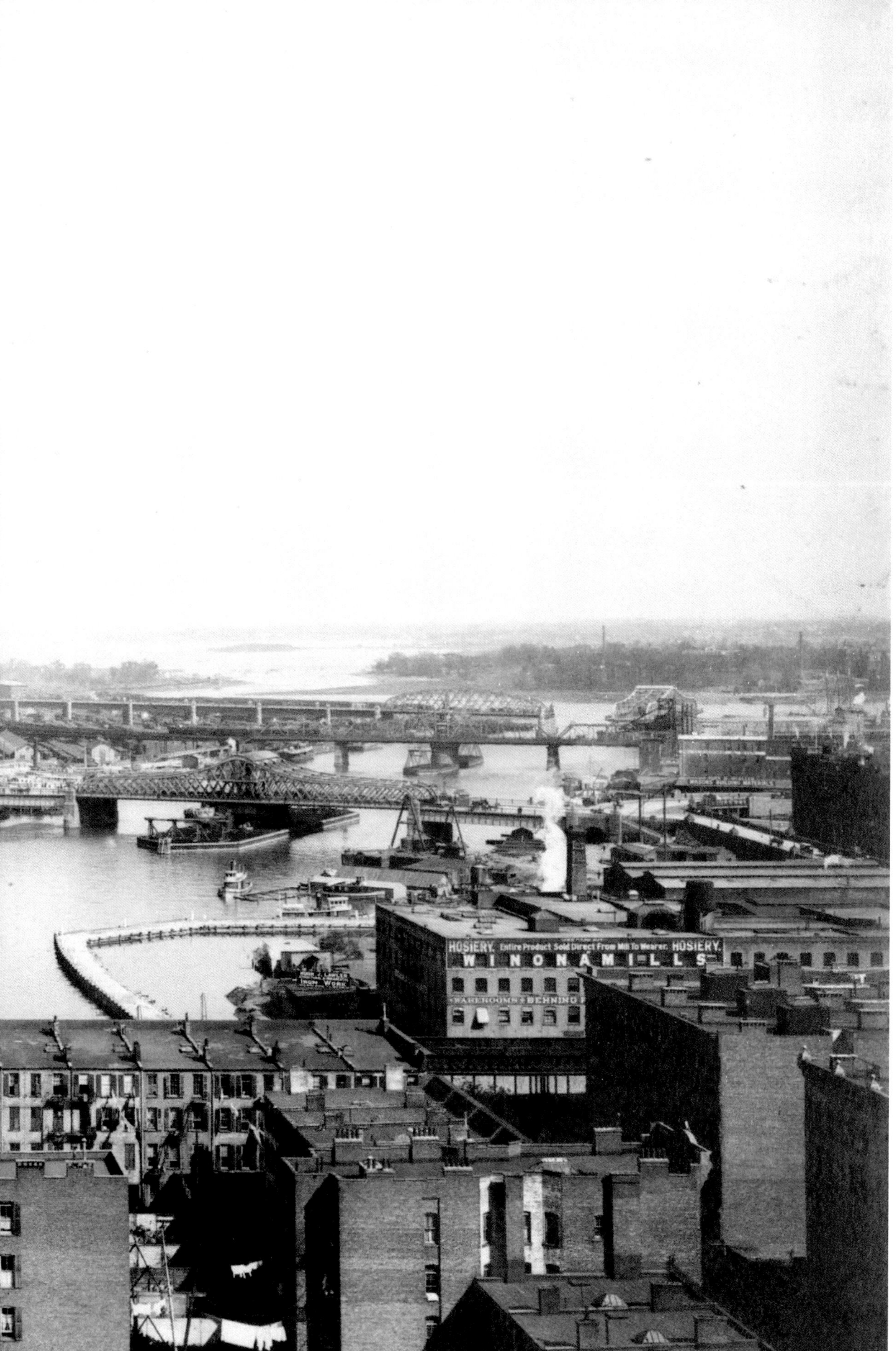

The bridges of the Harlem River are prominent in this 1902 view facing northwest. In the far distance, the junction of the Harlem and the Hudson can just be made out. A portion of the Bronx appears in the foreground.

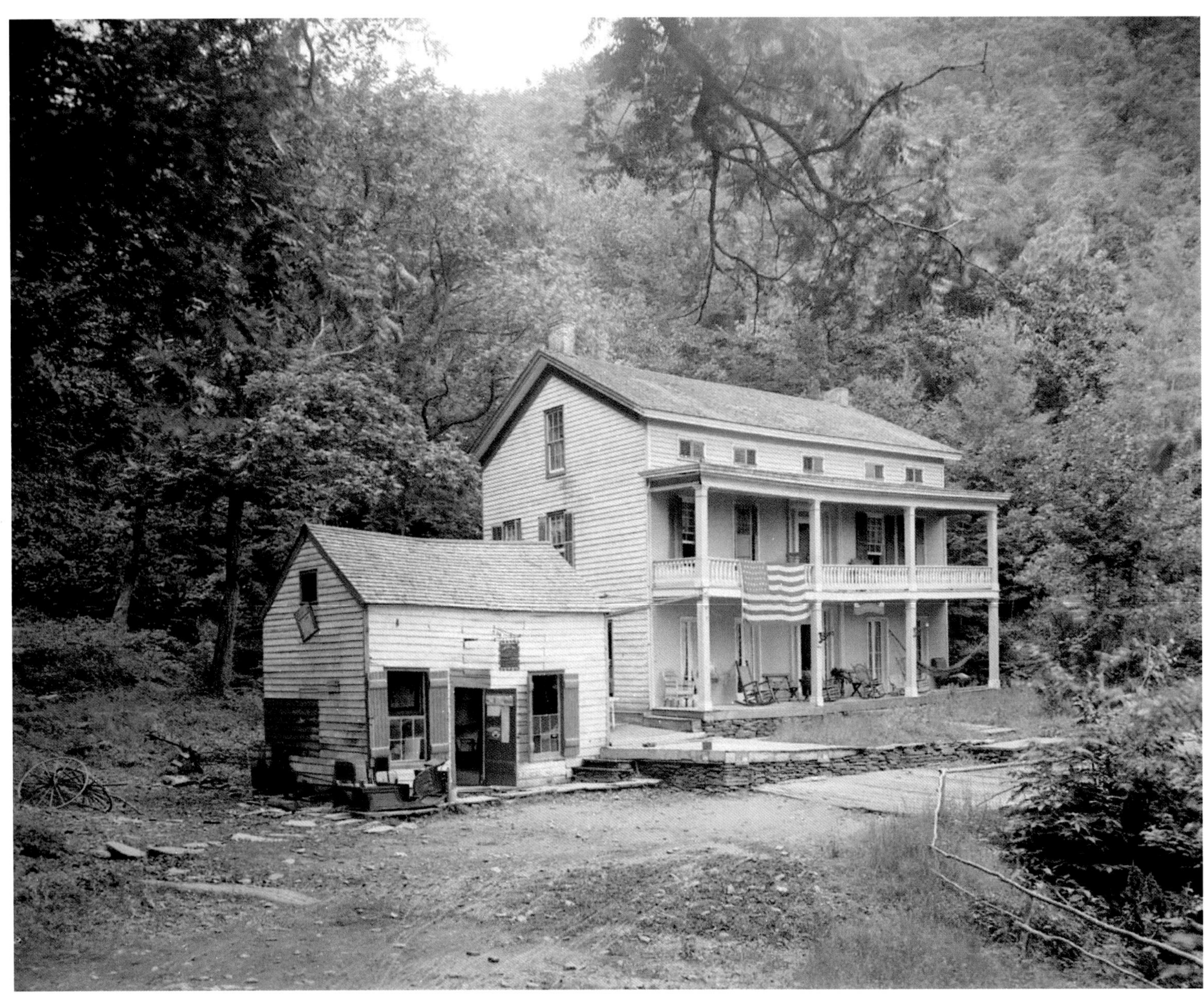

The Rip Van Winkle House, pictured here, stood about two miles from the famous Catskill Mountain House. The owner supplied refreshment to travelers. A visitor in 1900 wrote, "His hut is in a singularly romantic situation; built in a deep angle of the rock with a perpendicular ascent fifty feet directly above him." An earlier visitor's account suggested that this is where Rip drank with the ghosts of Henry Hudson's crew and slept for twenty years.

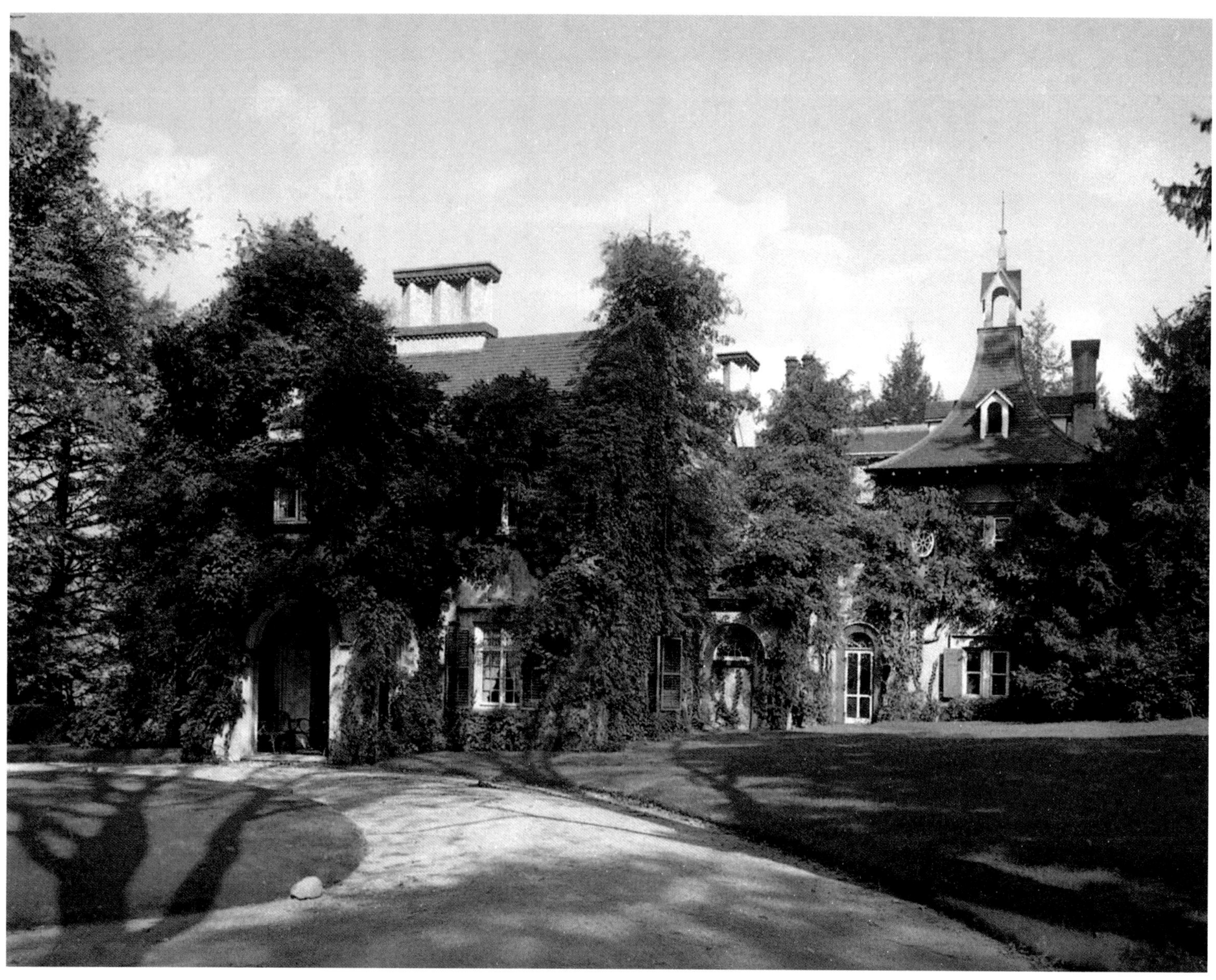

When this early-twentieth-century image was recorded, Washington Irving's Sunnyside was still a private residence owned by a member of the Irving family. In the mid twentieth century, it became a national historic landmark. This view shows the house as Irving intended it to be, a large and whimsical Victorian cottage. Irving inspired a generation of wealthy New Yorkers to find a similar nest along the Hudson.

Following Spread: Morris Park Racecourse was opened in 1889 in the Glendale section of the Bronx by businessman John A. Morris (d. 1895). The horseracing track closed in 1902 and was subsequently used for car racing, and then air shows. By the 1920s, it was the site of a factory. This photo of Morris Park track was taken by Benjamin J. Falk (1853–1925). Falk considered himself a photographer of theater, and he captured on film some of the greatest New York actors of his age.

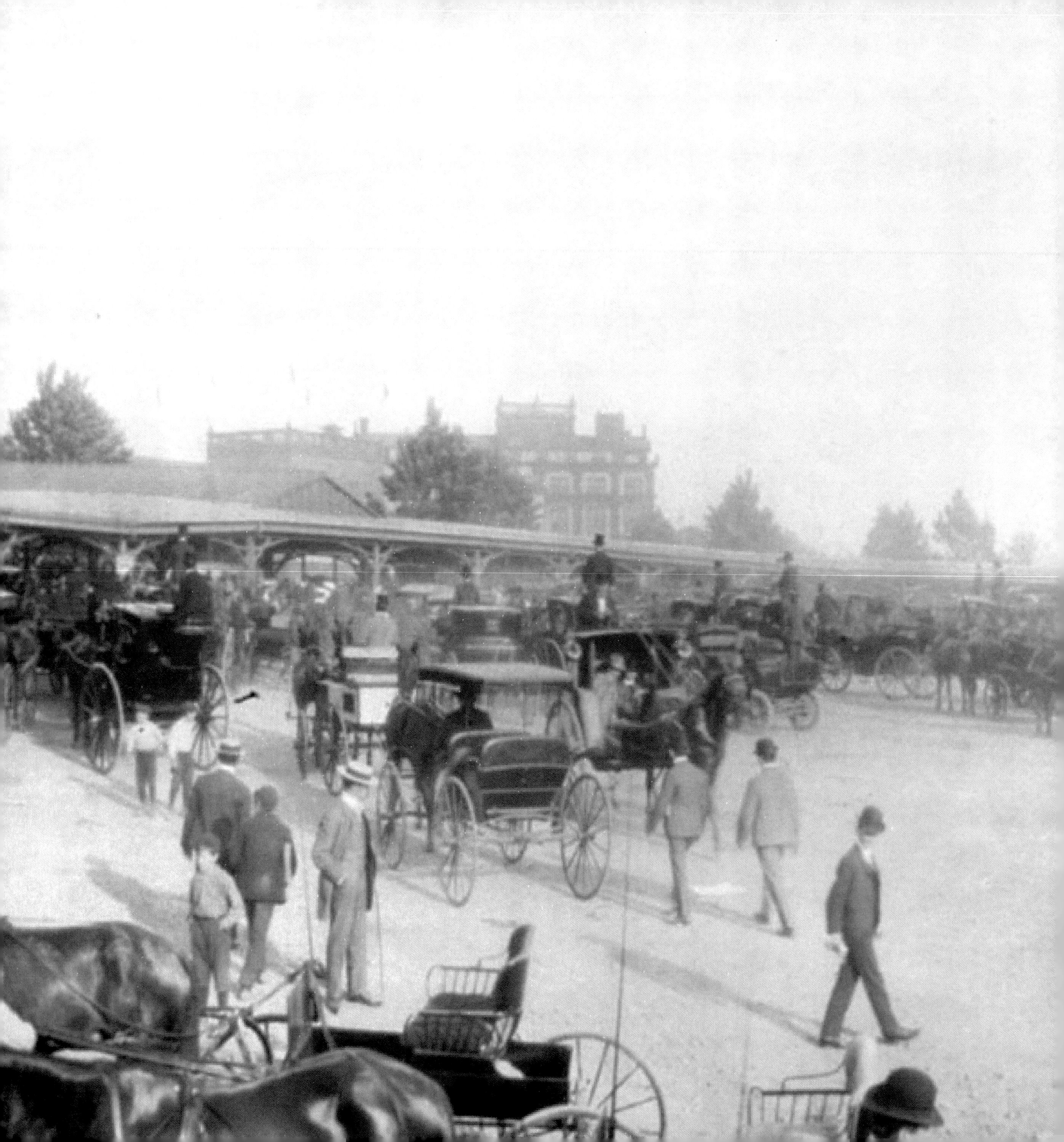

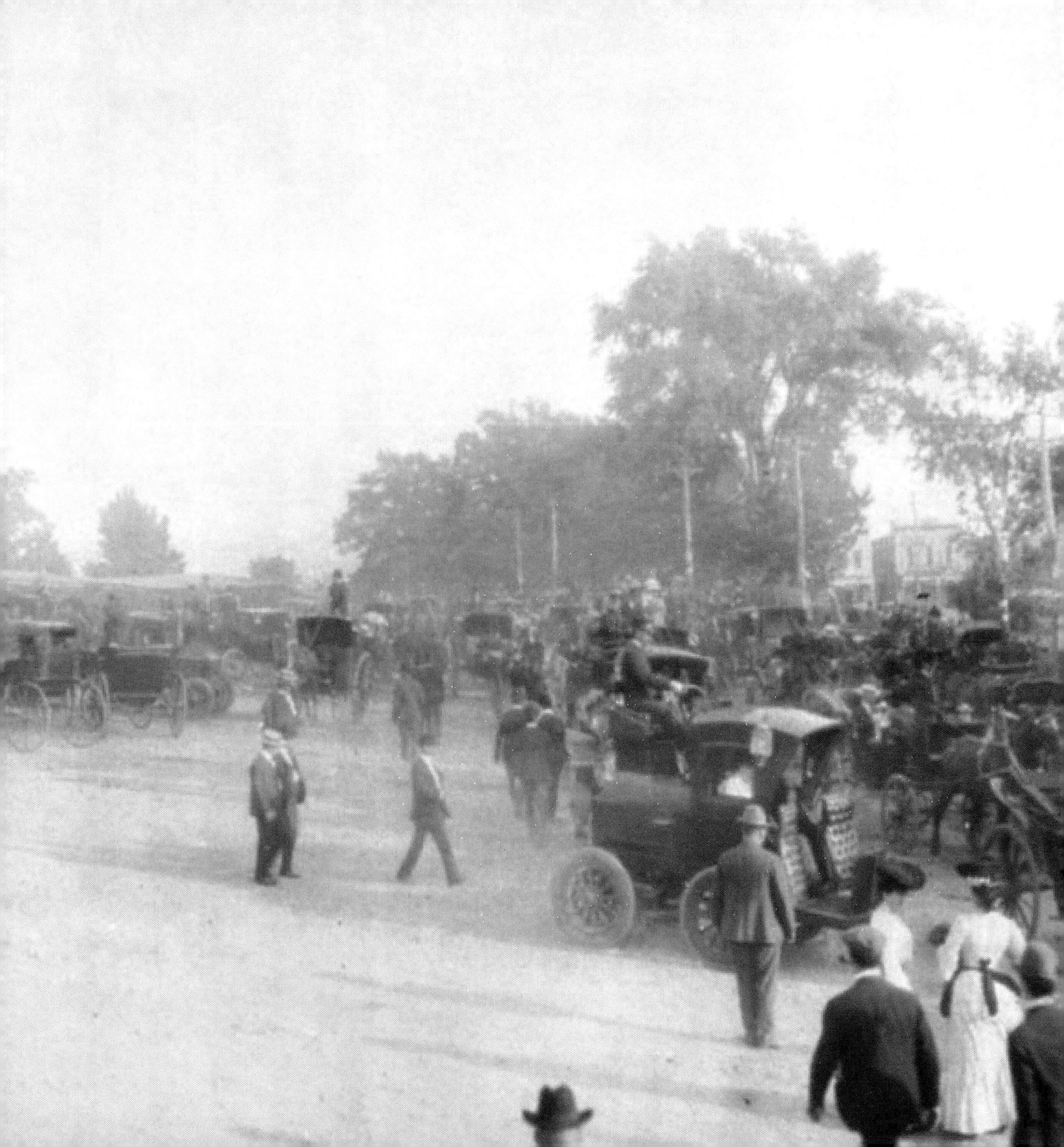

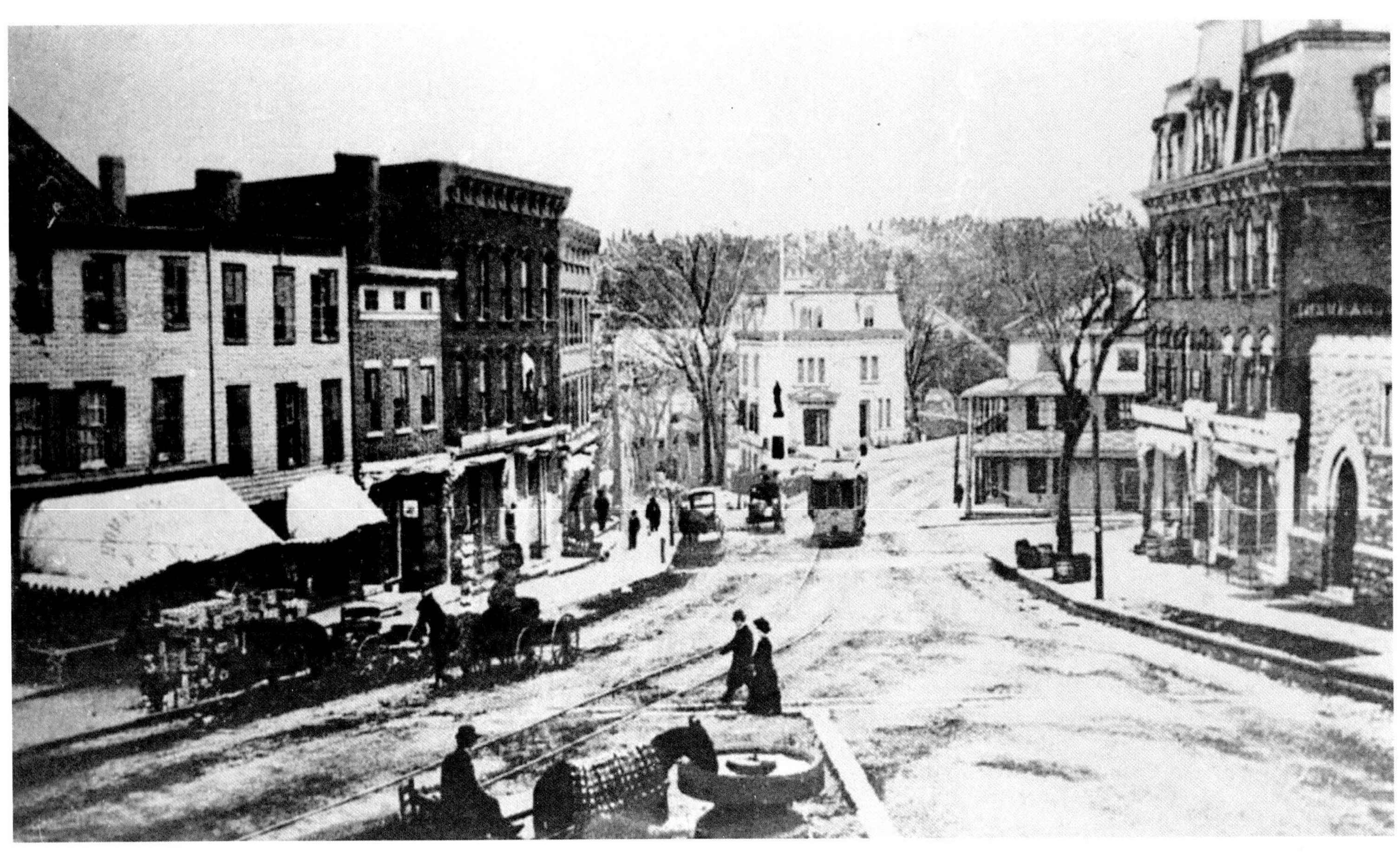

This early-twentieth-century scene of Main Street and Pleasant Square is similar in many respects to that of today. The first chartered village in Westchester, Ossining became a thriving commercial center with a riverfront port, stove factories, and of course, Sing Sing, a state prison. Vanished icon of American towns at the turn of the century, the fountain in the foreground is providing water for a thirsty horse. The buildings of the Main Street Crescent, at left, were constructed around 1874.

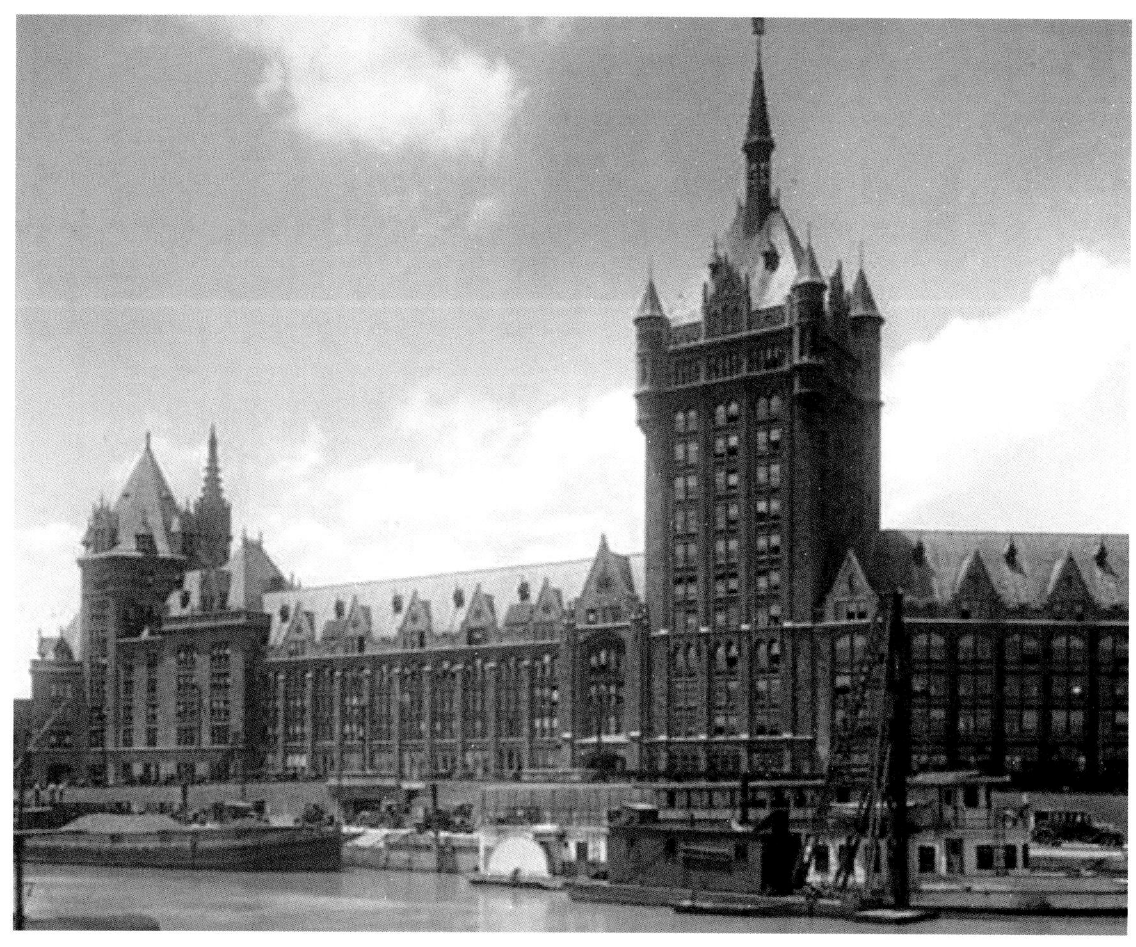

The Delaware and Hudson Railroad Building was designed by Marcus T. Reynolds (1869–1937) and completed in 1918. When erected, the building was actually intended to cut off the State Street view of Albany's industrialized waterfront. It is located at the State University Plaza and constructed of granite and slate. The D&H Railroad started out as the Delaware and Hudson Canal Company in 1823.

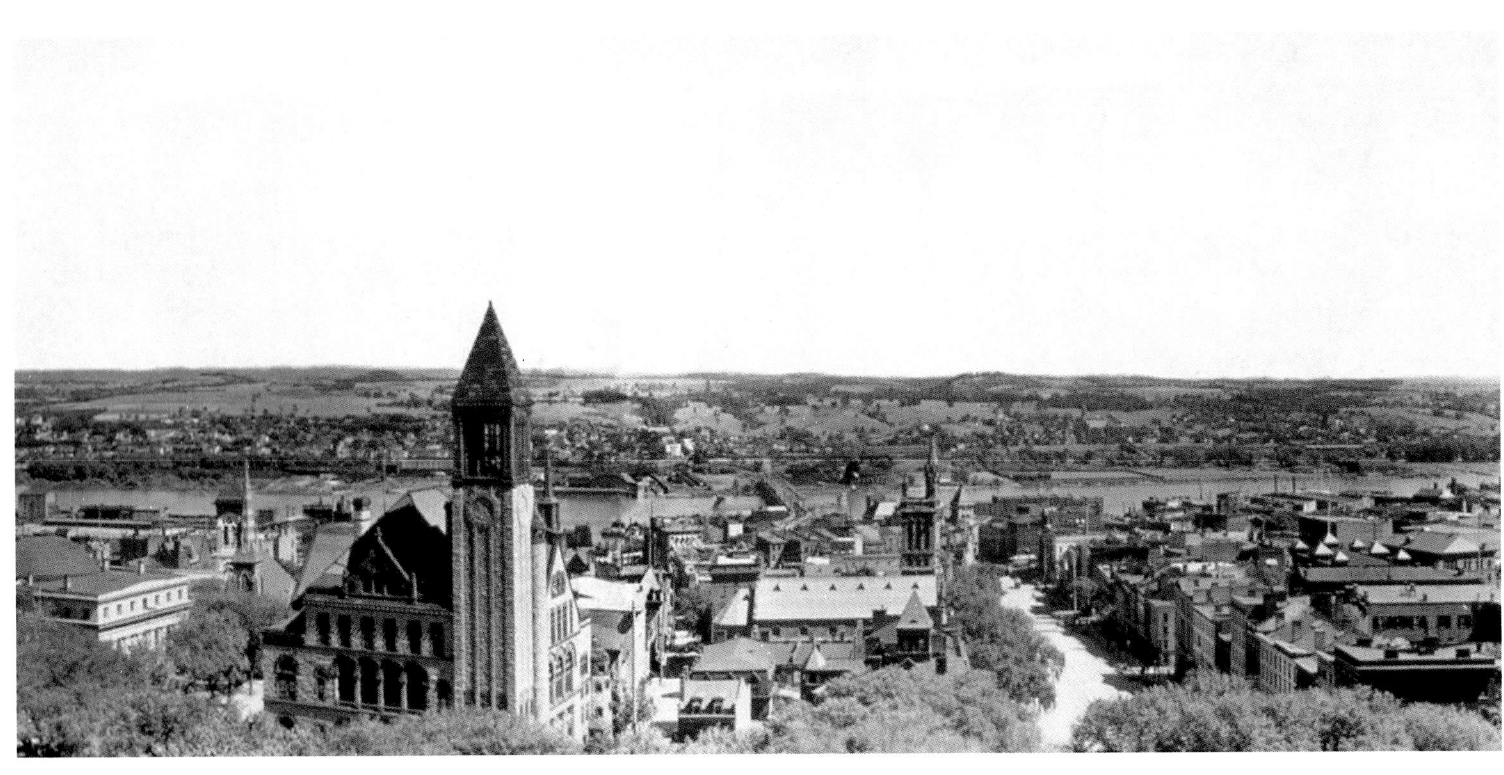

This panorama of Albany, recorded about 1906, shows City Hall in the left foreground and the 1866 Hudson River Bridge in the distance.

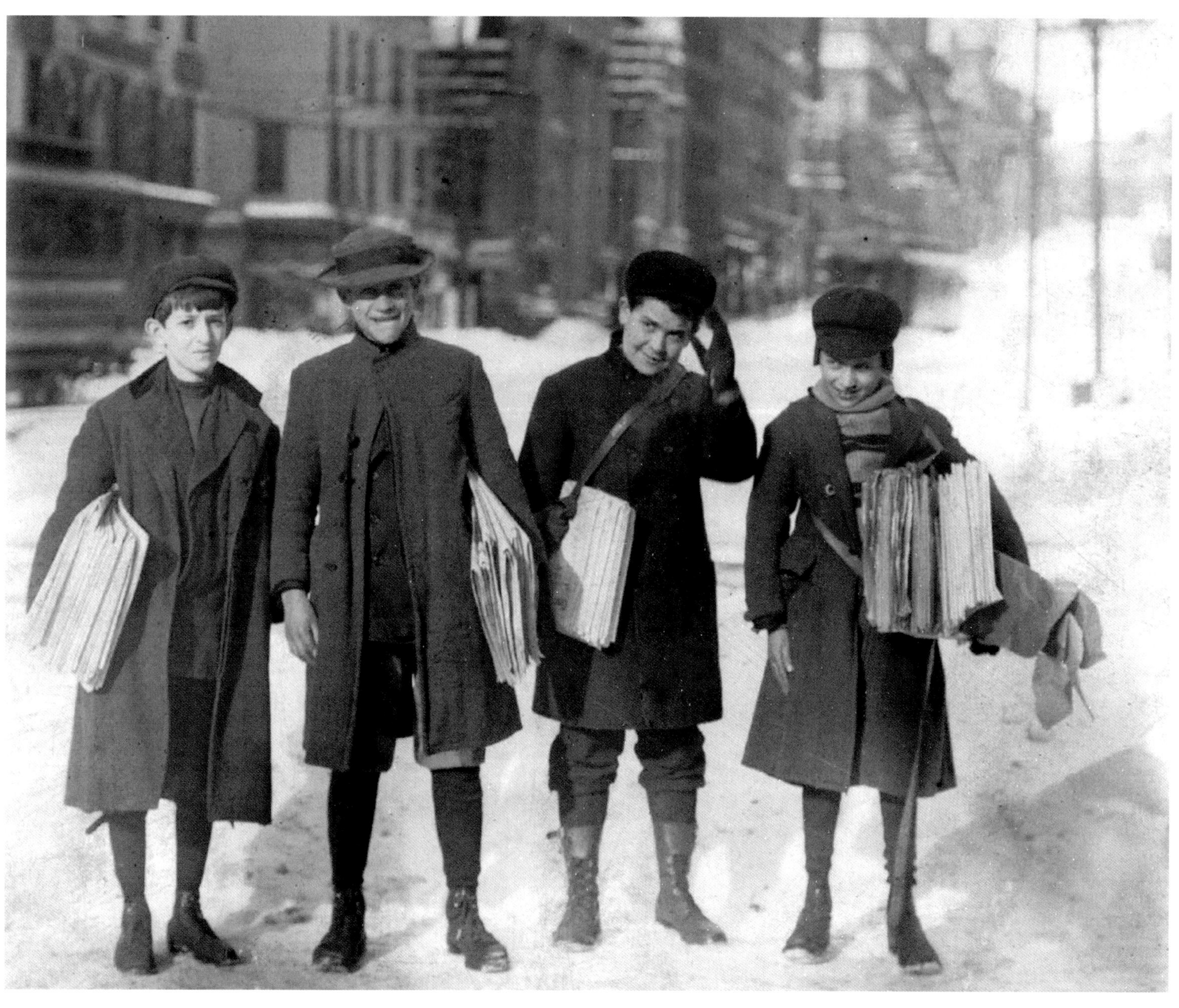

Working for the National Child Labor Committee in a coordinated effort to end the practice, Lewis Hine traveled the nation in 1910 recording images of children at work, many of them shown hawking newspapers as "newsies."

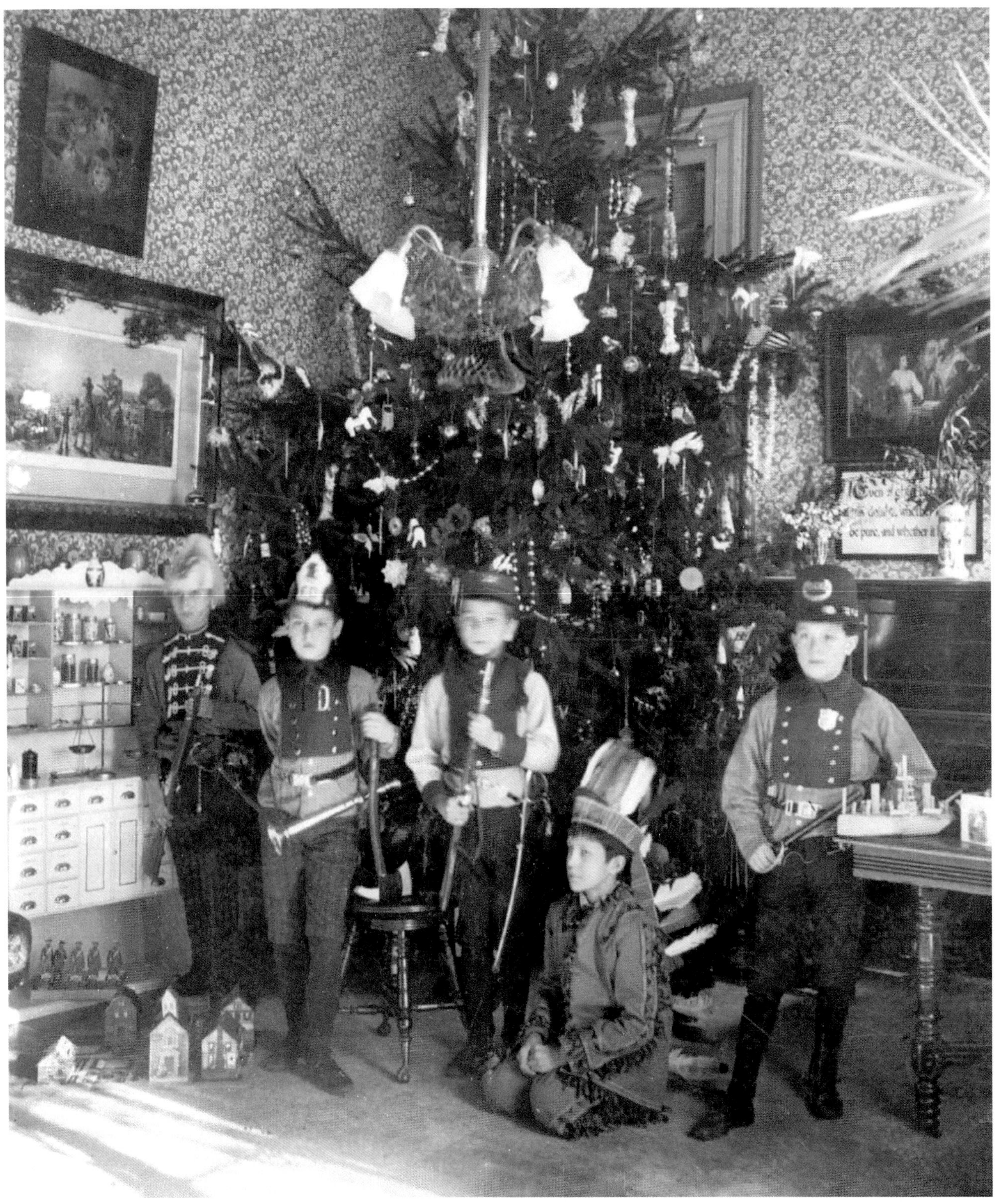

Miss Helen Gould, the daughter of railroad and telegraph tycoon Jay Gould, entertained city children at her estate, Lyndhurst, in Tarrytown. These children from Woody Crest are visiting the estate at Christmastime in 1905. Woody Crest, a home for "friendless children," was established in the Bronx.

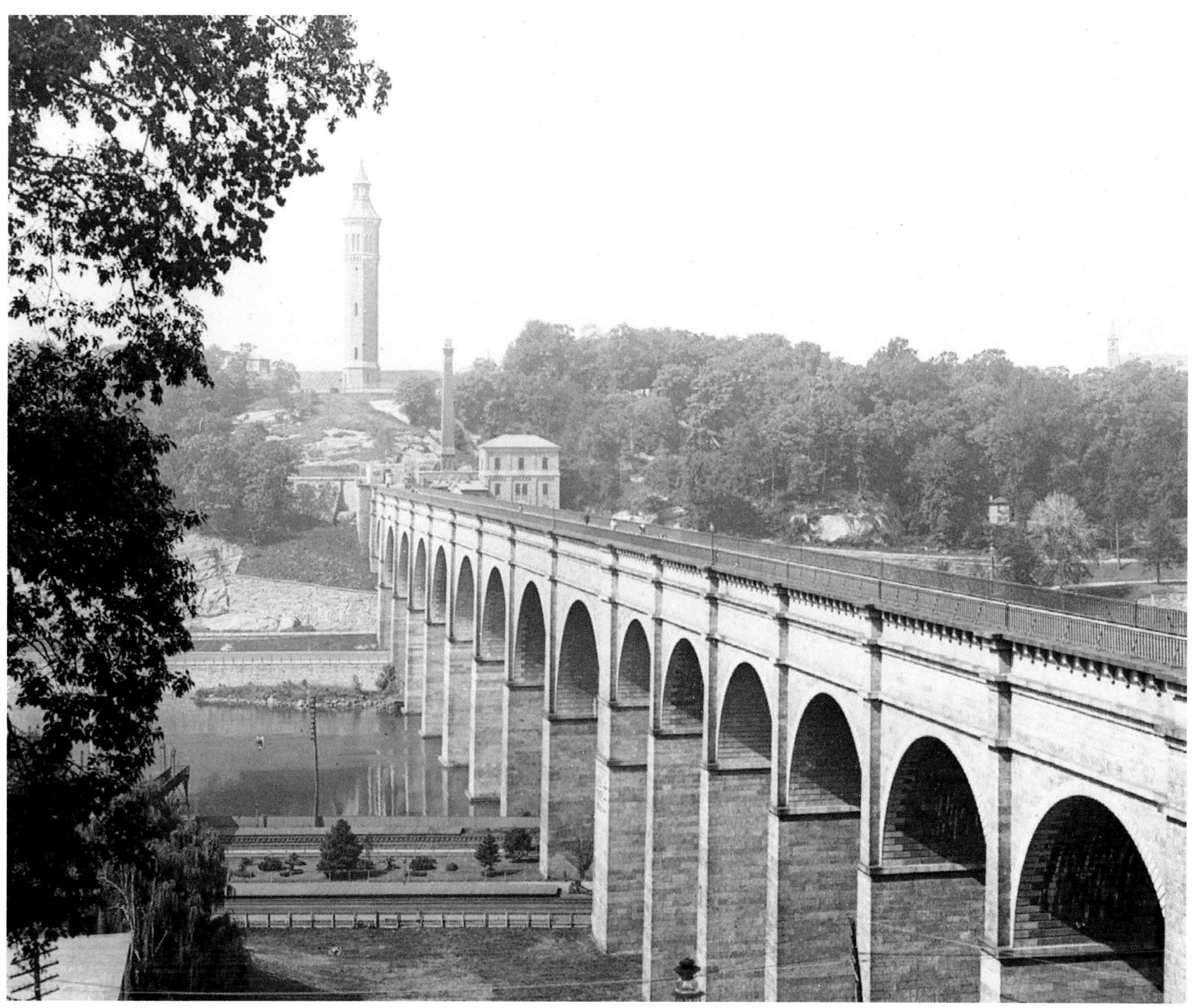

High Bridge, pictured here at the turn of the century, looked rather the same when it was completed in 1848. The one exception was the water tower that was added to the landscape in 1872, to supply water pressure for neighborhoods at higher elevations in the northern Manhattan districts of Harlem and Inwood. High Bridge is the oldest remaining bridge connecting the Island of Manhattan to the mainland.

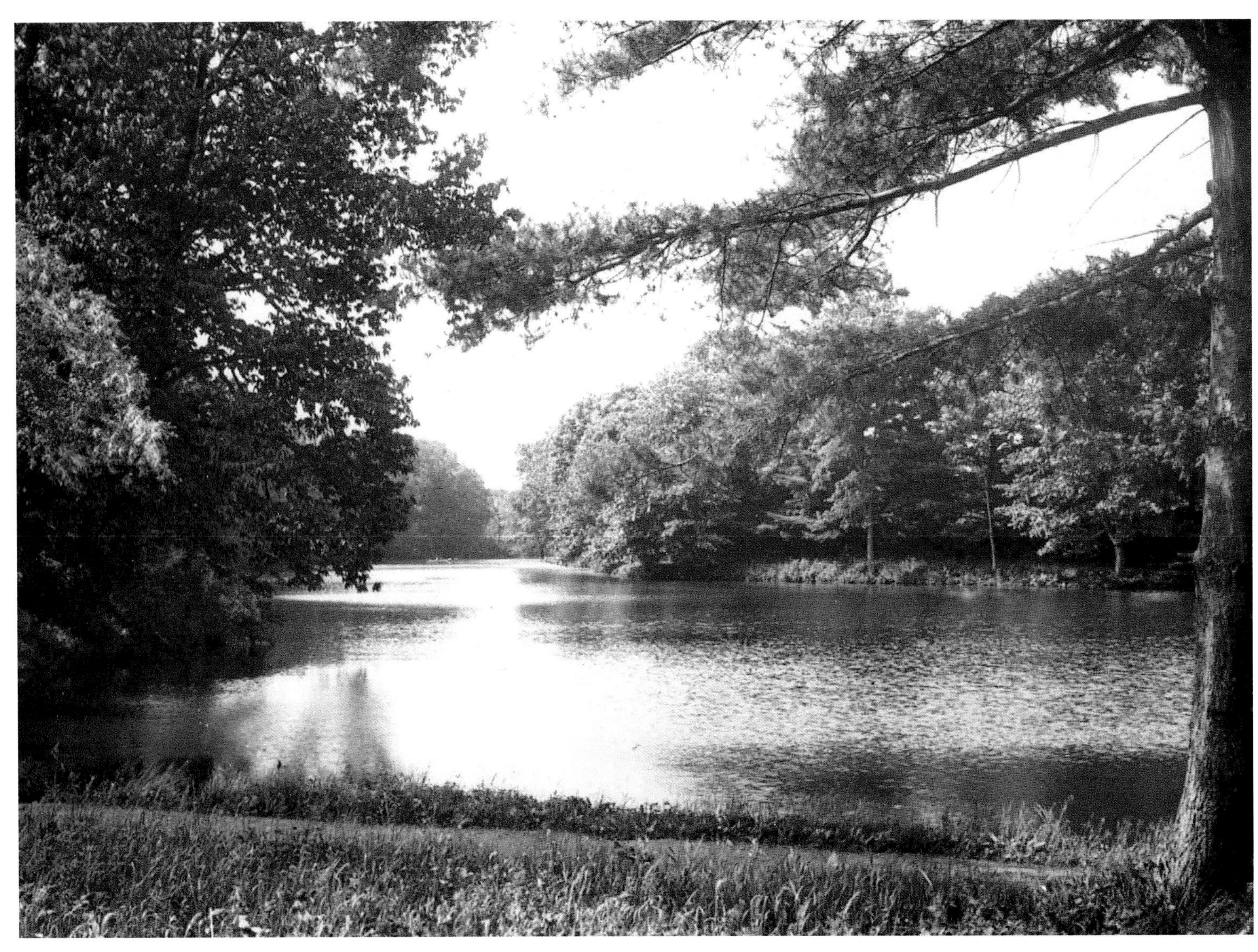

Vassar Lake at Vassar College, Poughkeepsie, is not to be confused with Sunset Lake, which was constructed about 500 yards to the southeast in 1912. Vassar Lake, shown here near the turn of the century, had a pump-house, icehouse, and rowboats.

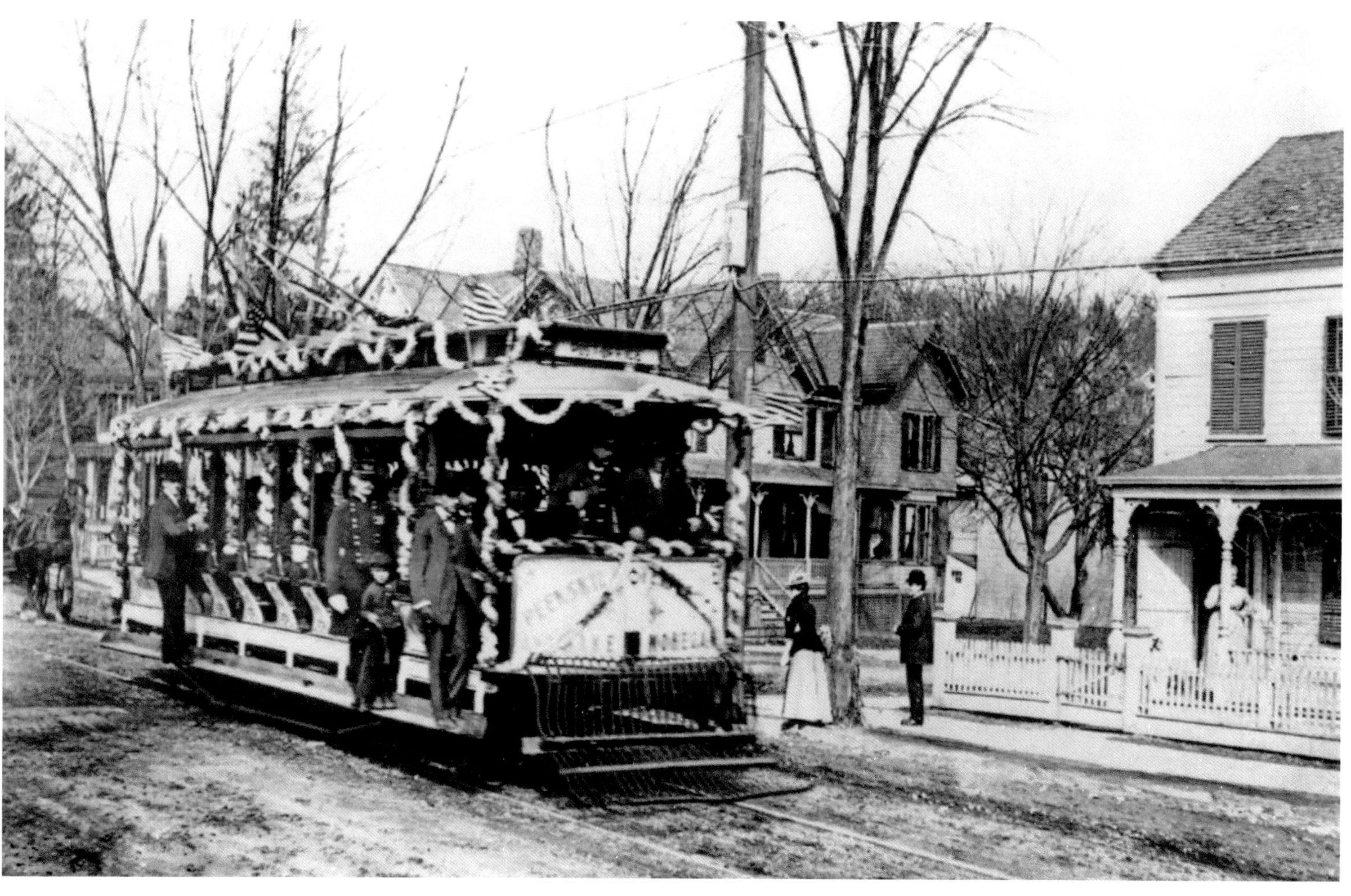

The trolley was a big innovation to an average Hudson River town. This one at Peekskill, running the tracks on March 23, 1907, decorated with tinsel and flying the Stars and Stripes, was the very first car on the Putnam & Westchester trolley line. Peekskill photographer A. B. Kennedy recorded the image.

These days Garrison Train Station houses a community performing arts center and is named the Philipstown Depot Theater. Here the station is shown in railroad service in the early twentieth century. The building was completed in 1893, the project of New York Assemblyman William H. LaDue. Garrison was the most convenient stop on the Hudson Line for visitors bound across the river for West Point. It is a quiet hamlet, once home to many railroad executives, and today associated with the performing arts.

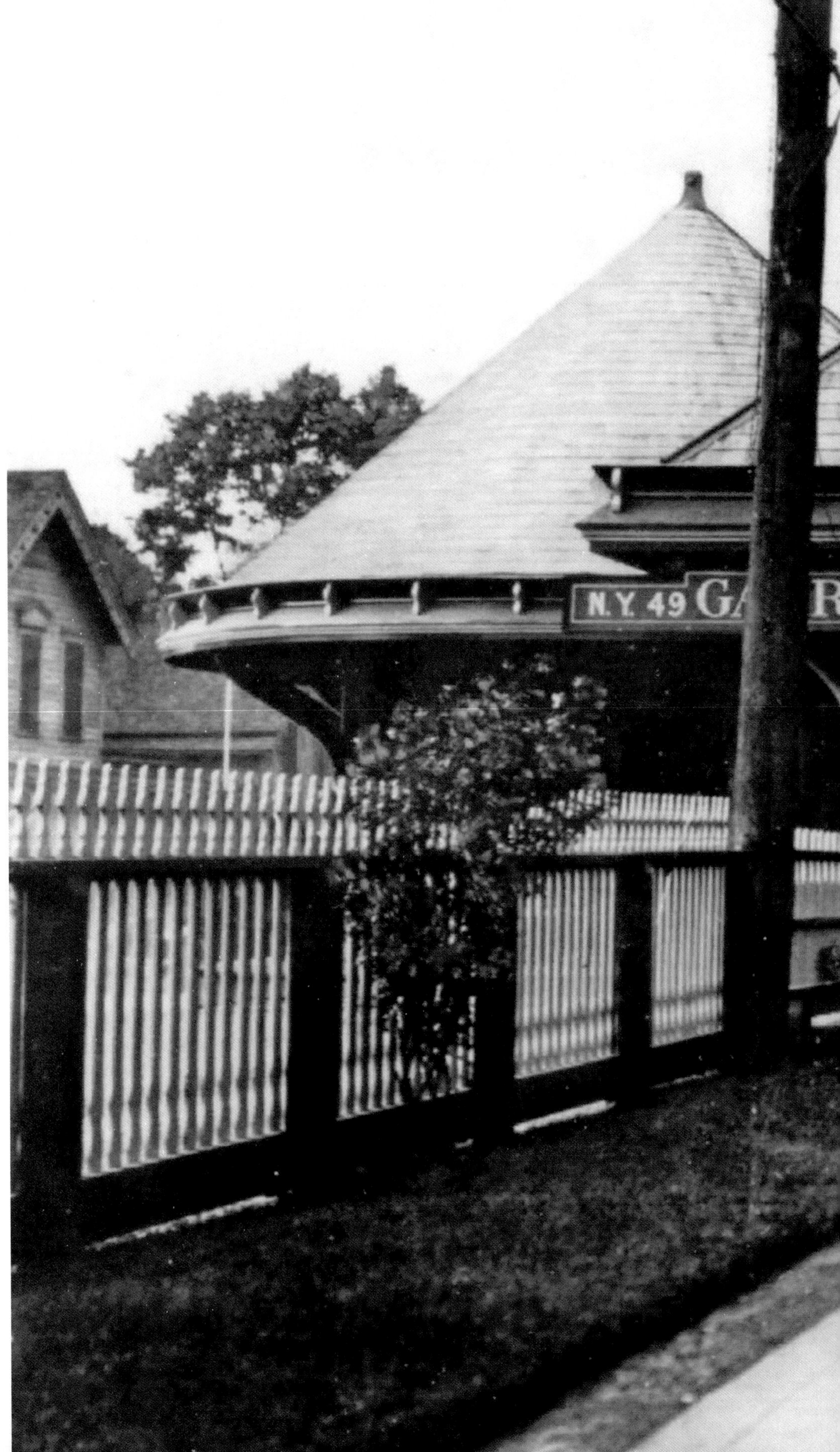

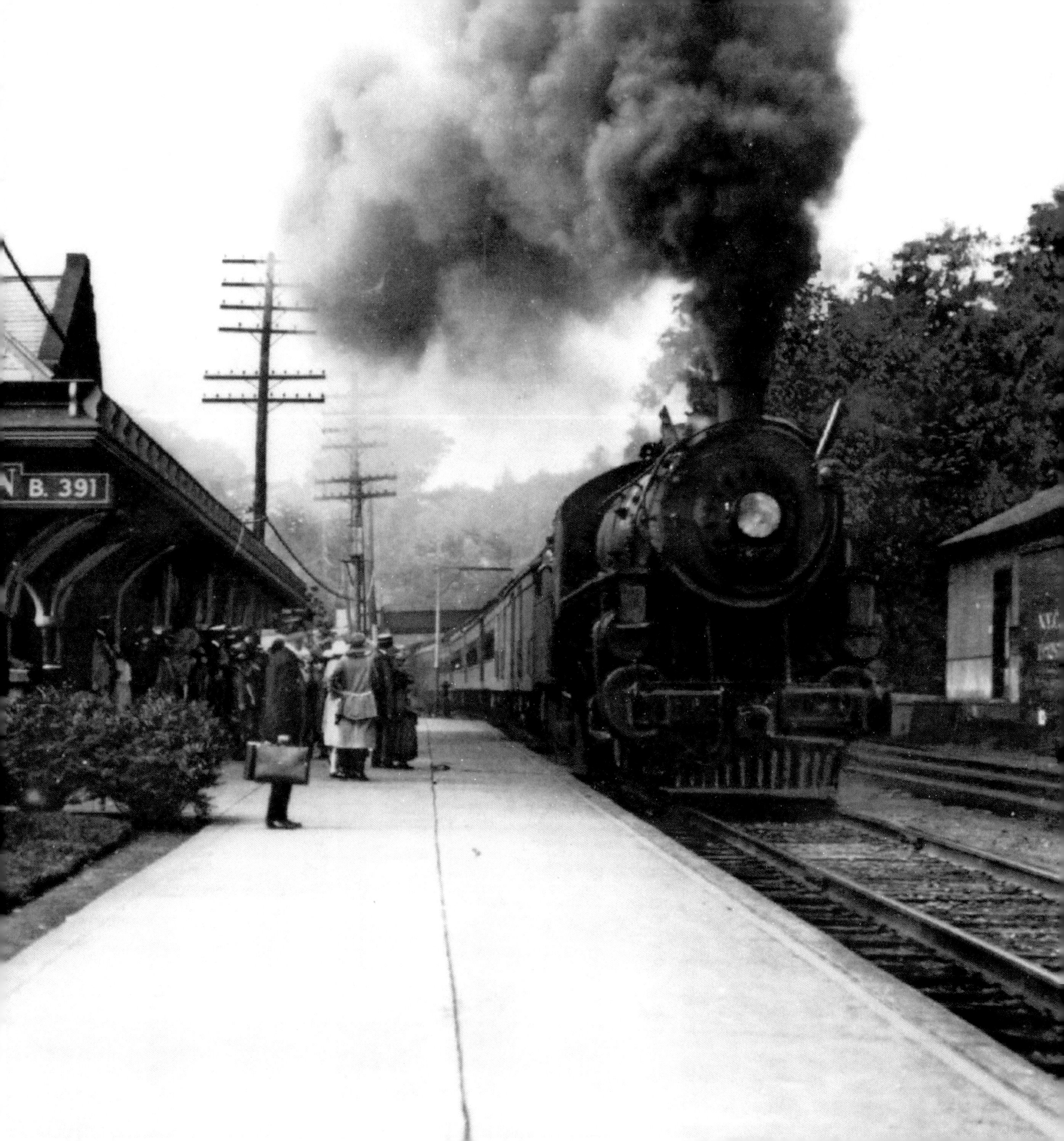
B. 391

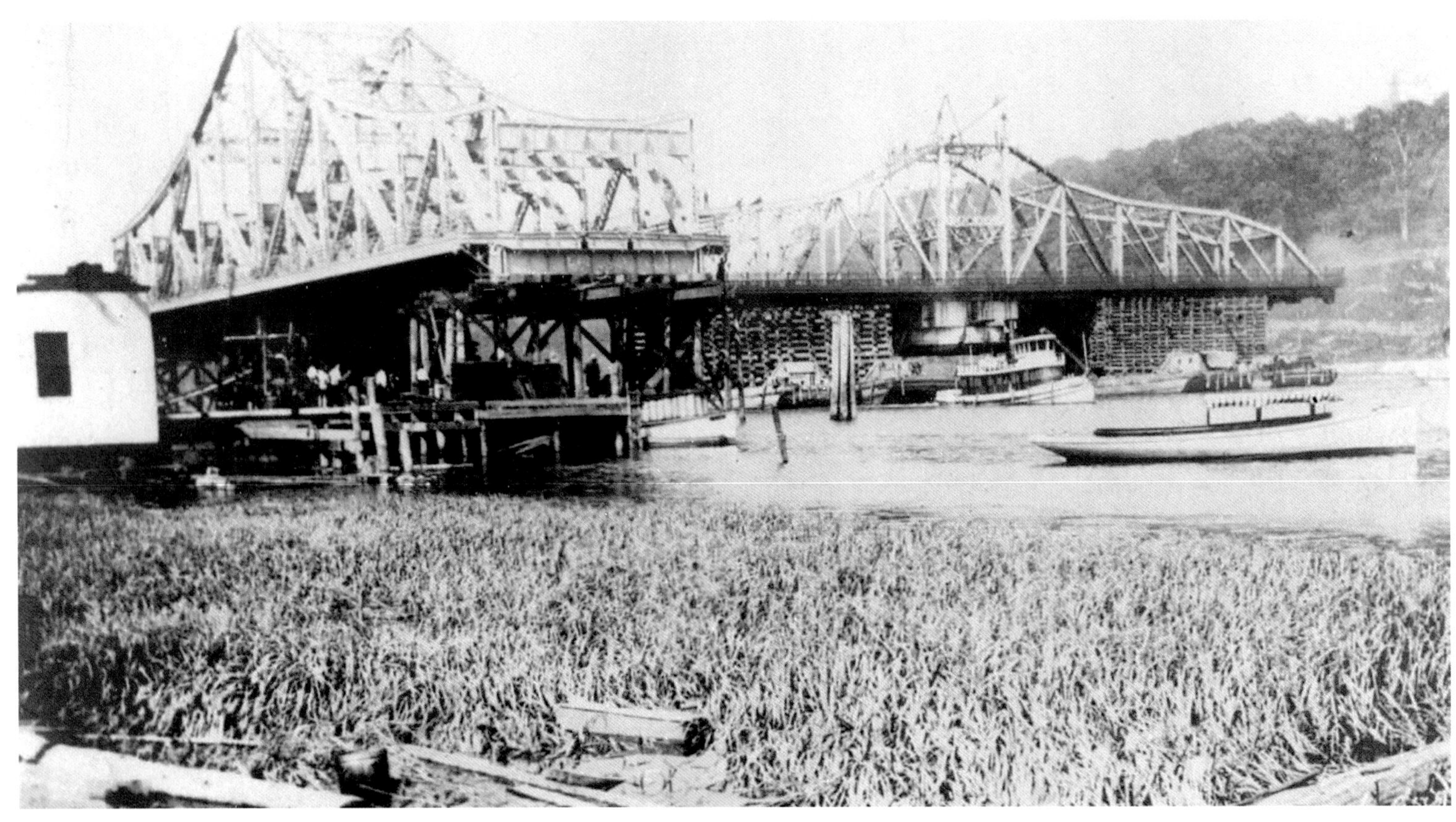

Here in 1906, the old Broadway Ship Canal Bridge is floated downstream to become the new University Heights Bridge, open to traffic in 1908. It was to be replaced with a new Broadway drawbridge, seen to the left, which was in use until the early 1960s.

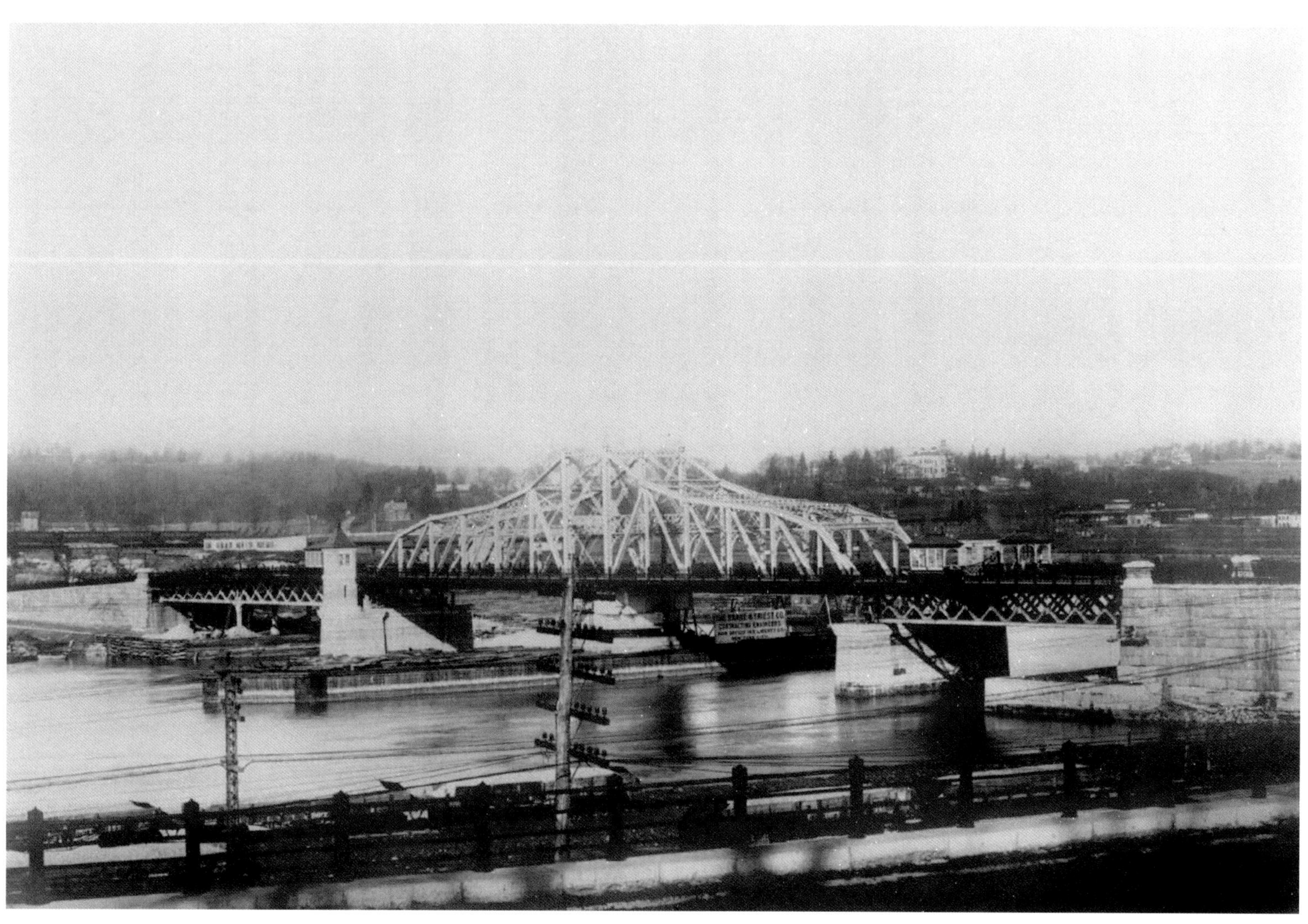

The University Heights Bridge at 207th Street in New York City, shown here on January 8, 1908, was "a steel Pratt/Howe, pin-connected, rim bearing swing span draw, with Warren truss approach spans." The bridge is the third-oldest in Manhattan and was key in facilitating the Harlem River Ship Canal shortcut between the Hudson and Long Island Sound. The bridge was designated a New York City Landmark in 1984.

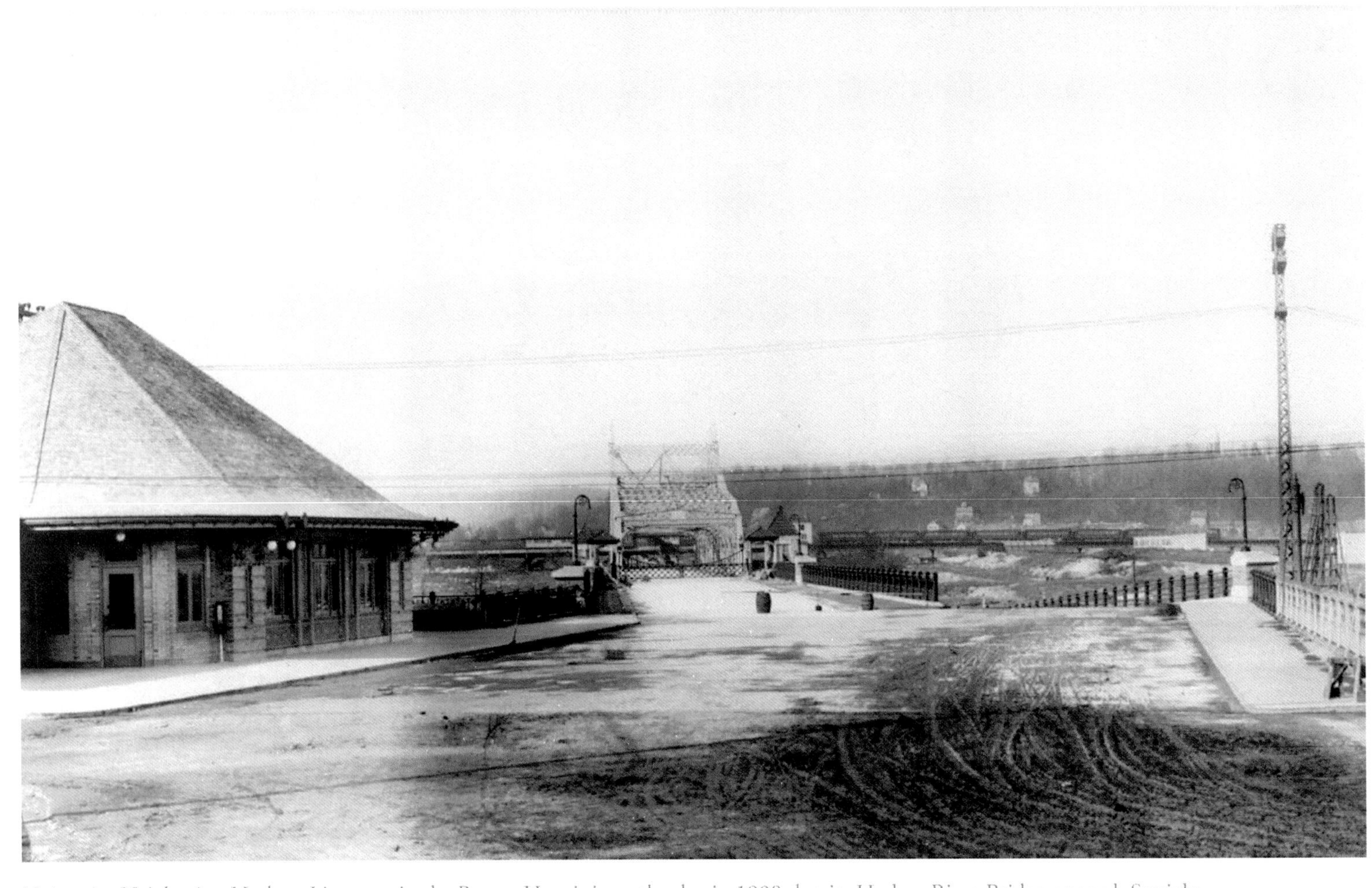

University Heights is a Hudson Line stop in the Bronx. Here it is on the day in 1908 that its Harlem River Bridge opened. Straight ahead, to the west, is the Inwood section of Manhattan. The bridge was designed by Alfred Pancoast Boller (1840–1912), founder of Boller and Hodge, a New York City engineering firm. Trolley service ran on the bridge from 1910 to 1940.

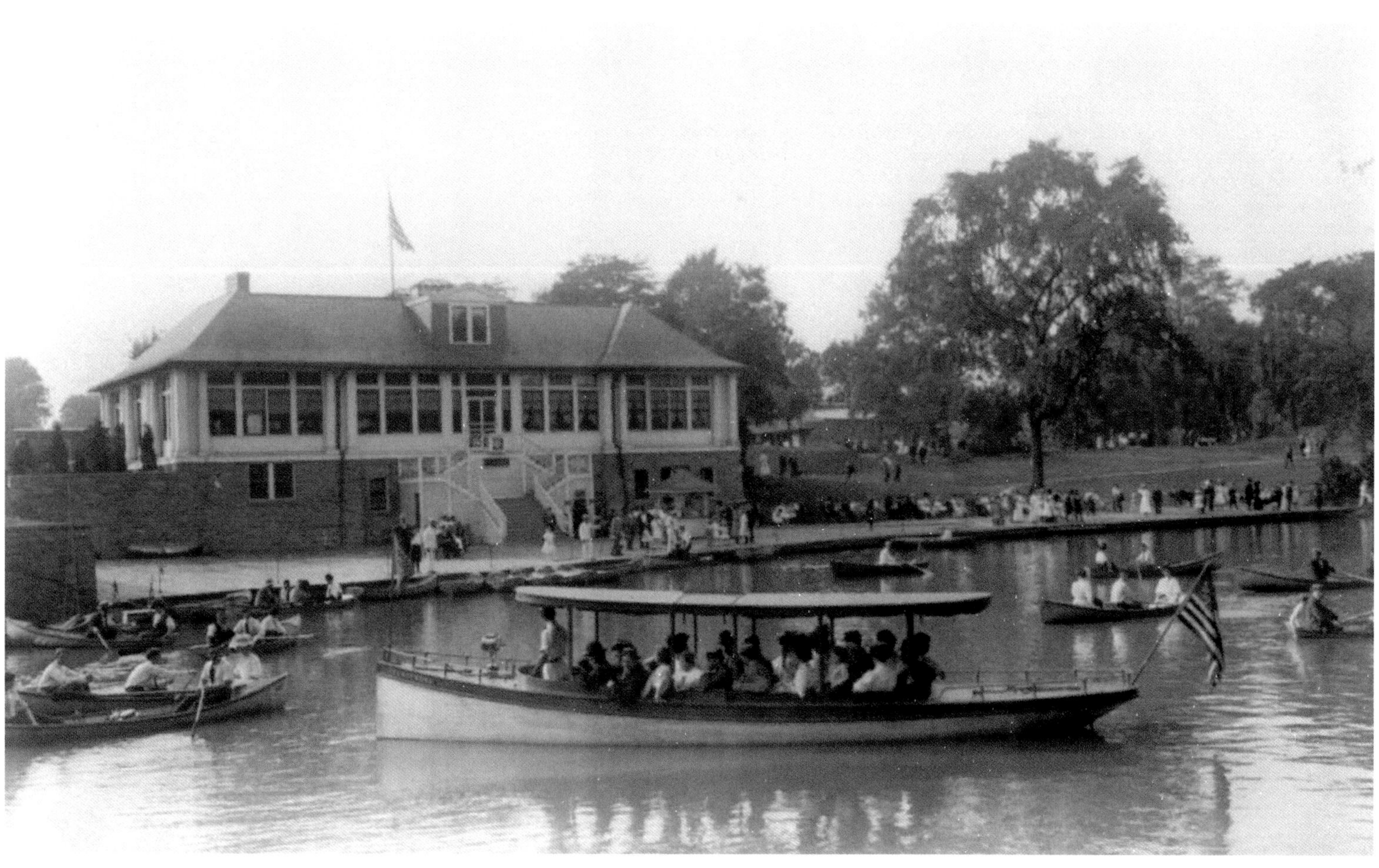

Bronx Lake is seen here on a busy day. Quiet electric launches made regular trips between the boathouse and Bronxdale Landing; adults 10 cents, children 5 cents. The round-bottomed rowboats rented for 35 cents an hour.

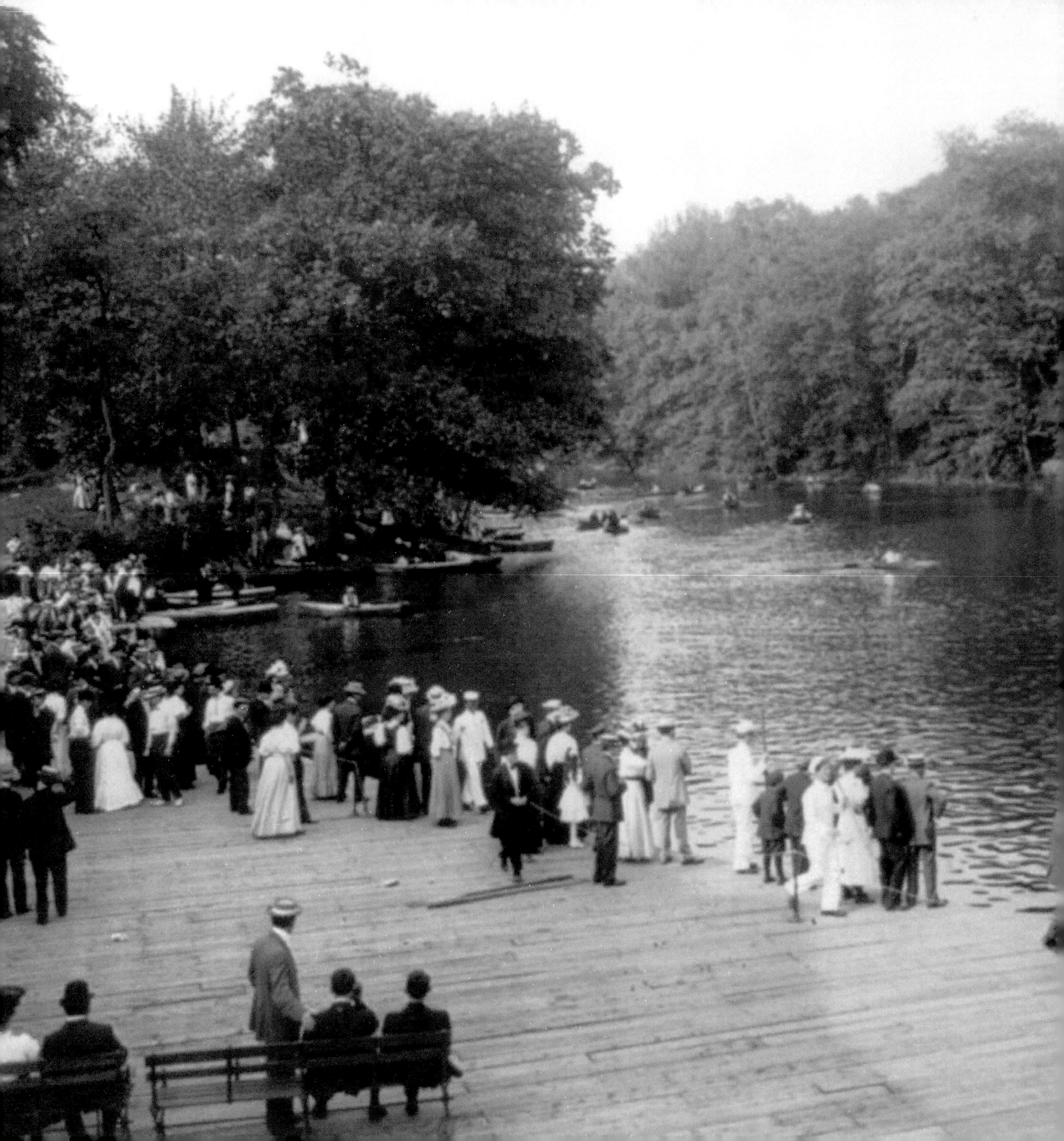

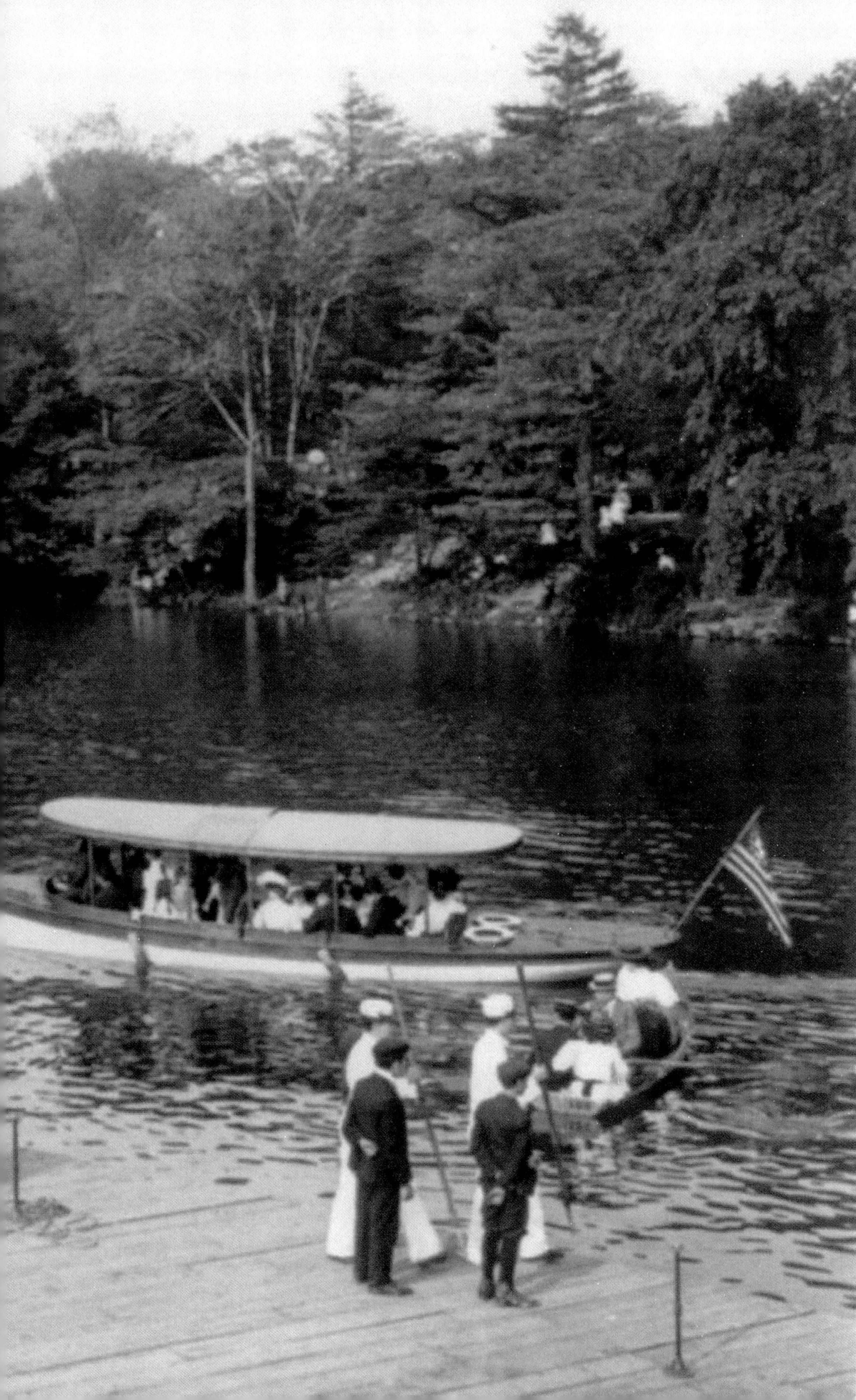

A large boathouse built on Bronx Lake was completed in 1906. The lake was created on the Bronx River and measured one mile in length, with an area of 25 acres. Bronx Park, including the lake, the zoo, and the botanical gardens, was created as a public park in 1888. This view dates from around May 1908.

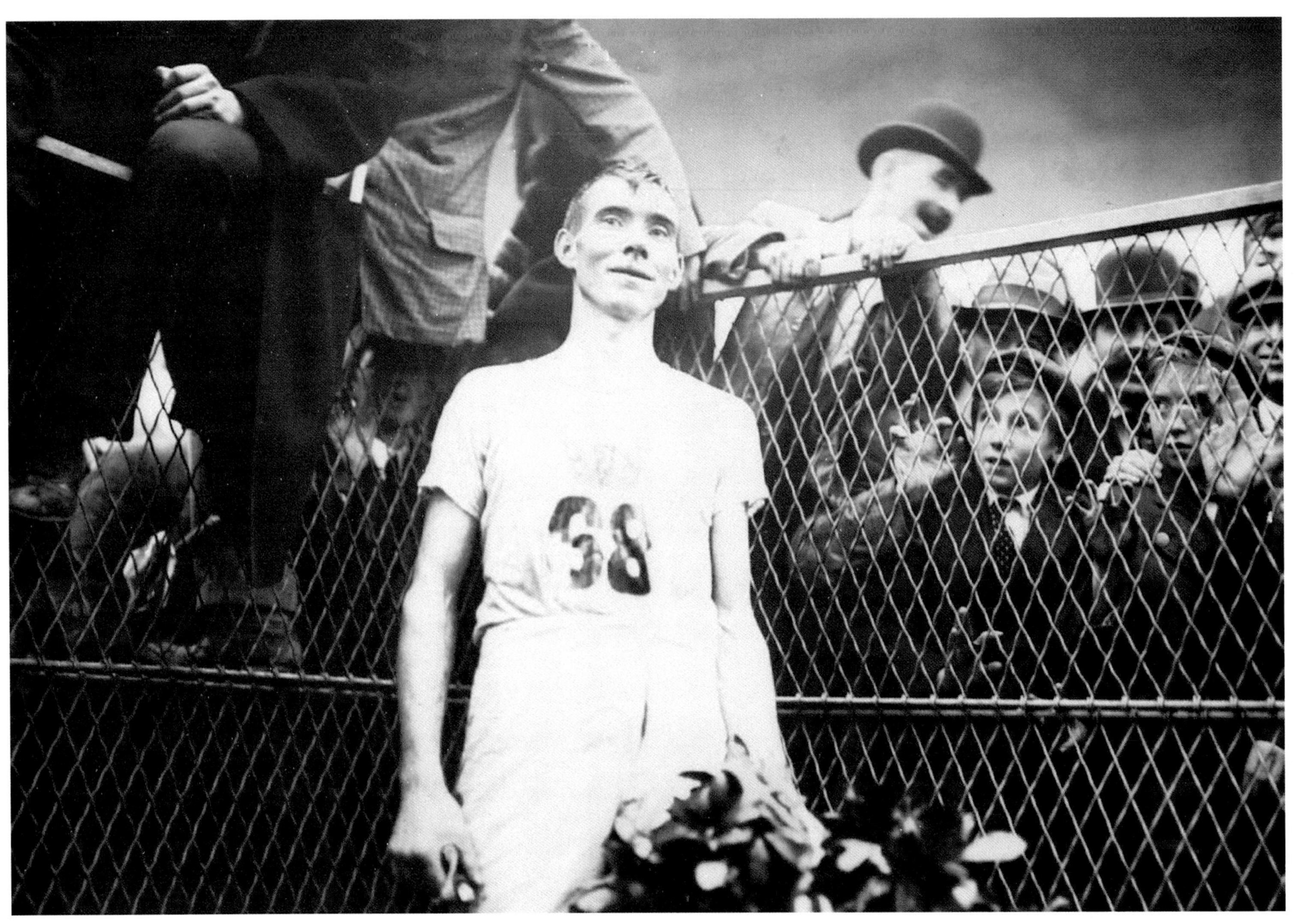

Owing to its demanding terrain, few records are broken at the Yonkers Marathon. The Yonkers race is the second-oldest marathon in the United States, after the Boston Marathon. Dubbed "King of the Marathoners," Irish-American champion James Crowley won more marathons than any other runner in his day. Here he is being congratulated on November 27, 1908, by some of the 20,000 fans attending the event that day.

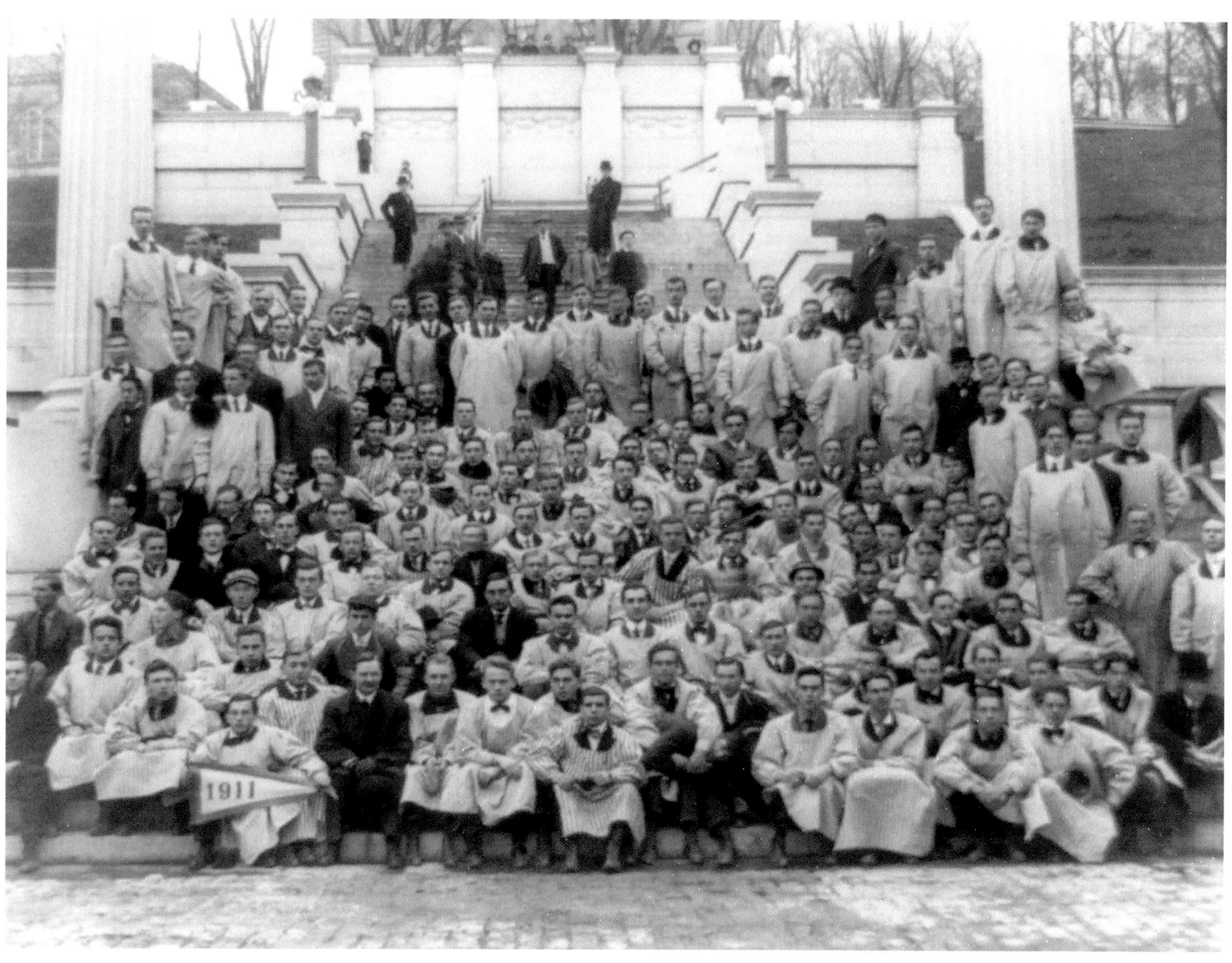

Rensselaer Polytechnic Institute's class of 1911 is shown here about 1908. Stephen Van Rensselaer established the school as a science institute in 1824, and in 1835, the college awarded the first civil engineering degrees in the United States. George Ferris, inventor of the Ferris wheel, attended the school. Rensselaer and Russell Sage College, founded in 1916, are both located in Troy, New York, which is situated on the banks of the Hudson.

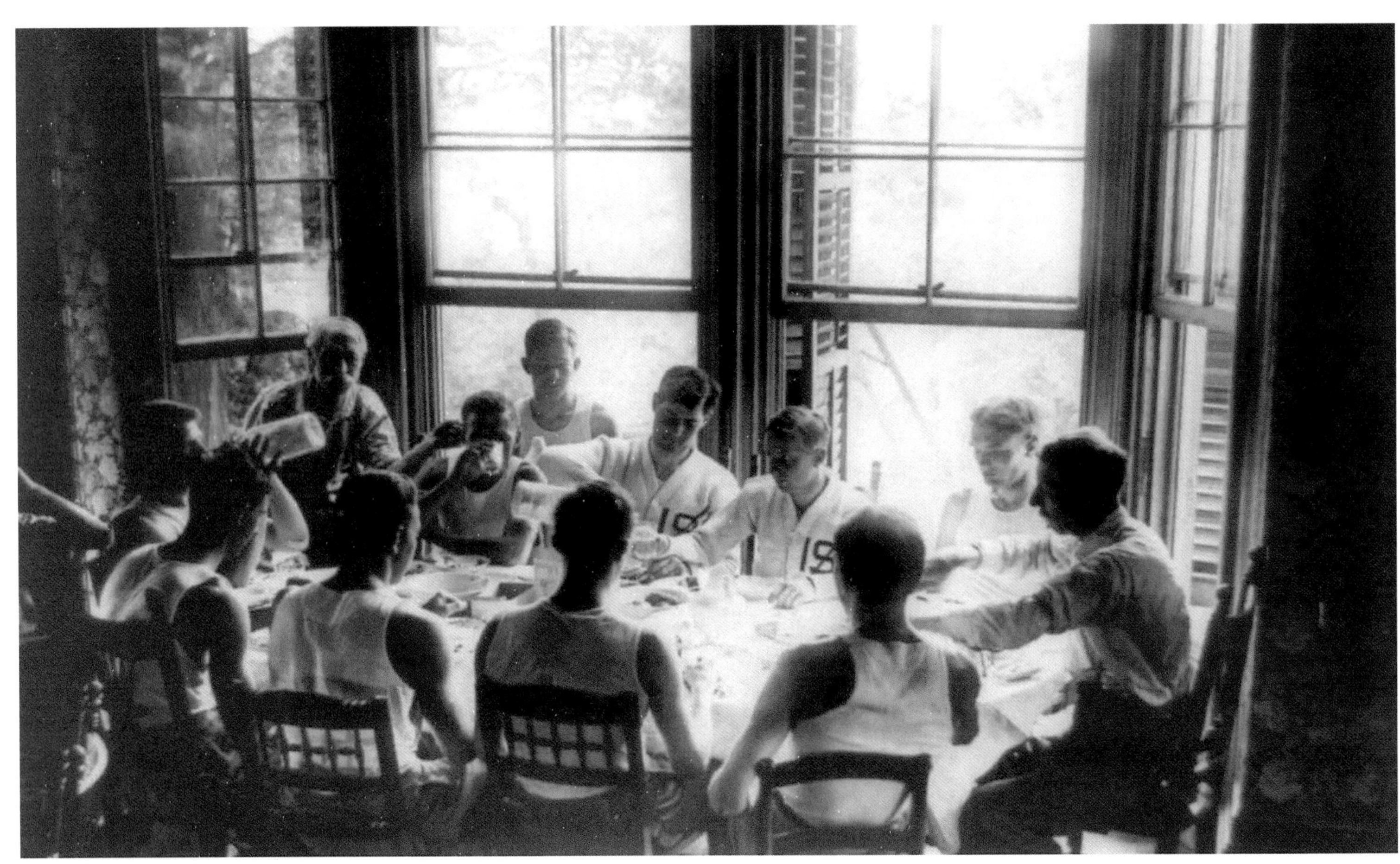

Syracuse University freshman rowers are shown here at dinner in Poughkeepsie on June 19, 1908. The Poughkeepsie four-mile course below Krum Elbow on the Hudson was a traditional racing stretch for rowers, dating back to 1837. In 1908, the freshmen took second place to Cornell, but the Syracuse varsity was victorious. Poughkeepsie was also a center for Hudson River ice yachting, with yachters occasionally racing the Hudson Line trains.

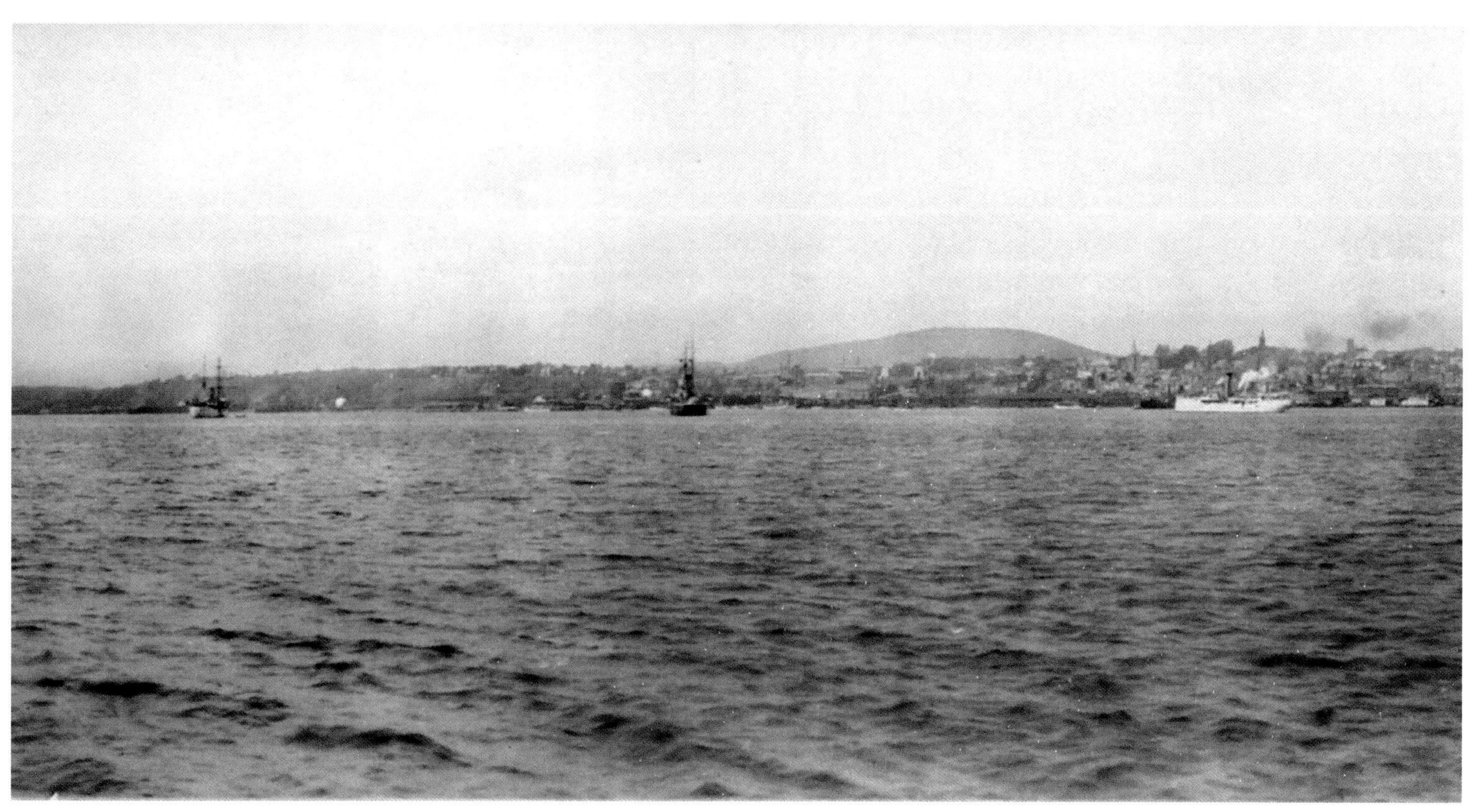

This is a view of the Newburgh waterfront about 1909. The city lies on the west side of the Hudson. It was here that General George Washington encamped with the Continental Army between 1782 and 1783, after the decisive Battle of Yorktown, while peace was being negotiated in Paris. A number of German settlers arrived in Newburgh in the early eighteenth century, displaced soon after by groups of Scottish and English colonists.

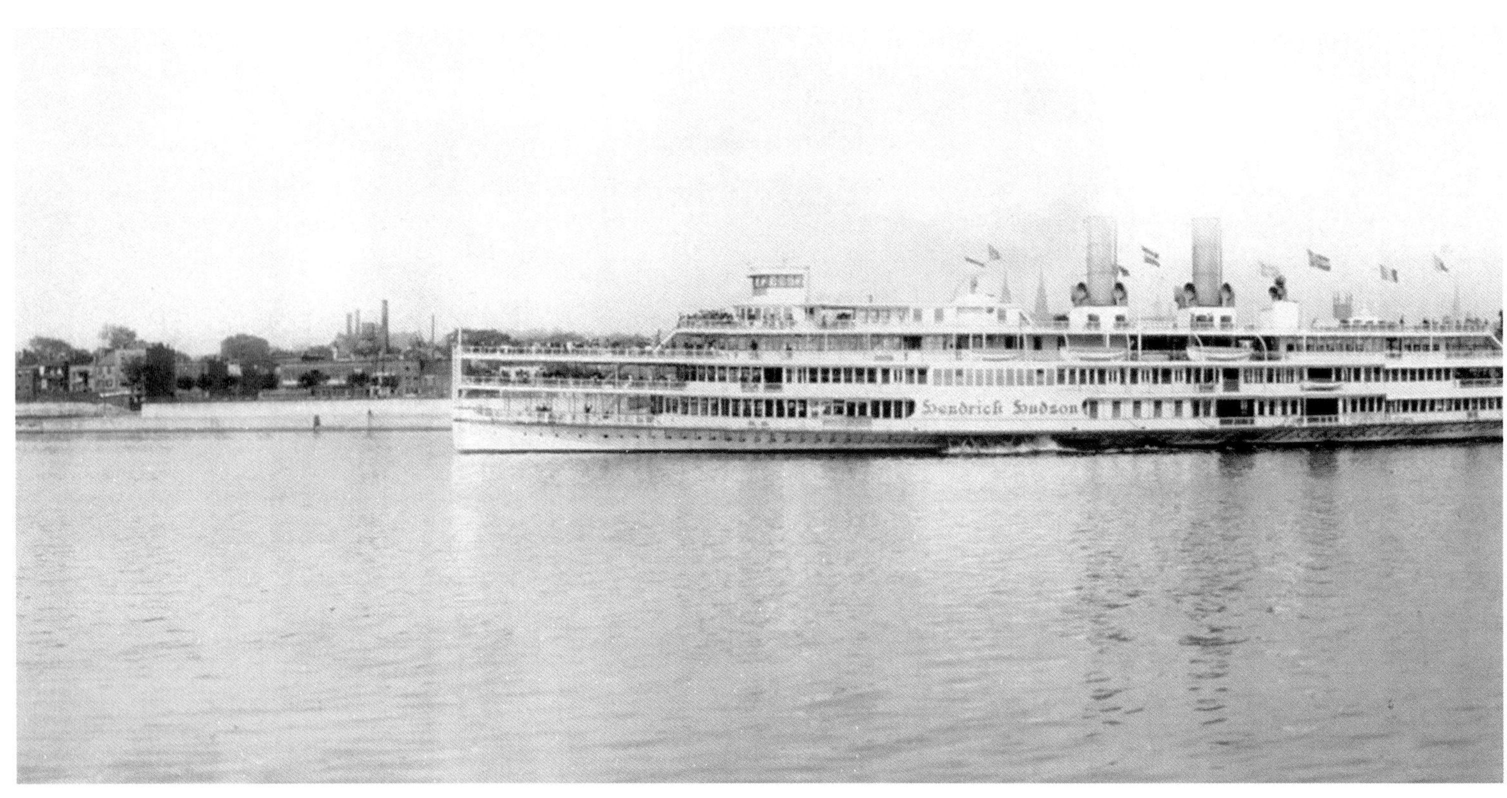

The steamer *Hendrick Hudson* is seen under way at Albany about 1909. The steamship was built at Newburgh in 1906 and equipped to accommodate 5,500 passengers on its run between New York and Albany. It was taken out of service in 1951.

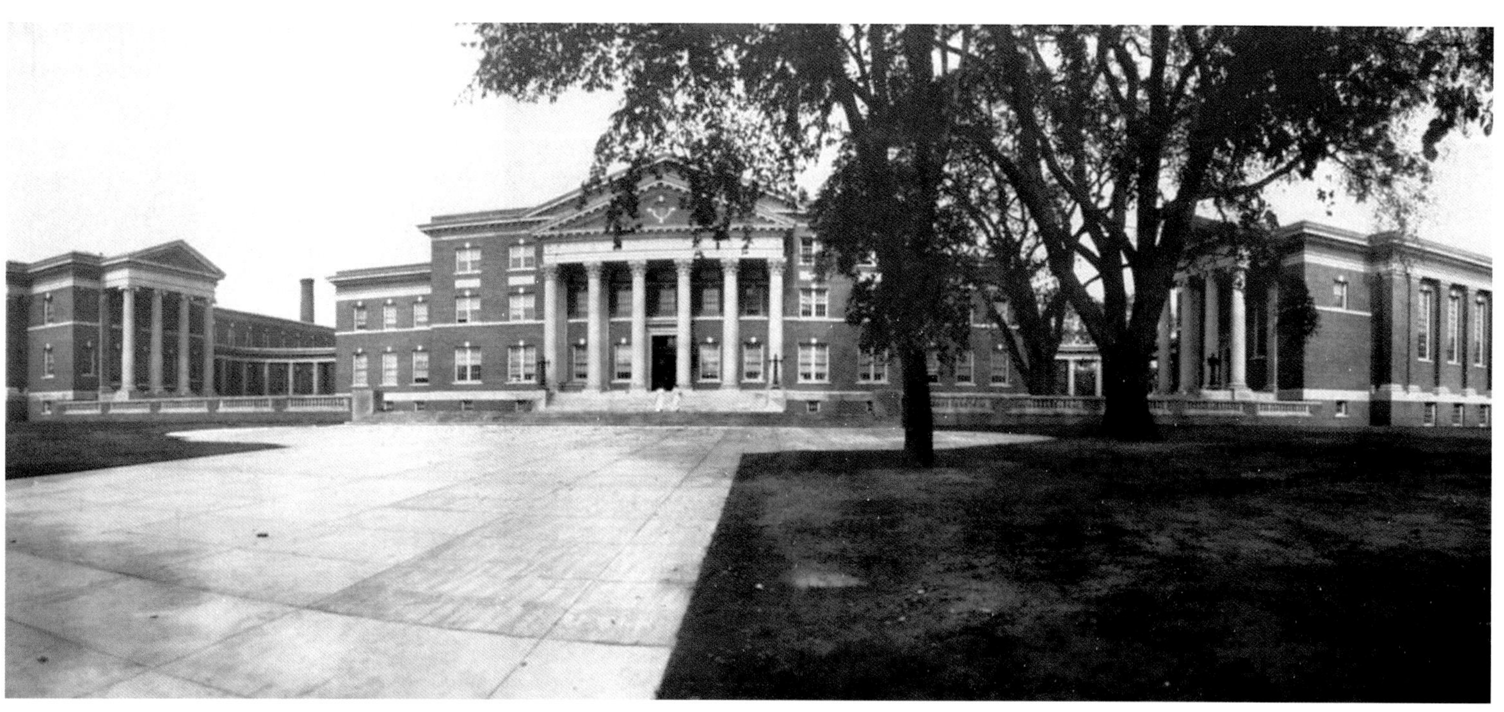

As the first institute of higher learning to be chartered by the state of New York, the State Normal School at Albany began with 29 students in 1844. The school trained high school graduates for careers in education, and by the early 1890s the name "school" had been changed to "college." The campus seen here was completed in 1909, the year this photograph was taken, and serves today as the Albany downtown campus of the State University of New York.

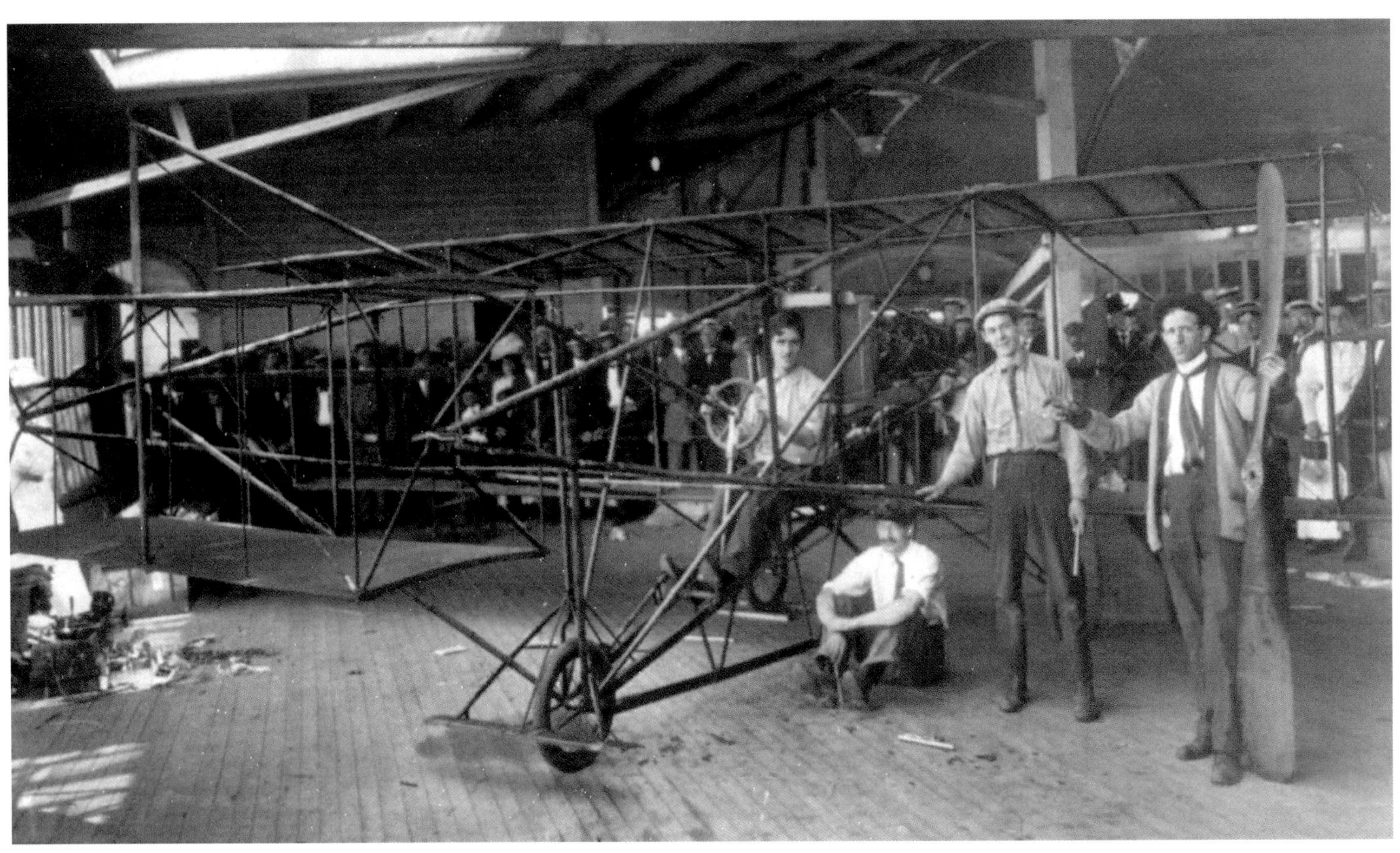

Glenn Hammond Curtiss (1878–1930) was a distinguished aviator and engineer. In 1910, he flew the airplane shown above from Albany to New York City, marking the first flight between two large American cities. Joseph Pulitzer, who established the Pulitzer Prize, awarded Curtiss a $10,000 grant in recognition of his feat. Nine years later, Curtiss would top himself by designing the first aircraft to cross the Atlantic Ocean.

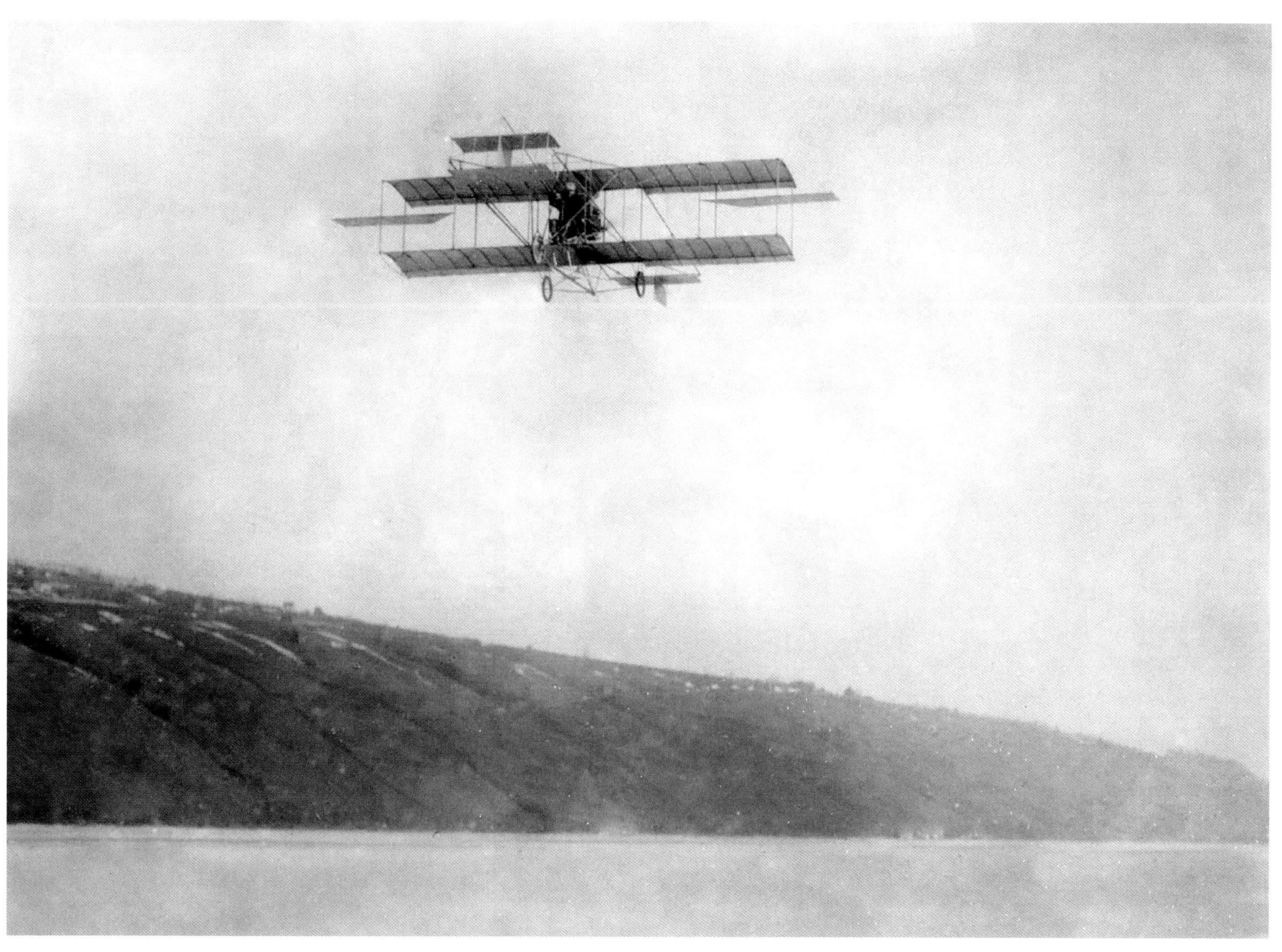

The Curtiss airplane en route from Albany to New York City. Glenn Curtiss proved himself integral to the war effort, building some of the earliest seaplanes and establishing the first American flying school in 1909. After World War I, Curtiss turned his talents toward recreational flying. Curtiss seaplanes won first place in the Schneider Cup for 1923 and 1925.

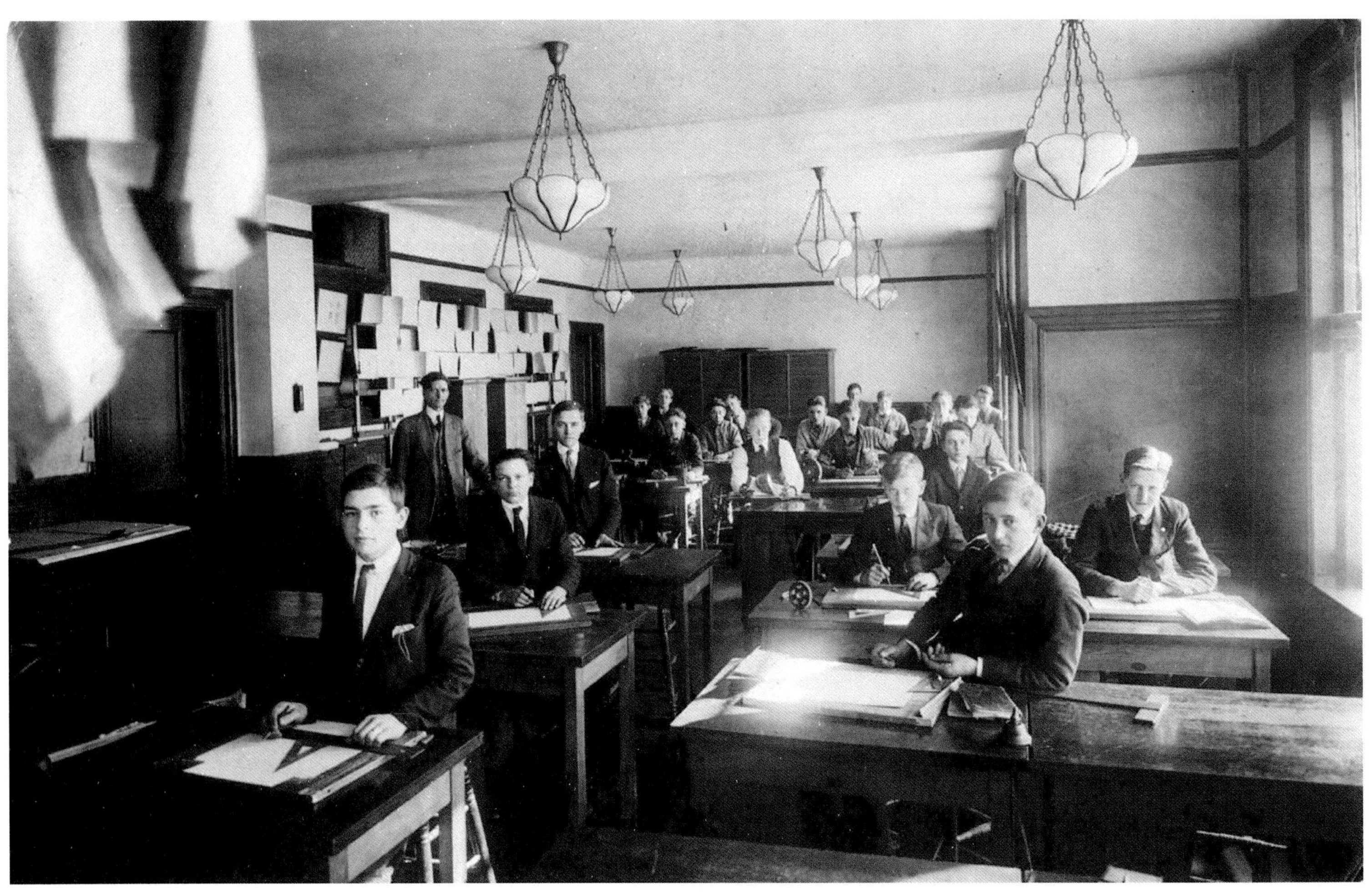

This is a classroom at Saunders Trade School in Yonkers about 1910. At this time classes were held in the basement of Yonkers High School, but in 1912 they were moved to a new building endowed by Erwin Saunders. Here the students are seen in mechanical drawing class. The school specialized in "pre-vocational instruction" and "manual training," in addition to academics.

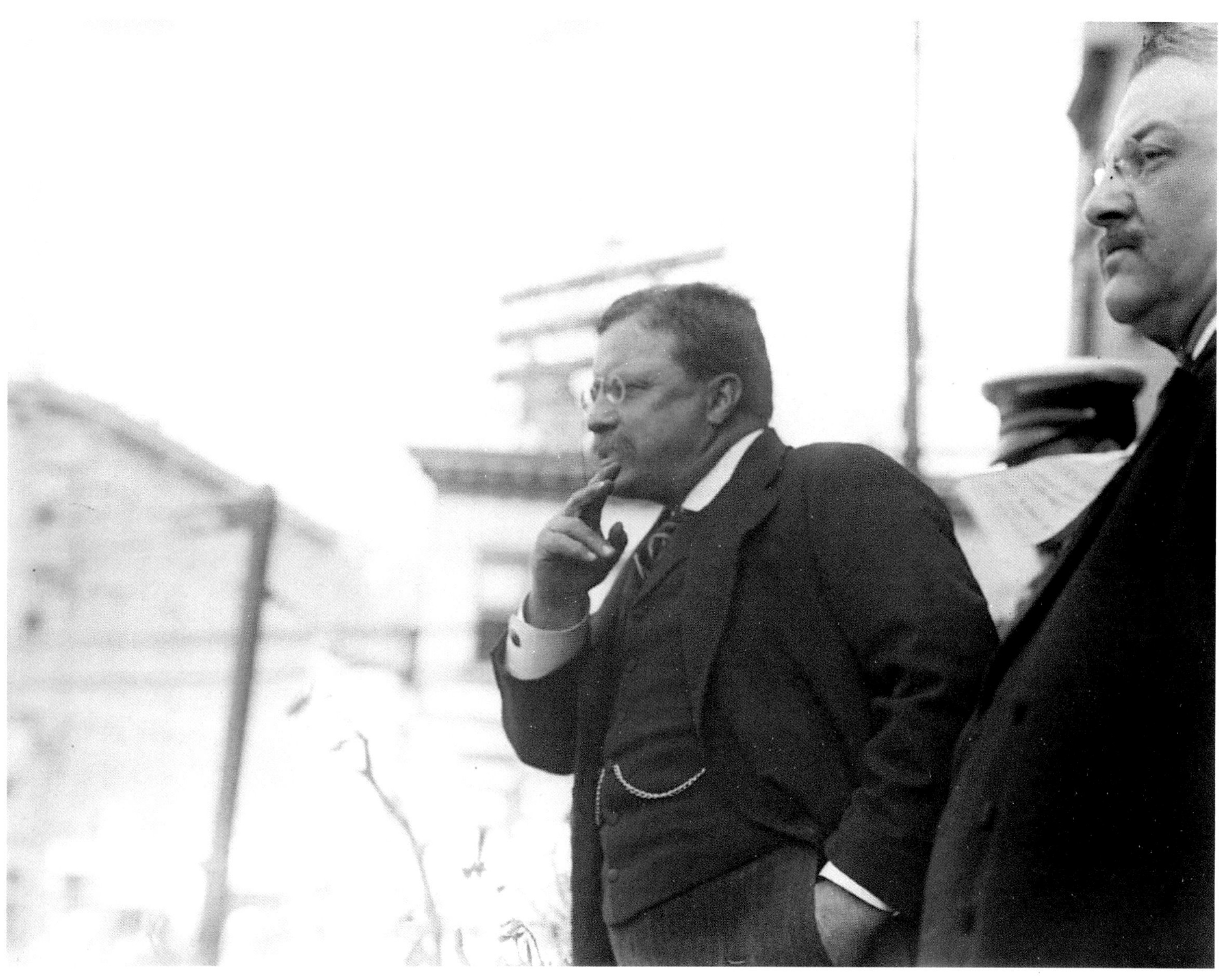

Theodore Roosevelt (1858–1919) is seen speaking at Yonkers in October 1910. Roosevelt served as New York City Police Commissioner and New York State Governor before becoming President of the United States. Here in Yonkers, the former president is stumping for Henry L. Stimson, who was to be defeated in his race for New York governor.

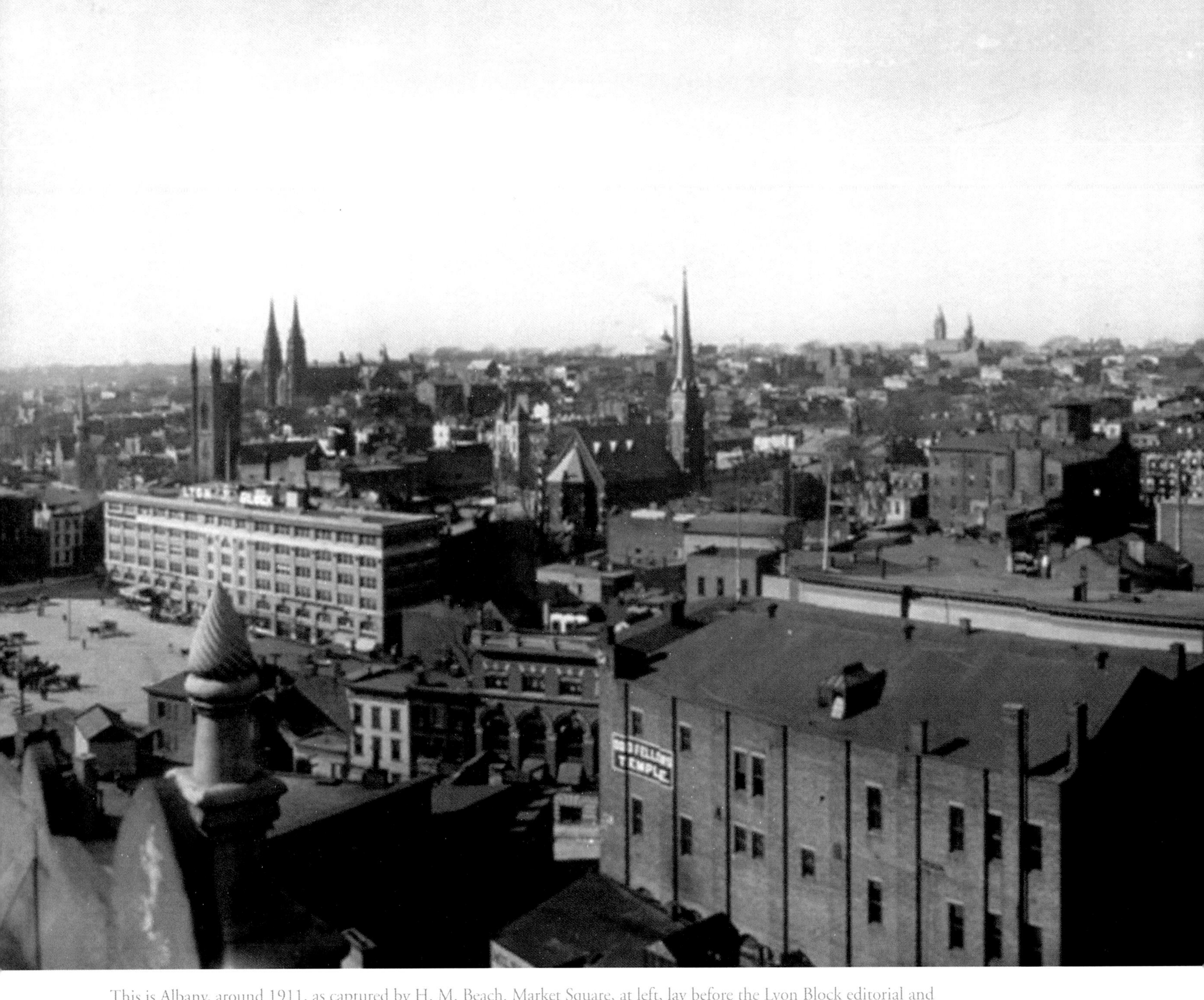

This is Albany, around 1911, as captured by H. M. Beach. Market Square, at left, lay before the Lyon Block editorial and production offices, built in 1909 on Hudson Avenue. Visible at right are the State Capitol and City Hall.

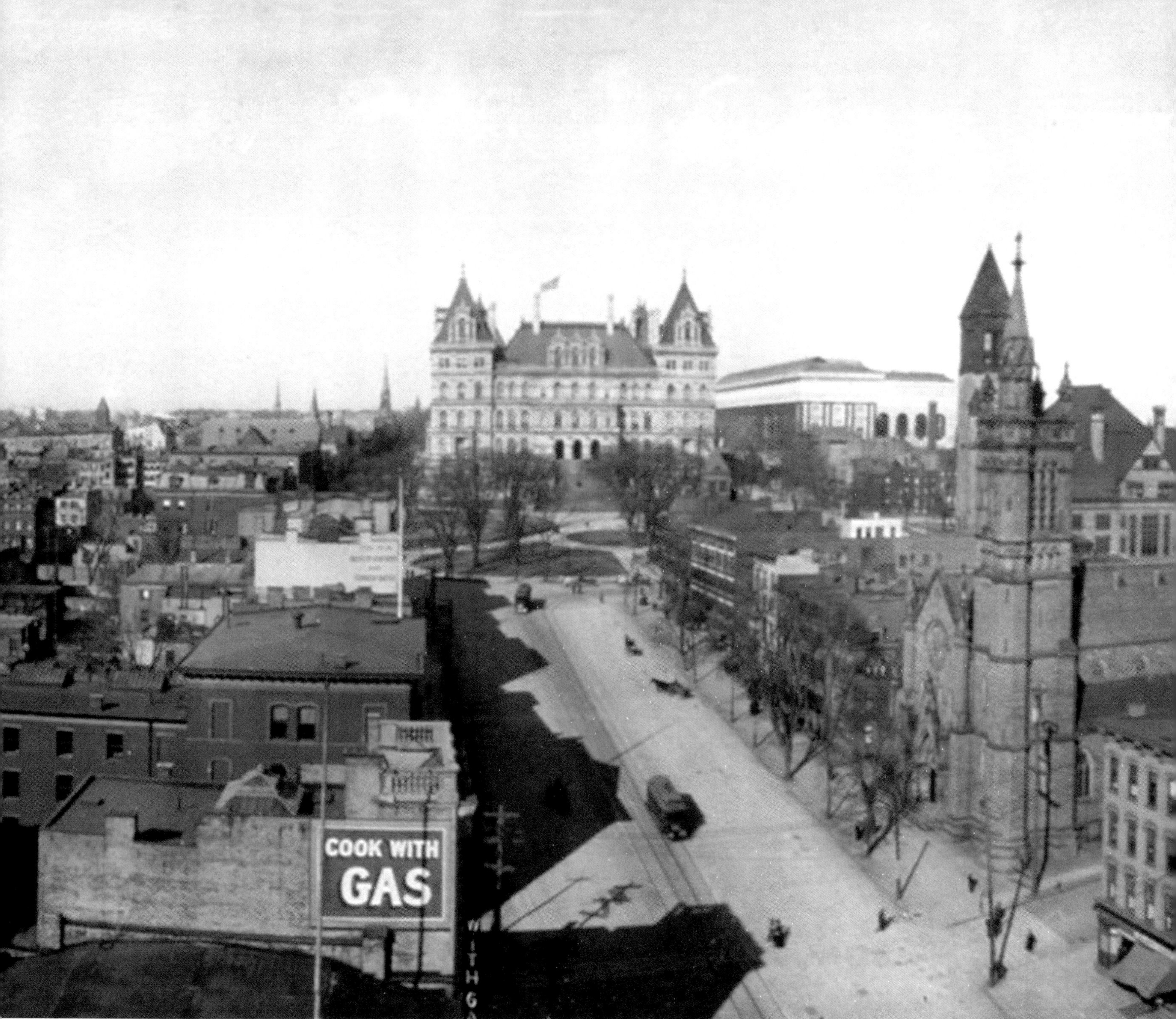
COOK WITH
GAS

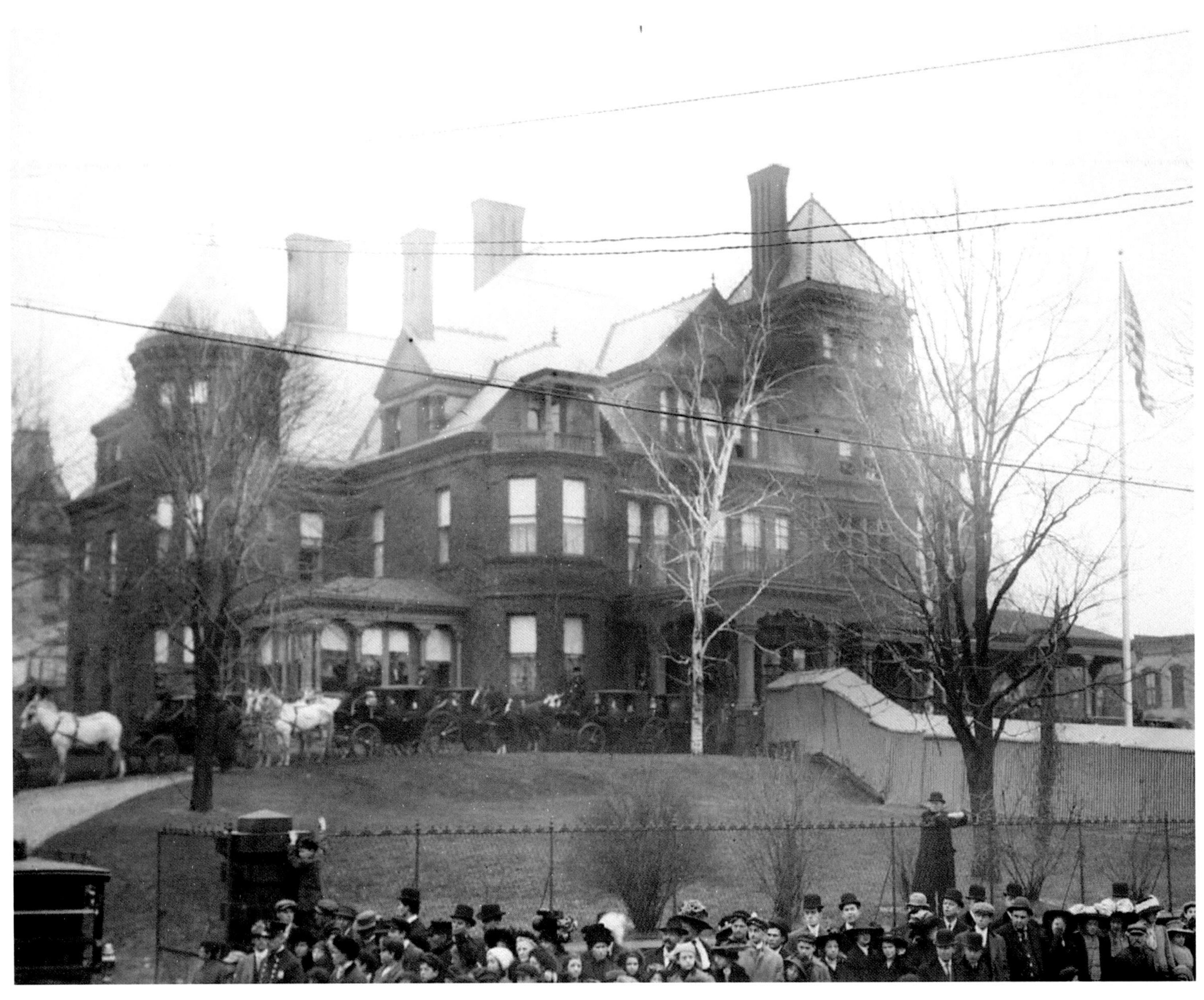

The executive mansion in Albany was the new home of Governor John A. Dix on January 3, 1911. It is shown here surrounded by a crowd of well-wishers. The house on Eagle Street was built as a private residence in 1856.

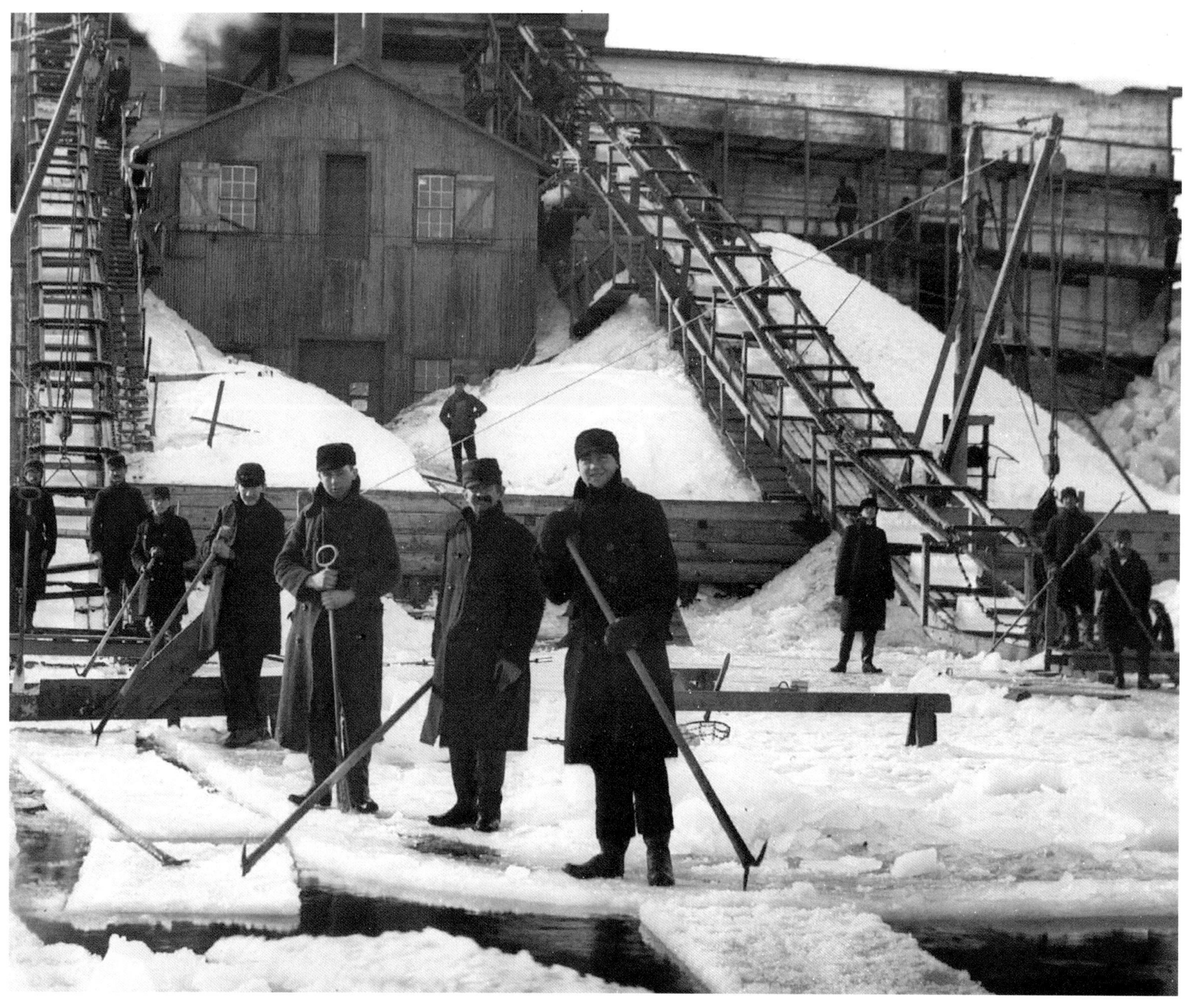

Ice harvesting looked very much the same no matter where it was done. This photograph was taken in early January 1912, when the ice cutting began. With a "twelve-inch crop," the Knickerbocker Ice Company could harvest more than three and a half million tons from its ice fields on the Hudson alone. They had other fields at "Croton Pond" and Rockland Lake. When the ice was ready, the company employed up to 10,000 men.

The New York Motorboat Club had an annual meeting on the evening of January 6, 1910, at 147th Street and the Hudson River in Manhattan. On the agenda was the election of officers and a report that the club had added nearly 100 new members, as well as 100 feet of waterfront. The club was the sponsor of boat races, including a very successful New York to Albany competition held the previous year as part of the Hudson-Fulton Tricentennial Celebration.

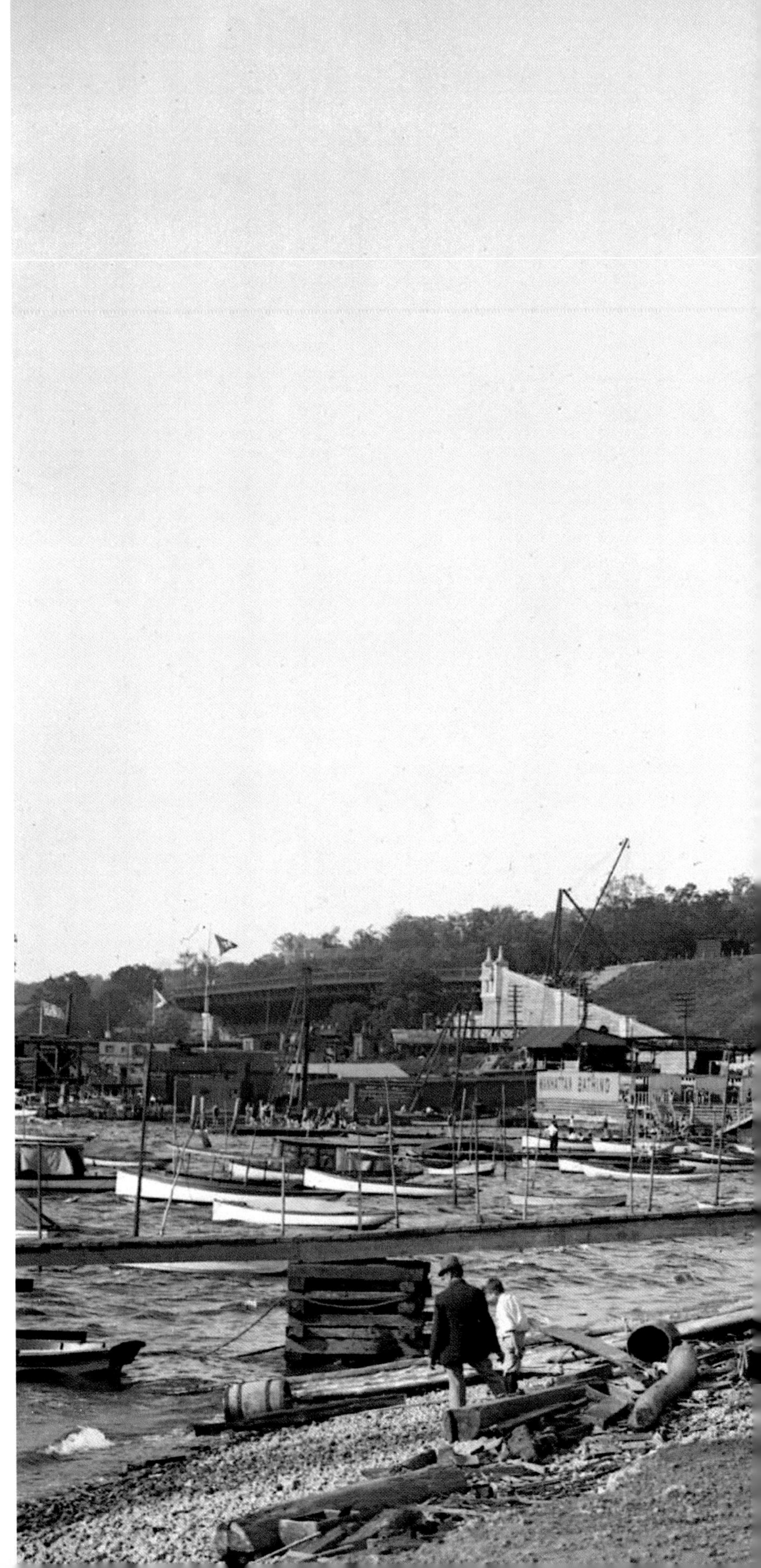

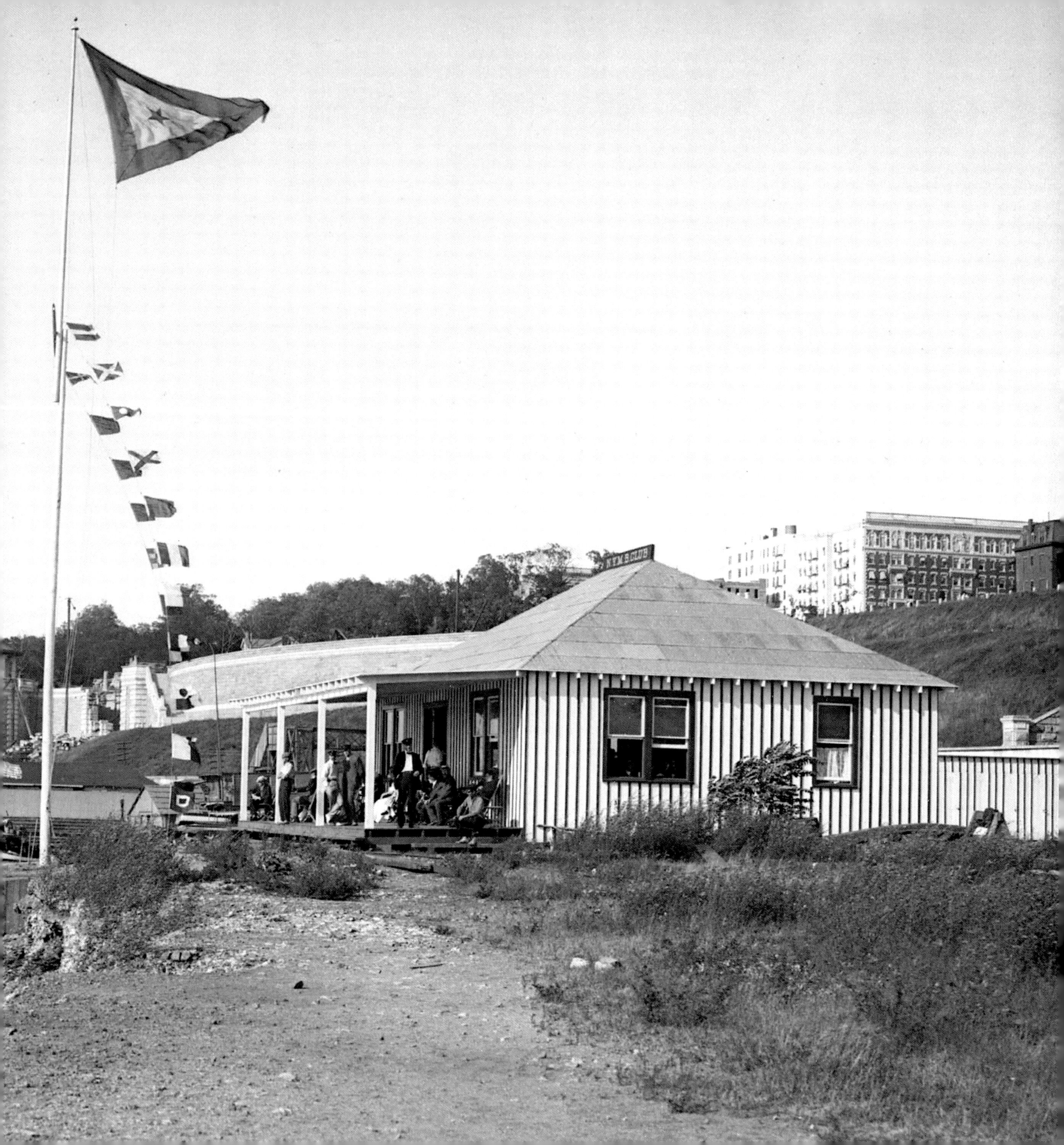
N.Y.M.B.CLUB

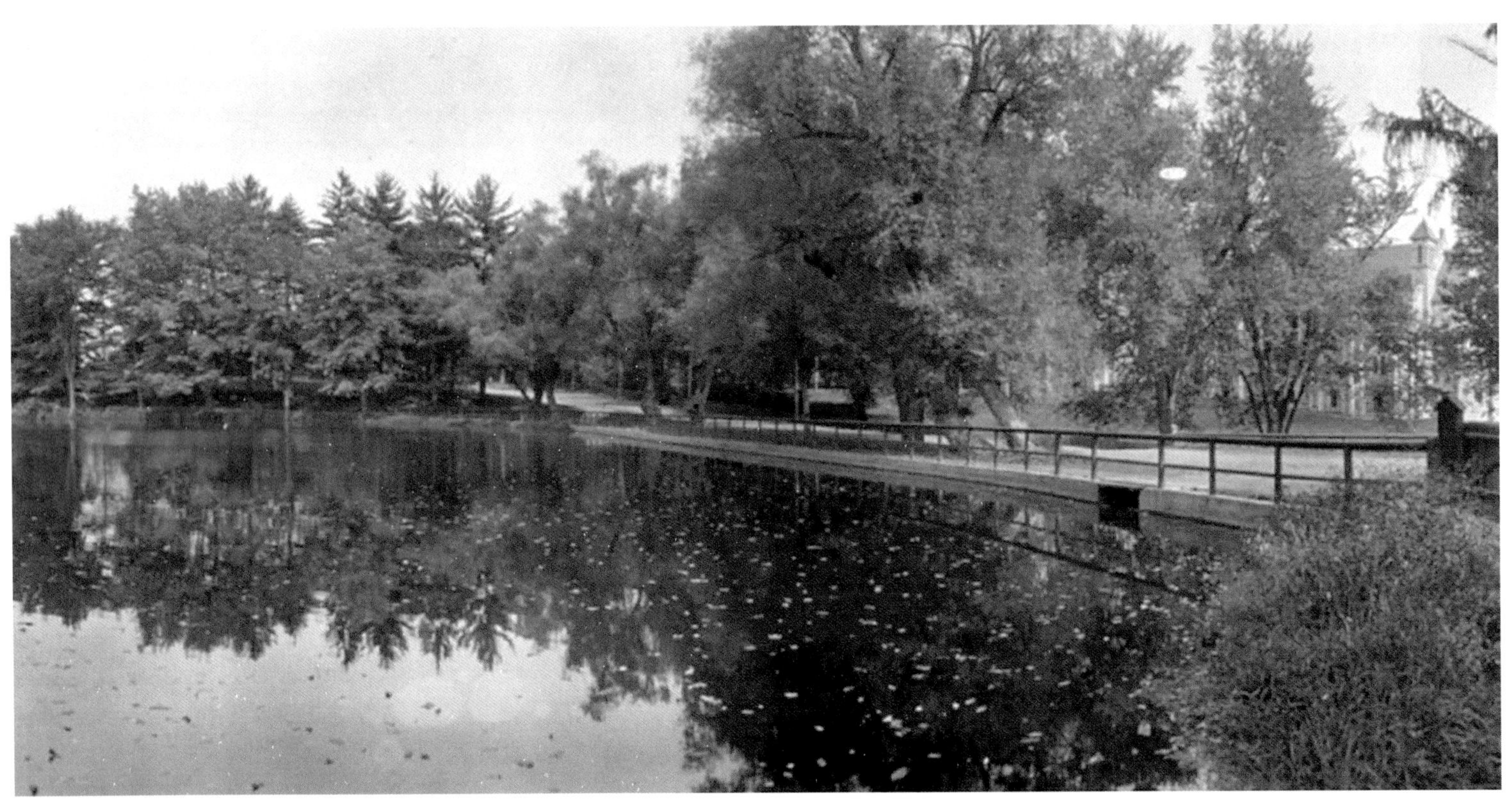

This is a 1912 shot of Sunset Lake at Vassar in Poughkeepsie. The drive to the right leads to Main, the large, original all-purpose building at Vassar, about 300 yards northeast. Originally named Pratt Lake after the donor who provided funds for construction, the lake soon acquired its current name. It was popular among the students for ice-skating and ice festivals.

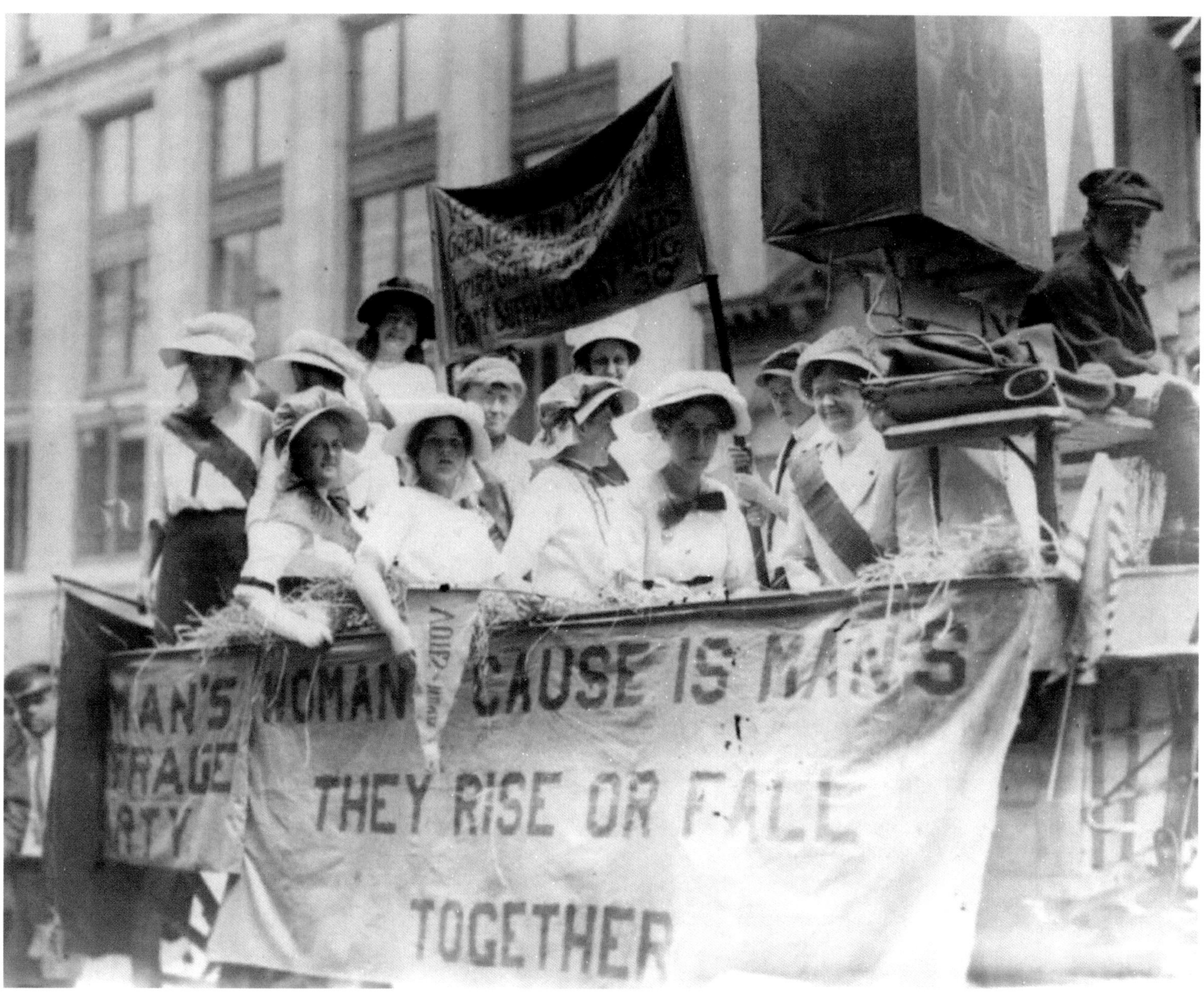

On August 10, 1913, this band of intrepid women campaigned for women's suffrage in Yonkers. The movement in Westchester County began in Yonkers, with a group of 12 women who met in 1909. By 1917, women had won the right to vote in New York State, and four years later, women's suffrage prevailed in the United States. The electric sign in the front of the float reads, "Stop, Look, Listen."

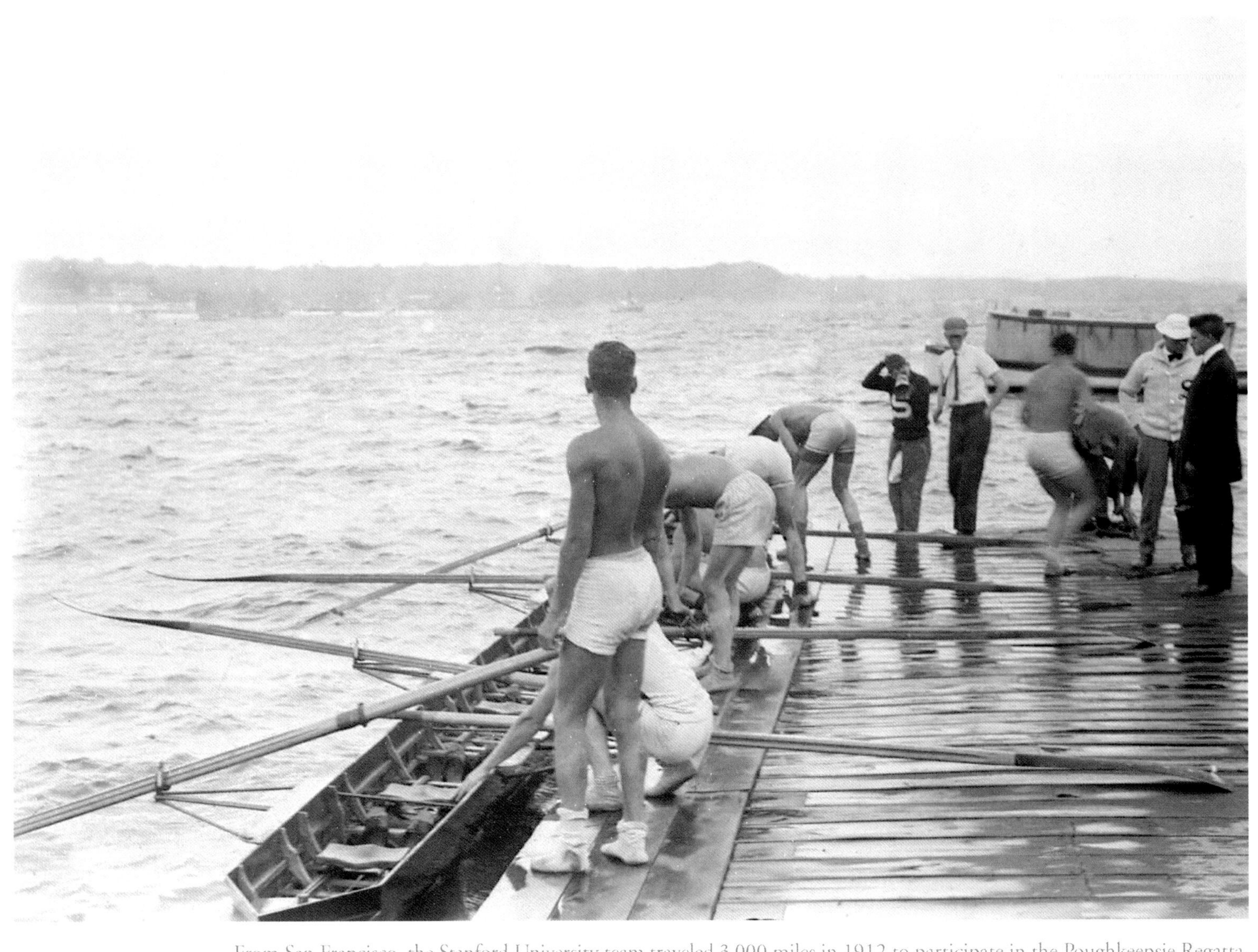

From San Francisco, the Stanford University team traveled 3,000 miles in 1912 to participate in the Poughkeepsie Regatta. Owing to a dock strike, it appeared at first that the team would have to borrow a boat from Columbia University, but they managed to compete in their own craft.

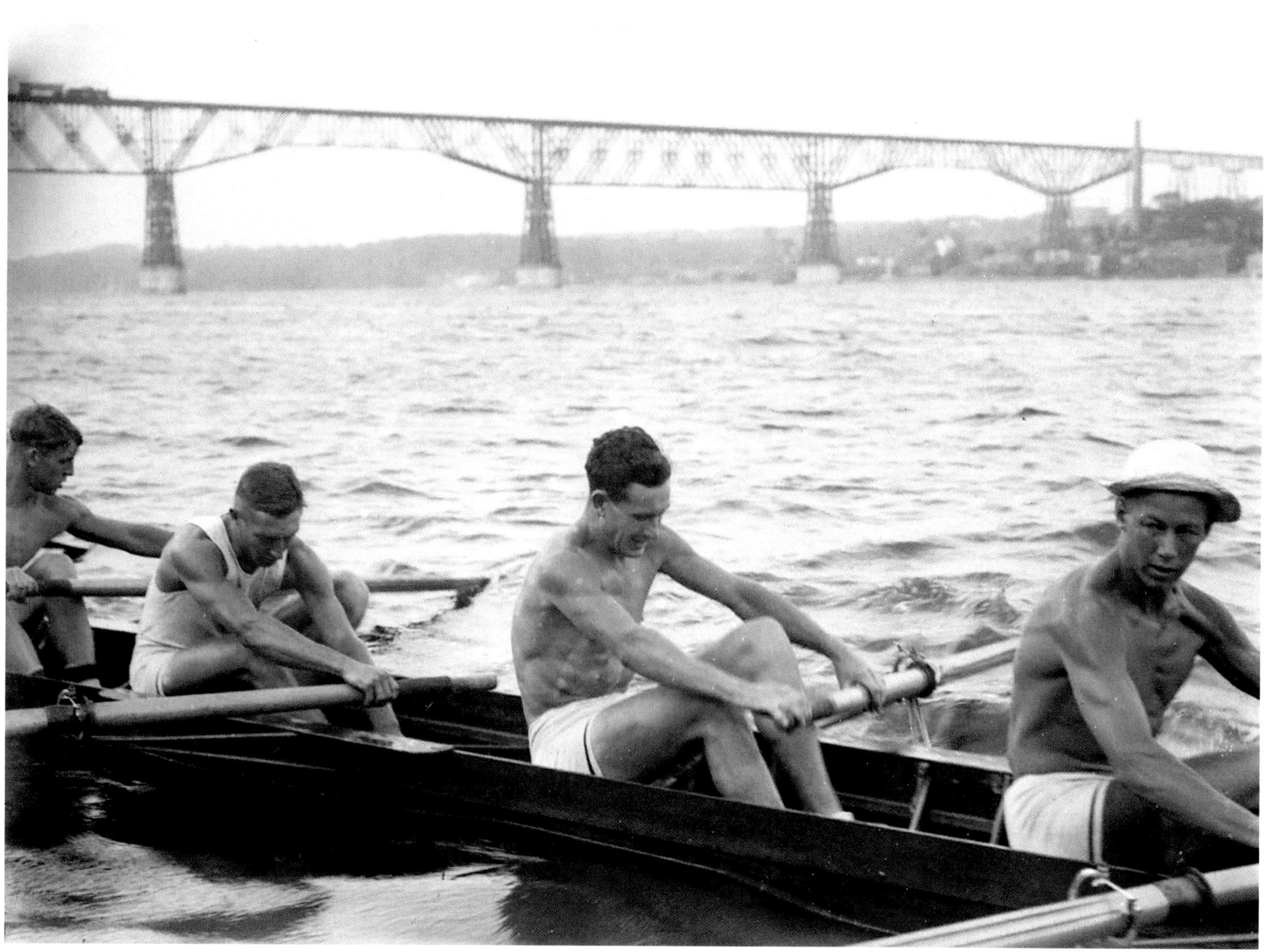

The Poughkeepsie Bridge, shown here with the Stanford University crew in the foreground, was completed on January 1, 1889. It served as the main Hudson River crossing below Albany until the Bear Mountain Bridge was constructed in 1924. Though taken out of service in 1974, it was to be reopened as a pedestrian bridge across the Hudson in 2009.

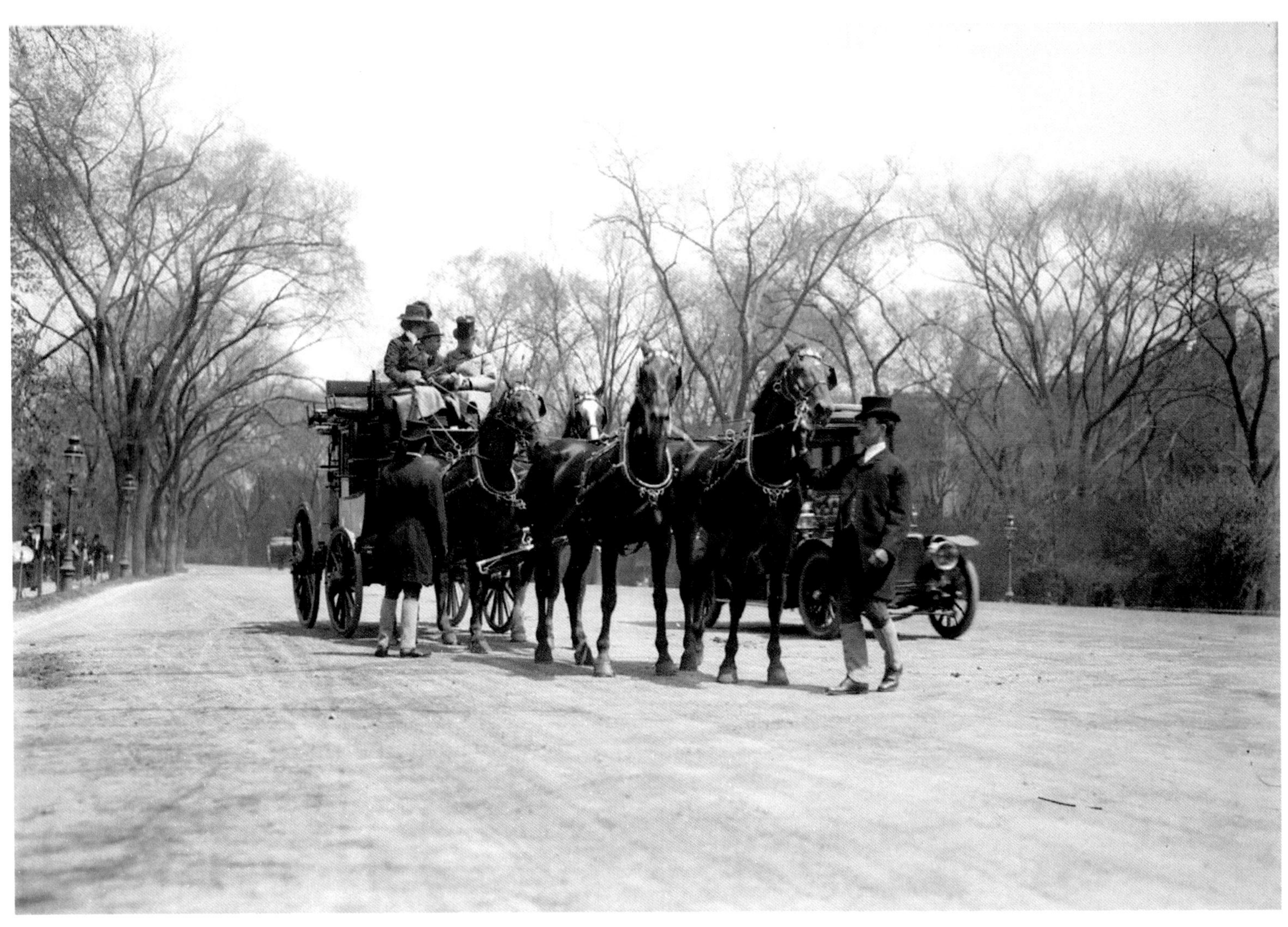

Mrs. Thomas Hastings was avid about her four-in-hand coach, and is seen here driving in New York's Central Park well after the advent of the automobile. Helen Benedict Hastings (d. 1936) founded the Ladies Four-in-hand Driving Club in 1901. Her husband, Thomas Hastings (1860–1929), was a famed architect who designed the Tomb of the Unknowns at Arlington, the New York Public Library, and the Frick Mansion on Fifth Avenue.

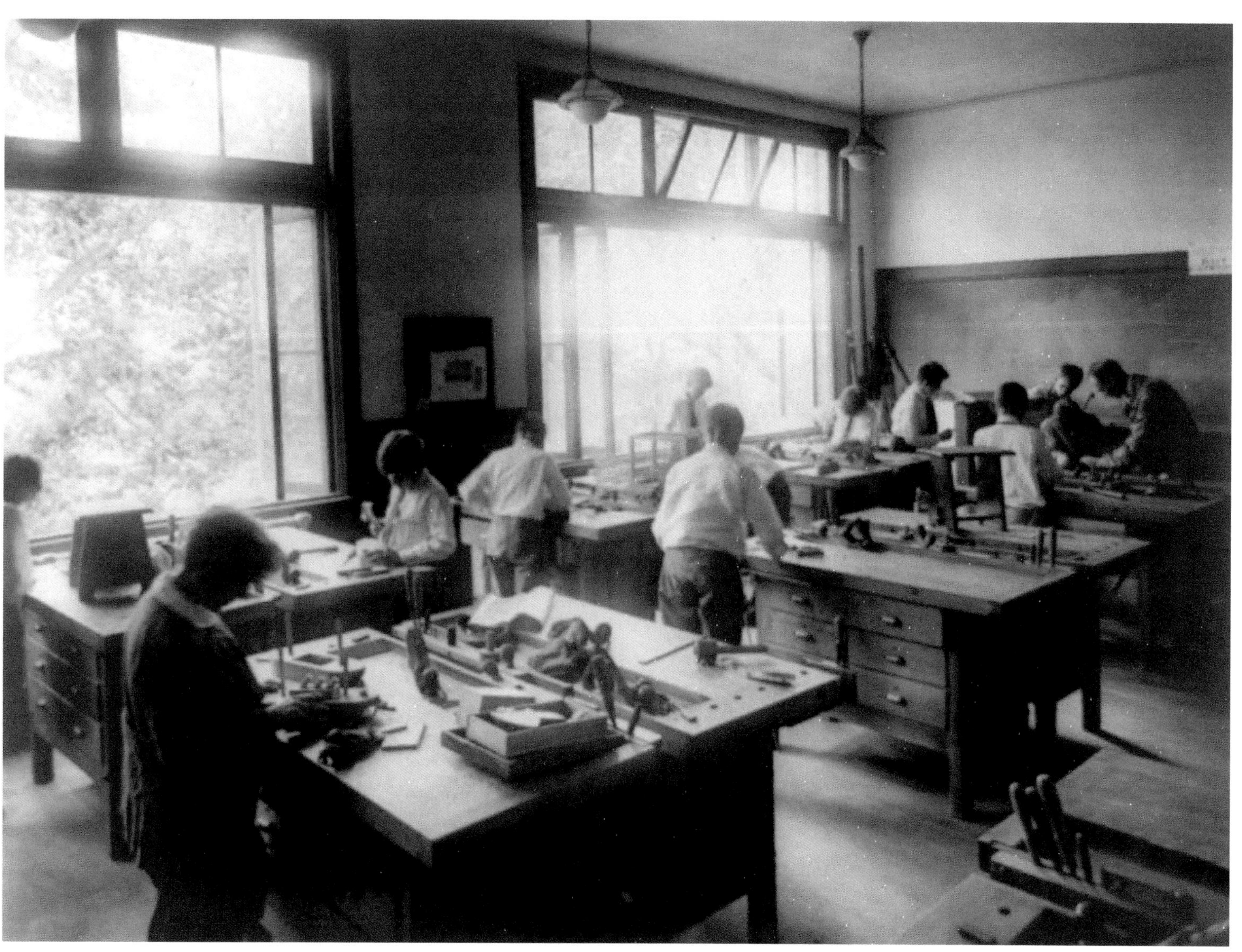

Boys study carpentry in this image of Riverdale Country School. Dr. Frank Sutliff Hackett founded the school in 1907, beginning with only 12 students and 4 teachers. At first, it was named Riverdale School for Boys and located near Van Cortlandt Park in the Bronx. In 2009, tuition costs were $35,000 a year. Riverdale was the nineteenth-century estate district of the Bronx; its affluence has continued to the present.

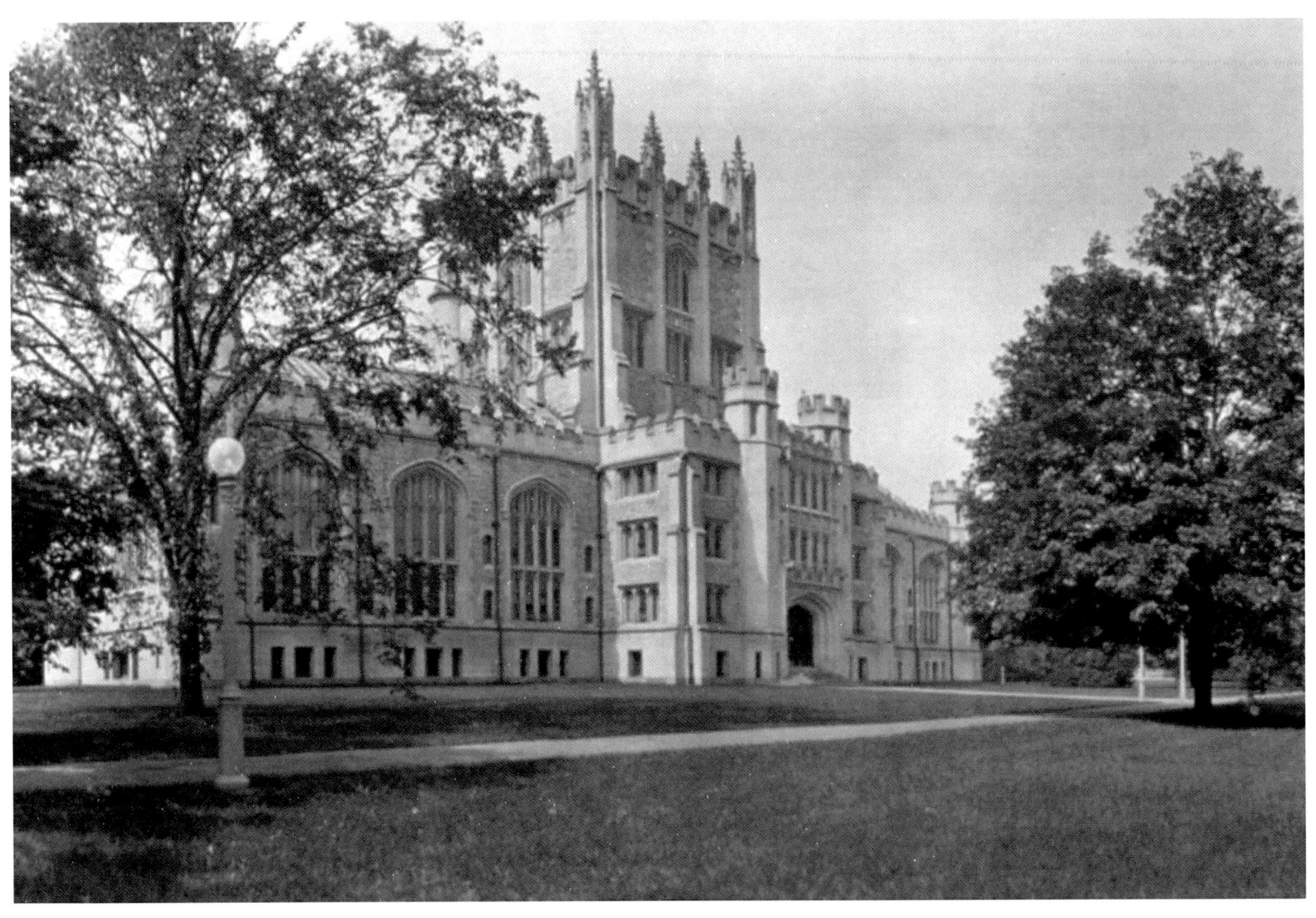

Poughkeepsie's Vassar College boasts the largest undergraduate library collection in the United States. The Thompson Library, seen here in 1912, was completed in 1905 with donations from Frederick Ferris Thompson and his wife, Mary Clark Thompson. Allen & Collens designed the building in the collegiate Gothic Revival style. The firm was also responsible for Riverside Cathedral and the Cloisters in New York City.

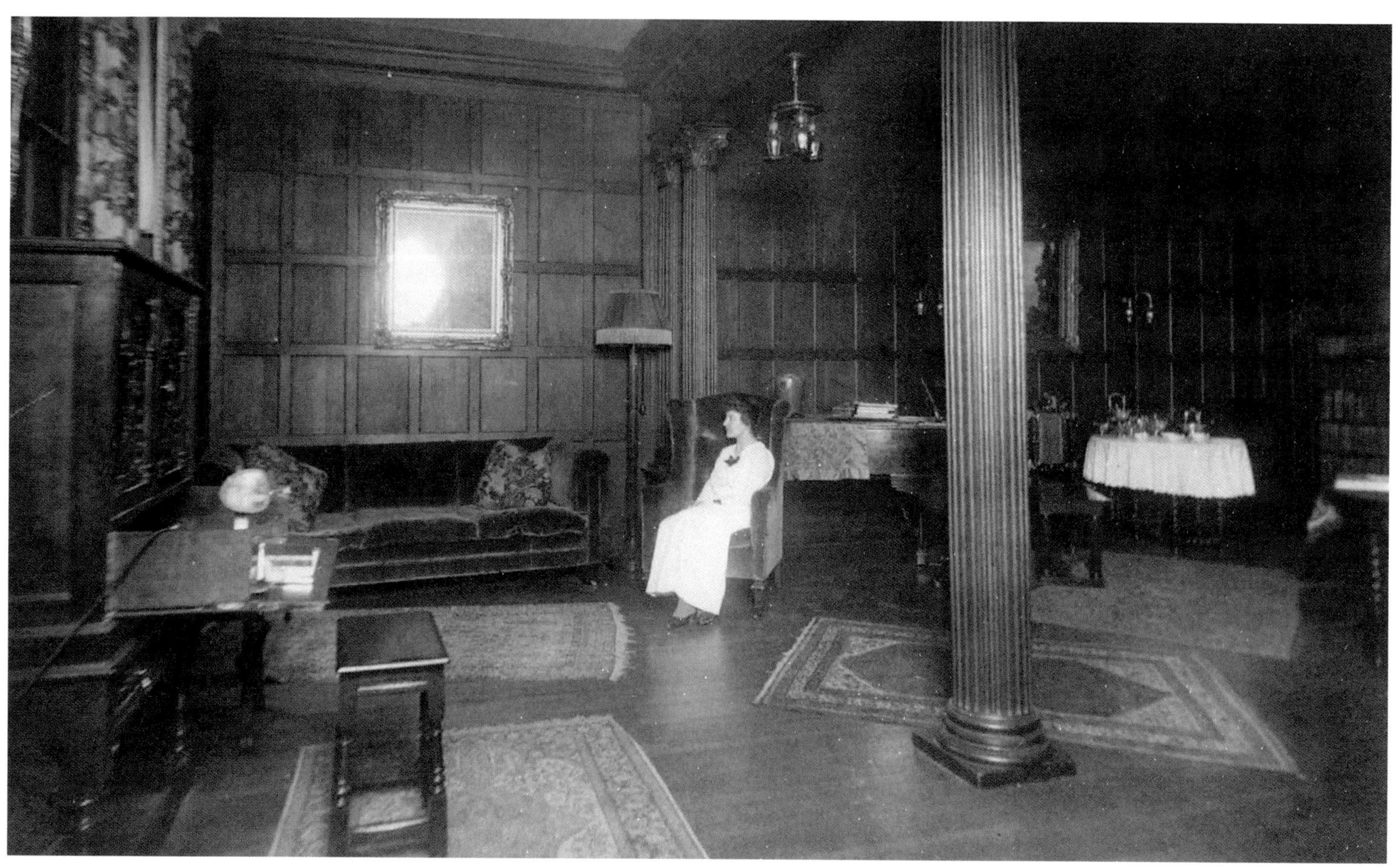

The old "Main" building at Vassar College held a senior parlor, its quiet surroundings enjoyed by this senior around 1915. The parlor featured a piano, curtains of Nottingham lace, and other handsome appointments. For 70 years, until 1943, the annual "opening" of the senior parlor was an important on-campus social event. Poughkeepsie photographer Edmund L. Wolven captured this image.

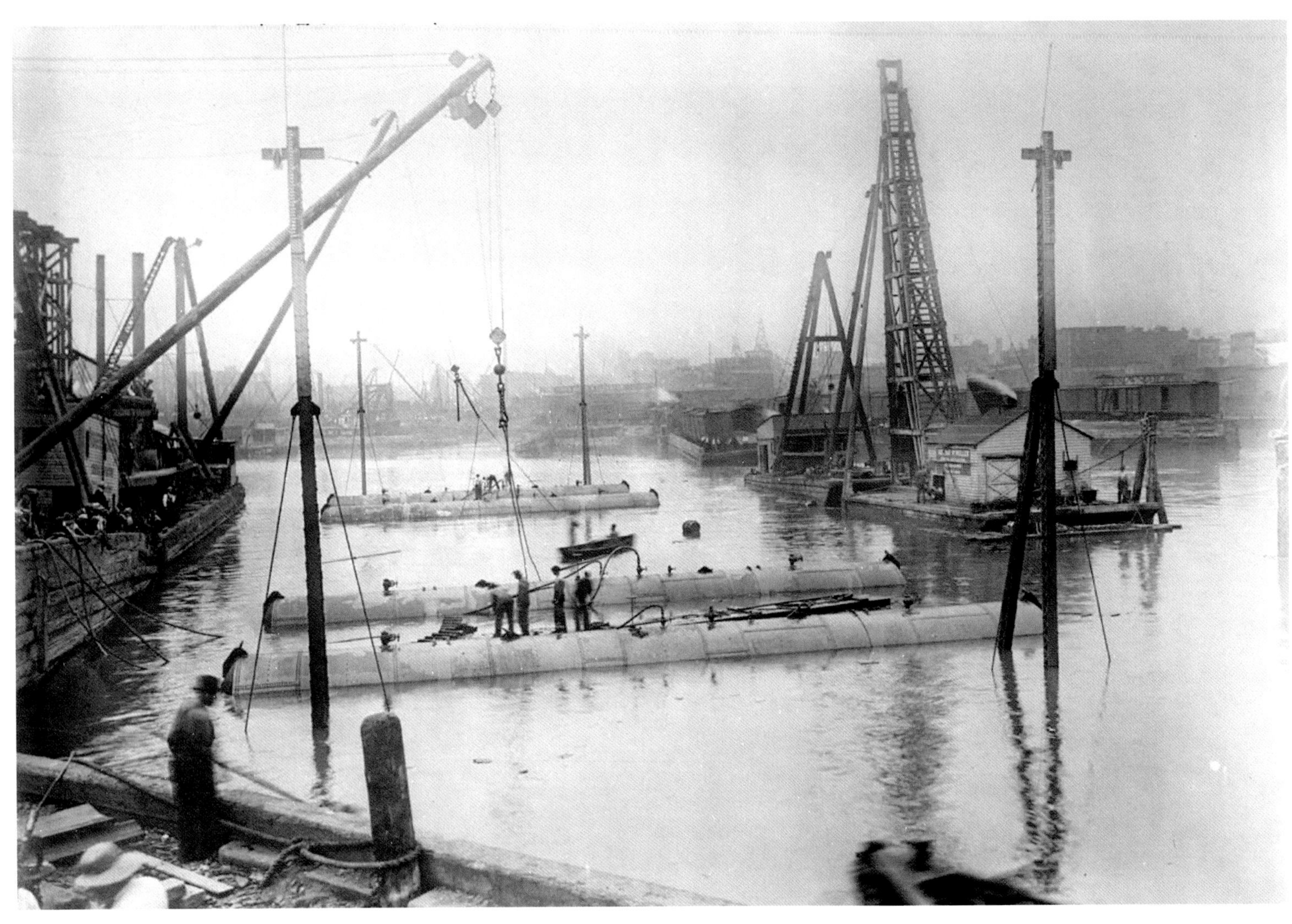

On August 29, 1913, these buoyancy chambers were in use in the Harlem River during tunnel construction for the Lexington Avenue Subway Line. At this point, the river was about 400 feet wide and 20 feet deep. Dredging operations began in March 1913 and were completed in September 1914.

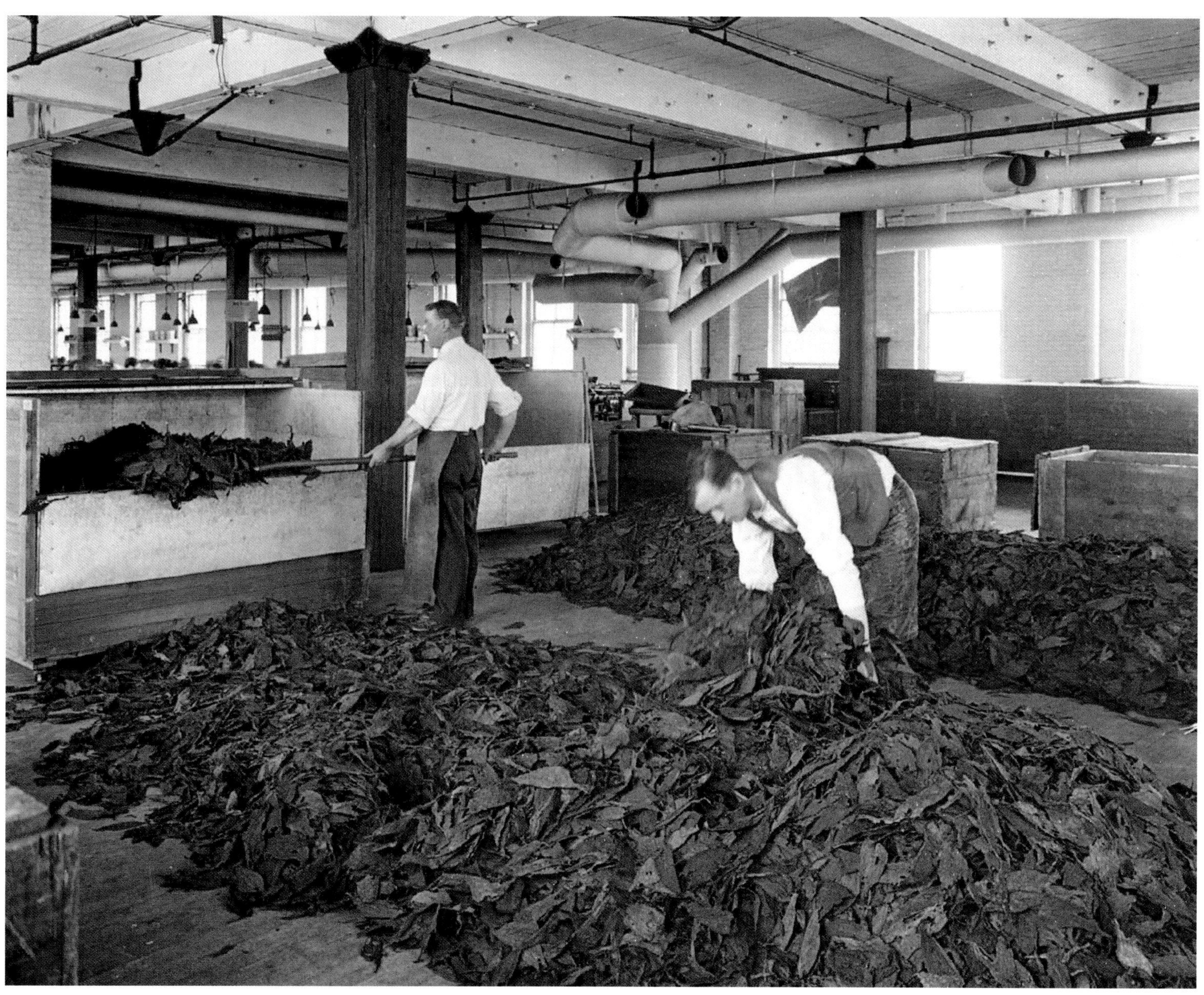

George W. Van Slyke was born in 1831, in New Baltimore, New York, and became the senior partner of Van Slyke and Horton, tobacco manufacturers. His son, by the same name, was born and educated in Albany and later managed his father's business as president of the company. The business was based in Albany, but the factory, shown here in 1913, was located in Kingston. In early times, tobacco was grown in the Catskill Mountains by the indigenous inhabitants.

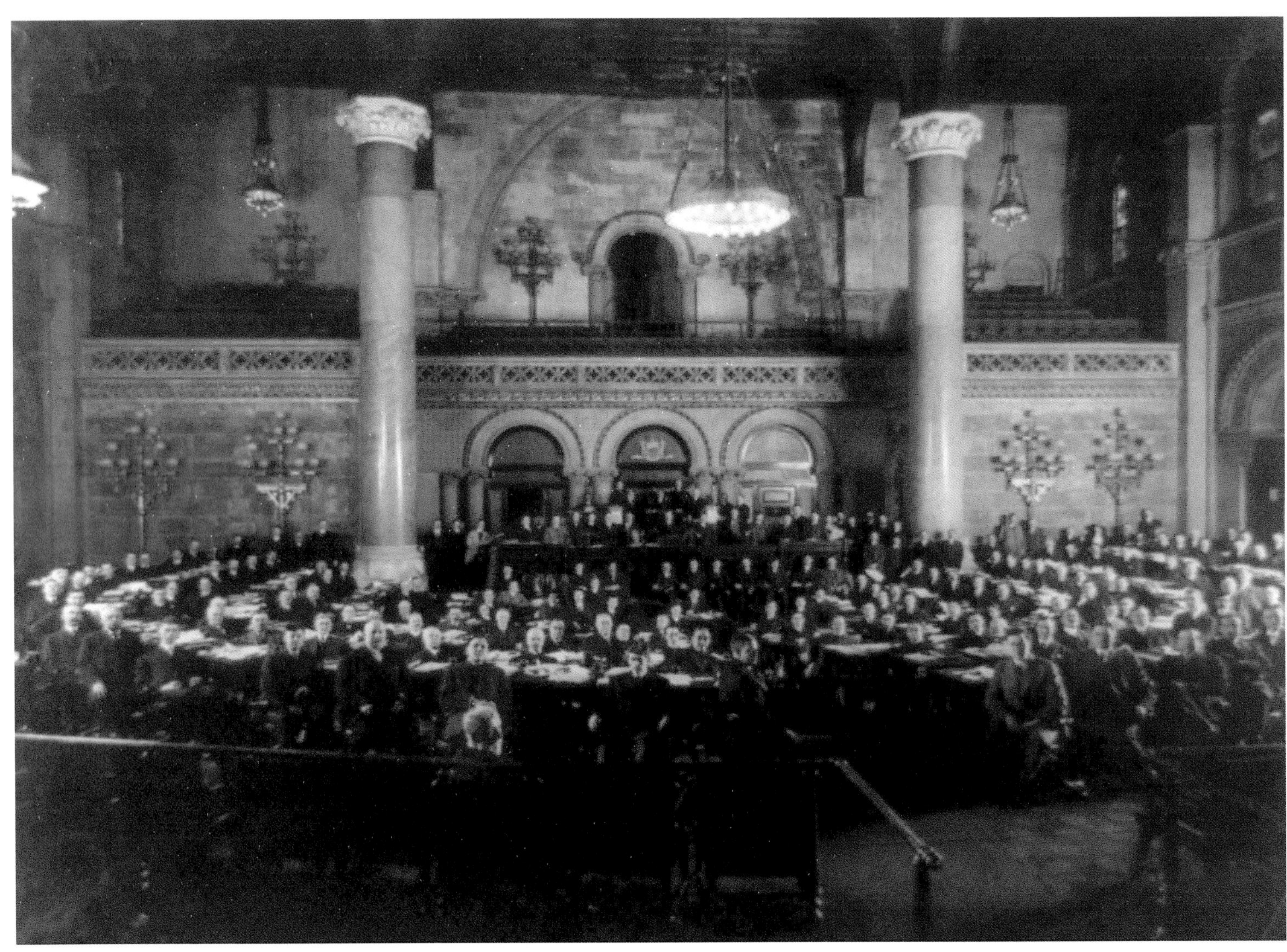

The State Assembly of New York had a perfect setting for this official photograph in 1913. The State Capitol, completed in 1899, was the most expensive public building in the United States in its day. A fire that swept through parts of the structure in 1911 was stopped before it could engulf the entire building.

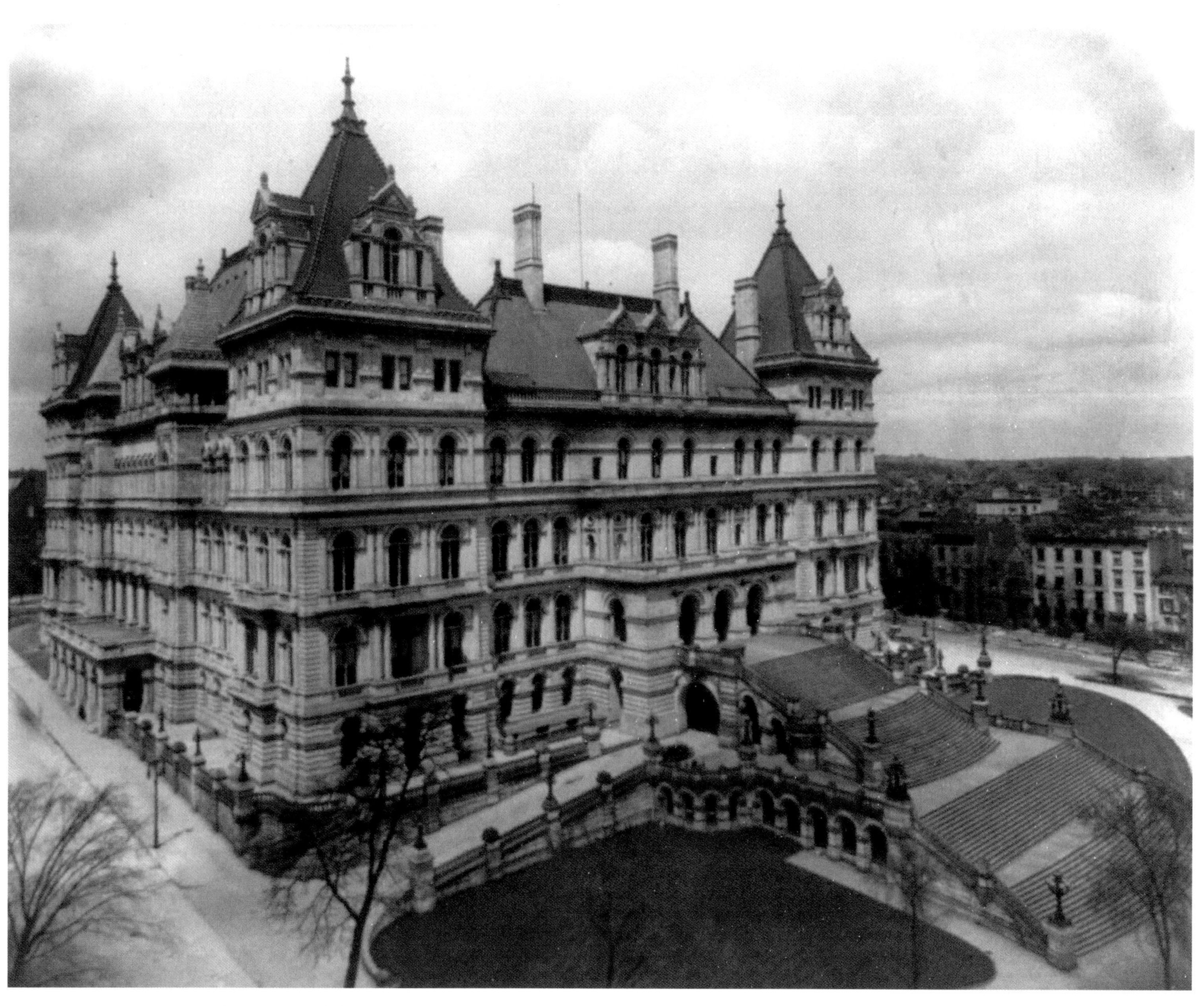

The exterior of the New York State Capitol sits prominently in Albany's landscape about 1915. The "million-dollar staircase" within was even more impressive than the palatial steps in front of the building.

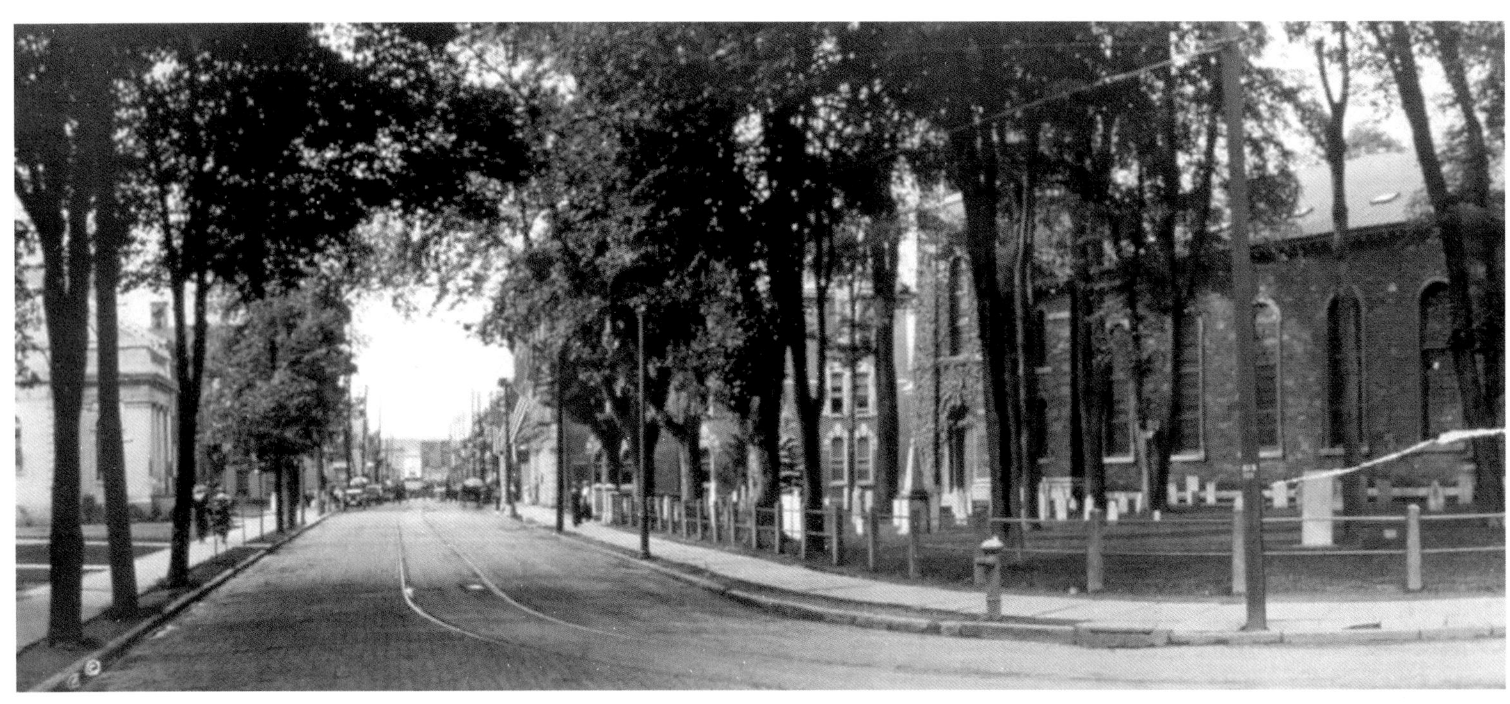

Among the burials at the Old Dutch Church of Kingston is that of George Clinton, first governor of New York and vice-president of the United States under Jefferson and Madison. Clinton's remains were moved there from Washington, D.C., in 1908. The church was designed by Minard Lafever (1798–1854) and completed in 1852. It is the sole remaining example of his work in the Renaissance Revival style, photographed here in 1916 by Arthur Church.

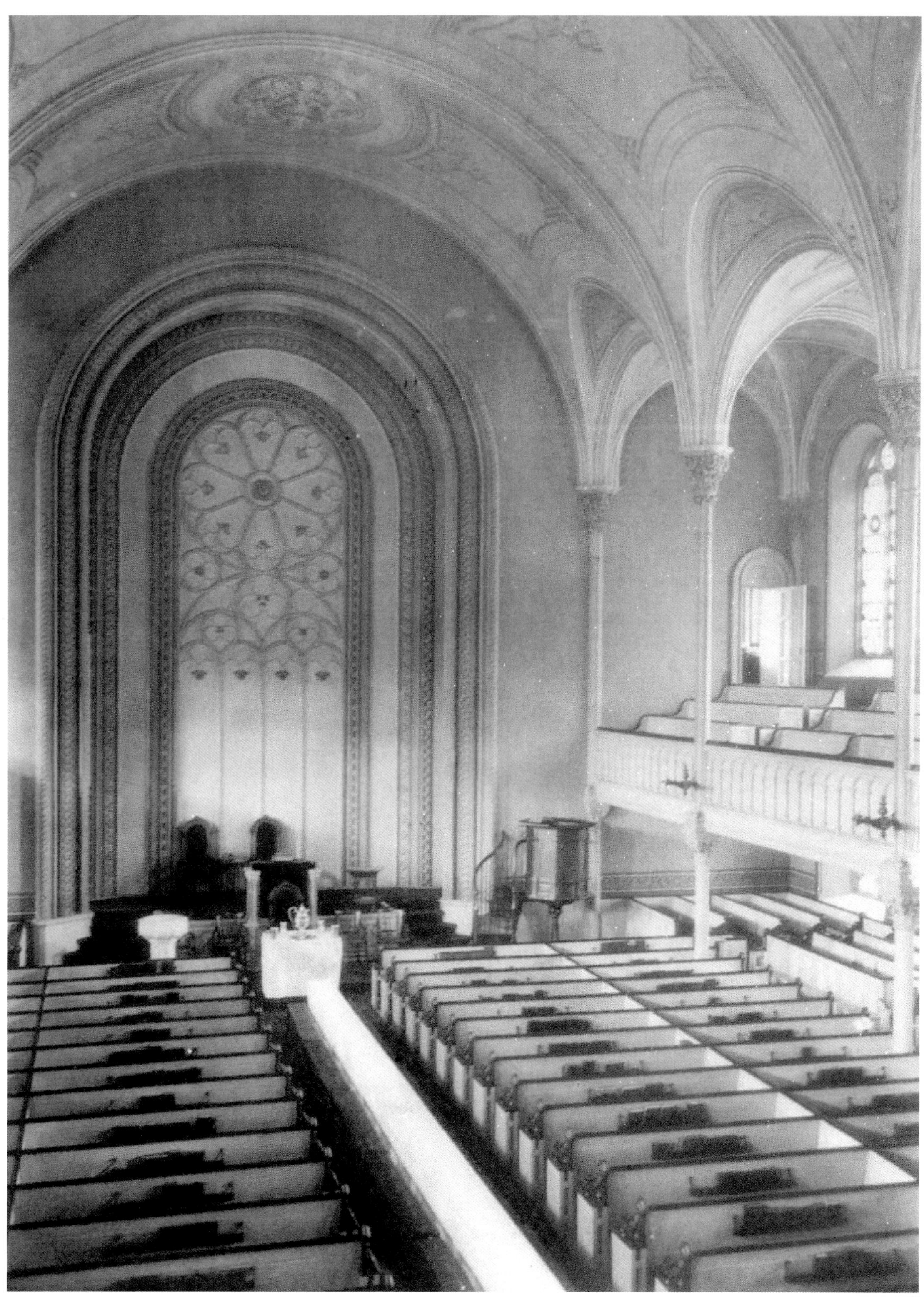

Interior view of the First Reformed Church, at North Pearl and Orange streets in Albany.

A military parade is captured on State Street in Albany, around 1917. World War I had begun in 1914 with the assassination of a Serbian archduke, and the United States would enter the fray in April 1917.

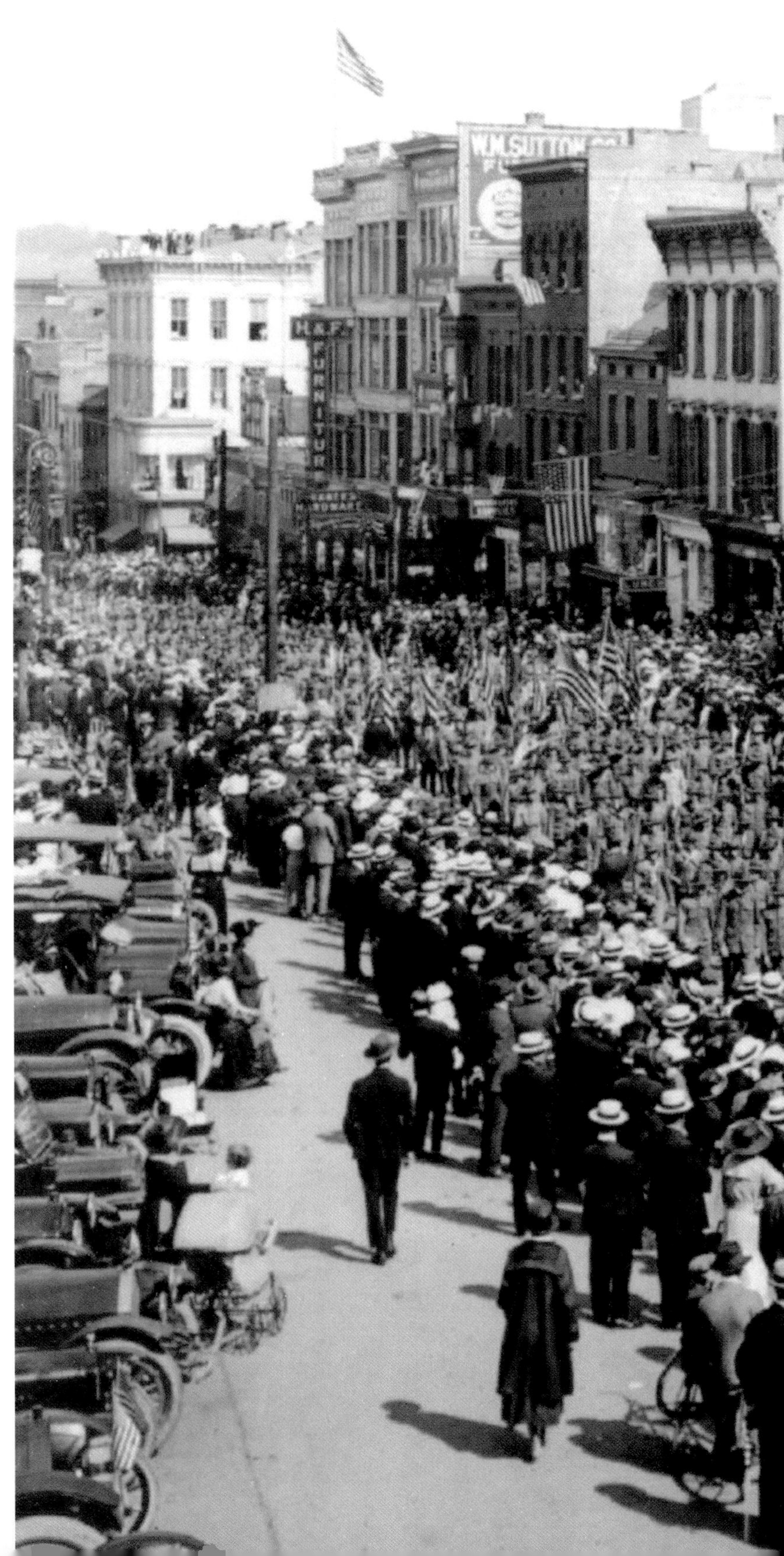

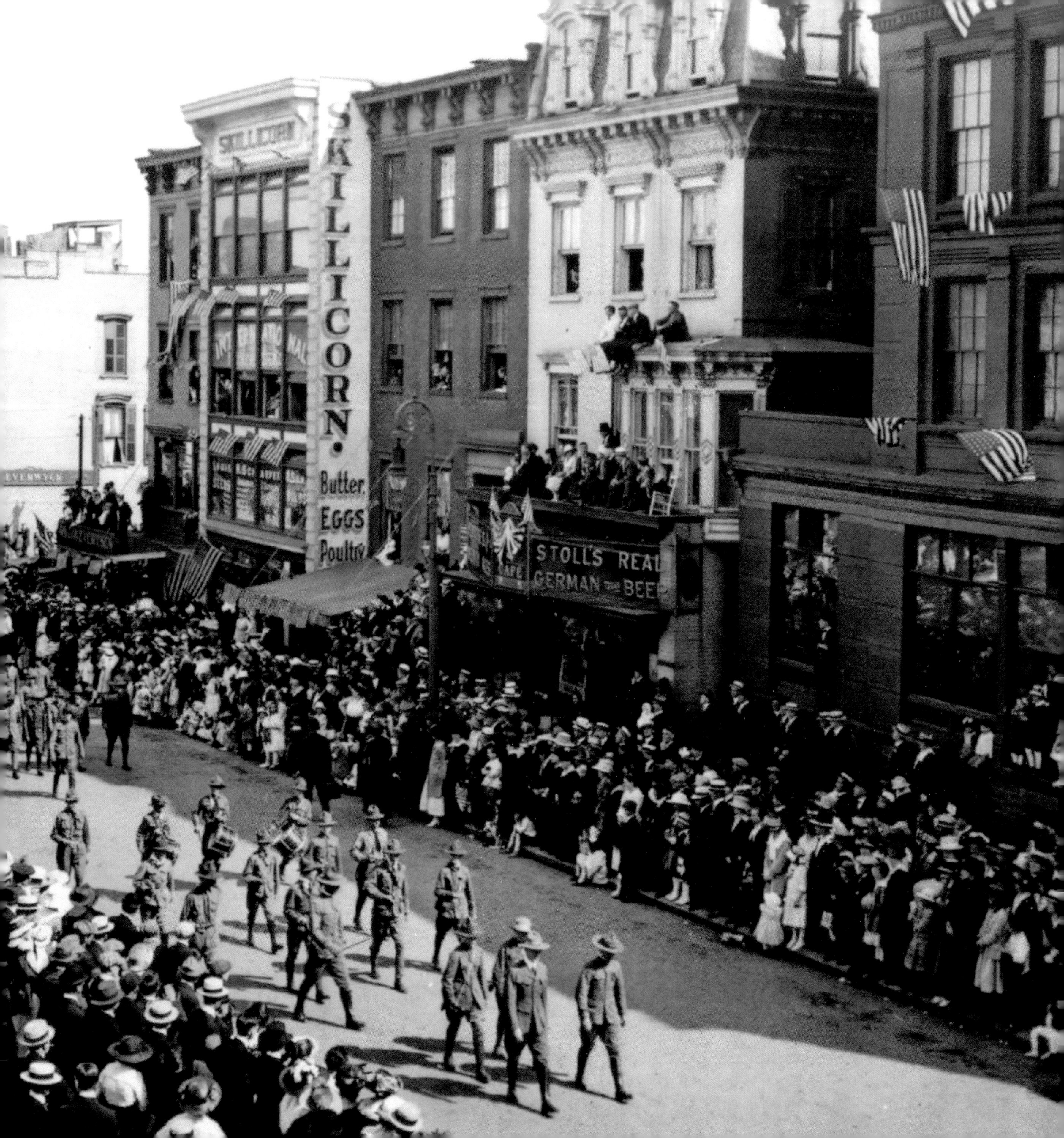
SKILLICORN
SKILLICORN.
Butter,
EGGS
Poultry
STOLL'S REAL
CAFE
GERMAN BEER
EVERWYCK

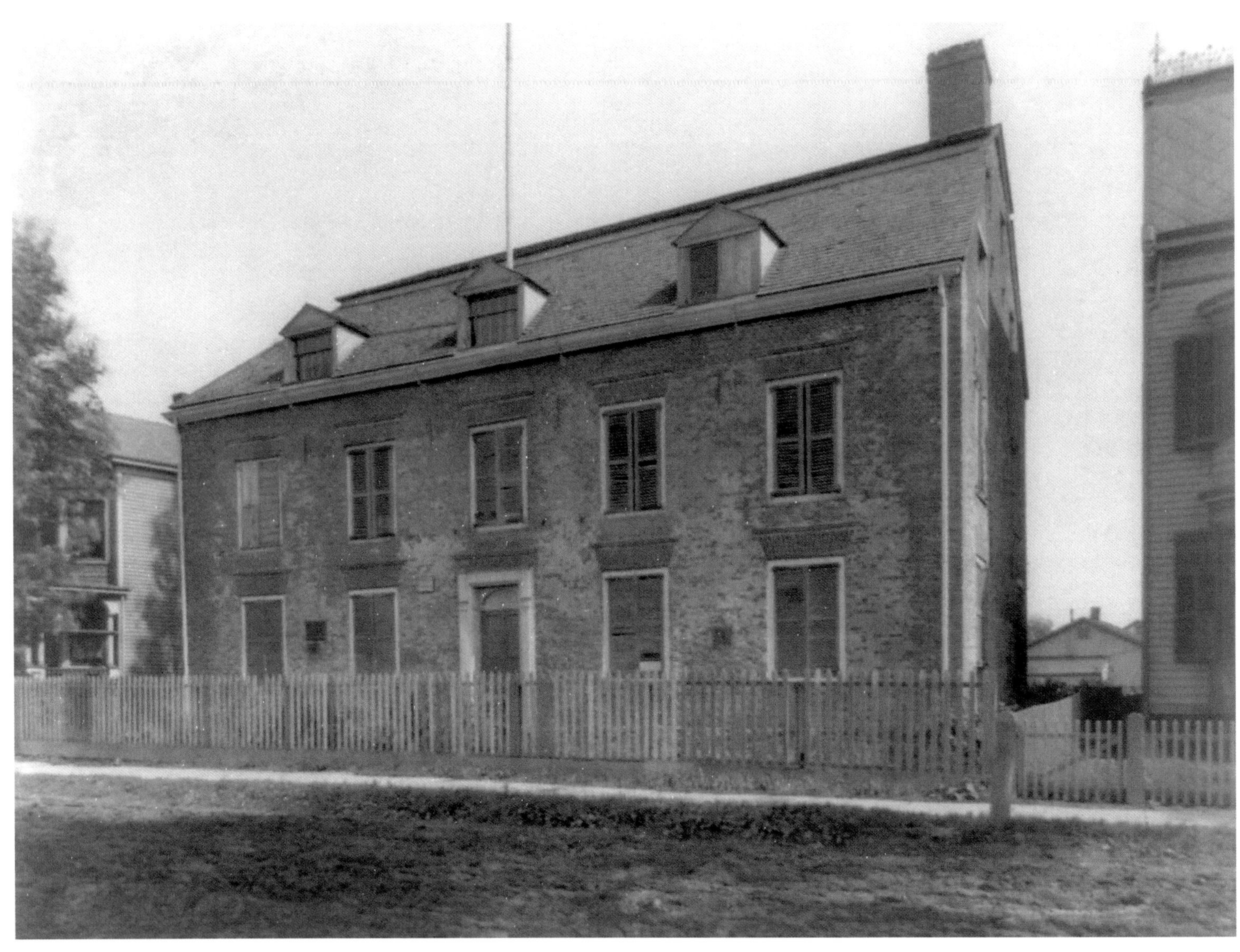

Shown here about 1917, Fort Crailo in Rensselaer, across the Hudson from Albany, dates from about 1712. It was the home of Hendrick Van Rensselaer, the grandson of Dutch patroon Killian Van Rensselaer, and is reputedly the place where the song "Yankee Doodle" was composed during the French and Indian War.

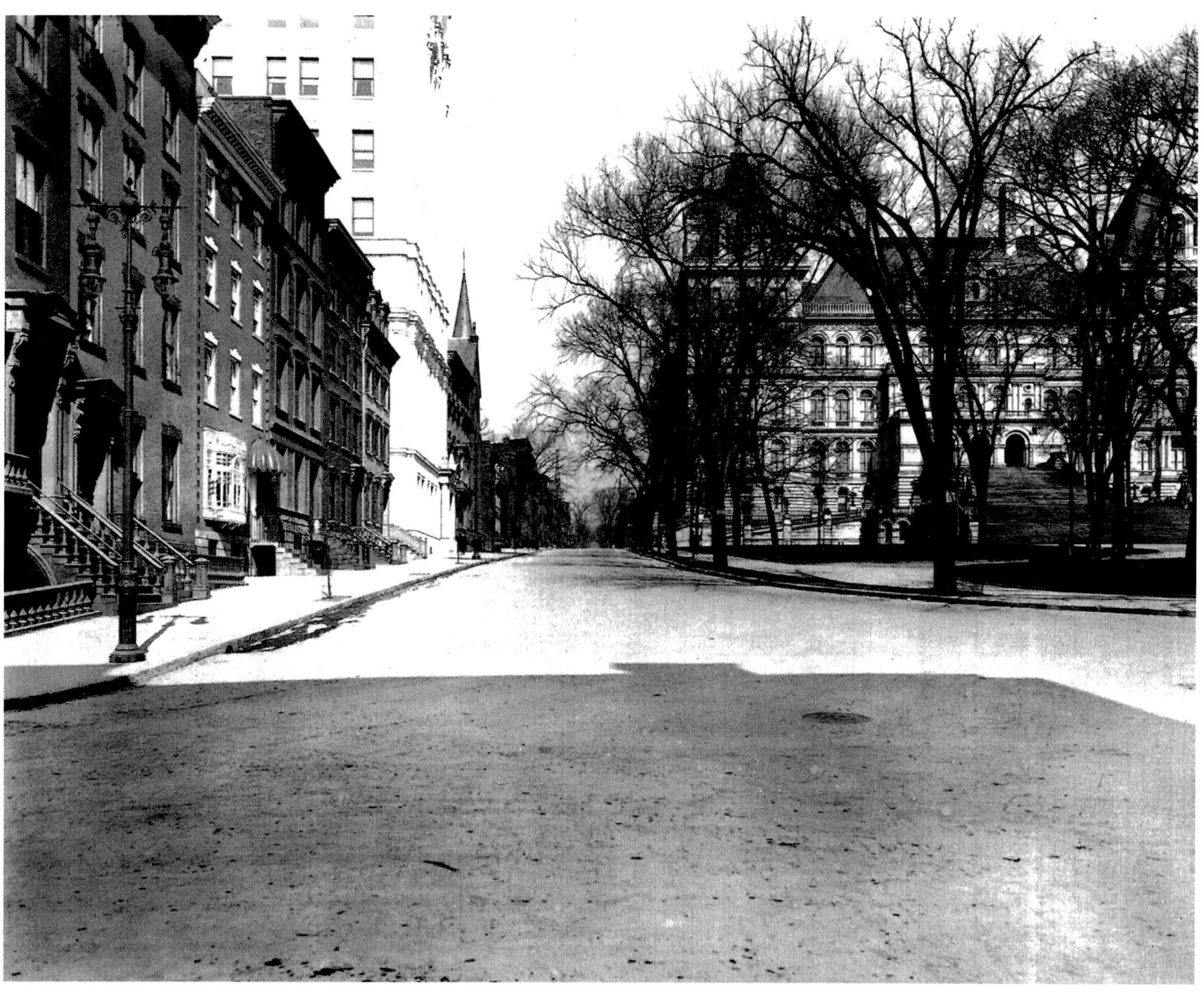

This is a 1917 view of upper State Street in Albany, facing north from Eagle Street. The State Capitol appears to the right. All the buildings shown at left, including the church, were to be taken down in twentieth-century efforts to modernize the capitol city.

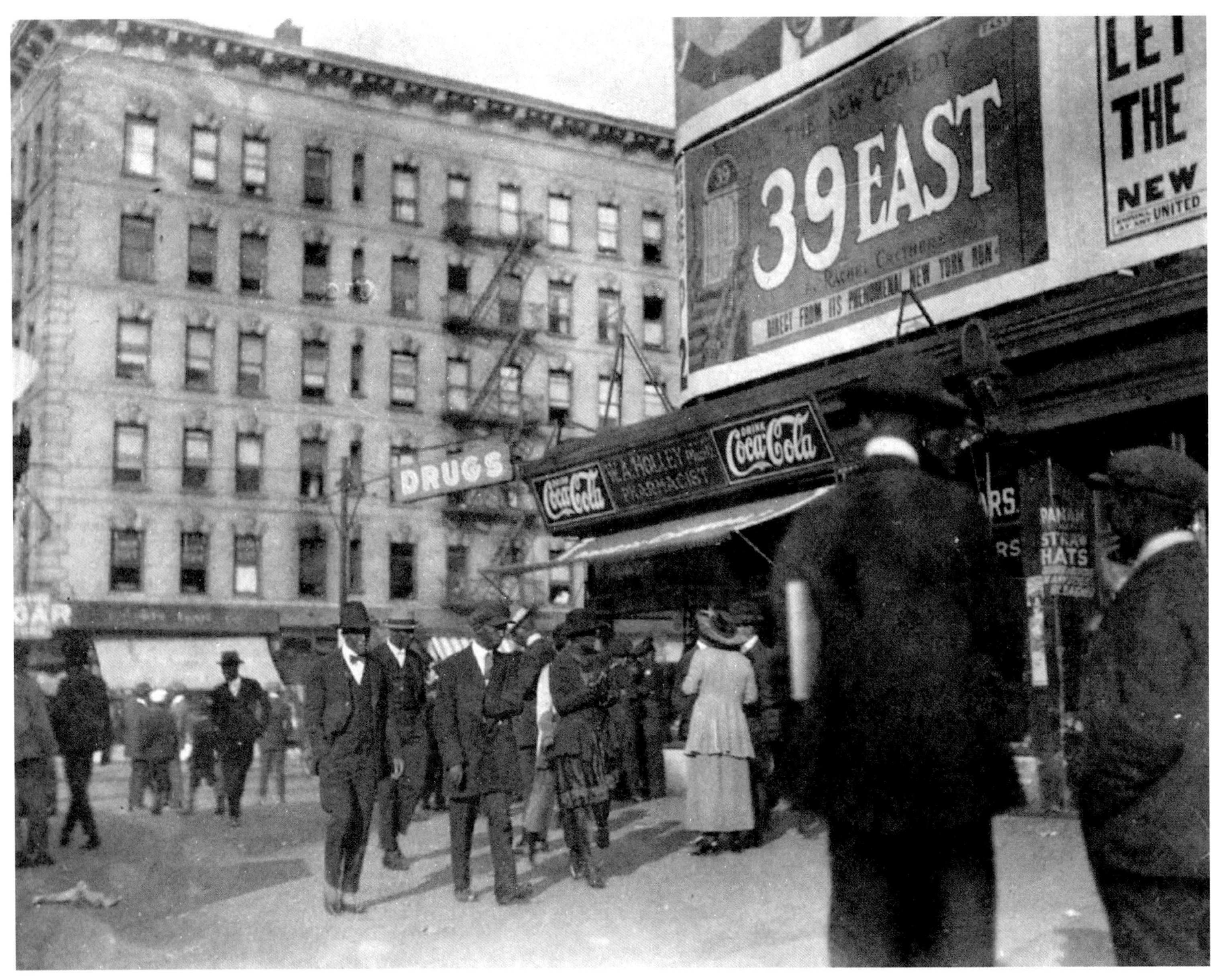

Here is Harlem on 135th Street, between Fifth and Madison, sometime in 1920. In the 1920s, the 139th Street Branch of the New York Public Library, between Fifth and Lenox, was a strong influence in the Harlem Renaissance. The library's book collection was an important link between the people of Harlem and their past. The librarian, Ernestine Rose, scheduled literary gatherings and theatrical performances as part of the library's fare.

Through Roaring Times and Ruined

(1921–1940)

To the automobile of the 1920s, the Hudson River represented not a highway, but a barrier. Well before the turn of the century, New York City had spanned both the East River and Harlem River with multiple bridges. Bridging the lower Hudson was another story. The Bear Mountain Bridge, the George Washington Bridge, and the Rip Van Winkle Bridge at Catskill-Hudson created a more immediate connection with places west of the Hudson—a direct connection that had been wanting since steamboat and sloop days. Until this time the car ferry and the foot ferry connected the two banks of the lower Hudson.

The post–World War I boom of the Roaring Twenties was a time of economic prosperity and a near-giddy optimism, soon to be dashed by the Great Depression. In 1930, the Bronx was home to more than 1.2 million people. The population explosion there was indicative of increases occurring farther up the line, particularly within commuting distance of the city. The need for expanded infrastructure and housing was evident. Now the middle class and least affluent citizens had their chance to seek a suburban home. Neighborhoods sprang up outside the centers of towns and villages.

The depression era was the day of the "pre-war" apartment building in New York and in Hudson River cities like Yonkers, Poughkeepsie, and Albany. Manufacturing in these cities was hurt by the depression, and their economic futures as factory towns became uncertain. In the wake of commercial decline, poverty and other social issues came into sharper relief, and communities began to wonder how their own "stranded" populations should be treated.

With automobile ownership on the rise, it was necessary for large population centers, like the Bronx, to build roads connecting their various districts, and link them with the emerging parkway systems. Among these projects were Pelham Parkway, the Saw Mill River Parkway, the Hutchinson River Parkway, the Bronx River Parkway, and the Taconic State Parkway.

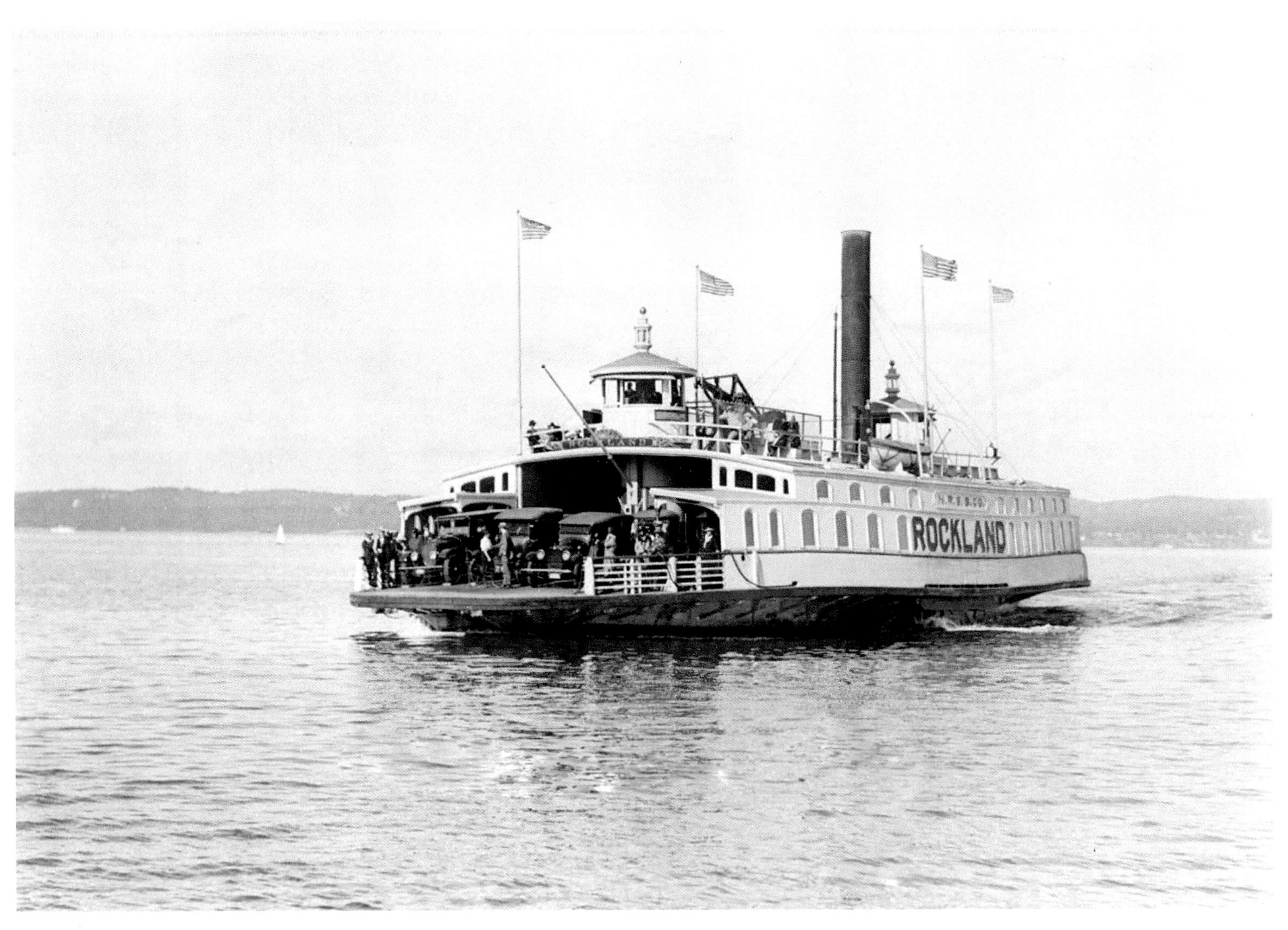

The *Rockland* was a passenger ferry running between Tarrytown and Nyack. It crossed the Tappan Zee in the days preceding the completion of the Tappan Zee Bridge in the mid-1950s. It is shown here around 1921. Sleepy Hollow's John Lyon was the skipper until his death in 1923, at the age of 89.

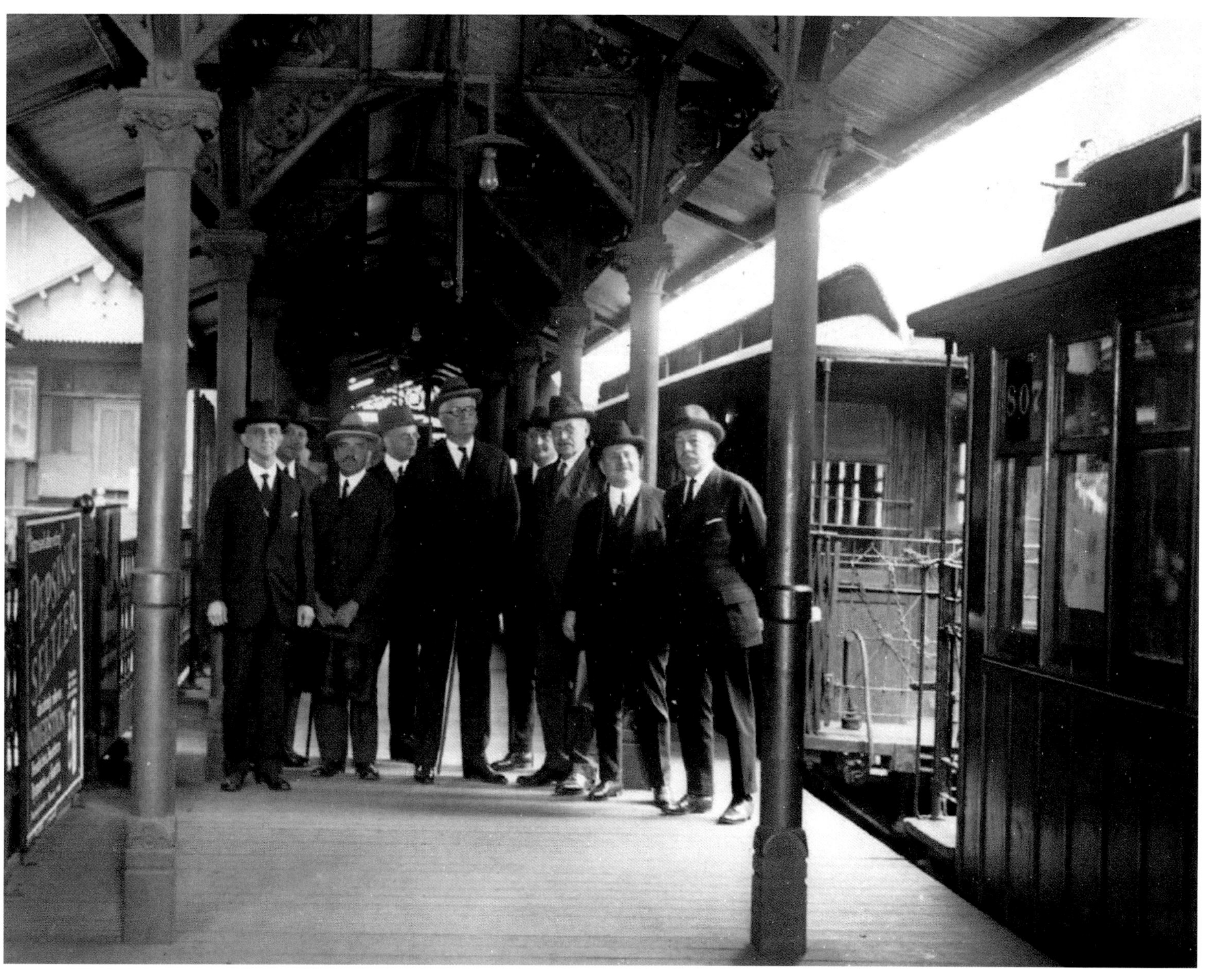

Justice James O'Malley (at center) of the New York State Supreme Court on an inspection tour. The group is examining Grand Central Station's elevated rail spur at 42nd Street, on September 27, 1923.

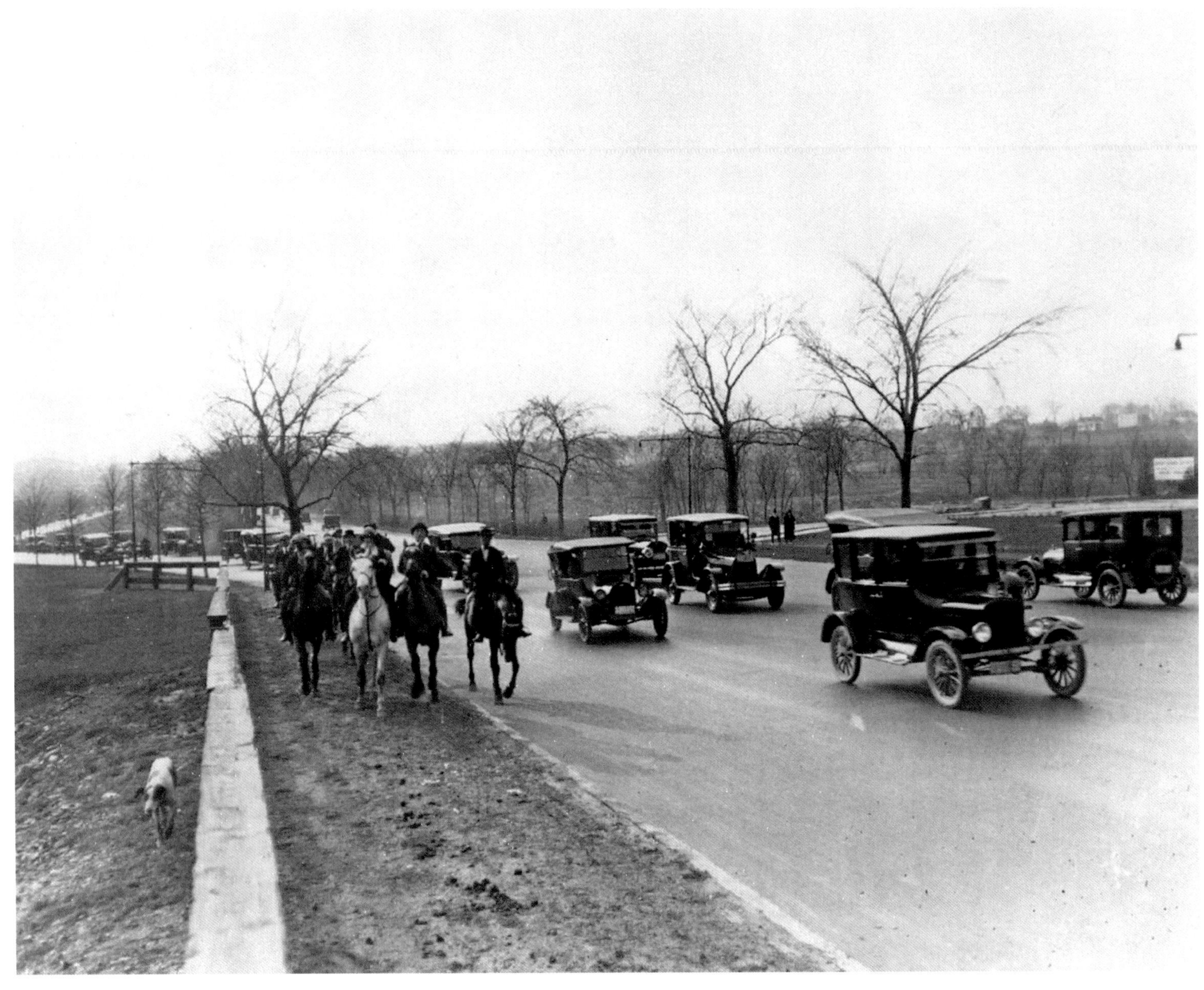

The Bronx and Pelham Parkway connects the Bronx River Parkway and Pelham Bay Park, New York City's largest park. The road is the dividing line between the Bronx Zoo and the Bronx Botanical Garden, shown here at Eastchester Road in 1923. The parkway was established in 1911 with only a single lane; it was enlarged in the 1930s.

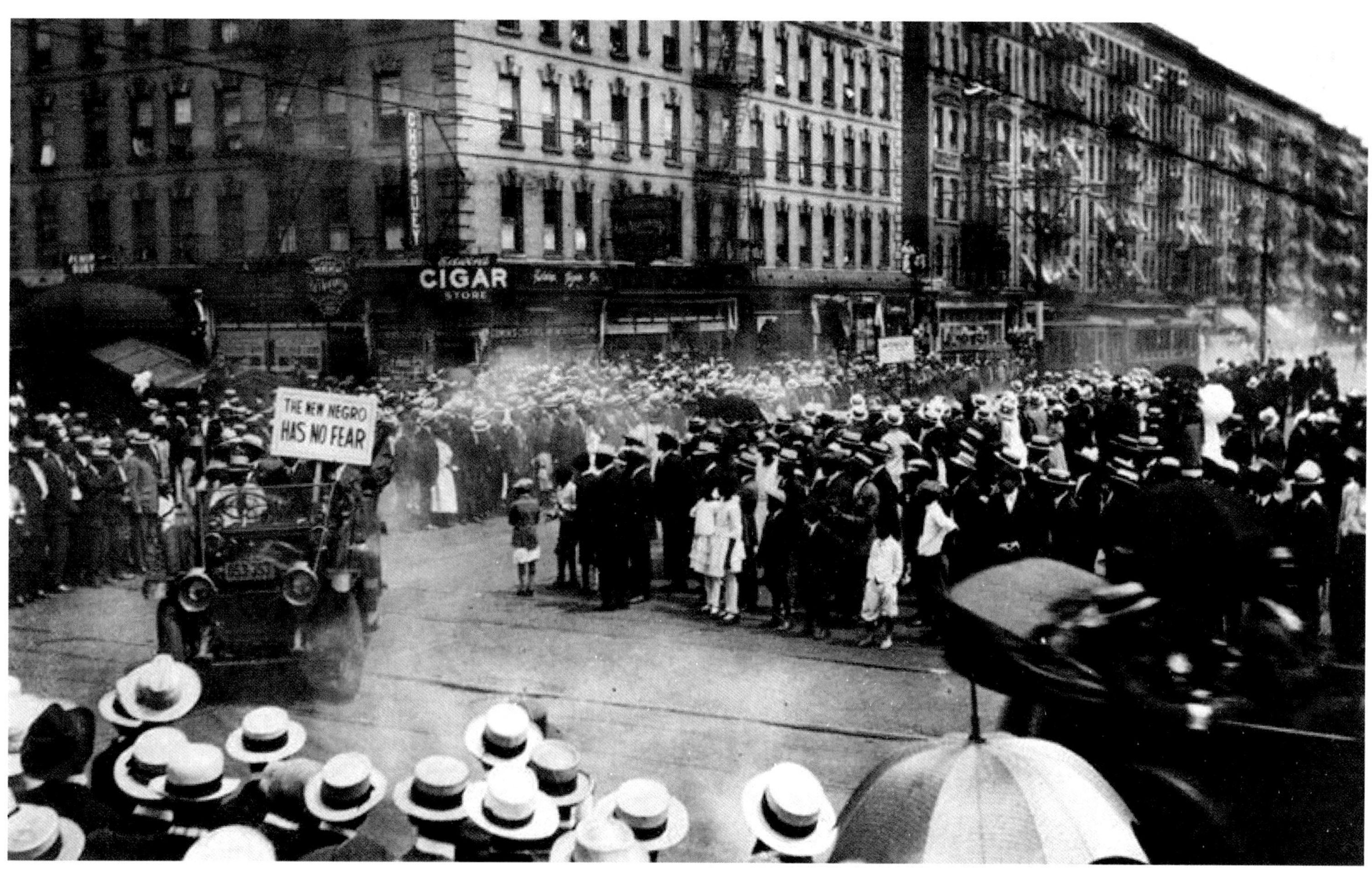

The activist Universal Negro Improvement Association (UNIA), led by charismatic Marcus Garvey, was fast organizing during the early 1920s. The group raised eyebrows and objections in the more mainstream and intellectual NAACP. The banner reads, "The new negro has no fear." This parade is taking place at the corner of Harlem's 135th Street and Lenox Avenue in 1924.

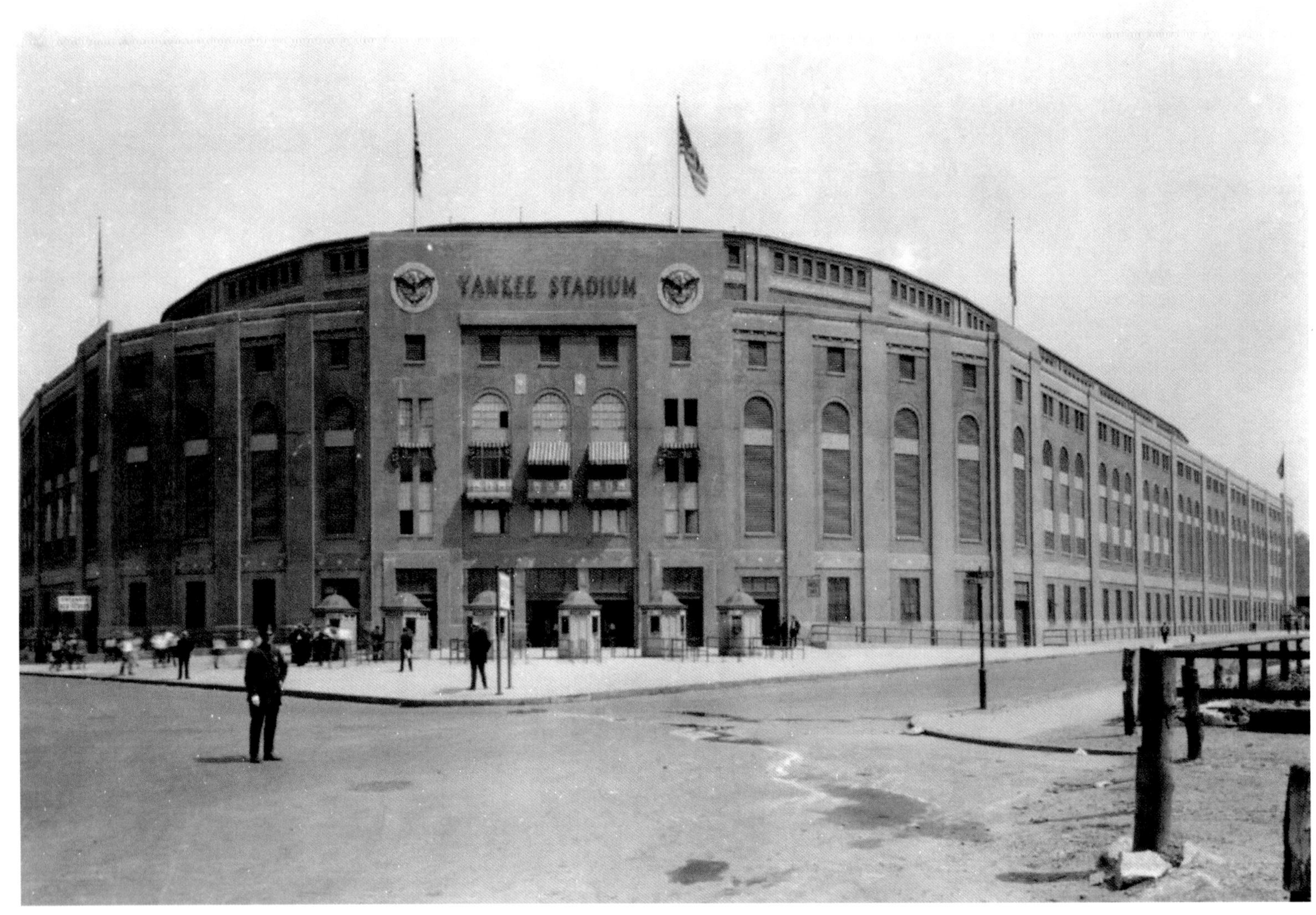

The original Yankee Stadium is located at 161st Street and River Street in the Bronx. Dubbed "the House That Ruth Built," it was home to the New York Yankees from 1923 to 2009. On opening day, New York governor Al Smith threw out the first ball, and Babe Ruth, when asked what he thought of the stadium, responded, "Some ball yard!" He went on to hit a three-run homerun to beat the Red Sox, 4–1. A new stadium with a price tag of $1.5 billion opened in 2009.

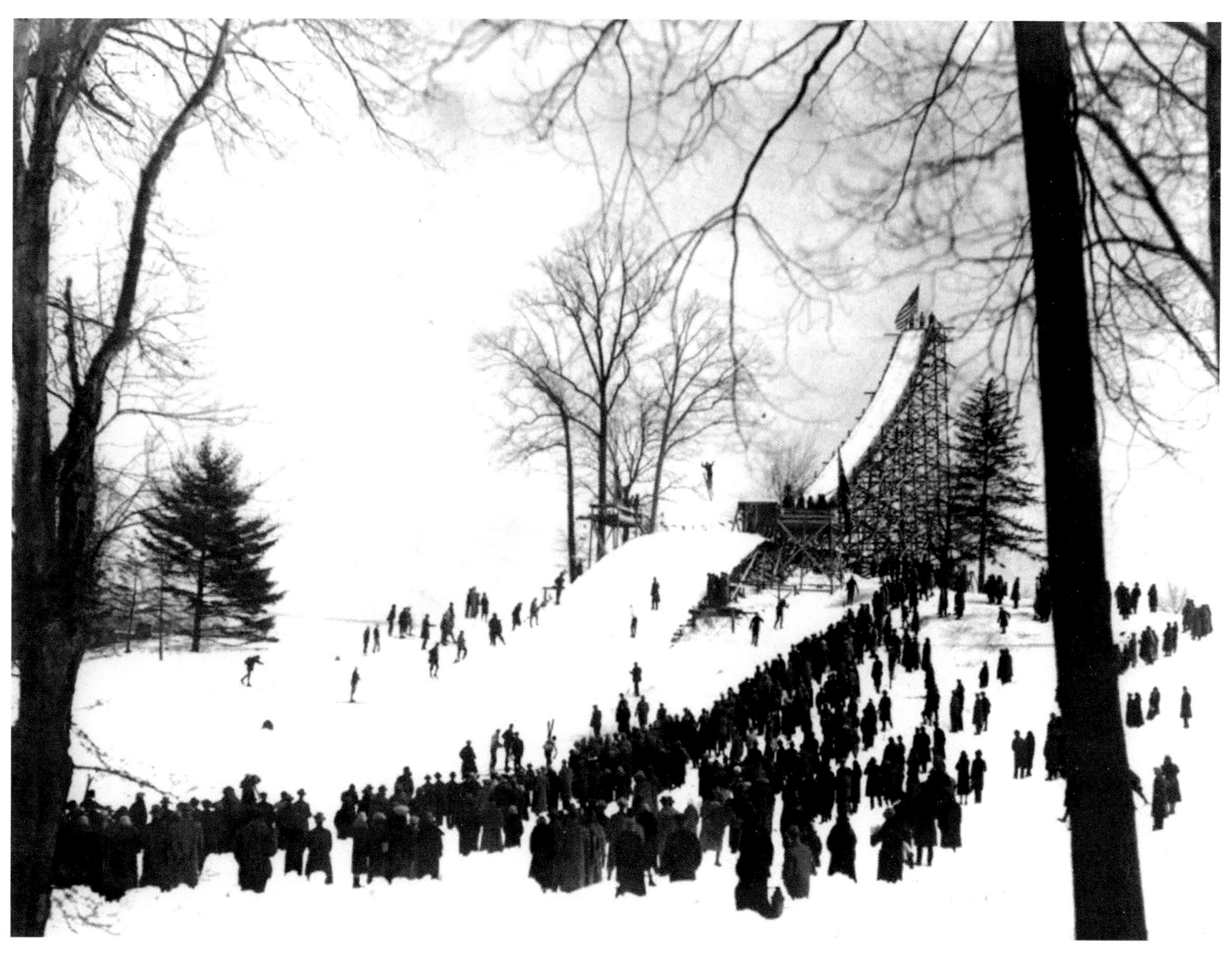

Rockwood was the estate of Standard Oil partner William Rockefeller (1841–1922), at the northern border of the Village of Sleepy Hollow. A few years after his death, the estate became a country club. Carl Stenset of the Norsemen Ski Club is seen taking a ski jump at Rockwood Hall Country Club. A portion of Rockwood was once the home of Commodore Matthew Perry. Today Rockwood Hall is a part of the Rockefeller State Park Preserve.

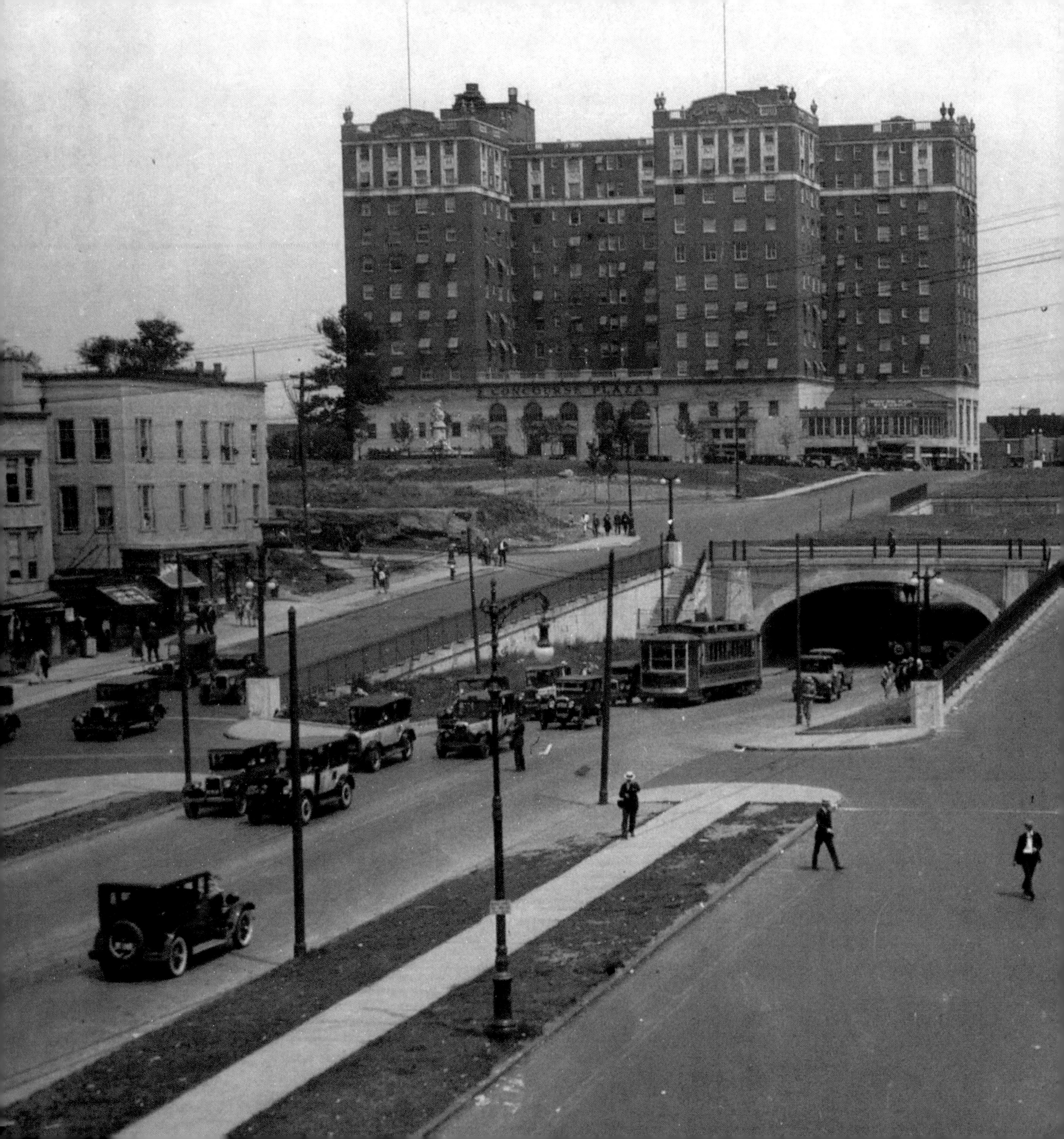
CONCOURSE PLAZA

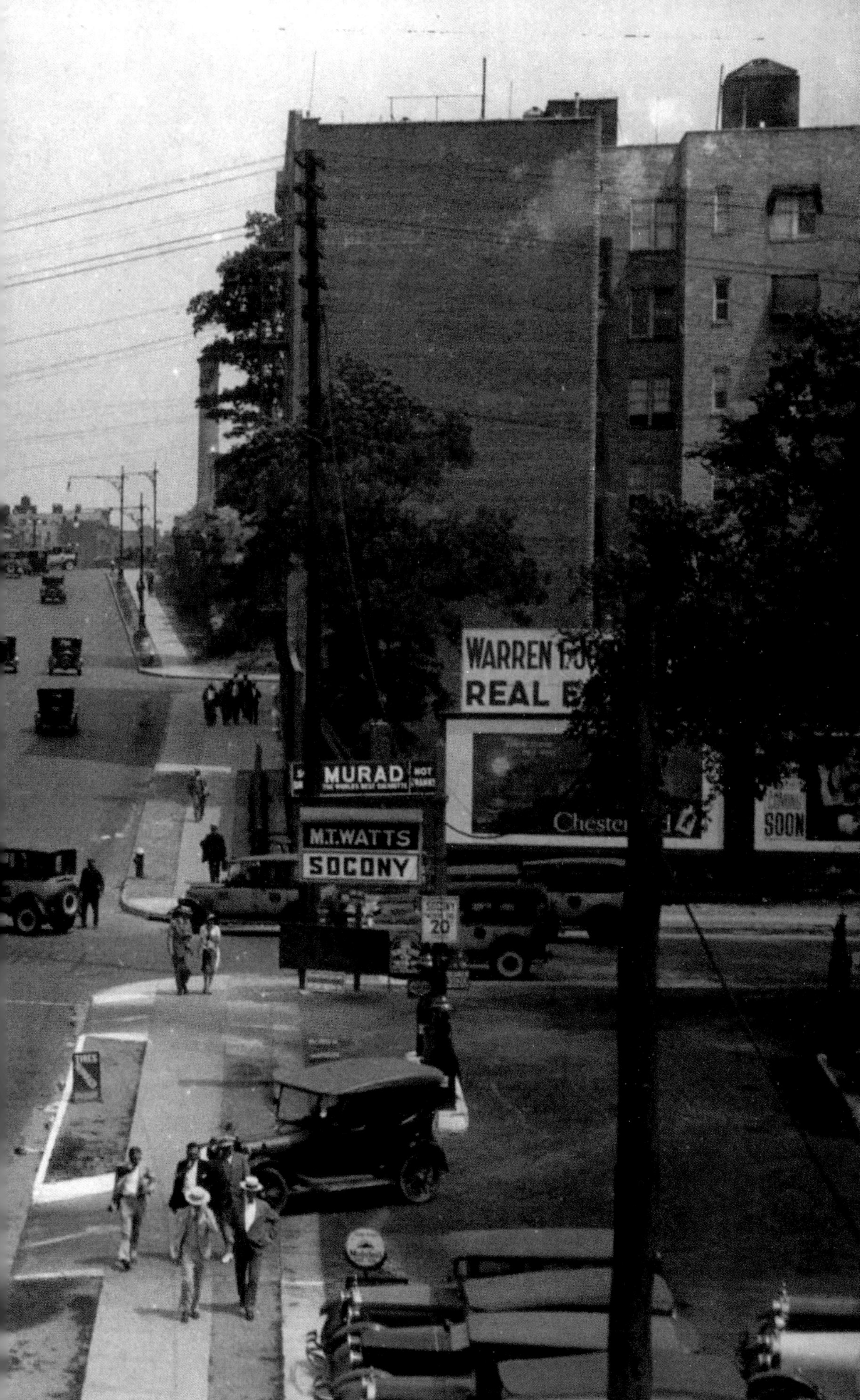

This 1926 photograph looks out from the Yankee Stadium elevated subway stop at 161st Street and River Avenue. The neighborhood was to become home to a commercial district, courts, and government buildings.

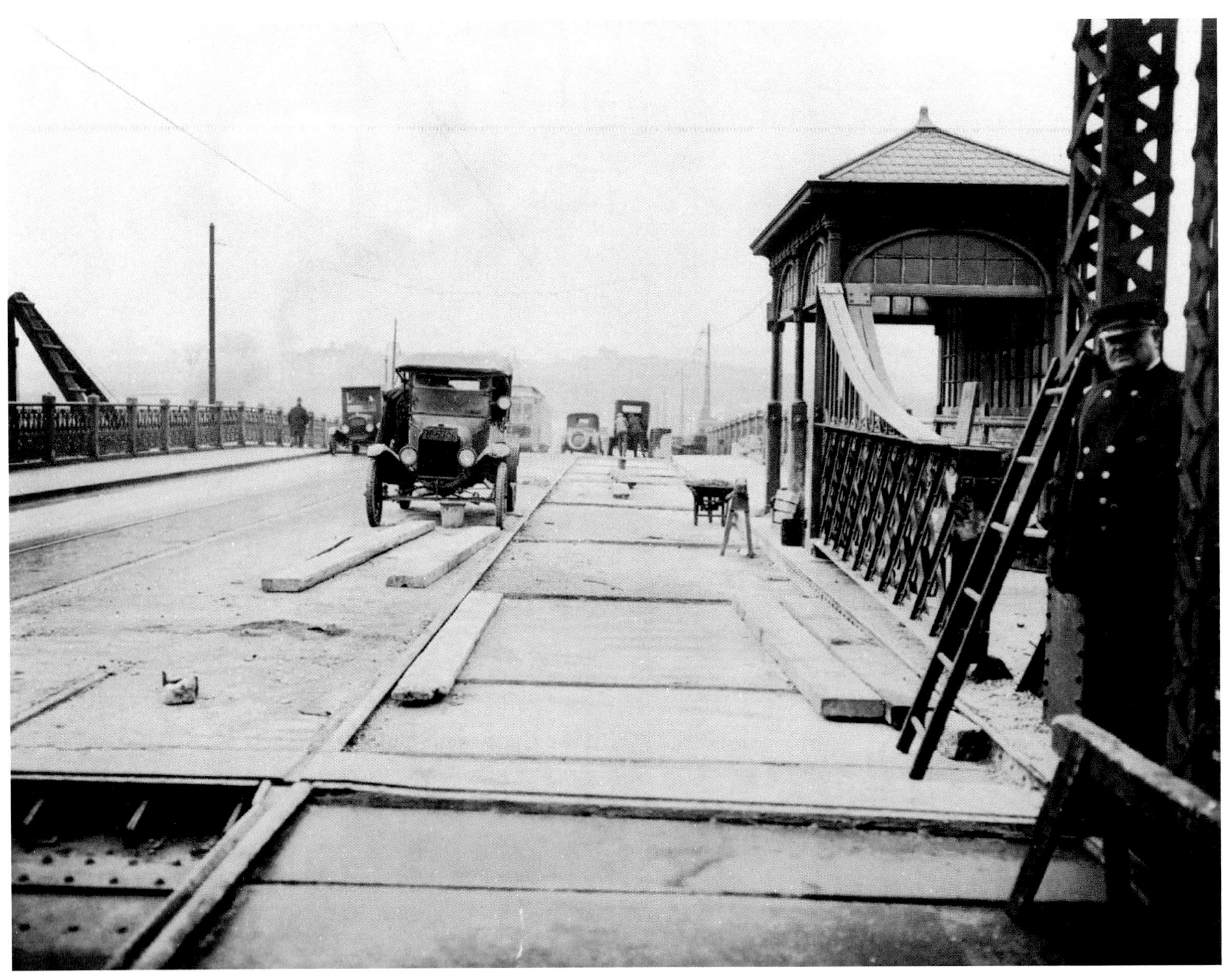

University Heights Bridge is shown here in December 1925, the year the roadway was reconstructed. The bridge opened in 1908, replacing a wooden footbridge between Inwood and University Heights, after being floated to this location from previous service at 225th Street. The camera looks west, toward Manhattan.

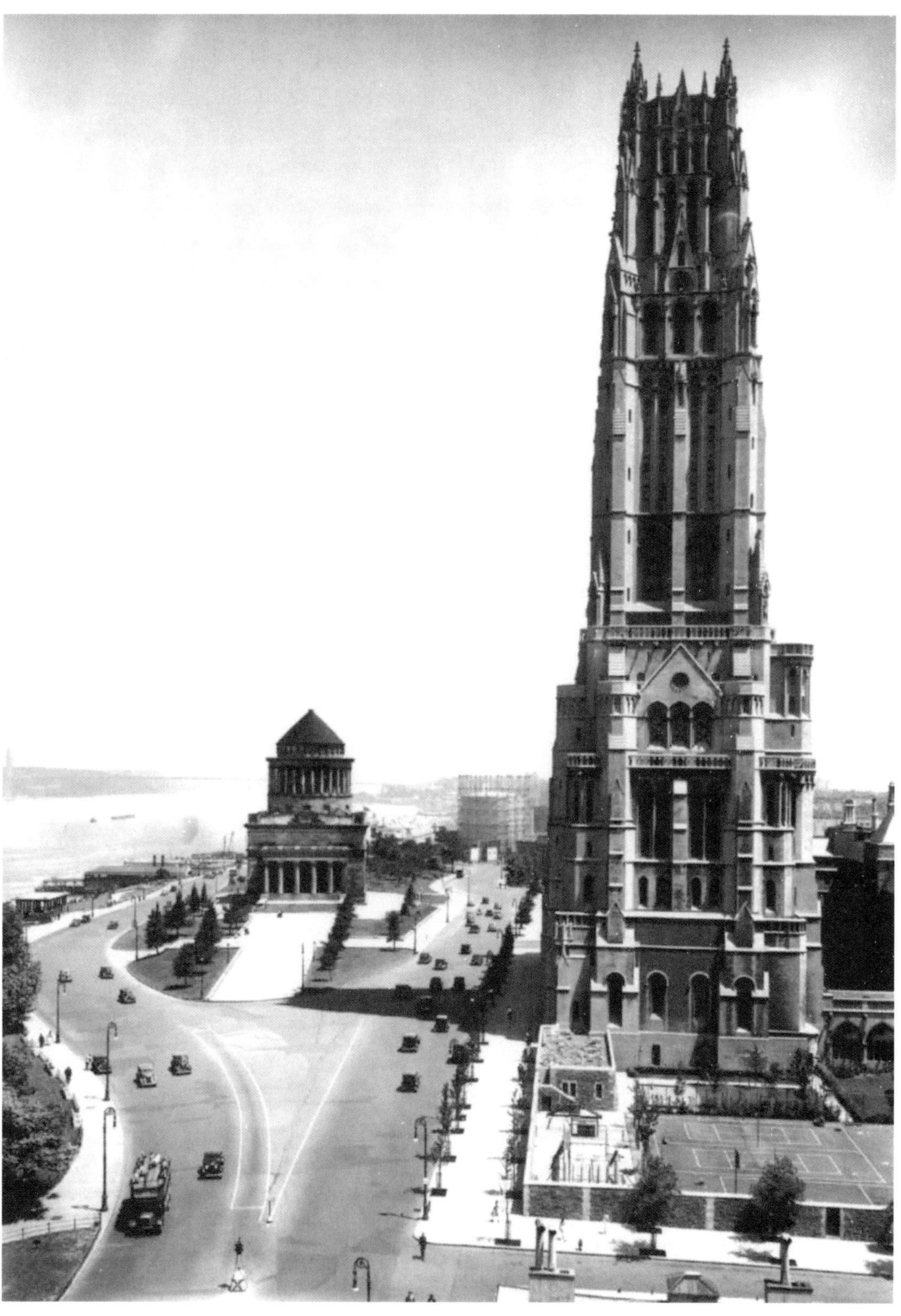

Riverside Church is seen here beside Riverside Drive and Grant's Tomb along the Hudson. The church was built in the Gothic style, opening in 1929. At 22 stories, it is the tallest church in the United States, and its carillon is the world's largest. Riverside is interdenominational and serves as a center for activist causes based on liberation theology and likeminded points of view. It was designed by Allen Pelton and Collens after the French Cathedral of Chartres.

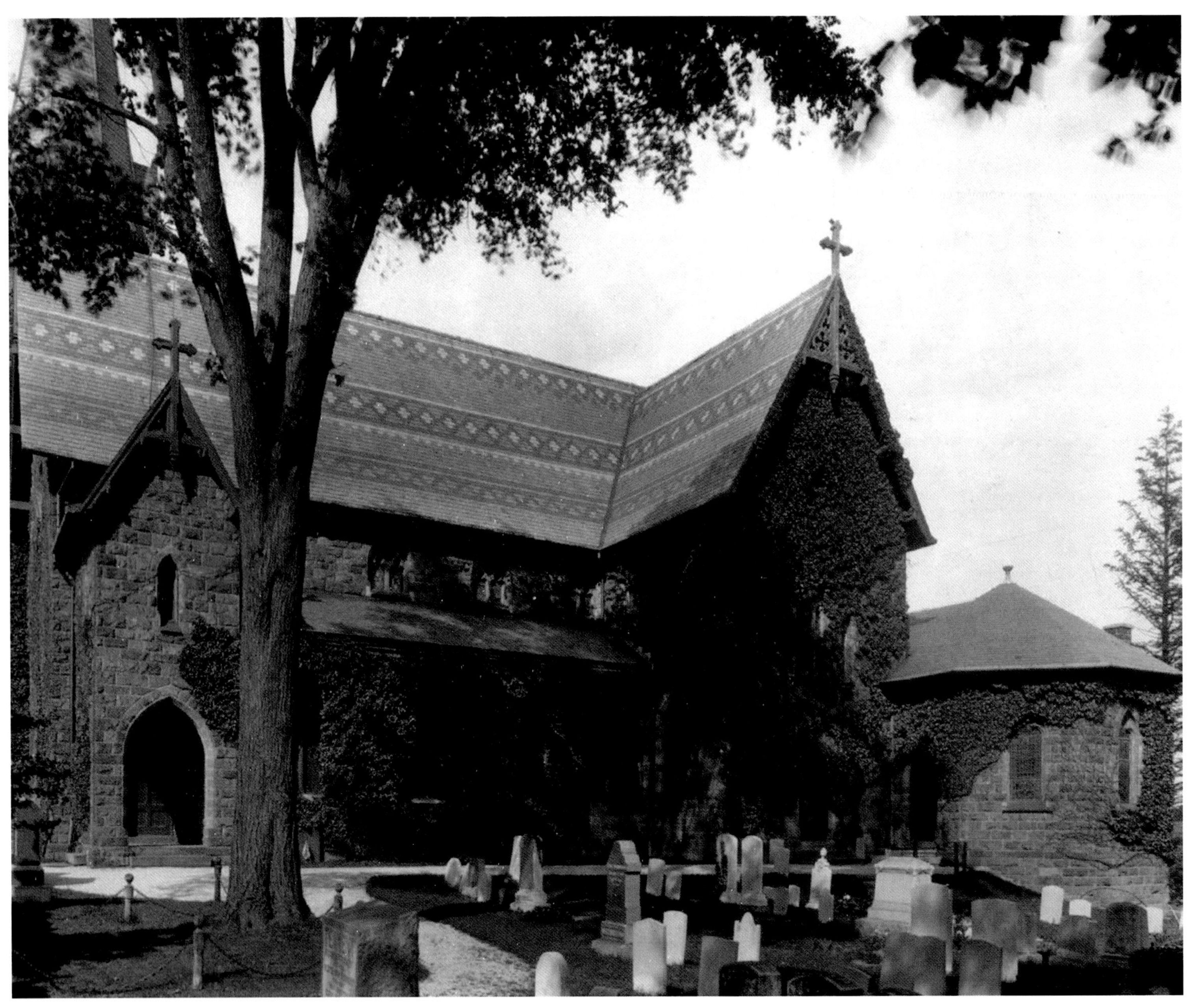

The latest of three Saint Peter's Episcopal churches is a Gothic Revival structure completed in 1855 near Seabury Avenue in the Bronx. It was designed by Leopold Eidlitz, who also designed New York's old Metropolitan Opera House. The original church was founded in 1693, at what was then the colonial village of Westchester. Samuel Seabury of Saint Peter's debated in print with young Alexander Hamilton, prior to the Revolution.

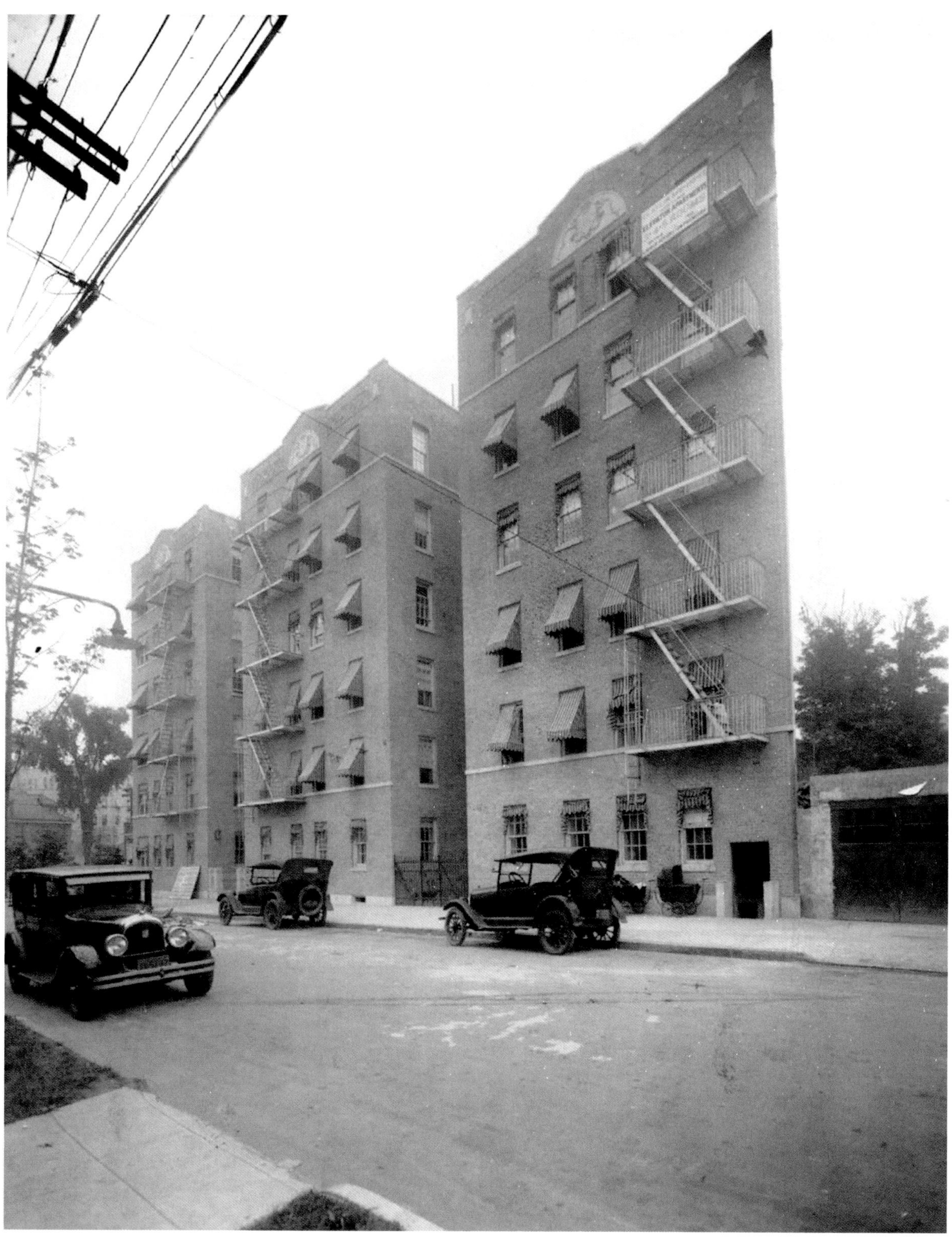

In the early days of the American Revolution, the American Army constructed forts in the Bronx anticipating a British onslaught. The Bronx was then part of lower Westchester County. These residential buildings at Claflin Avenue and 195th Street were built near the site of "Old Number Four Fort" in the 1920s. H. B. Claflin had purchased 500 city lots in 1866. His estate was auctioned off in 1919 and developed, contributing to the local building boom.

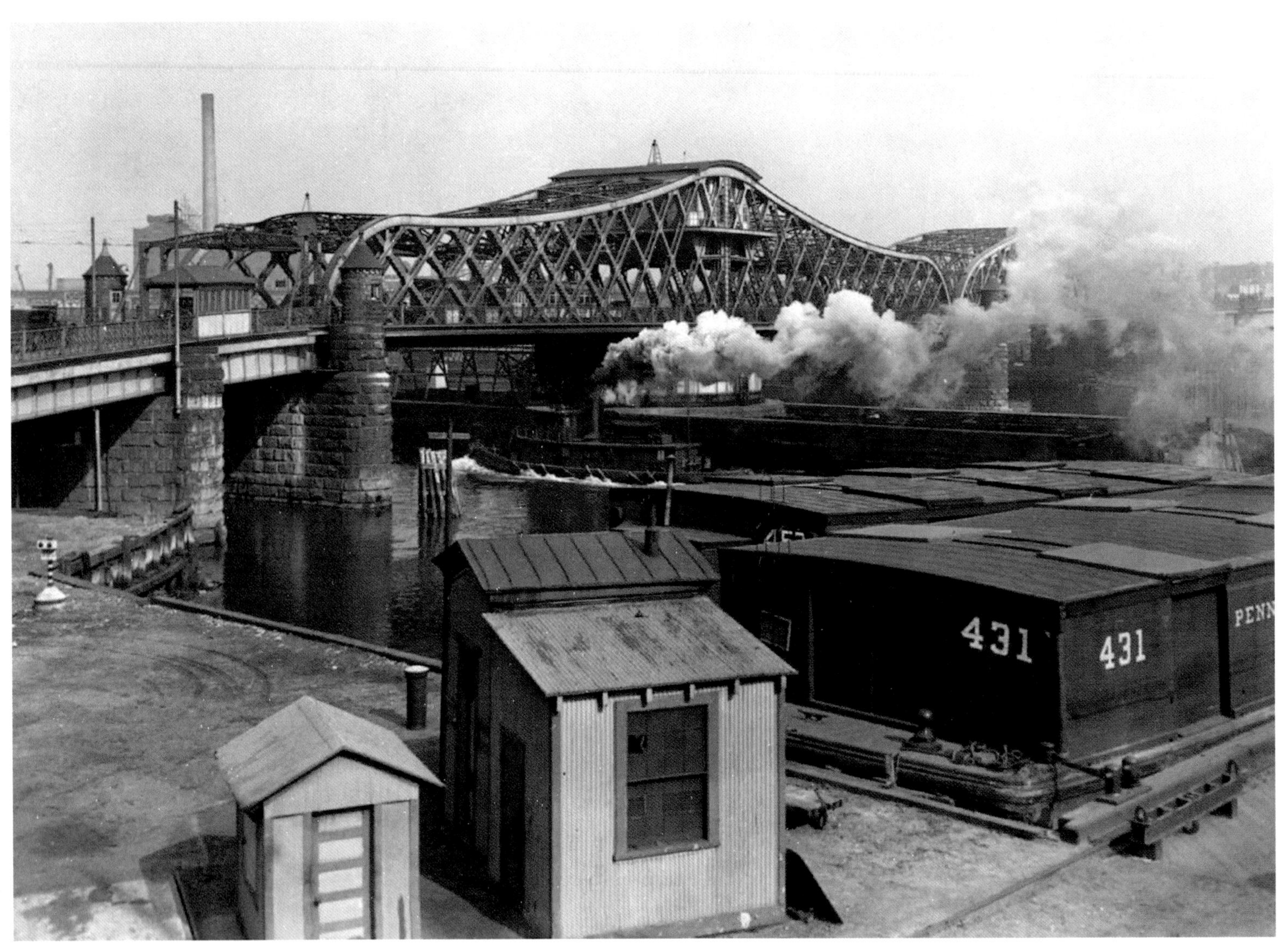

The Willis Avenue Bridge at 127th Street and 1st Avenue opened in 1901 at a cost of approximately $2.5 million. The bridge carries northbound traffic across the Harlem River to Willis Avenue in the Bronx. The avenue is probably named for Edward Willis, a local property owner in the 1860s.

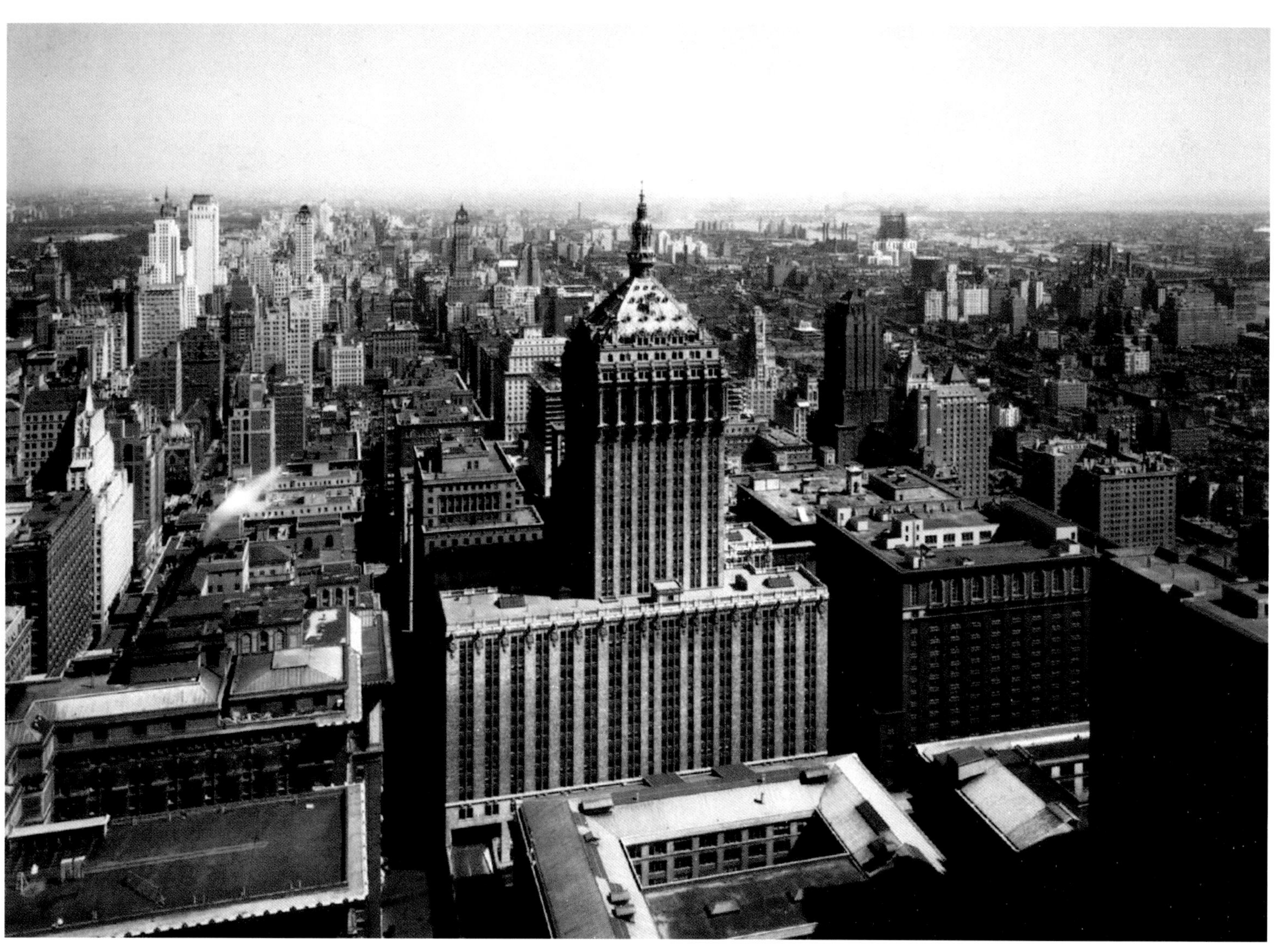

Now called the Helmsley Building, the New York Central Building was richly and ornately constructed to house the railroad goliath's headquarters. It also served as an ornate and imposing gateway for cars and pedestrians approaching Grand Central Terminal from upper Park Avenue. The building stands at 230 Park Avenue between 45th and 46th streets.

A bird's-eye view of Manhattan by Percy Loomis Sperr (1890–1964) shows Park Avenue South leading up to Grand Central Terminal at the lower left. Also prominent is the Chanin Building, completed in 1928. To the upper right is the Queensboro or 59th Street Bridge.

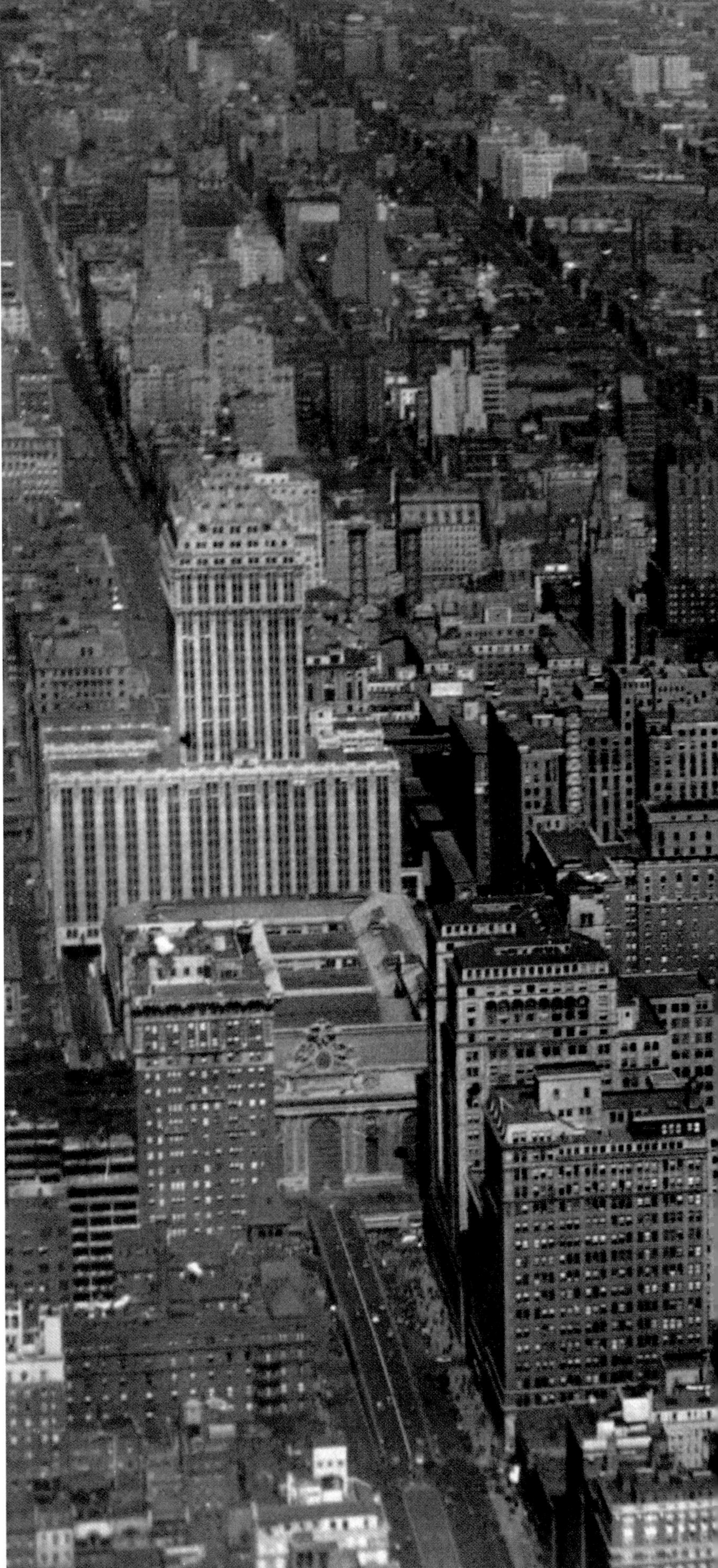

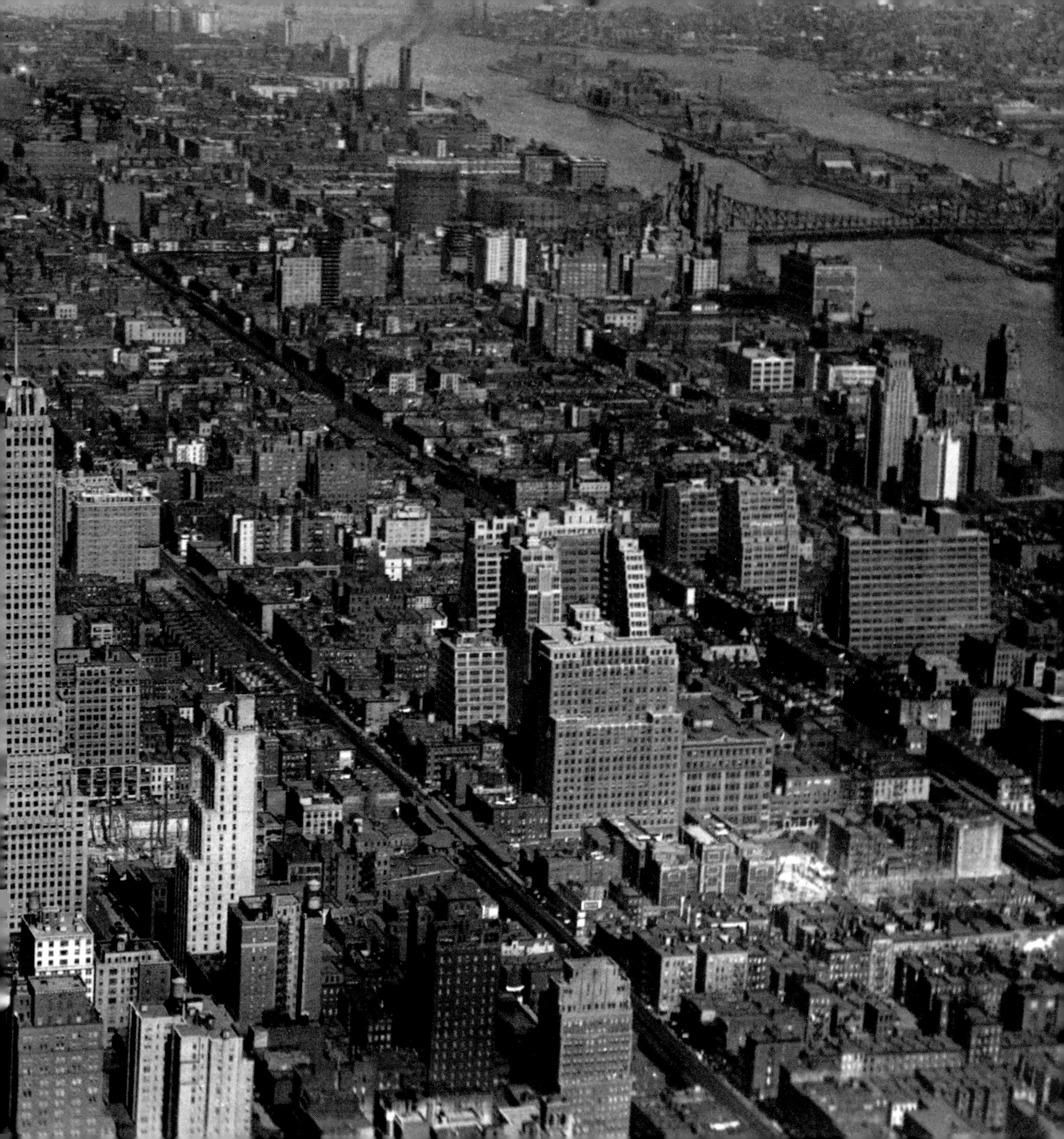

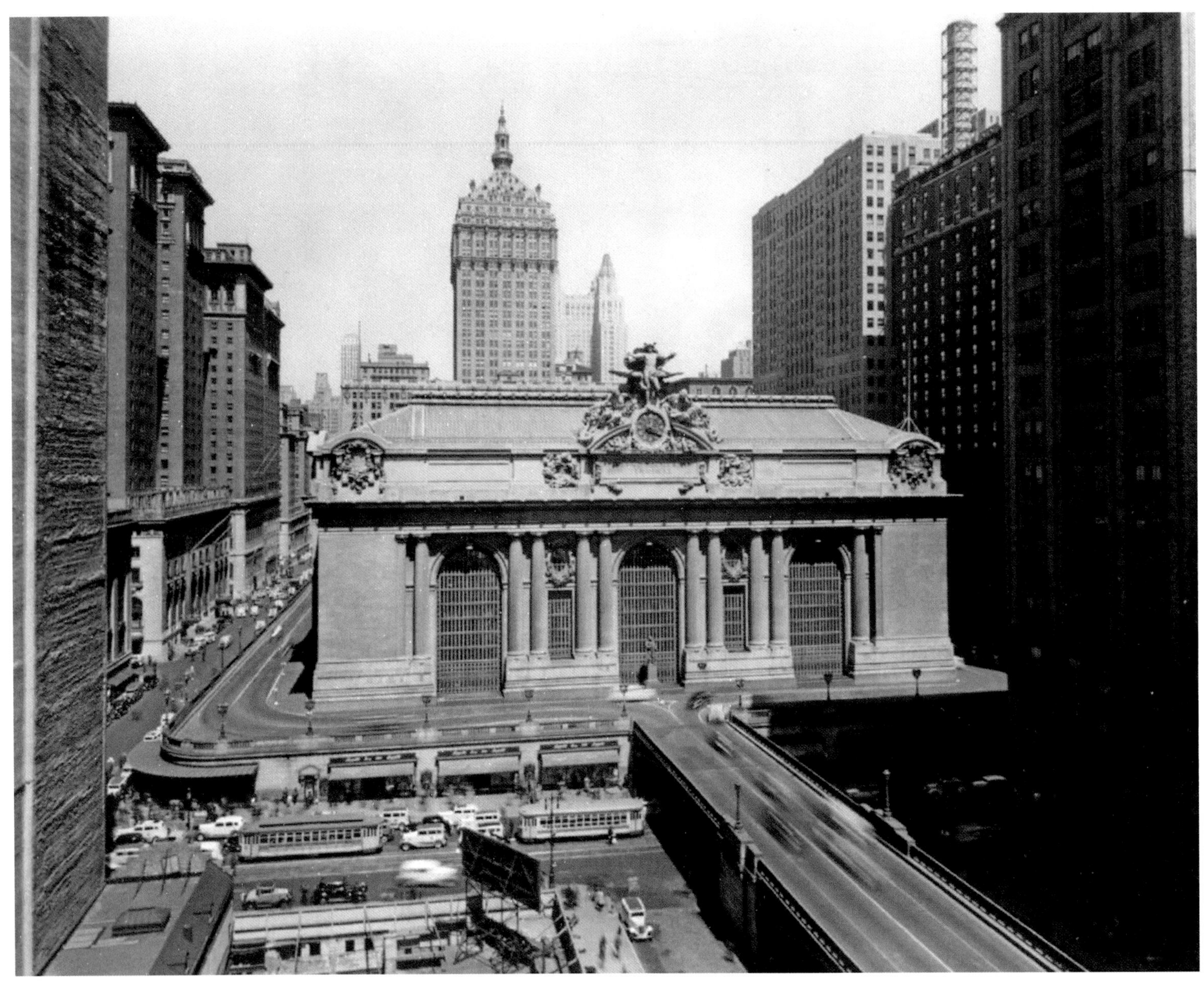

Grand Central Terminal is the southern terminus of the Hudson, the Harlem, and the New Haven lines. The three railroads all travel beneath Park Avenue on their approach to the terminal. Constructed in 1929, the New York Central Building—now the Helmsley Building—can be seen beyond and above Grand Central in this view from around 1931. Park Avenue wraps around the terminal and continues south at lower right. Forty-second Street runs horizontally past the facade of Grand Central toward the recently completed Chrysler Building to the east, and Times Square to the west.

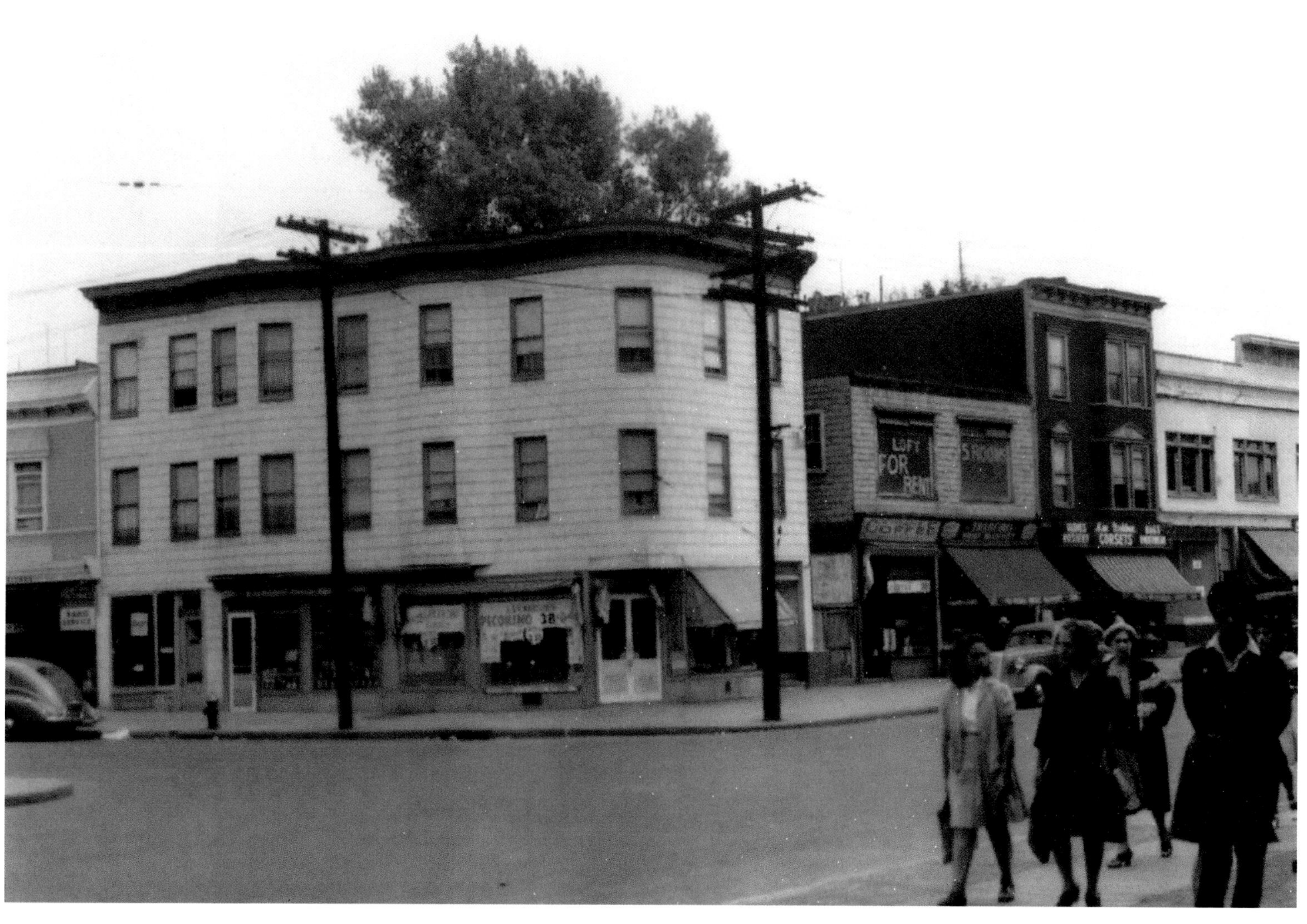

Hoffman Street in the Bronx is named for William B. Hoffman of West Farms, who owned an estate named Cedar Grove. This scene, shot by Percy Loomis Sperr about 1930, is at 184th Street.

Park Avenue Baptist Church at Park Avenue and 64th Street is shown here around 1931. The John D. Rockefellers, father and son, donated half of the $1.5 million construction costs. In 1922, the congregation moved to the new church building from its old location at 4 West 46th Street. The same congregation would soon move on to the splendid Riverside Church.

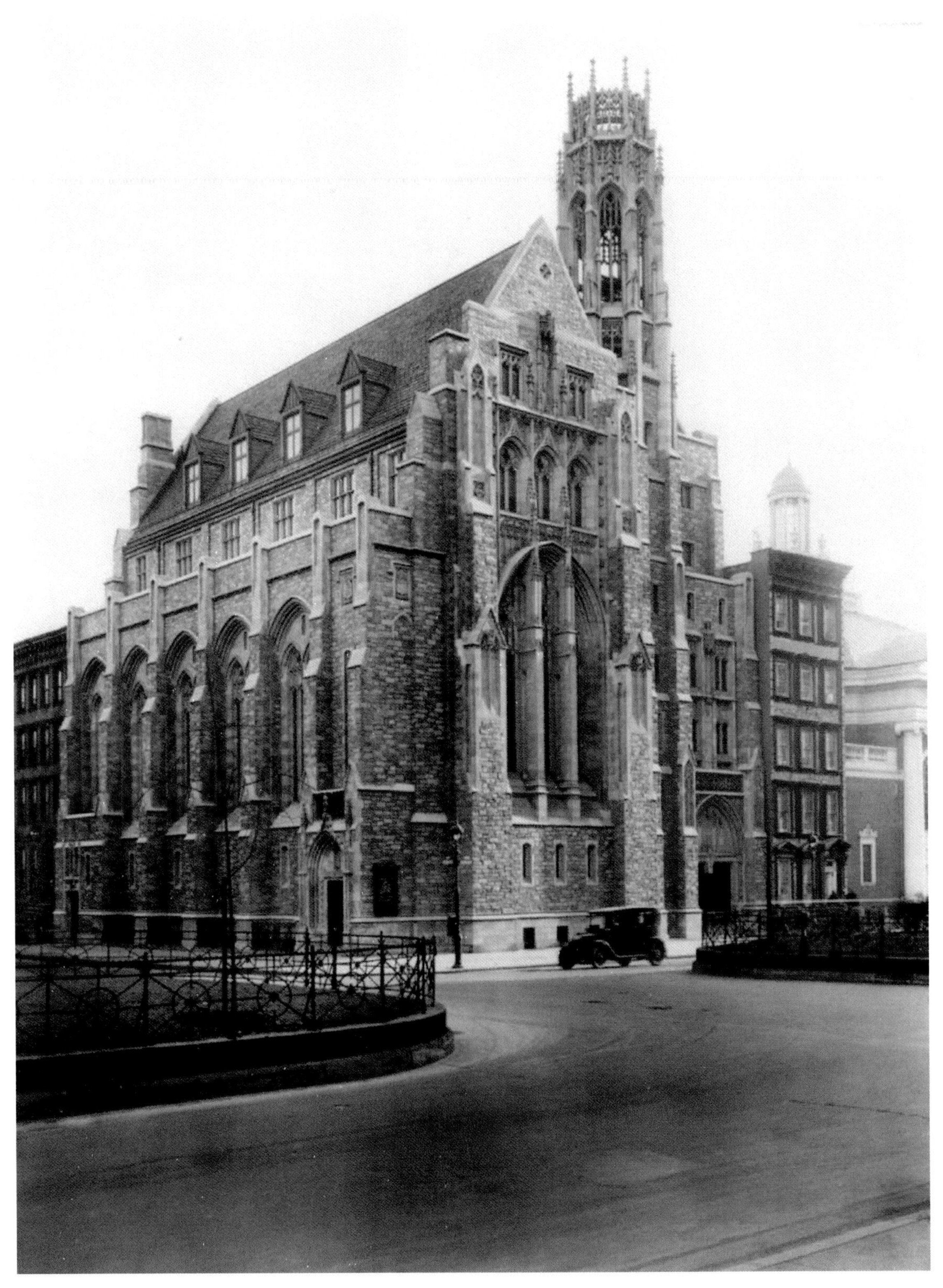

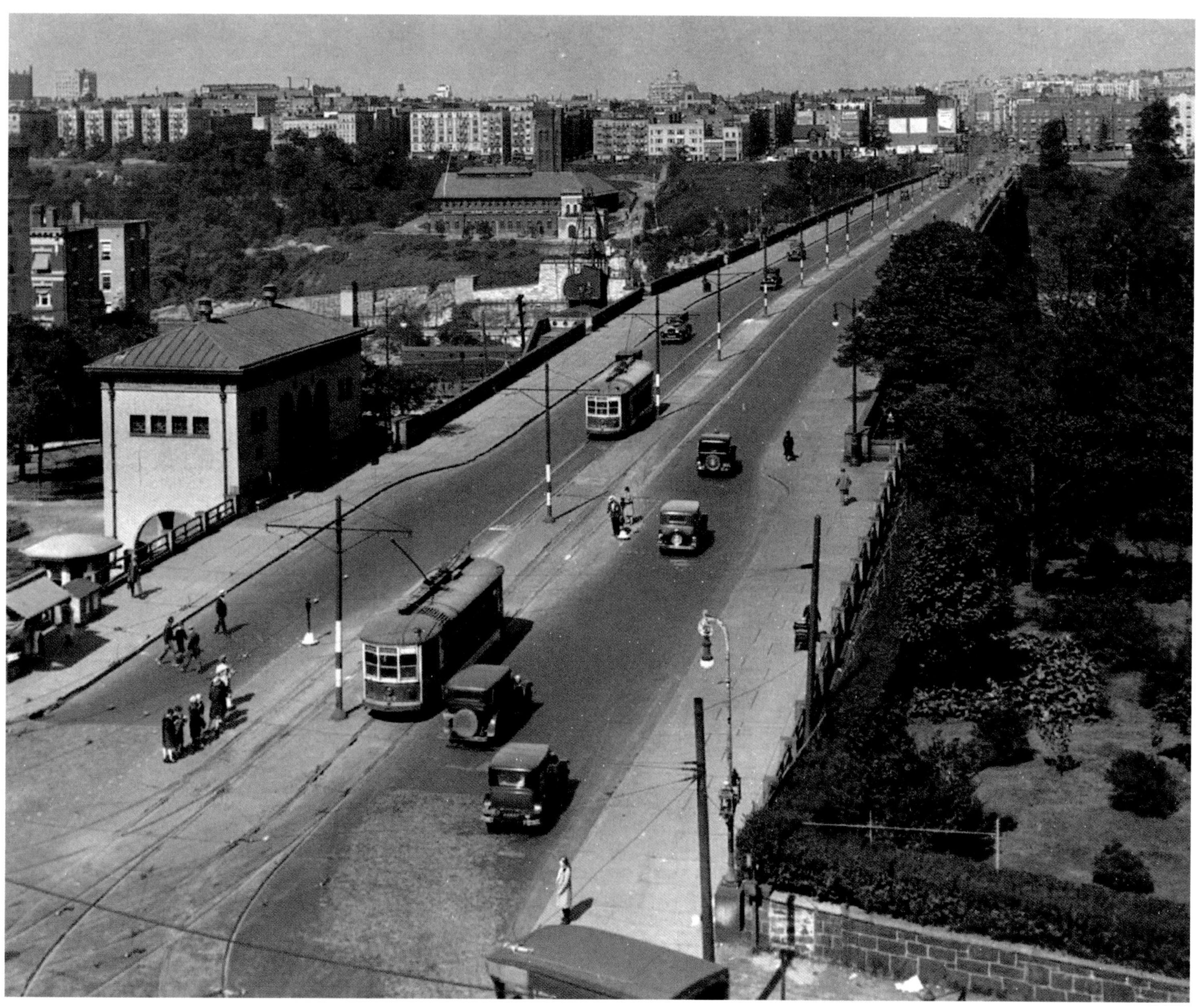

Except for the Eads Bridge in St. Louis, Missouri, the Washington Bridge had the widest steel arches of any American bridge when it opened in 1889. The Washington Bridge connects 181st Street with the Bronx. This photo was taken about 1932 by the Ewing Galloway Agency in Manhattan.

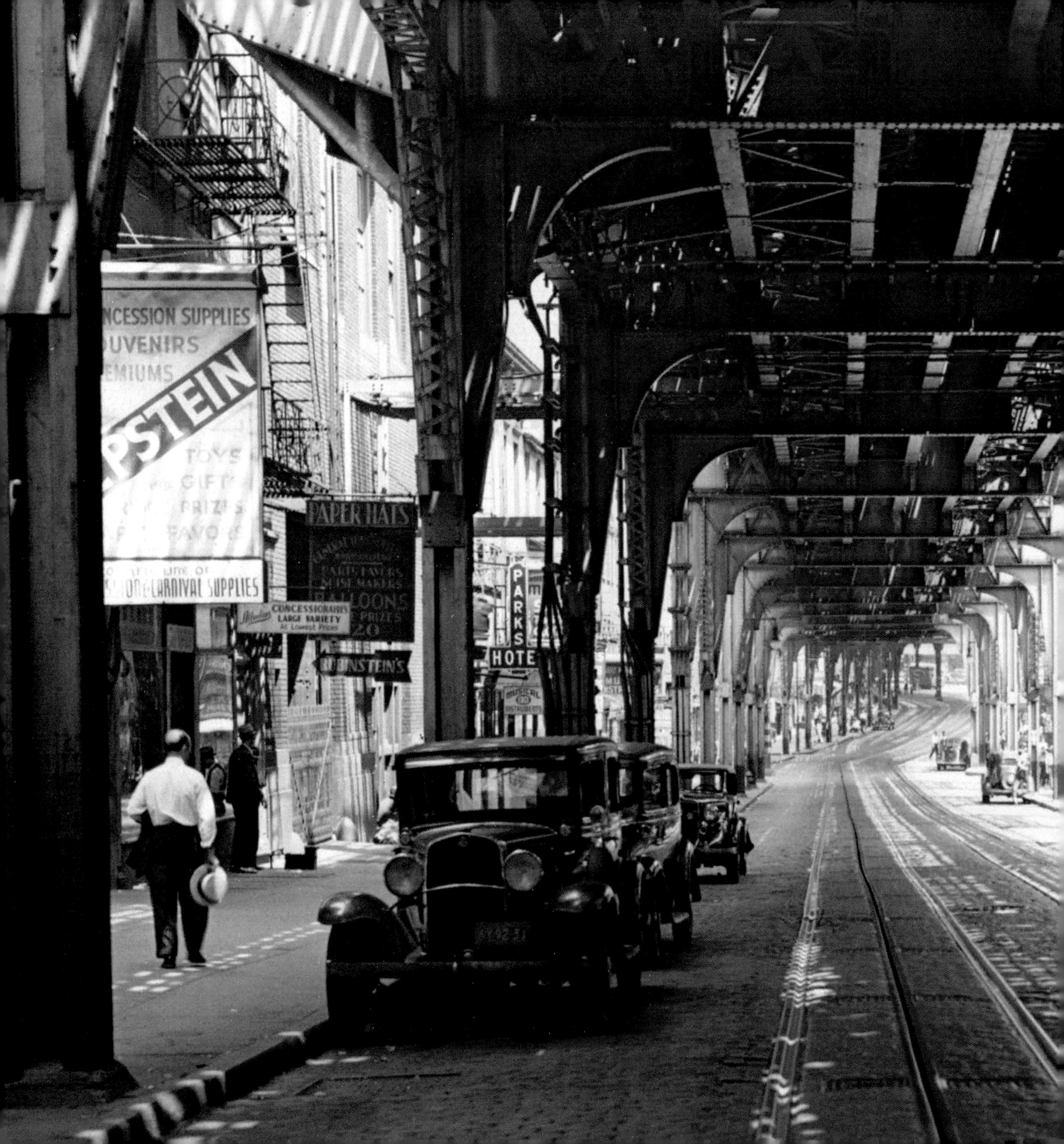
NCESSION SUPPLIES
UVENIRS
EMIUMS
PSTEIN
TOYS
PAPER HATS
BALLOONS
CONCESSIONAIRES
LARGE VARIETY
At Lowest Prices
PARKS
HOTE

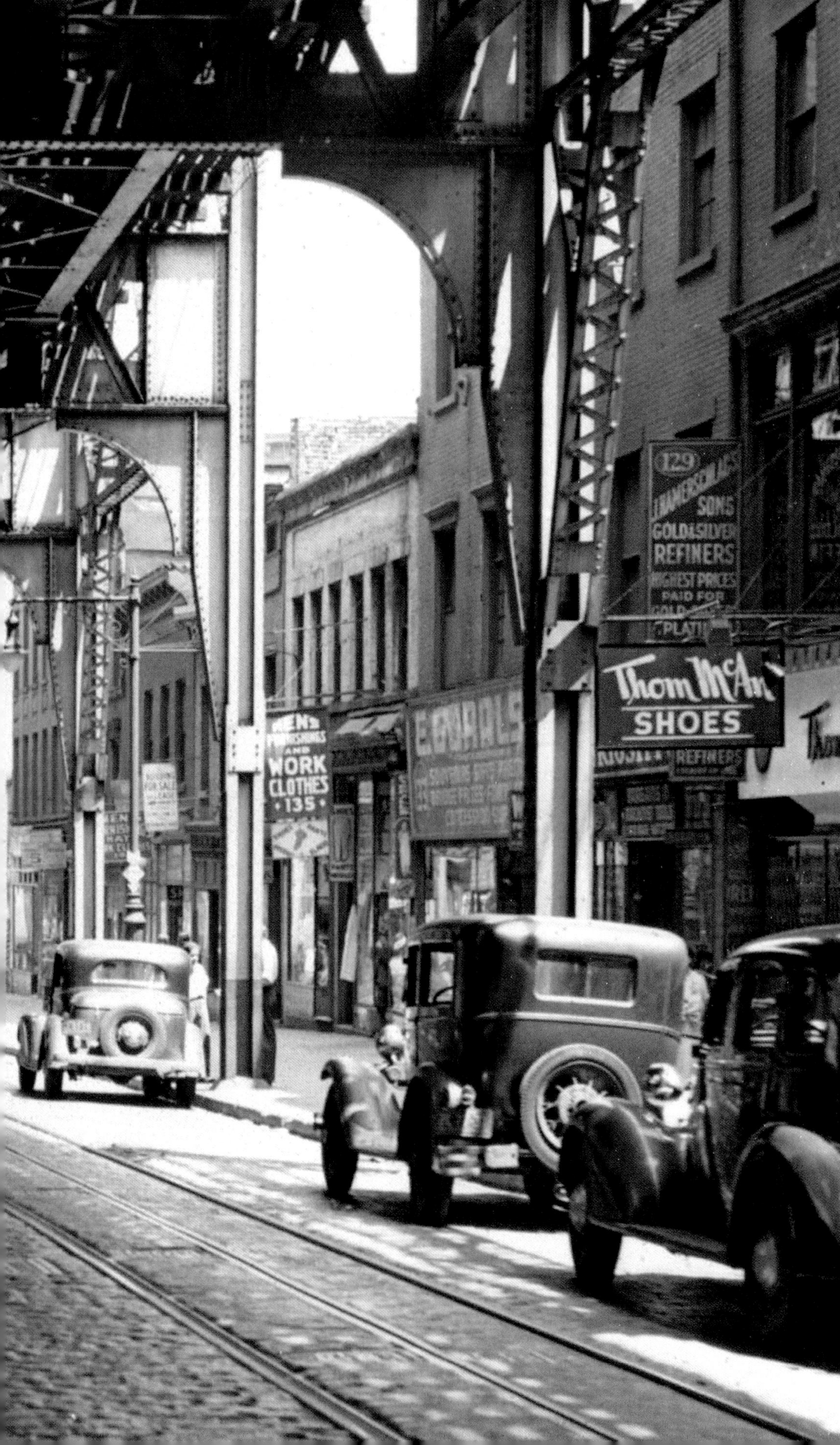

The First Avenue Elevated Railroad at Park Row illustrates how an "el" could literally take the sunshine out of a commercial district. The noise of the line for pedestrians and the residents of second-floor and third-floor apartments was another dubious "charm" of the elevated railroad. Park Row was a central hub for those bound for New York City Hall and Brooklyn. By 1944, all elevated lines had ceased to use Park Row Terminal. When first established in 1851, the "head house" of the Hudson Line was located in lower Manhattan at Chambers and Hudson streets, about five blocks west of City Hall and Park Row.

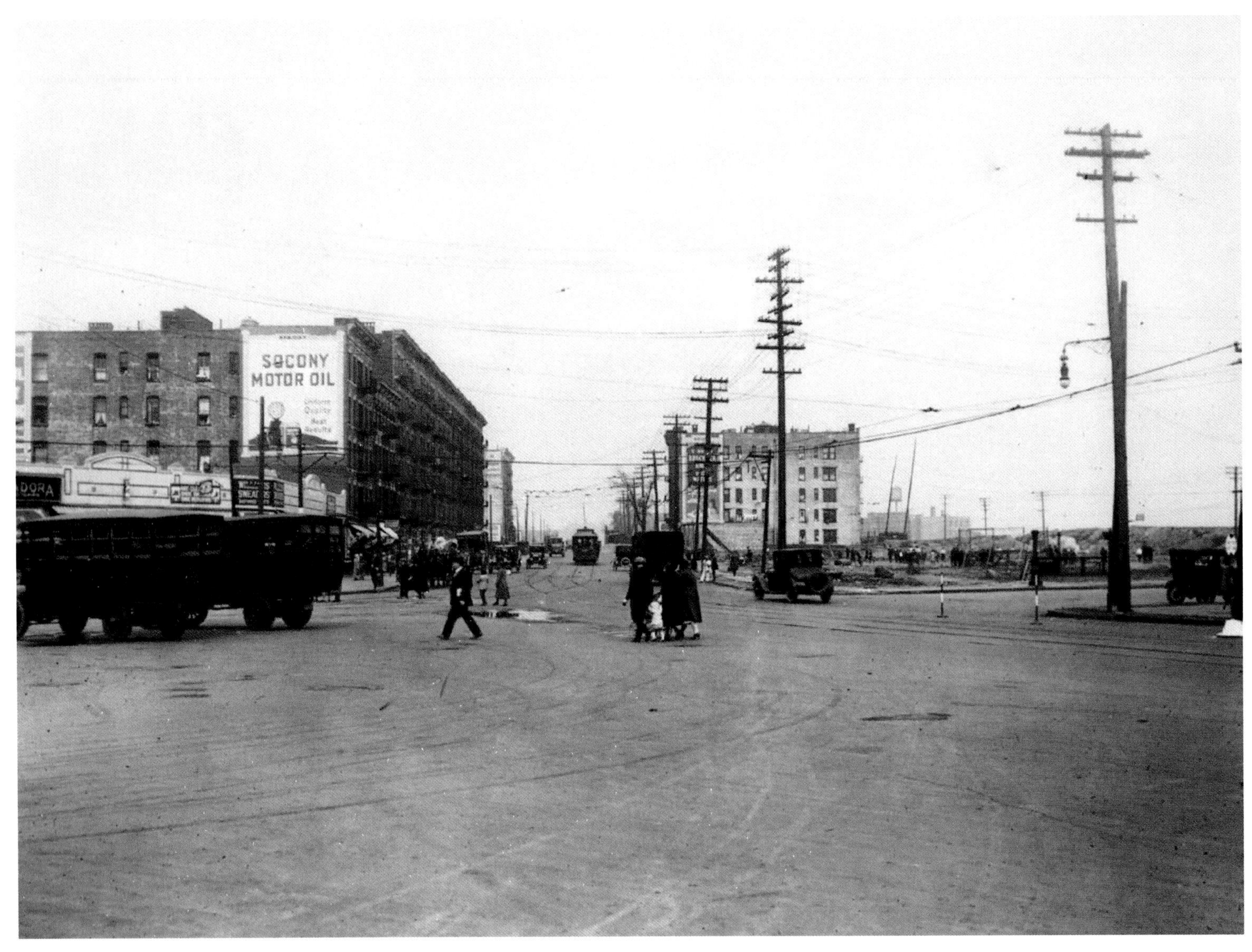

The Southern Boulevard in the Bronx is shown here at 149th Street, facing north. The boulevard was a wide, important, grand thoroughfare, as envisioned in the 1870s. Today it runs from the Mosholu Parkway south, along the western edge of the Bronx Botanical Gardens and the Bronx Zoo, ending at Boston Post Road.

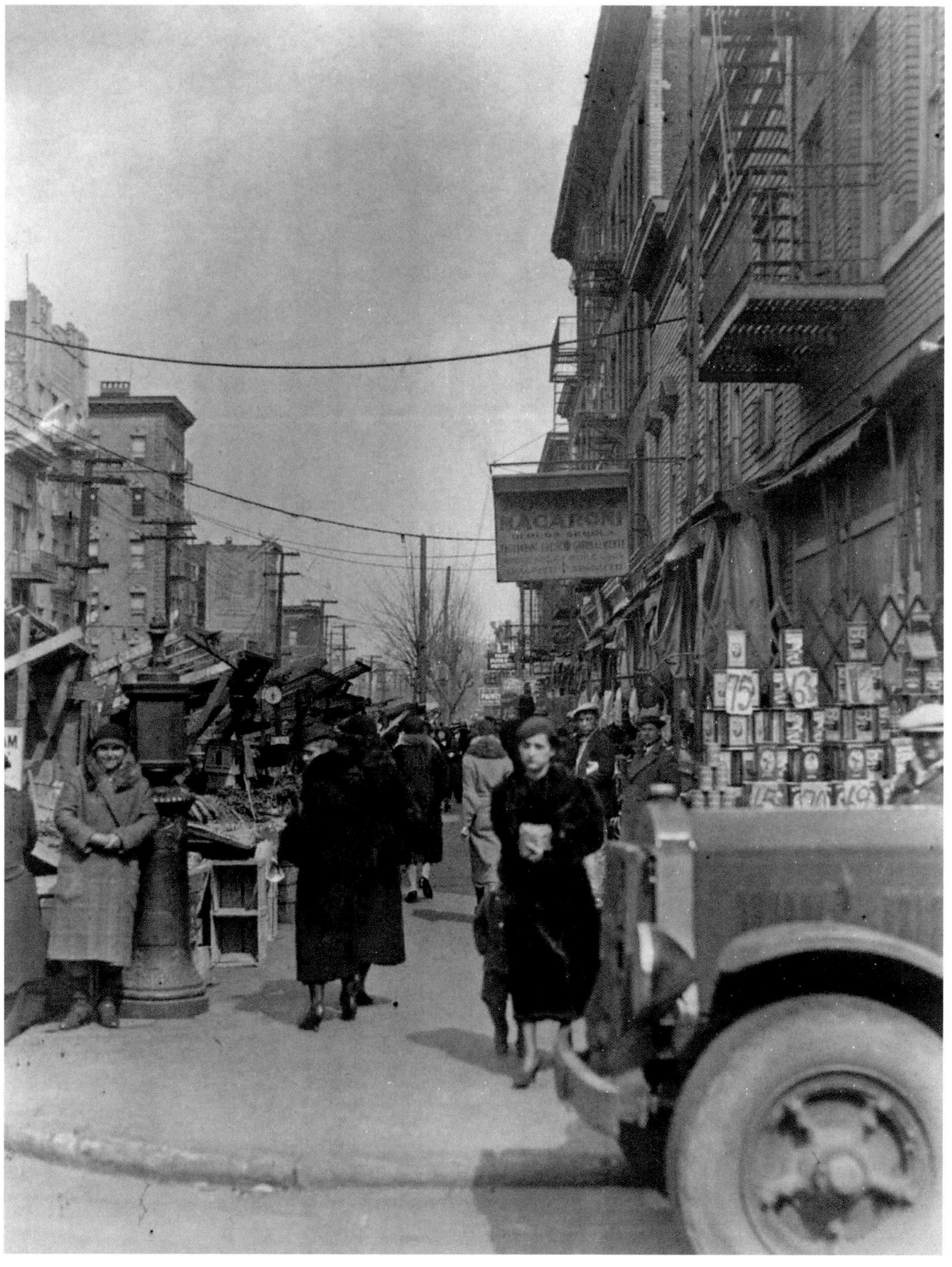

Probably named for President Chester A. Arthur, Arthur Avenue in the Bronx, seen here in 1930, was a predominantly Italian neighborhood. Today it is famous for its Italian cuisine. This image, recorded at 186th Street, shows some of the early vitality of the district. By 1940, pushcart vendors had been moved indoors, to the New York Retail Market building down the street.

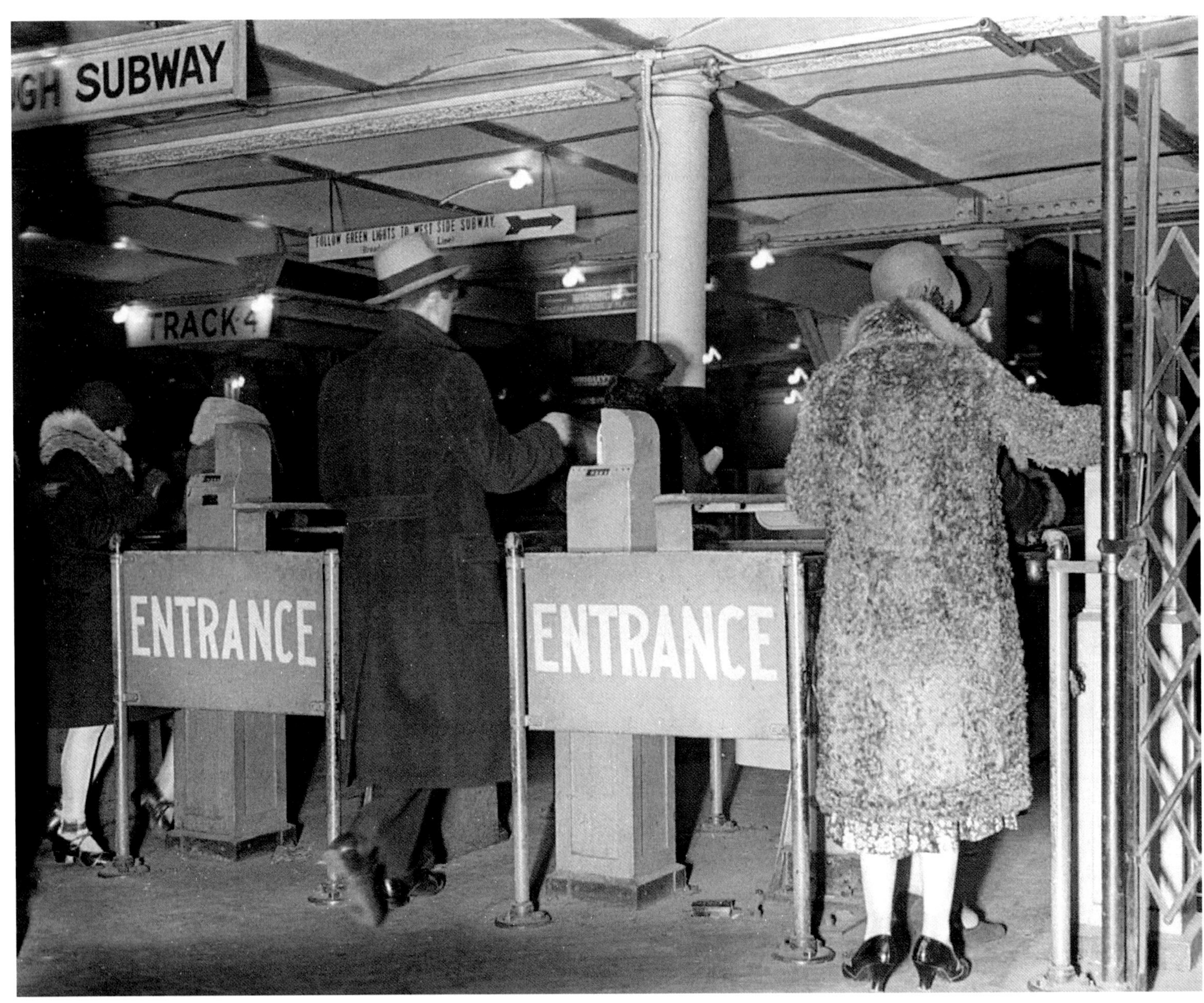

Commuters enter the subway turnstile at Grand Central Terminal in 1934. The busy stop on the Lexington Avenue Line still runs beneath the terminal at 42nd Street, between Park and Lexington avenues. It is also the terminus for a subway shuttle to Times Square.

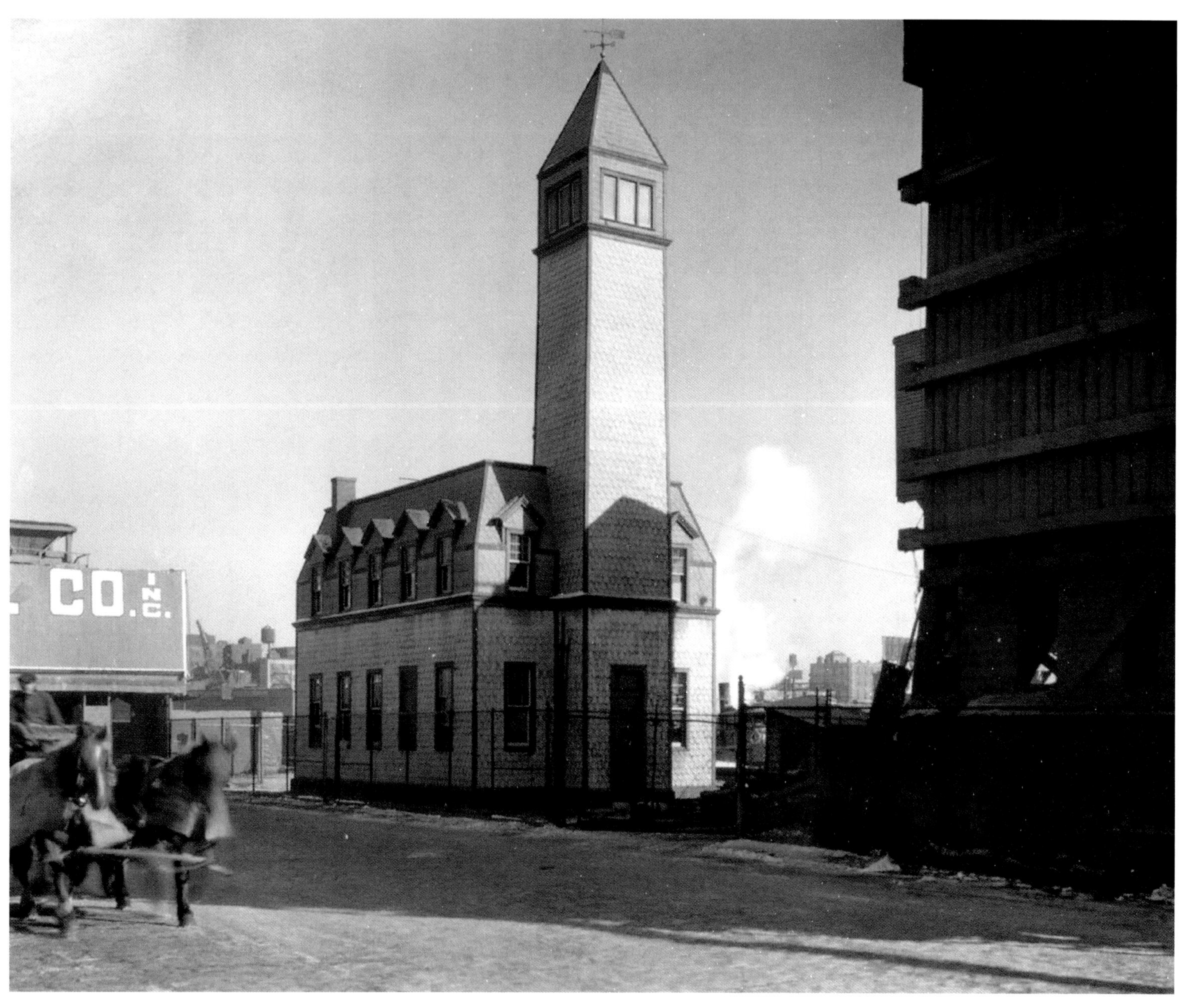

This firehouse at Park Avenue and 135th Street in Manhattan was photographed on December 19, 1935, by Berenice Abbott (1898–1991). The firehouse was specifically intended as a station for fireboats on the Harlem River. The structure, "neo-Victorian" in design, was built in 1909 and moved to this location from Lexington Avenue and 132nd Street. A horse-drawn wagon leaves Cullen Fuel Company on the left.

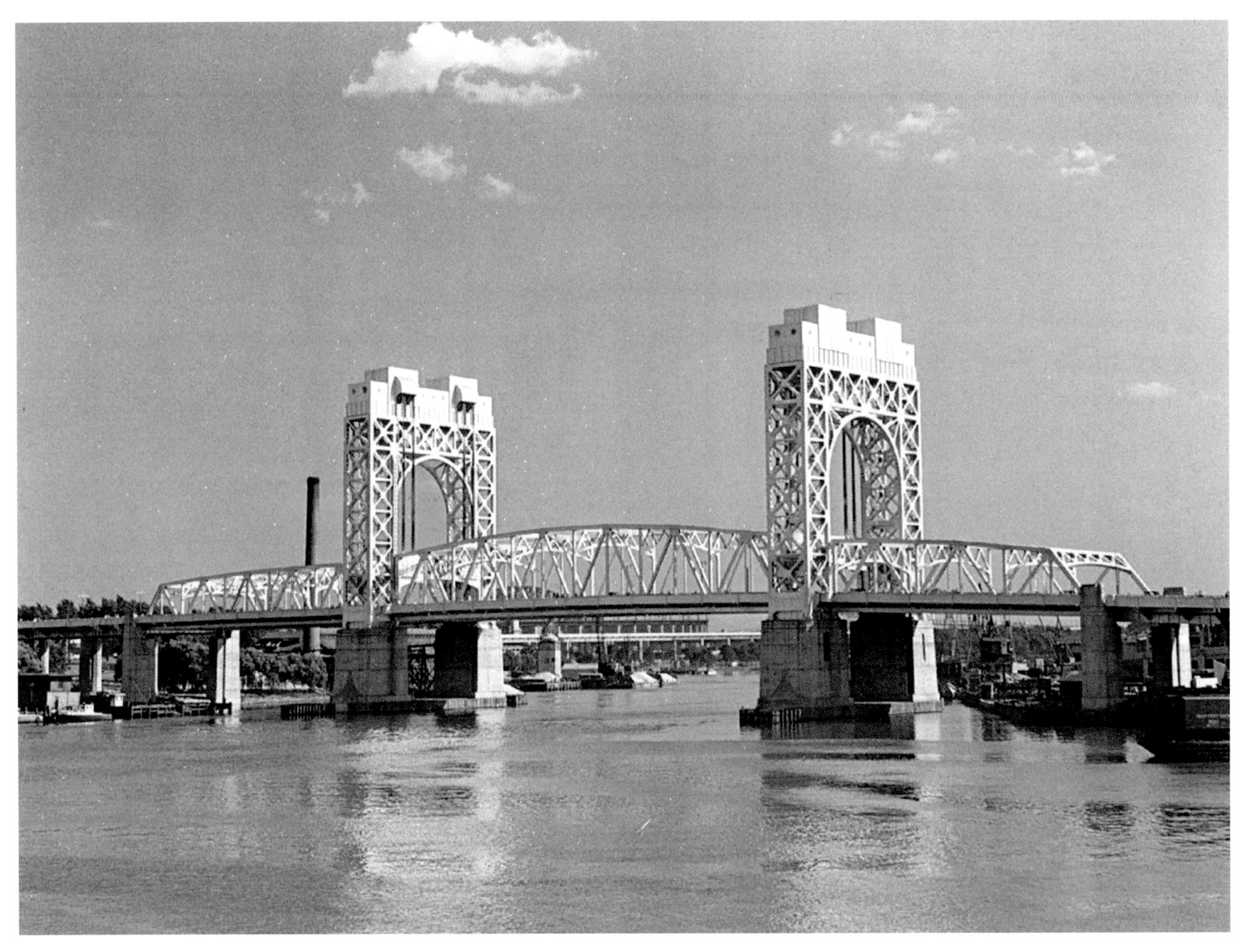

The Triboro Bridge was renamed the Robert F. Kennedy bridge in 2008. The bridge opened in 1936, built substantially with New Deal funds. Robert Moses was a driving force behind the project. This photograph shows the vertical lift section over the Harlem River.

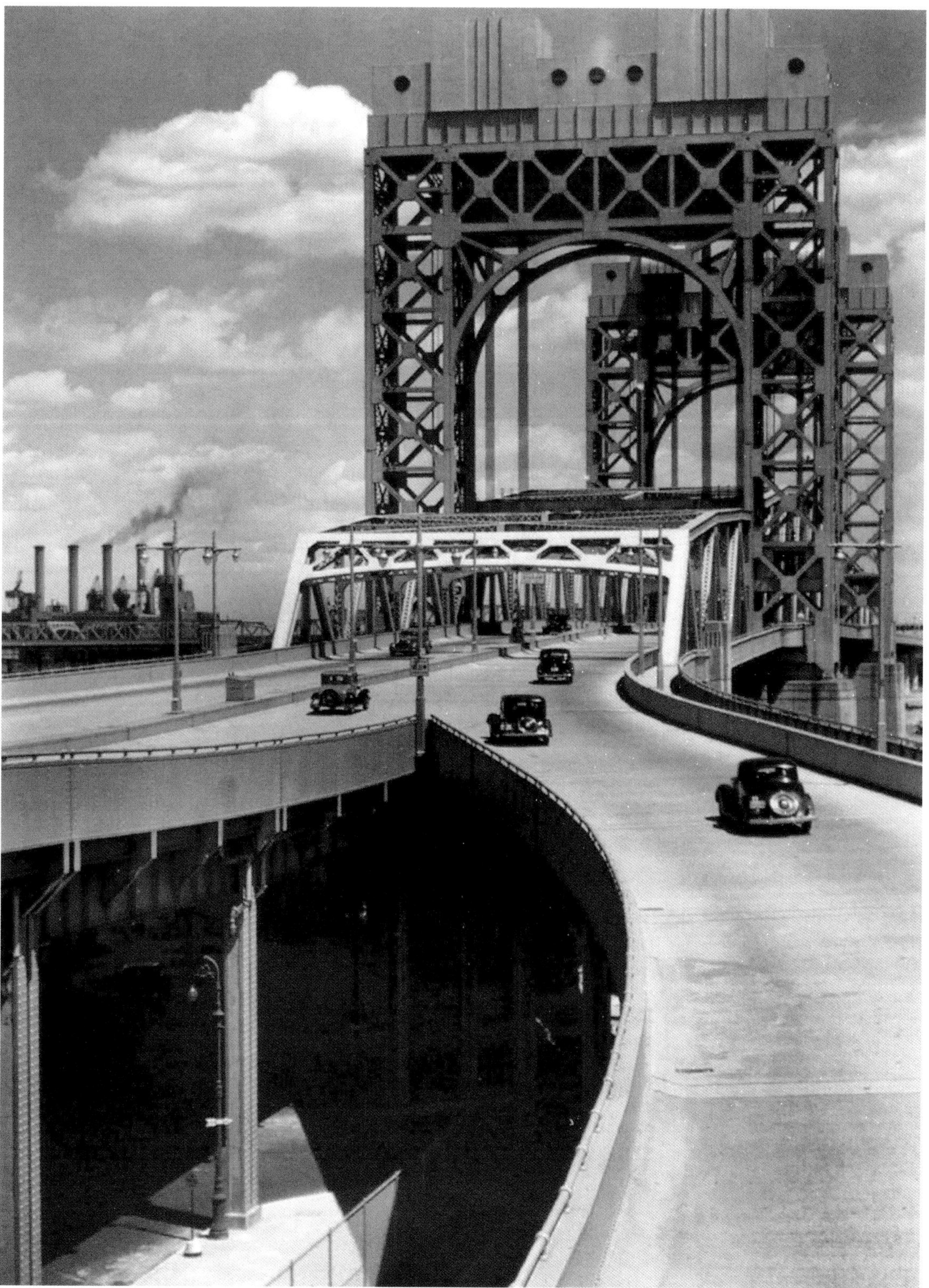

This is the 125th Street approach to the Triboro Bridge in 1937. The photograph is the work of Berenice Abbott. The bridge project was started in 1929, the year of the stock market crash.

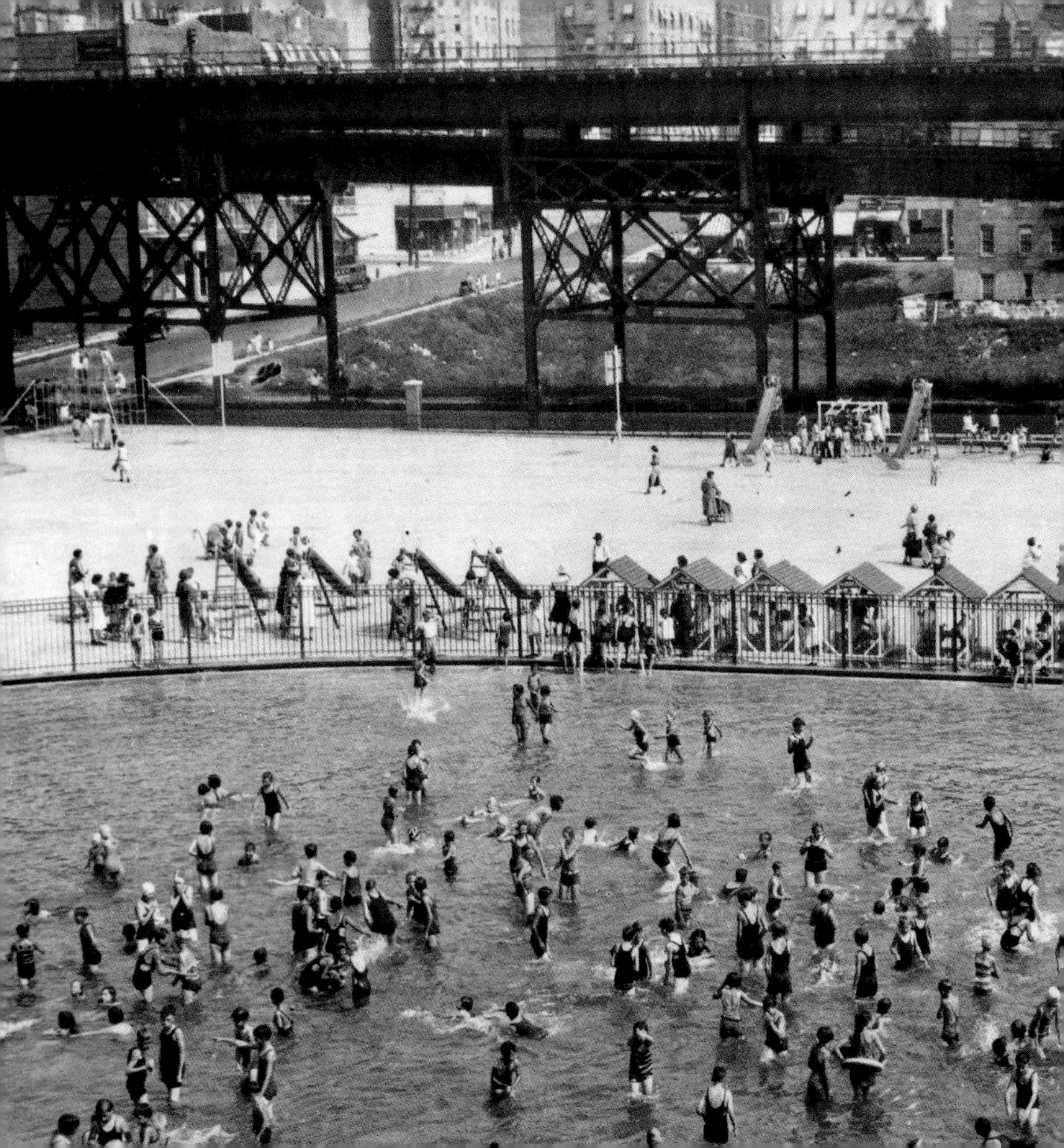

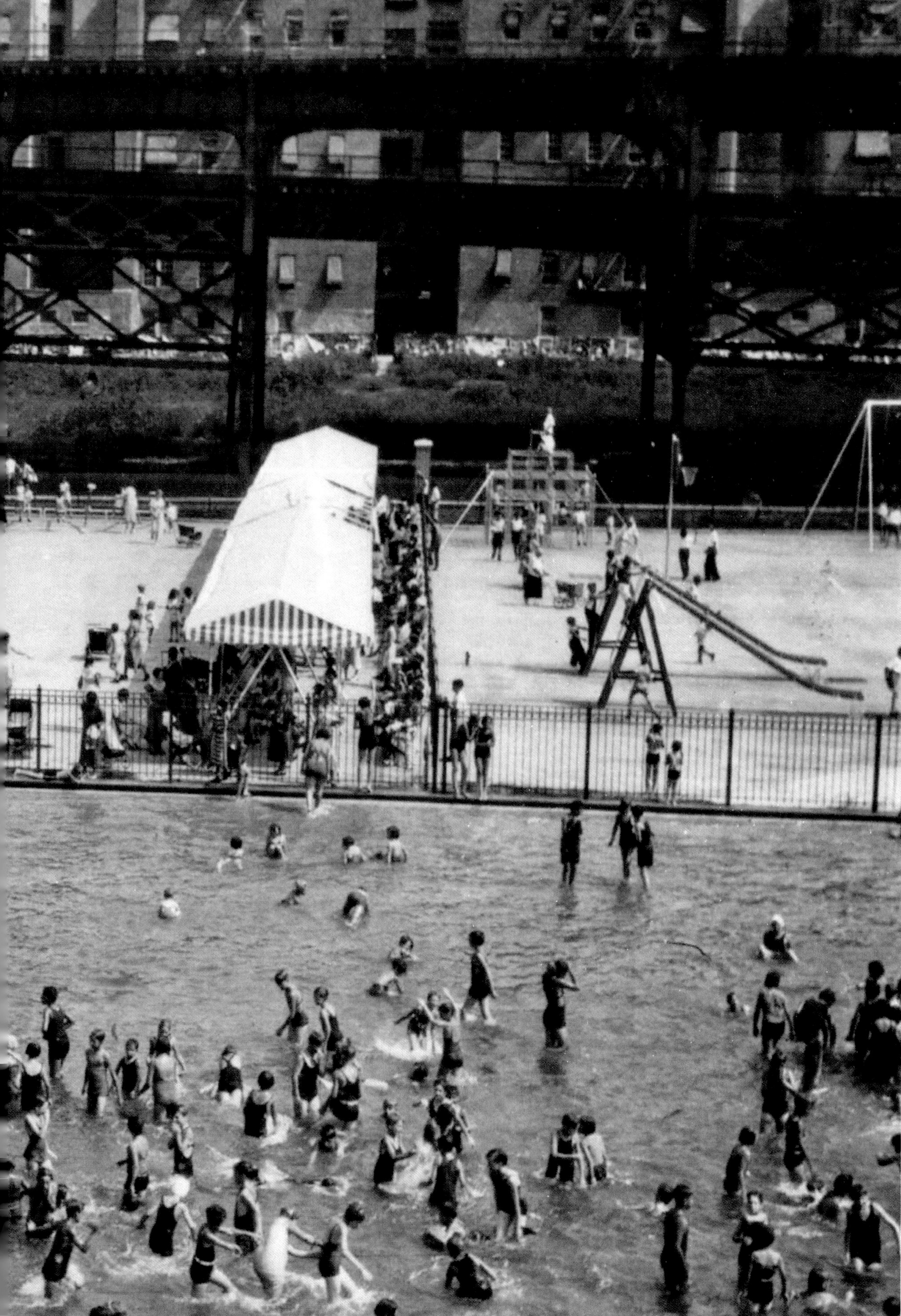

Named for John Mullaly (1835–1911), an early green space advocate, Mullaly Park is located at Jerome Avenue and 164th Street, in the Highbridge area of the Bronx. Land for the park was acquired by the city in the mid-1920s. This scene, photographed in 1936, shows the playground and park near the elevated railroad. The swimming pool doubled as a skating rink.

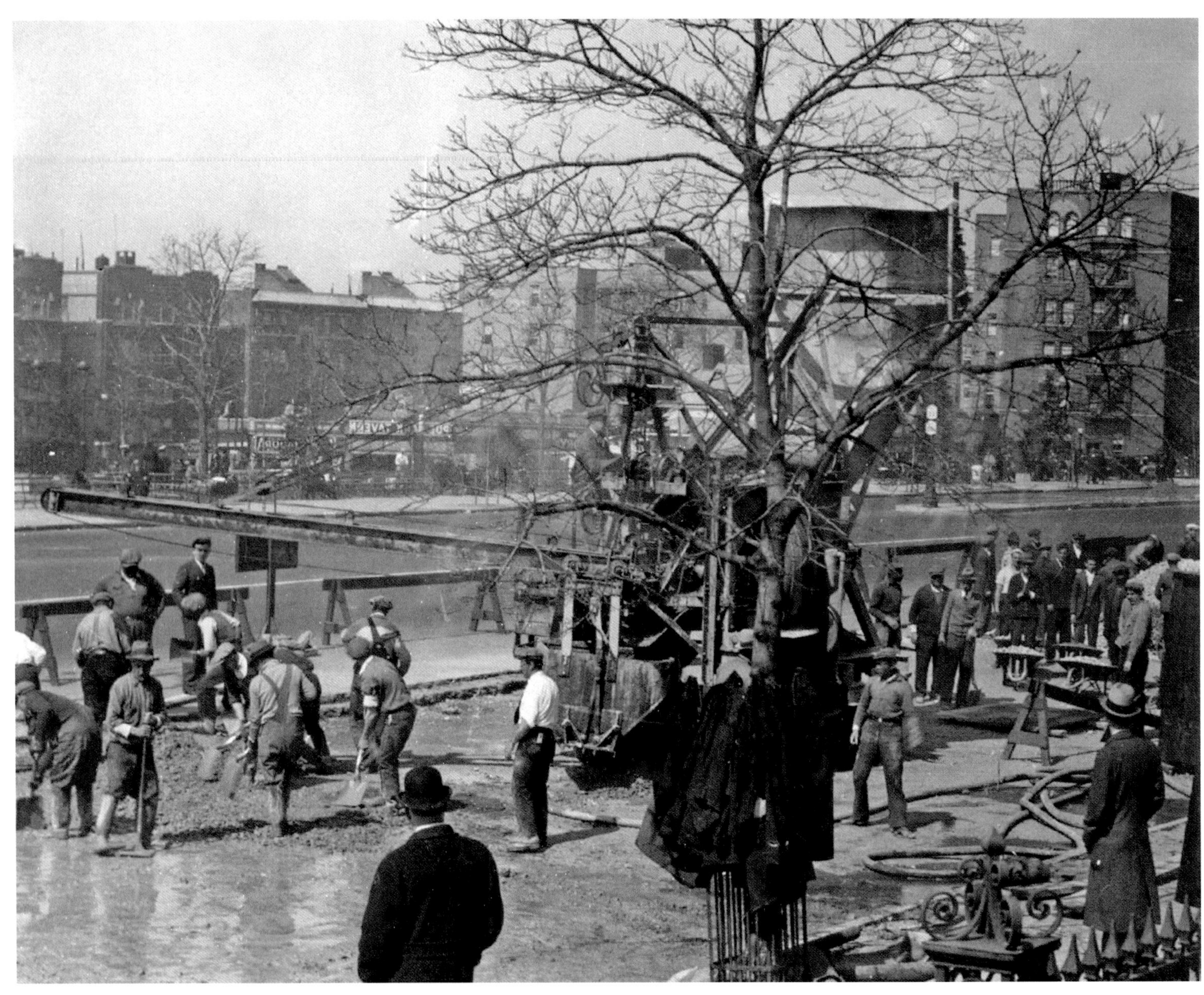

Louis Aloys Risse, an Alsatian immigrant, designed the Grand Concourse after the Champs Elysees in Paris. Opening in 1909, after 20 years of construction, it was originally four miles long but was later extended. Approximately 300 modern apartment houses were built along the concourse in the 1920s and 1930s. The area attracted many Jewish and Italian families from lower Manhattan.

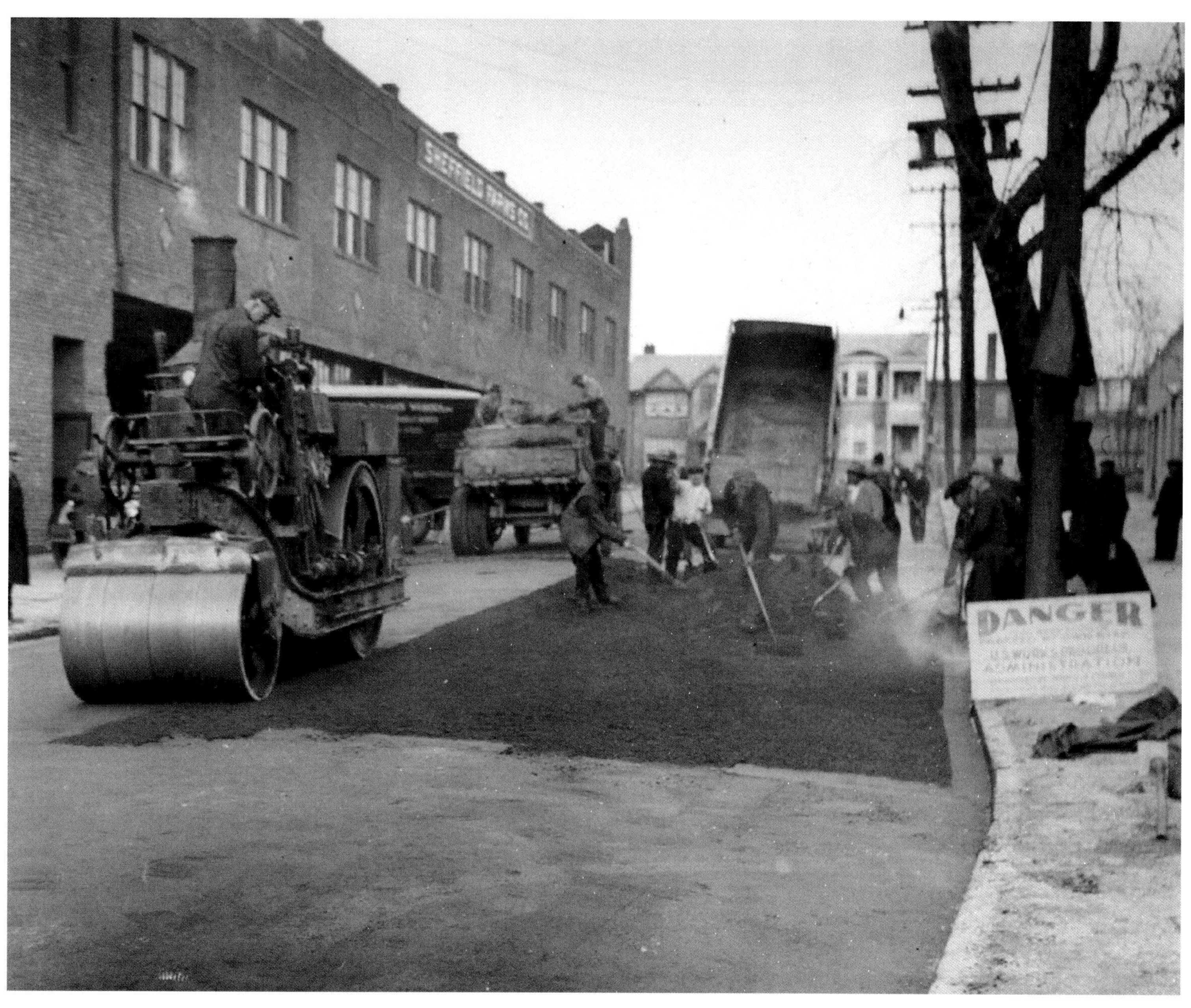

In 1936, signs of the Great Depression were visible everywhere. On Bronx Boulevard, south of East 242nd Street, a Works Progress Administration crew is paving the roadway. The boulevard parallels the Bronx River Parkway in the north Bronx.

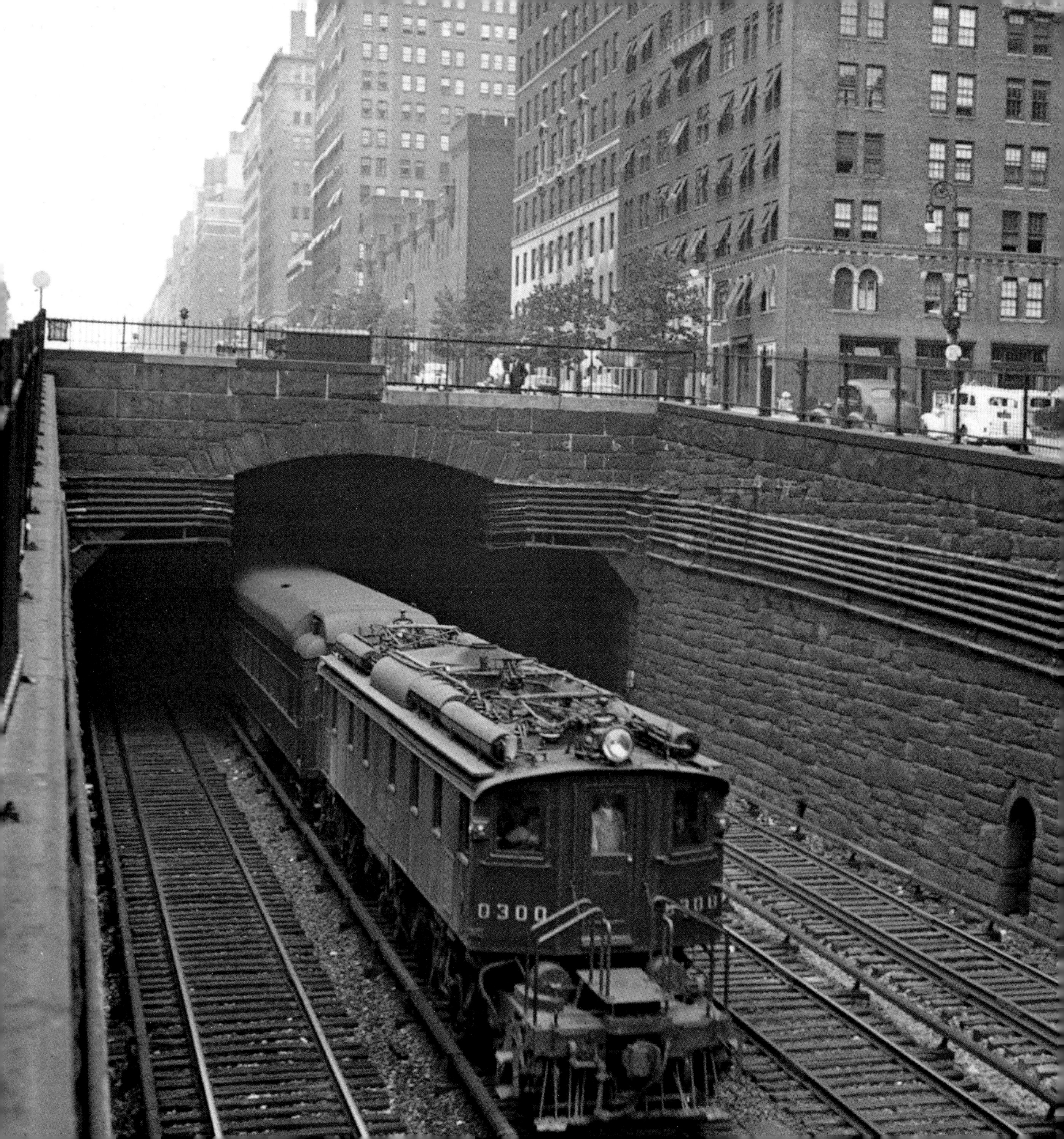
0300

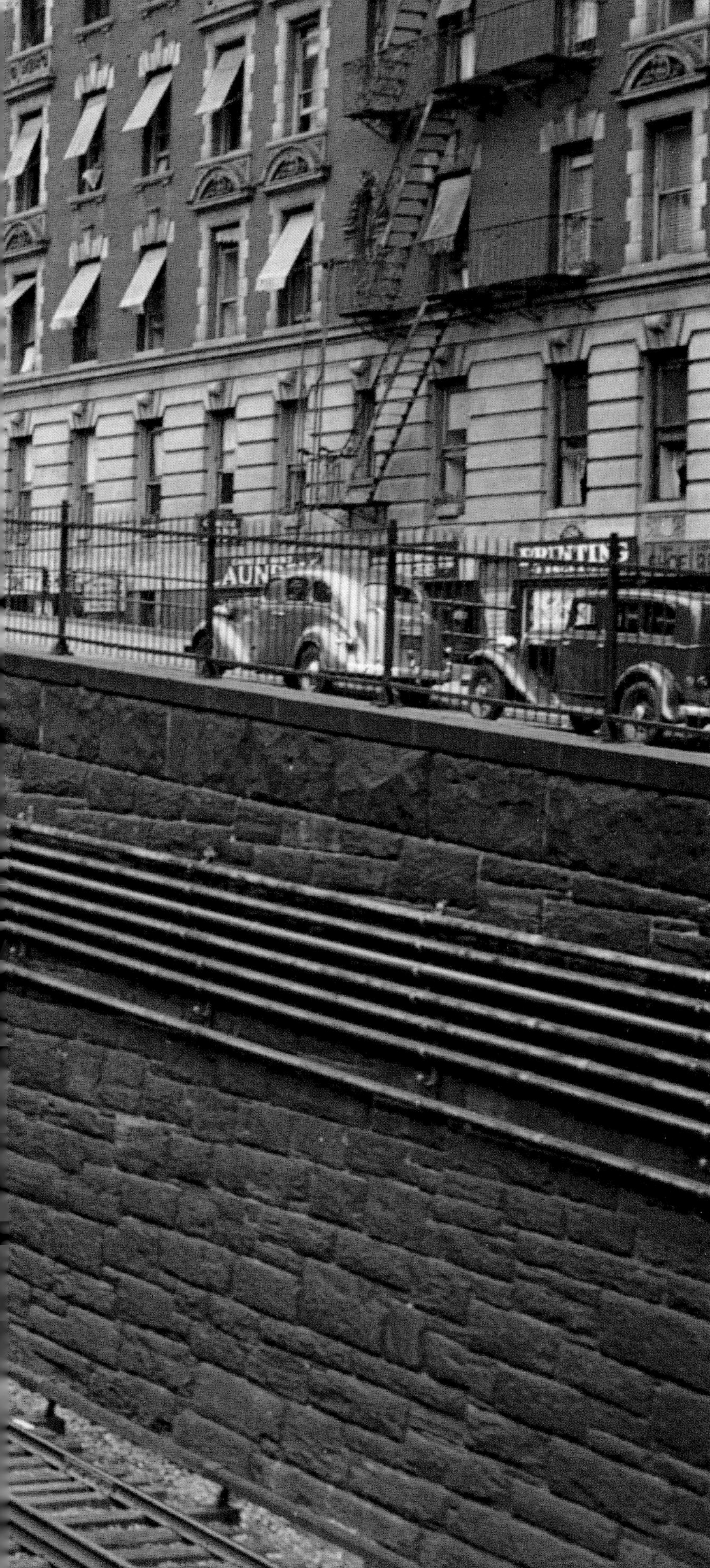

An electric locomotive exits the Park Avenue tunnel at 96th Street during the 1930s. At first, the Park Avenue section of the railroad lines ran through a cut above ground. The tunnel was installed between 1872 and 1876. Originally, there were three Manhattan stops within the tunnel. These were taken out of service before the trains were electrified in 1906.

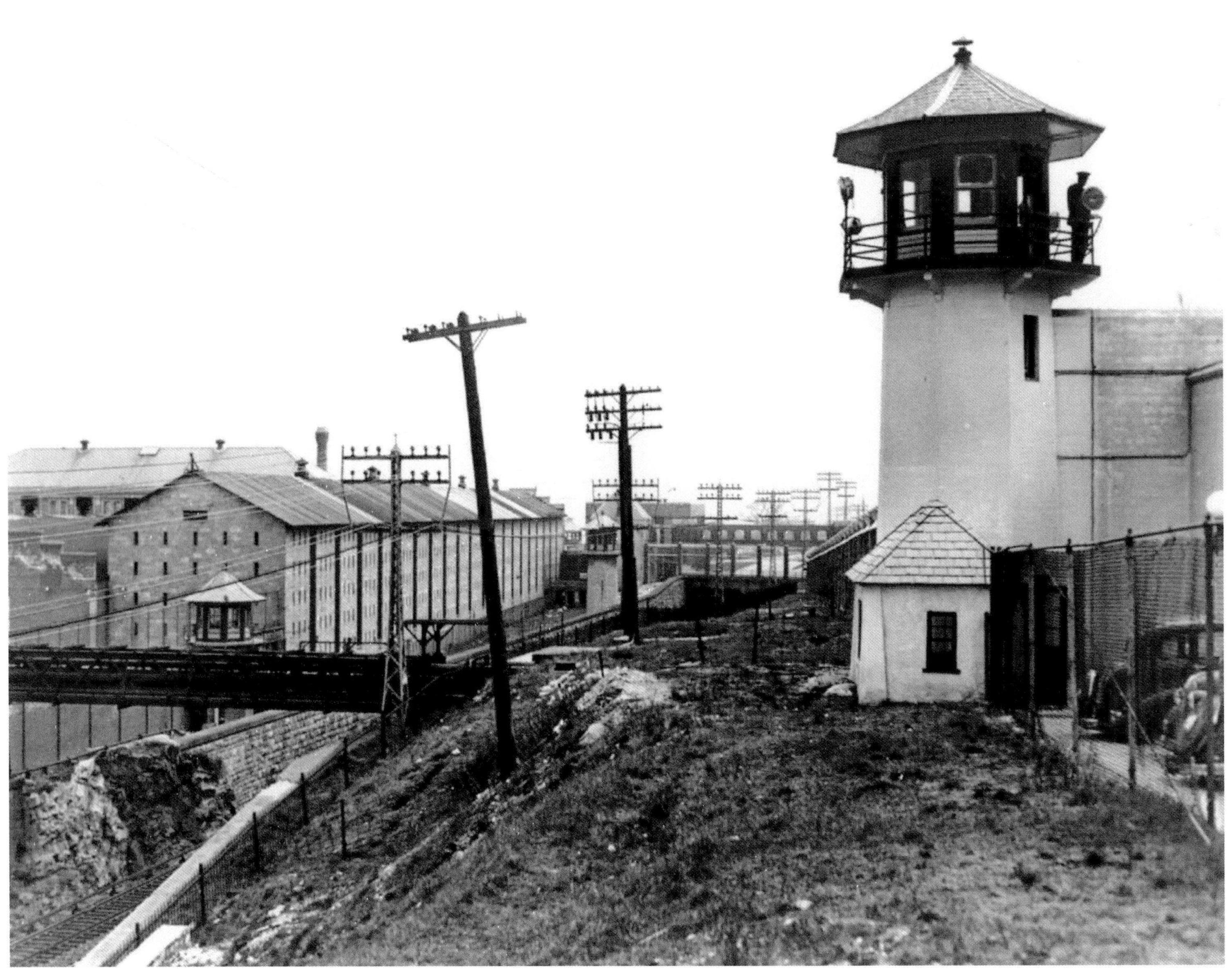

Sing Sing Prison stands on the waterfront in the town of Ossining. The town changed its name from Sing Sing to Ossining in 1845, and the village of Sing Sing followed suit in 1901. At that time, a boycott of prison-made goods hurt the village's economy by association. Guards on the Sing Sing guard towers had one of the finest Hudson River views in Westchester County. C. M. Stieglitz captured this view in 1938.

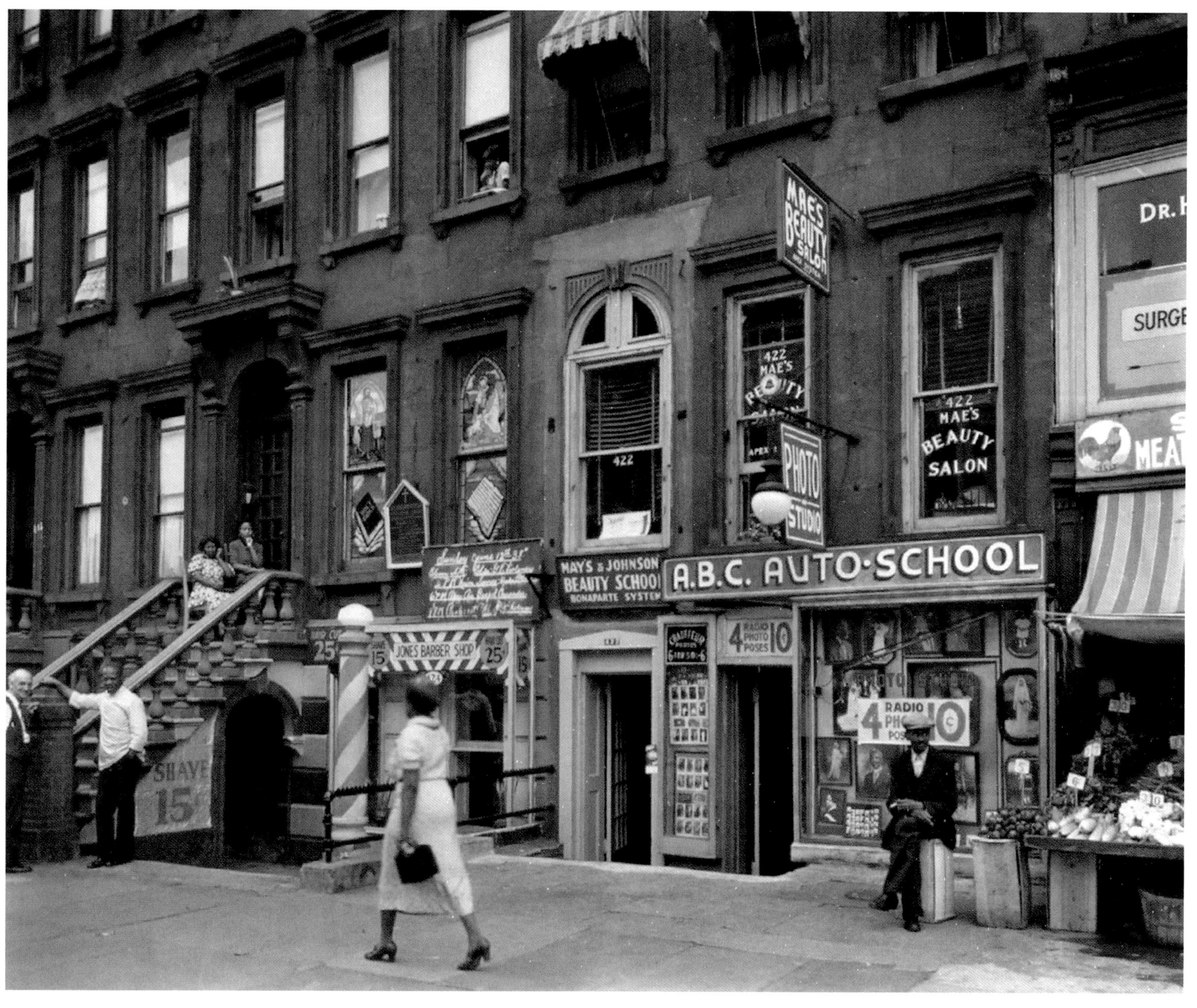

A day in the life of Harlem, June 14, 1938, is a tapestry of people and signs. Part of a produce stand is visible on the lower right, alongside a beauty parlor, a driving school, a barbershop, and a tiny church. Shown is 422-424 Lennox Avenue, photographed by Berenice Abbott.

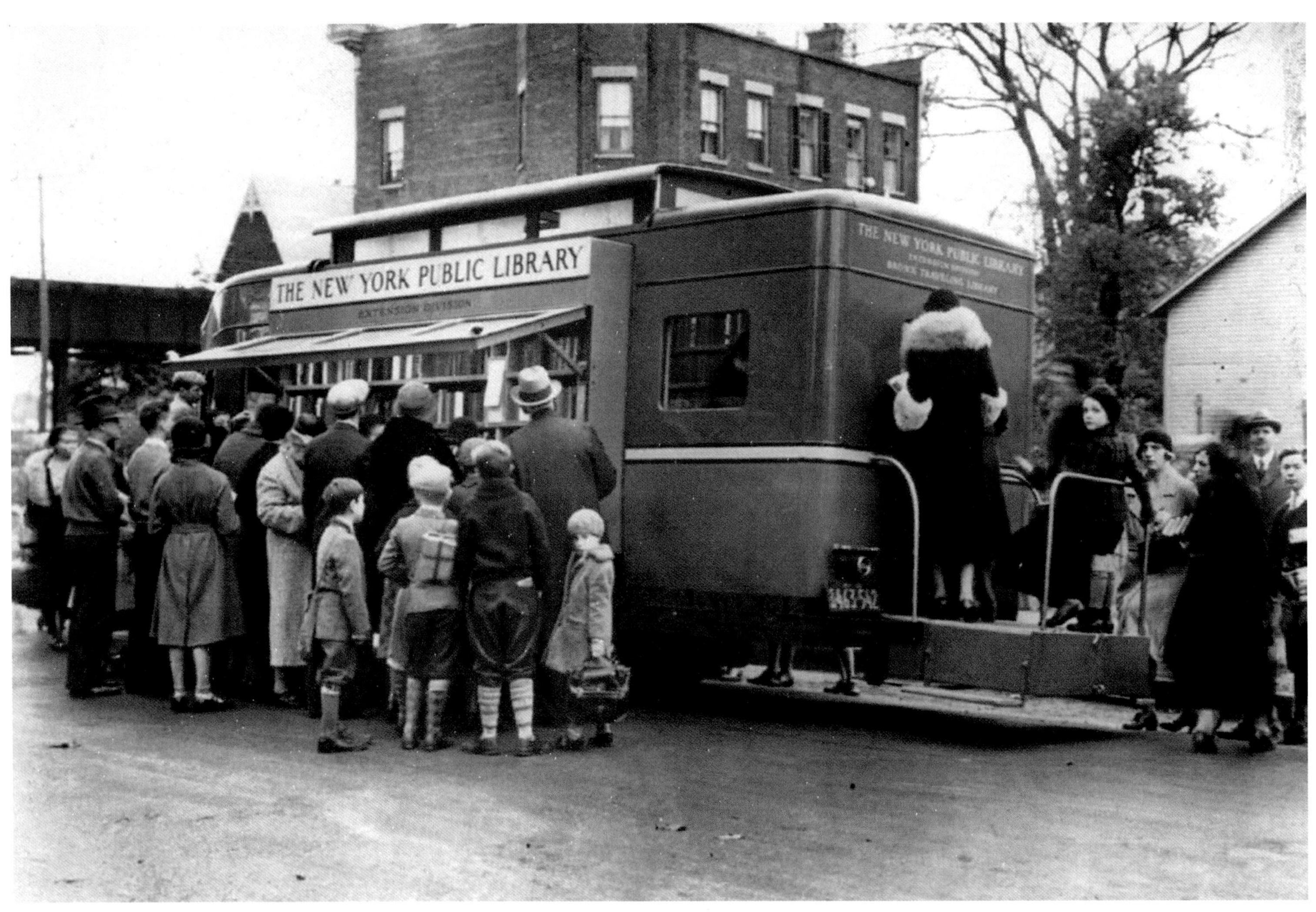

A bookmobile of the Bronx Traveling Library is shown circulating its book collection. The New York Public Library sent this vehicle out in the years of the Great Depression, although funding for the program was always uncertain.

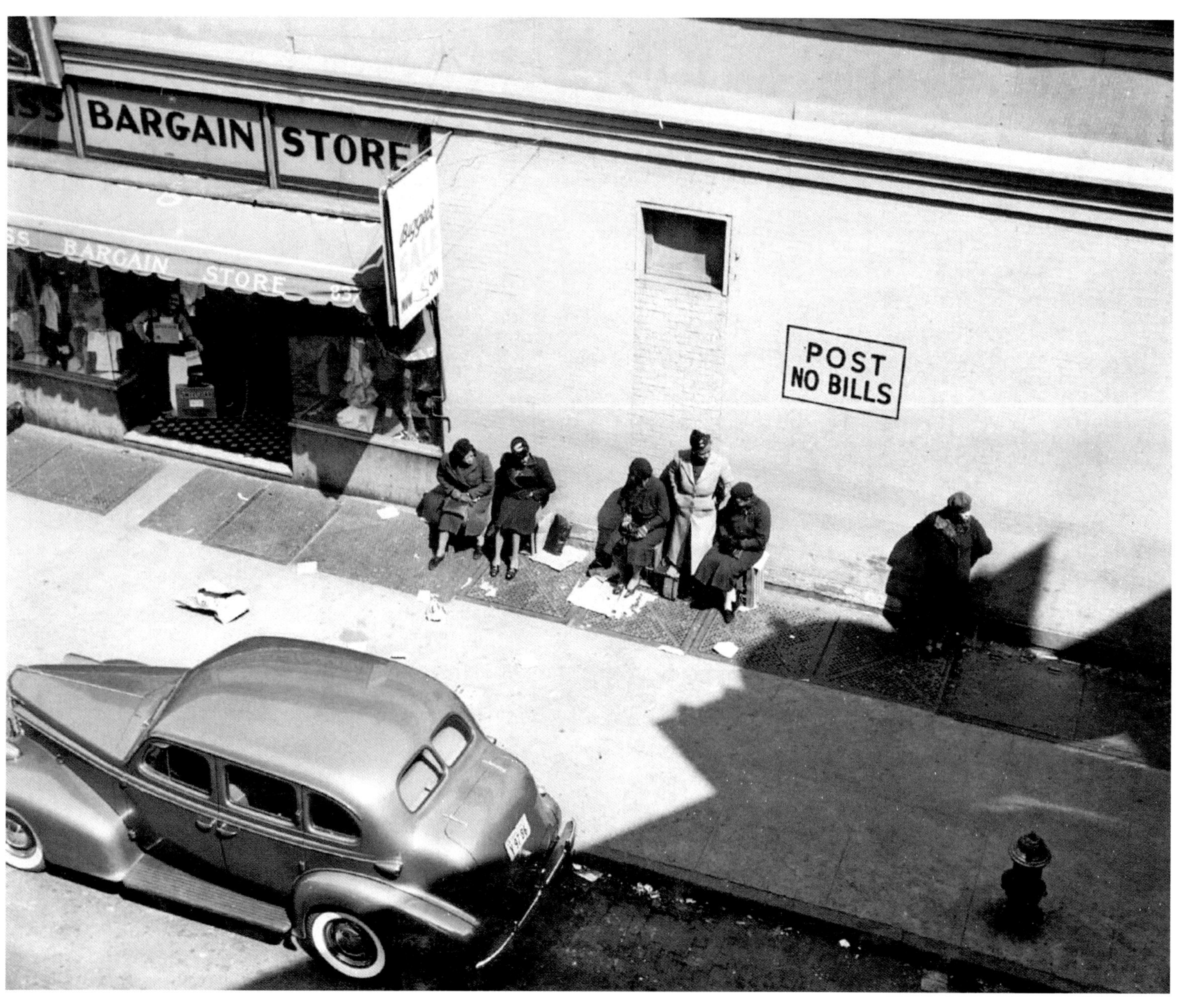

A glimpse of "the Bronx slave market" is shown here on April 12, 1939, at the corner of Jerome Avenue and 170th Street. The city curtailed the sidewalk employment practice about 1941 and opened a domestic employment agency in the neighborhood.

Generous deposits of clay along the shore of the Hudson River led to the prevalence of brick manufacturing in the Hudson Valley. Hutton Brickworks at Kingston is shown here in 1939. The Hutton Brickworks began operations in 1865 and closed in 1980. Its abandoned buildings are among only two brickworks still intact along the Hudson.

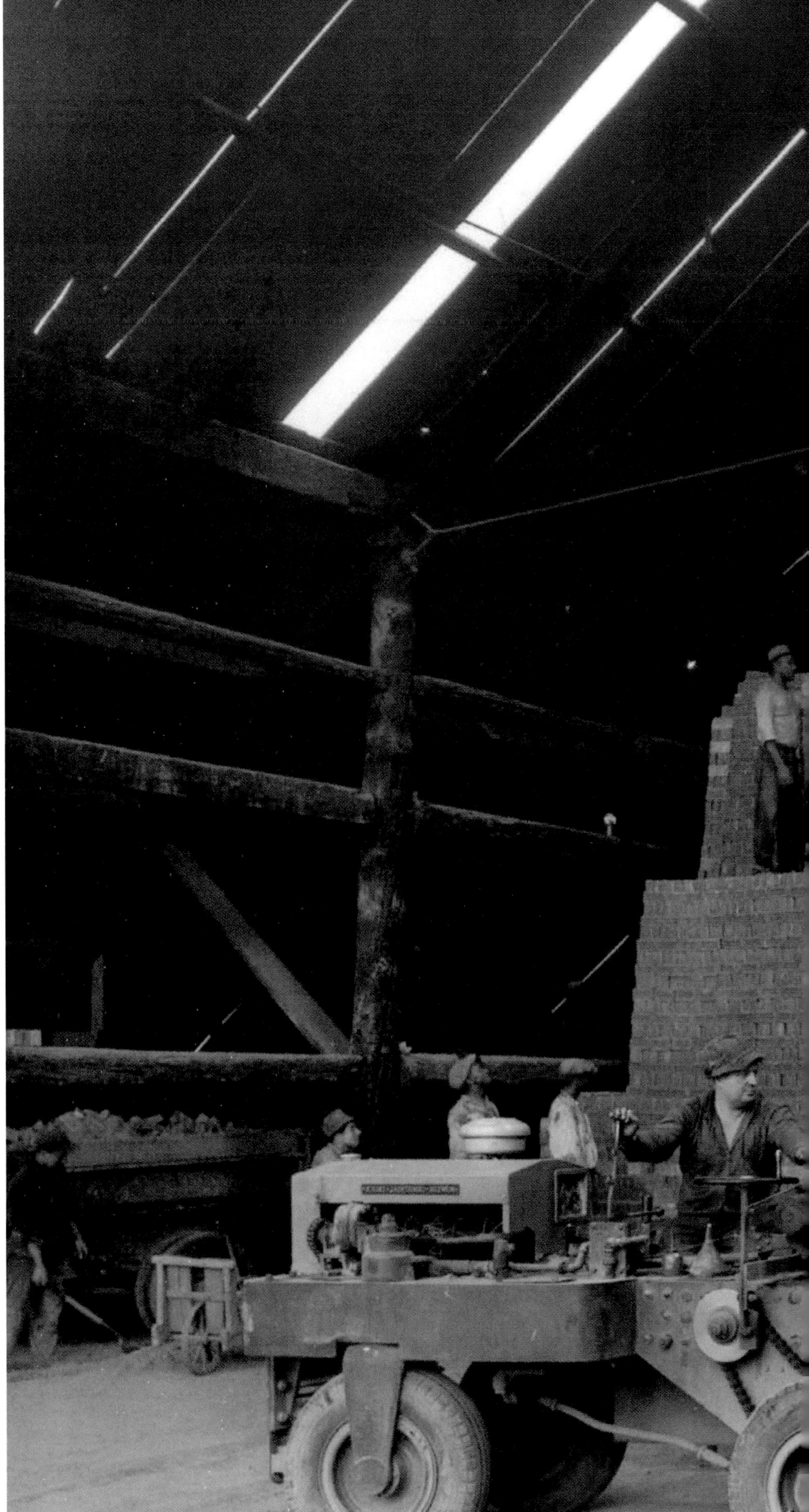

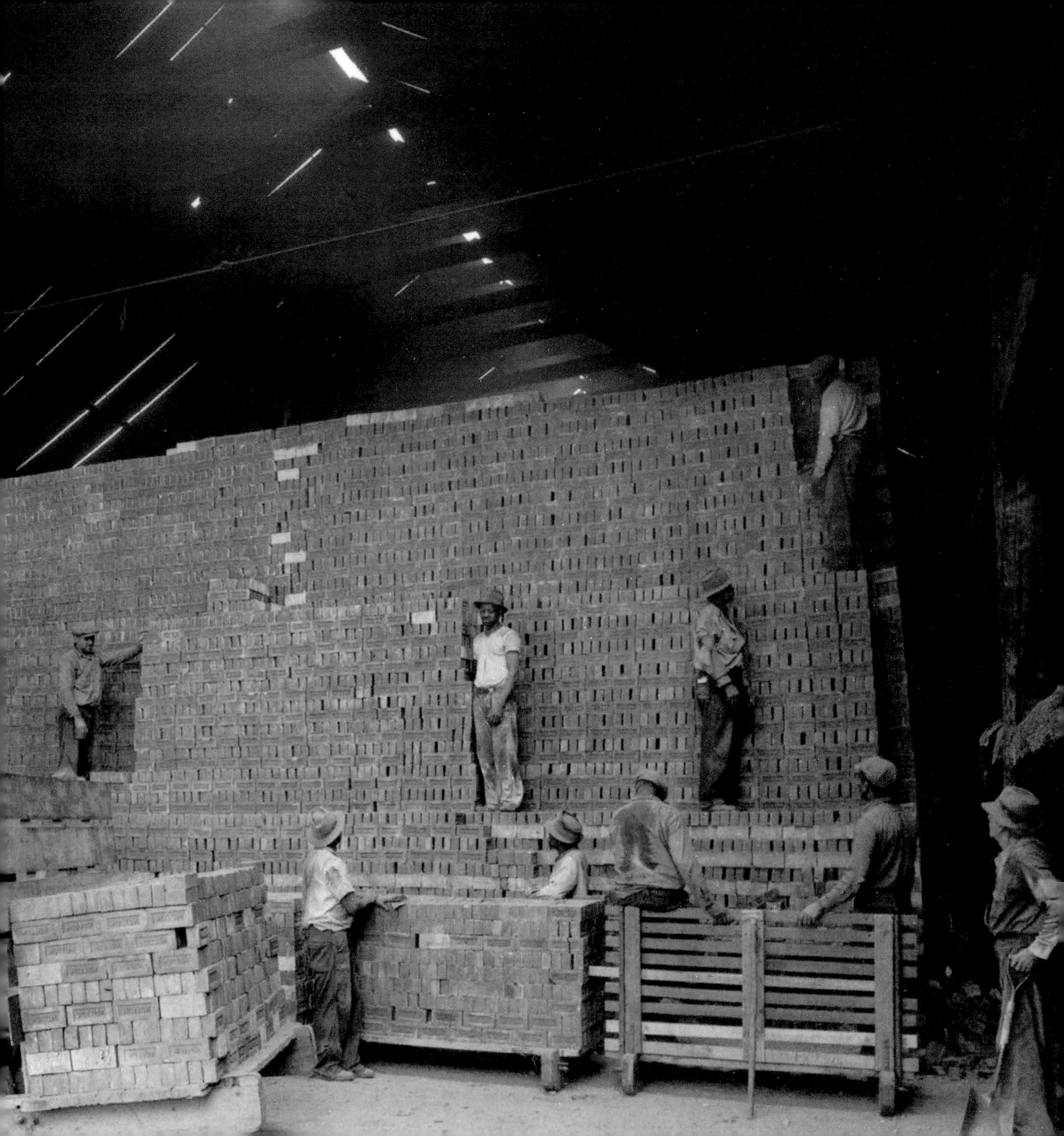

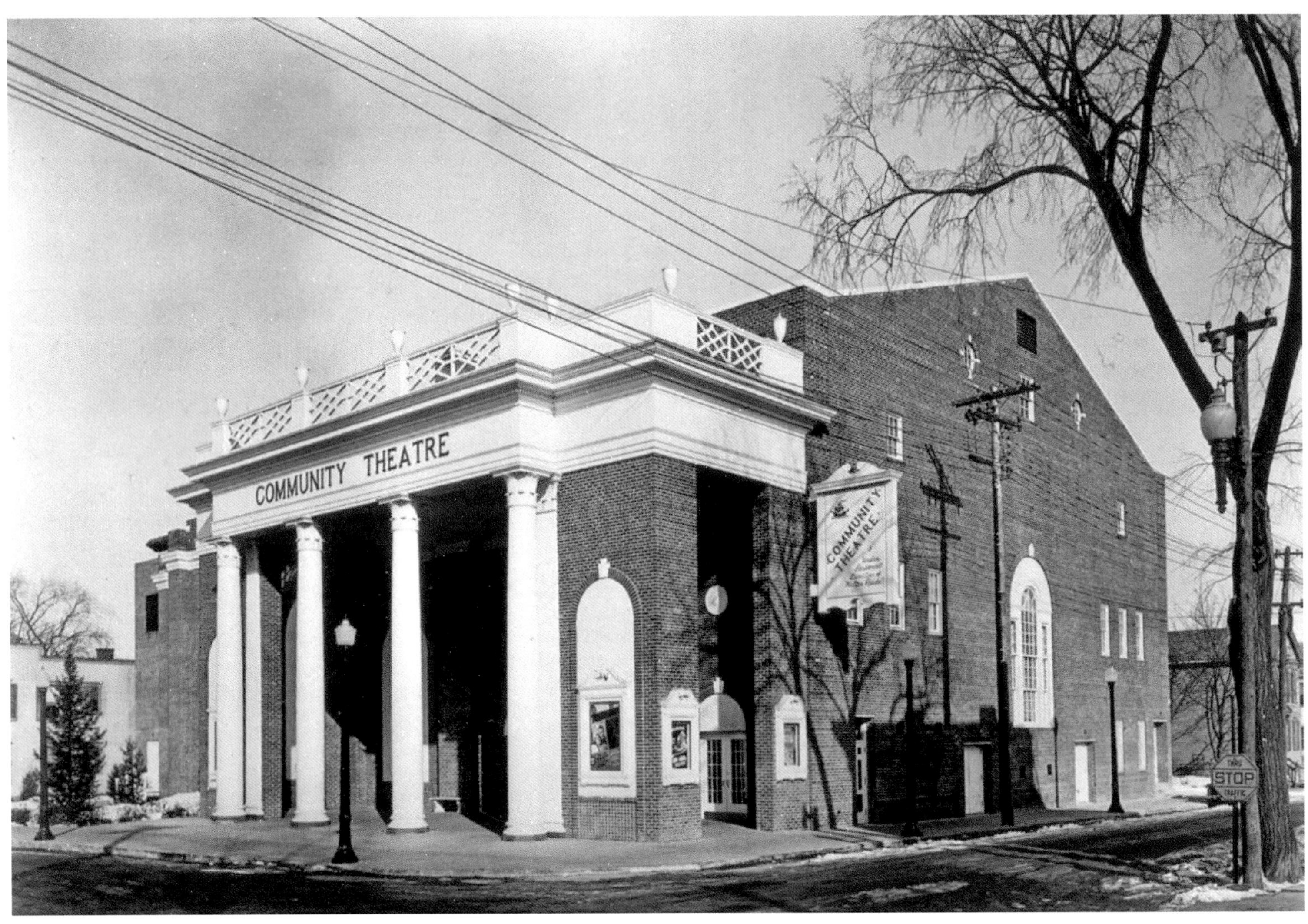

William I. Hohauser designed this community theater in Hudson, New York, as well as other theaters in Beacon, Stamford, Brewster, and Brooklyn. The Hudson theater building is shown here in 1939. Most of the theaters Hohauser designed have either been closed or demolished. A 1913 graduate of Stuyvesant High School in Manhattan, Hohauser was known for his theaters and Manhattan low-rise buildings.

The Ulster County architectural firm of Teller and Halverson designed the Myron J. Michael School in Kingston, shown here in 1939. Michael was a principal of Kingston Academy and Clinton Liberal Institute. He died in 1931 at the age of 80. Although the Michael school still stands, Teller and Halverson buildings in the area have not enjoyed a healthy detente with the wrecking ball.

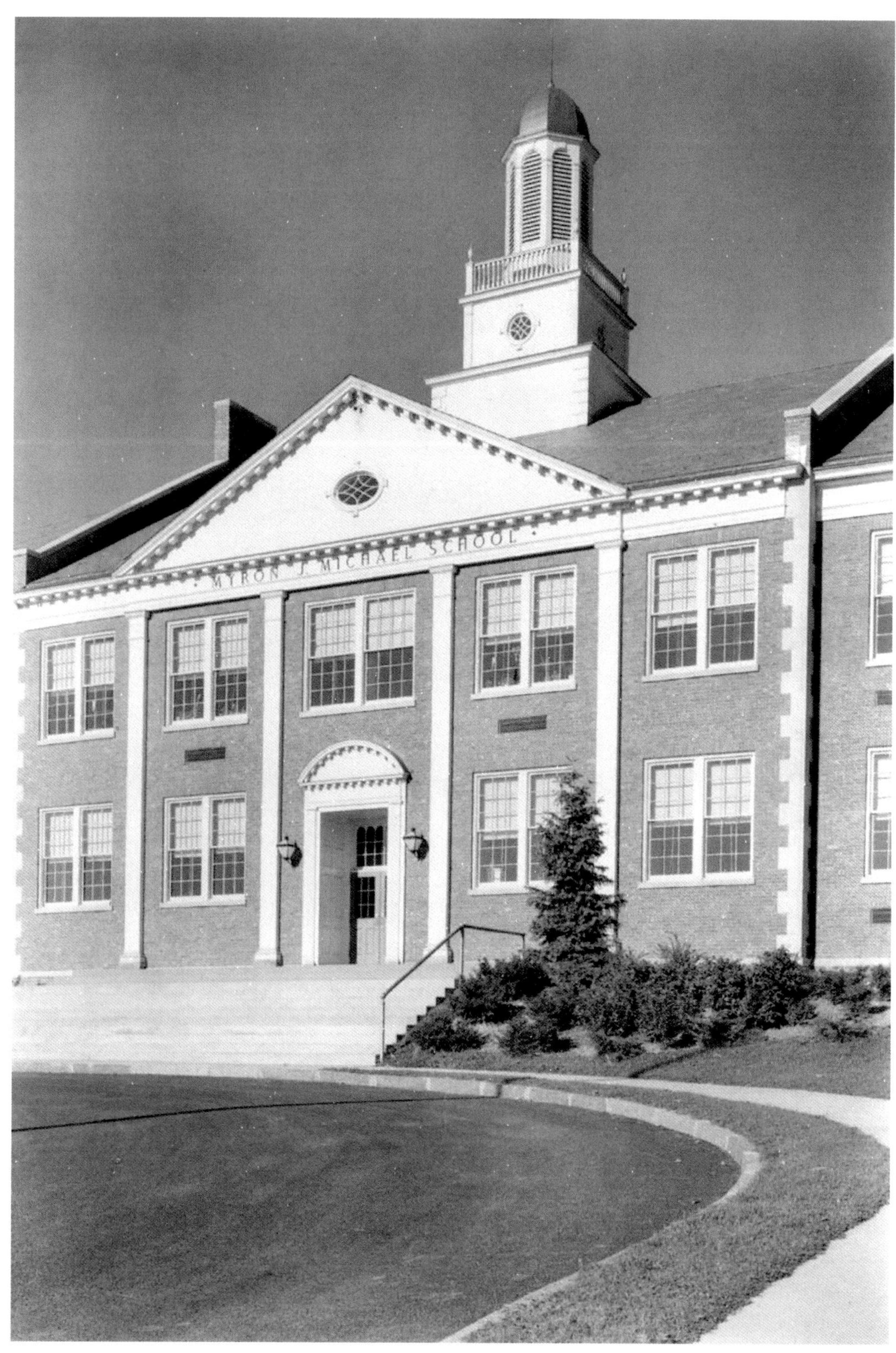

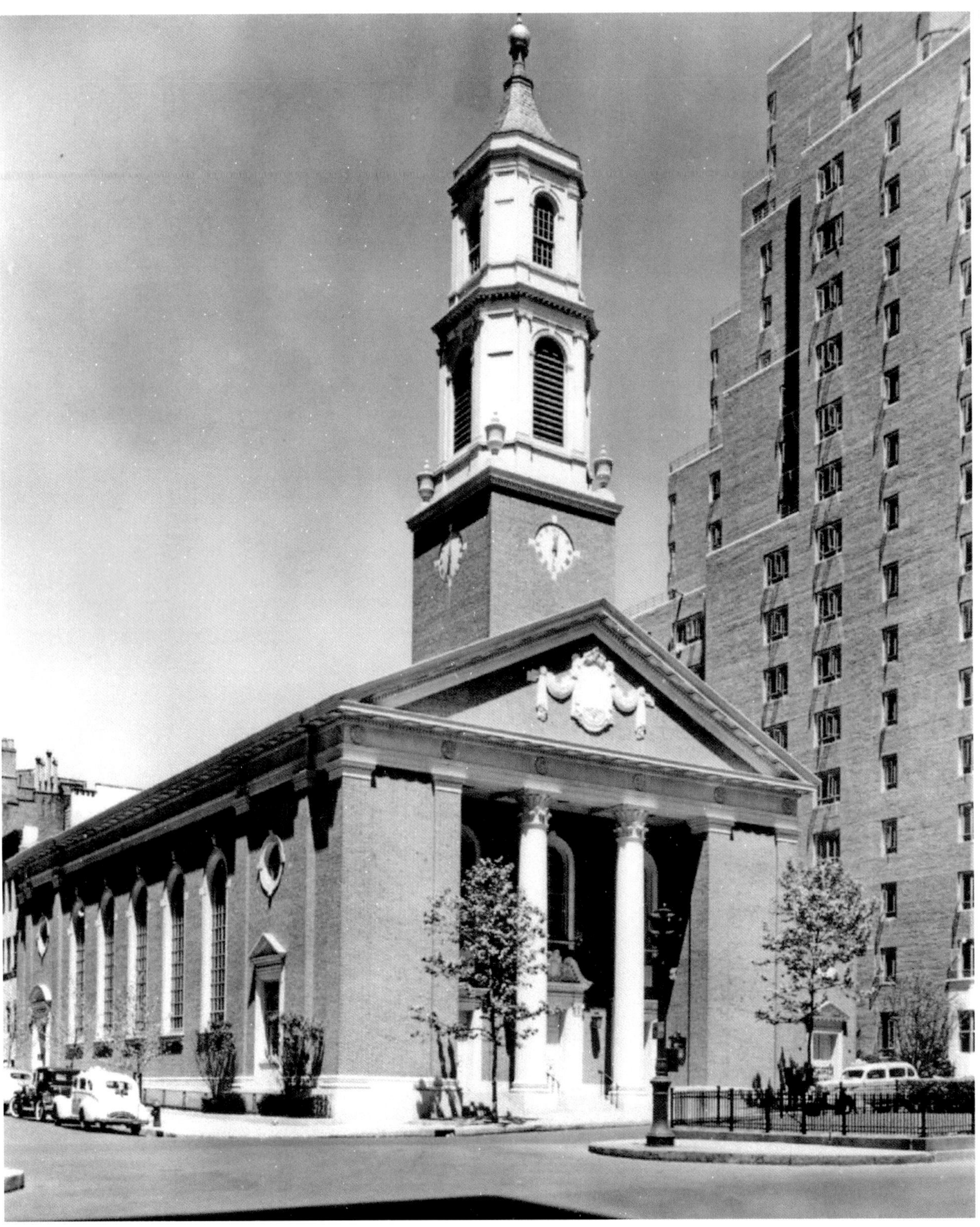

The Brick Church, on Park Avenue and 91st Street, is shown here in 1940. The church was built in 1938 and designed by Lewis Ayres. The church's bell and weather vane were taken from the congregation's original church building, located downtown at Park Row and Beekman Place.

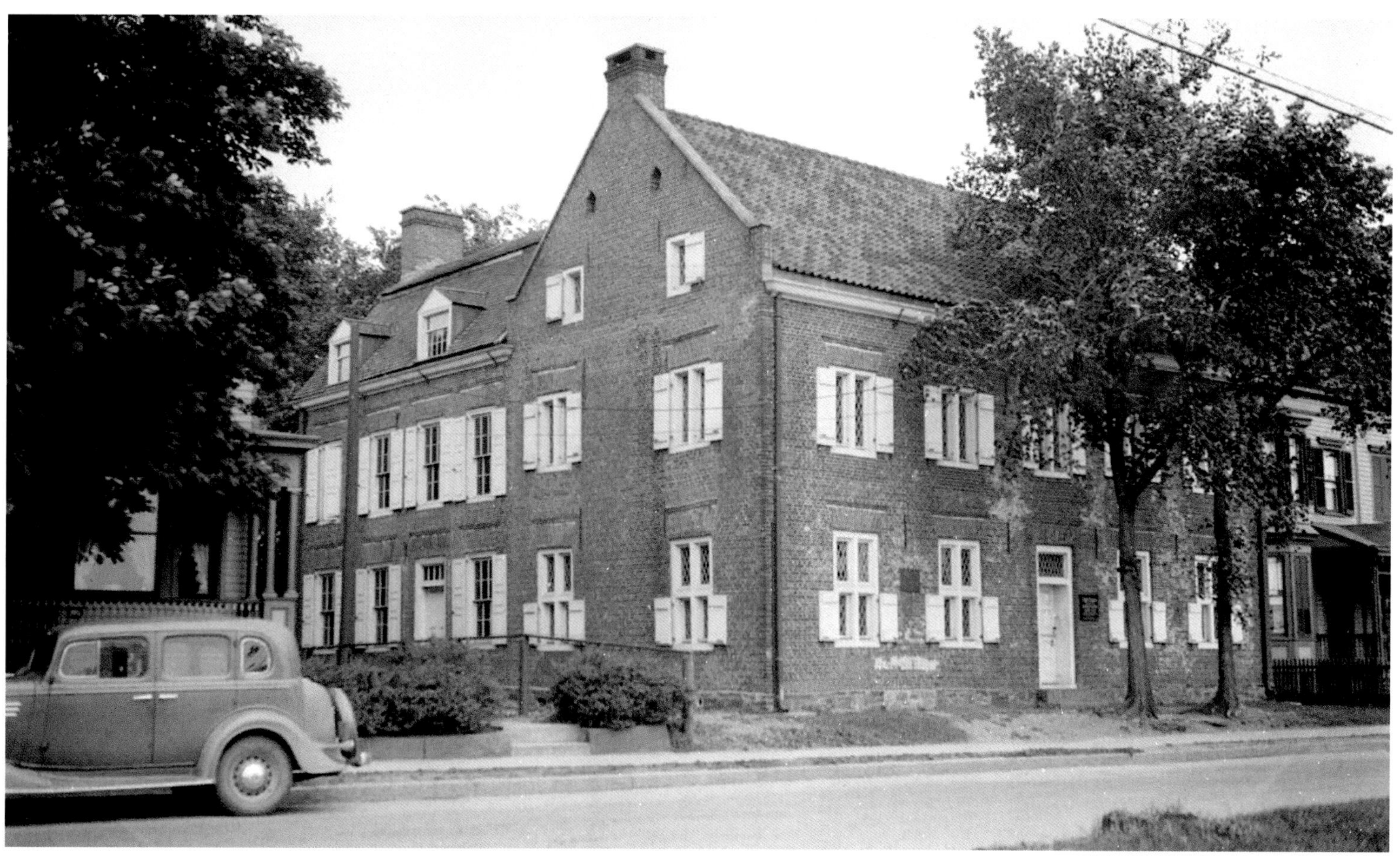

This is Fort Crailo at 10 Riverside Drive in Rensselaer, around 1940. The lands surrounding the building were often used for military encampments during colonial times. Catherine Van Rensselaer, the wife of Major-General Philip Schuyler, was born and raised at Fort Crailo. Catherine's daughter, Elizabeth, became Mrs. Alexander Hamilton.

Following Spread: C. M. Stieglitz took this shot of Arthur Avenue and Crescent Avenue in the Bronx. As a destination for Italian food, Arthur Avenue, "the Little Italy of the Bronx," still rivals Little Italy in lower Manhattan. Many Italian families were attracted to this district, known as Belmont, by landscape and carpentry jobs created by the construction of the Bronx Zoo.

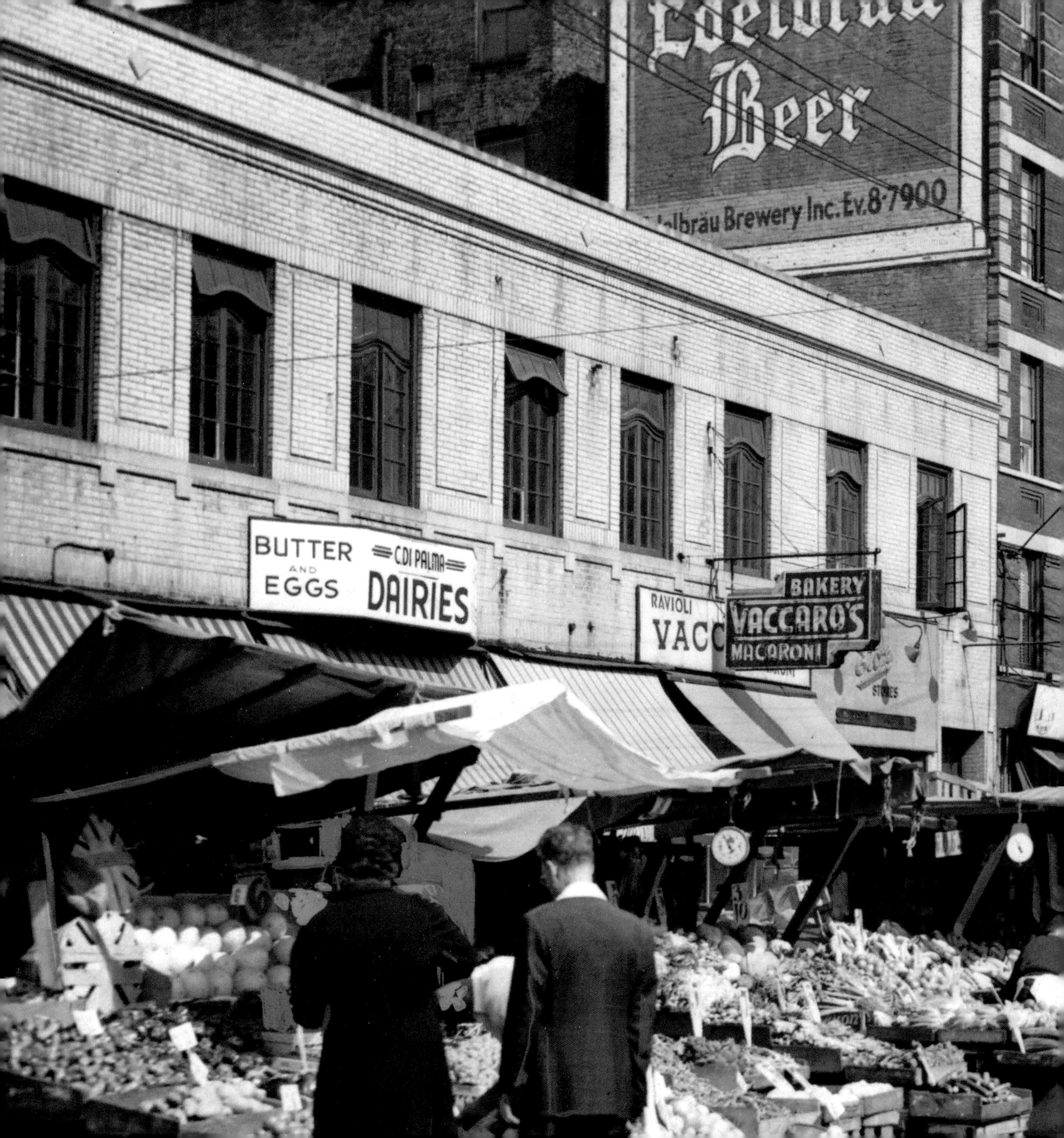
Beer
Brewery Inc. Ev. 8-7900
BUTTER AND EGGS
C. DI PALMA
DAIRIES
RAVIOLI
BAKERY
VACCARO'S
MACARONI

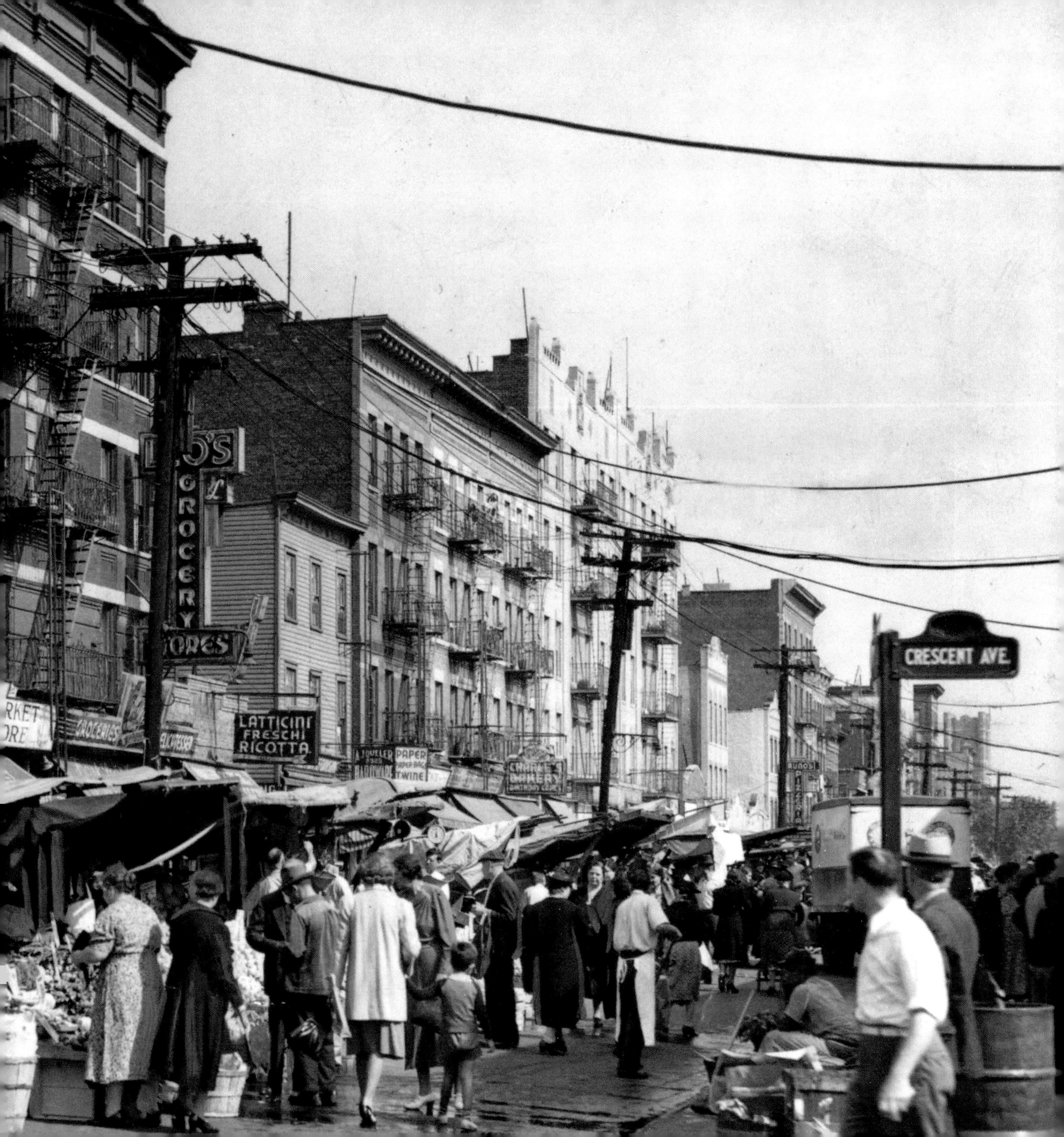

GROCERY
LATTICINI
FRESCHI
RICOTTA.
GROCERIES
PAPER
TWINE
BAKERY
CRESCENT AVE.

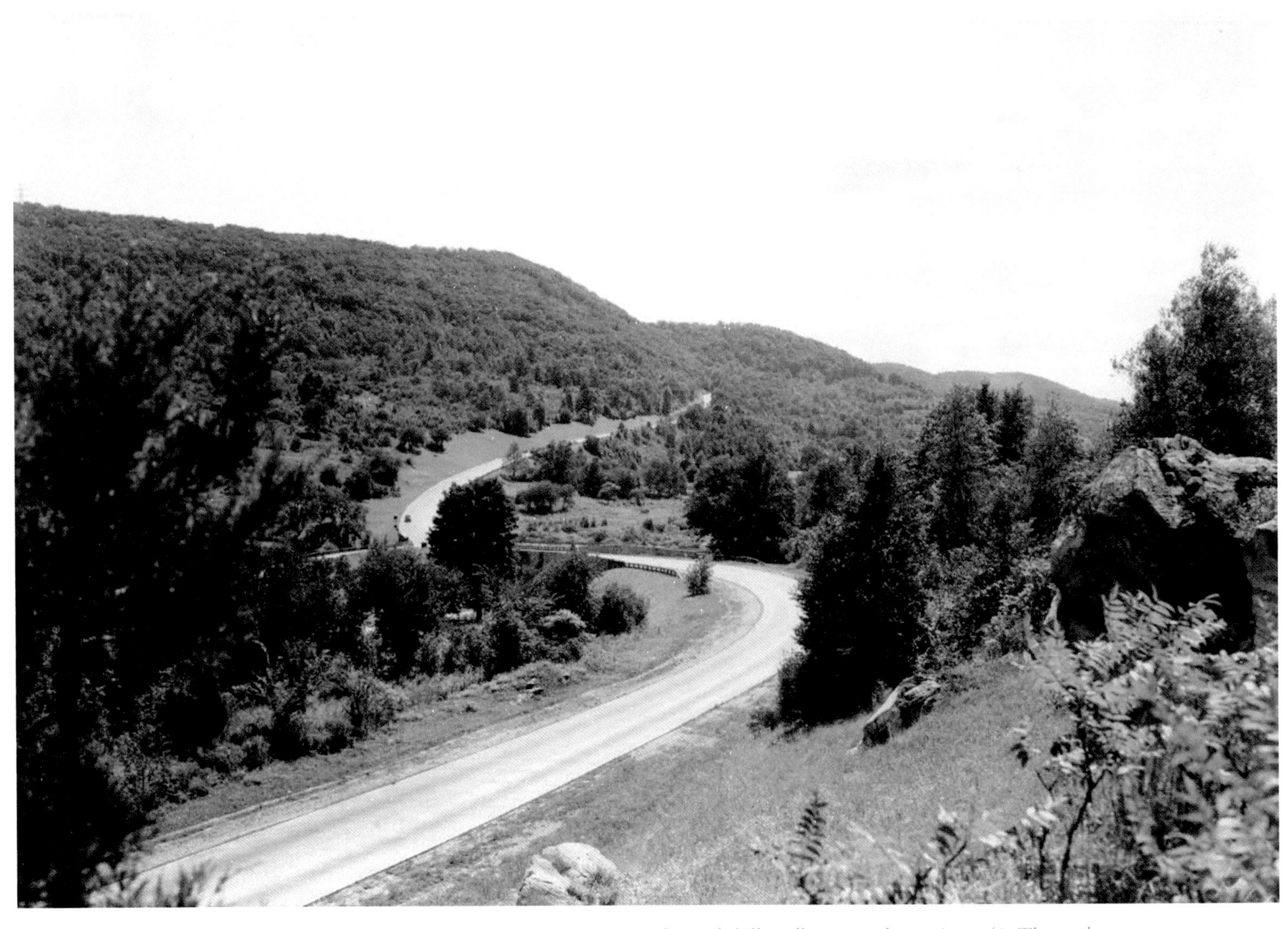

The Taconic State Parkway reached Peekskill Hollow Road in 1933. Here is the Peekskill Hollow interchange in 1940. The parkway was proposed by Robert Moses as a scenic and speedy way for New Yorkers to gain access to the newly built Bear Mountain Bridge. It was also to become a direct, convenient route to Albany.

THE WAR YEARS AND POSTWAR ERA

(1941–1960s)

World War II jump-started economic recovery, alleviating unemployment that in New Deal 1939 was still raging nationwide at 17 percent, and the United States emerged from the world conflict with undisputed economic preeminence. New York City continued its role as a mecca of finance, media, and the arts. Now colleges and universities in the river towns expanded as postwar affluence brought increased numbers of residents seeking higher degrees. Along the Hudson, local factories retooled for a new wave of consumer demand, and working families packed the family car for their first real vacation.

In transportation, the New York State Thruway became a new competitor of the Hudson Line, and the Tappan Zee Bridge now crossed the Hudson River at one of its widest points. The Hudson River Railroad and its parent, the New York Central, began to lose ground after four decades of great financial success, a situation aggravated by the automobile, trucking companies, and the airlines. Government was to take control of the line in the 1970s.

After the prosperity and promise of the 1950s, the times gave way to heightened racial tensions and a new sense of social conflict. In Yonkers, the largest Hudson River city after New York, plant closures and declining real estate values created large pockets of unemployment, followed by a steady rise of illegal drugs and violent crime. This scenario was mirrored on a much greater scale in New York City itself, where racial tensions had been mounting since the Harlem riots of 1964.

The late sixties also saw a new trend in social policies and outlook that placed greater value on regional historic legacies. The sloop *Clearwater* was an emblem of a movement to reclaim the Hudson River in the coming, post-industrial period, and the Hudson River Fishermen's Association and the Riverkeeper went beyond symbolism by successfully suing large river polluters. The larger river towns began to assess the value of their historic districts and place new value on their regional legacies, creating a kind of Renaissance on the Hudson. In the twenty-first century, communities are confronting new issues of large-scale waterfront residential development and riverfront preservation and access.

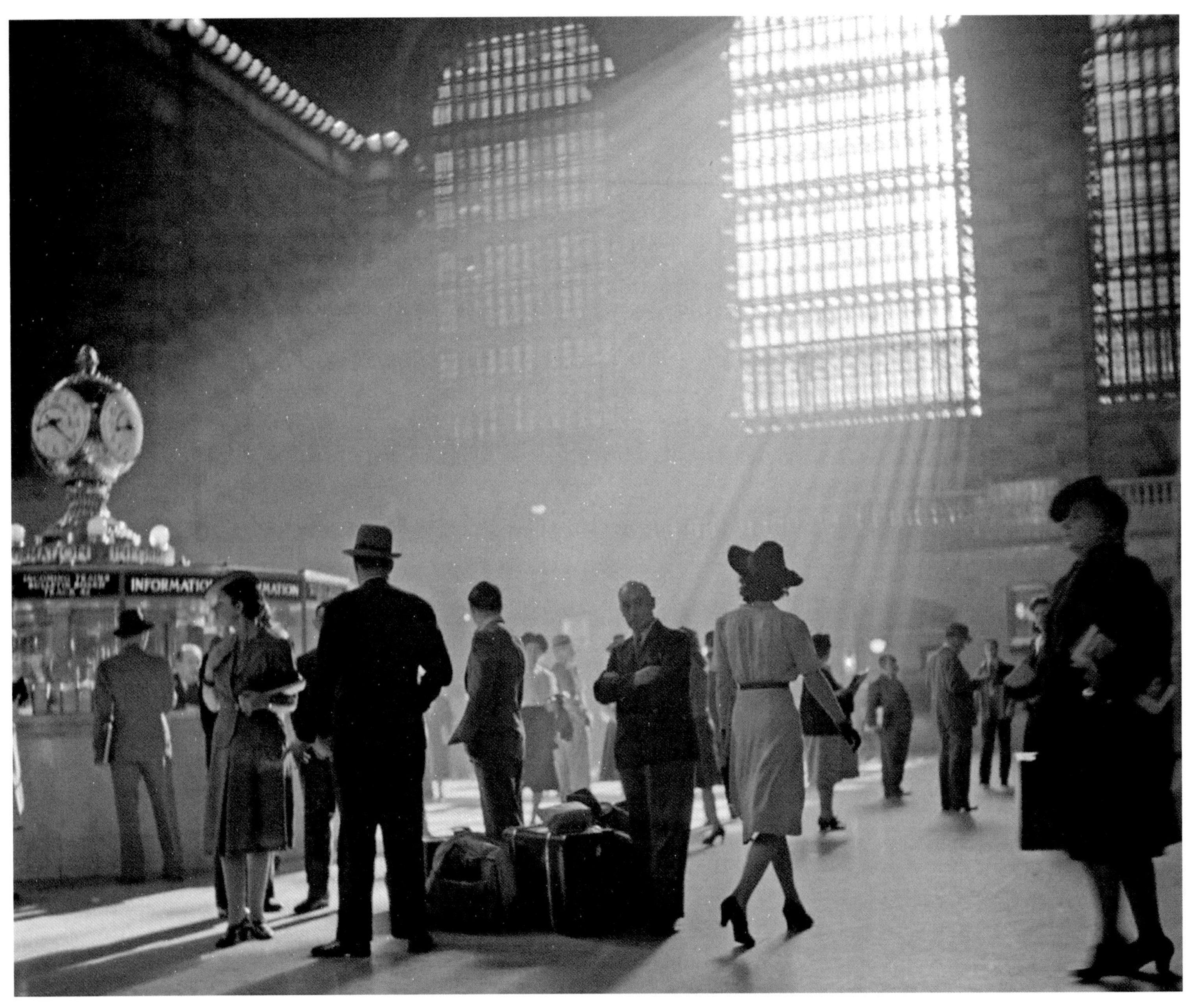

An iconic and evocative image of Grand Central Terminal was created by photographer John Collier (1913–1992) in 1941. Collier is associated with his work in rural New Mexico—geographically and thematically remote from these New Yorkers at the terminal's main information booth.

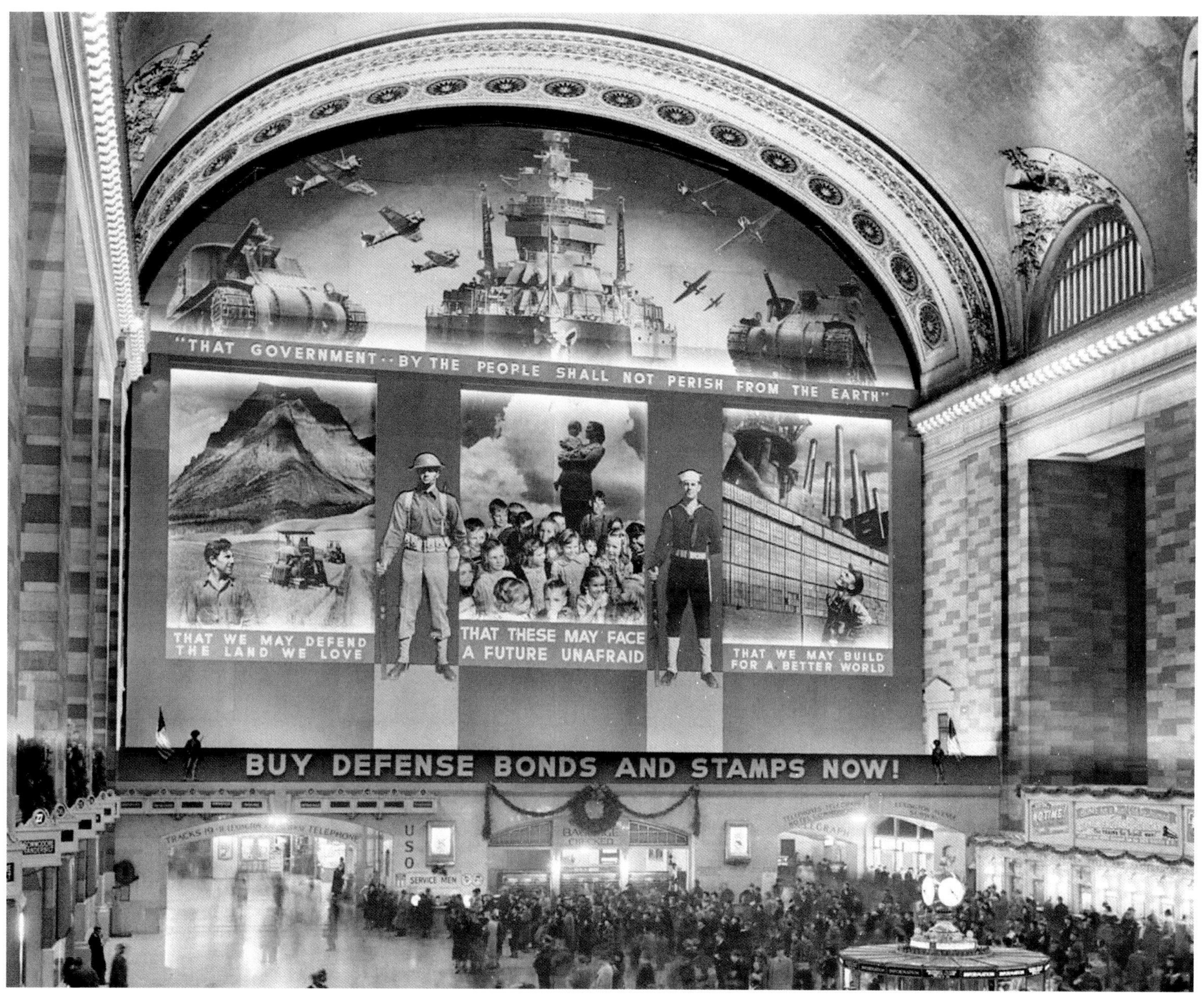

The grandeur of Grand Central is seen here on the eve of war in 1941. The photograph is by Arthur Rothstein (1915–1985), a photographer better known for his Great Depression images of America's rural poor. The Farm Security Administration for which Rothstein worked created the War Bond display seen here.

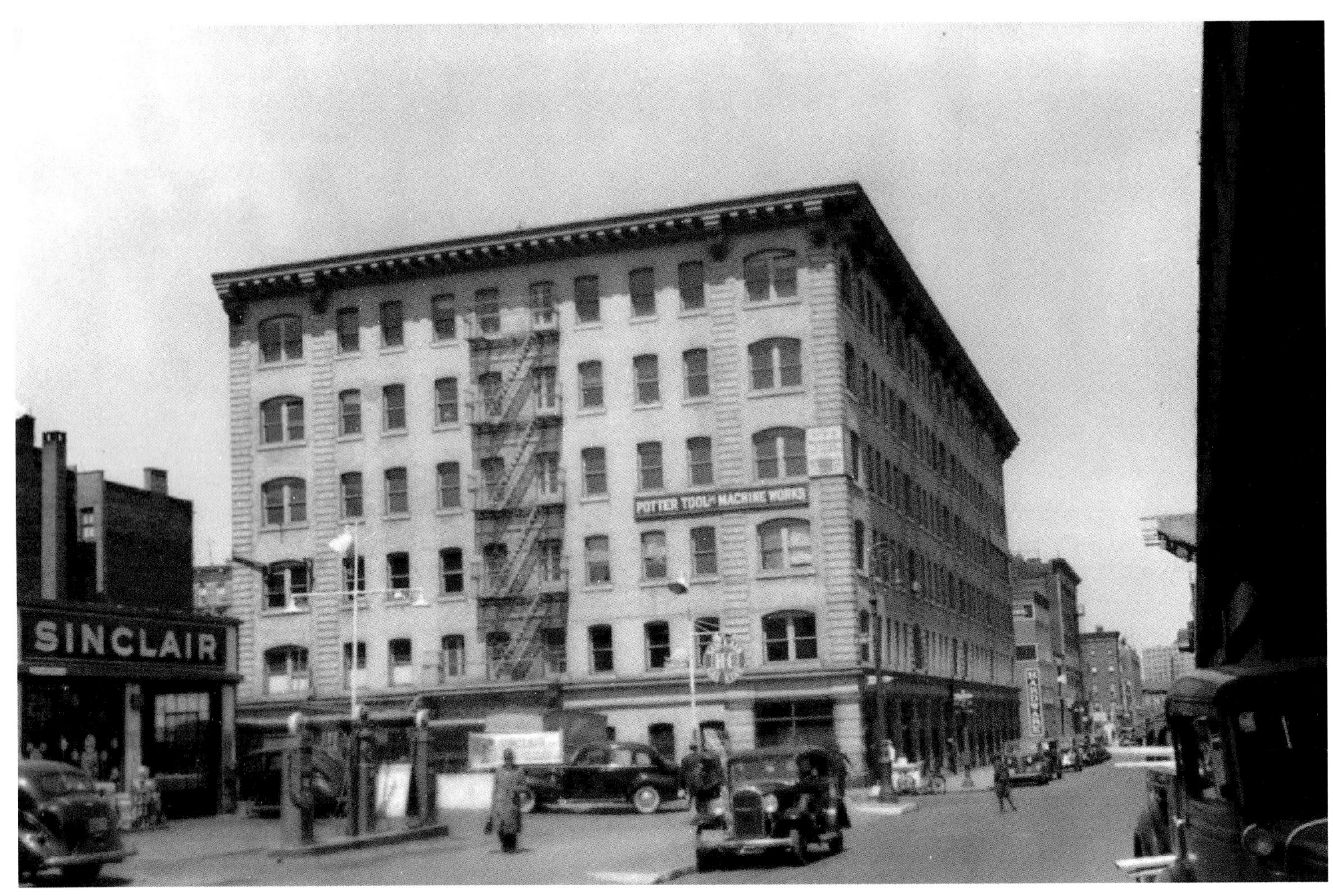

Percy Loomis Sperr photographed the corner of Park Avenue and 136th Street in the Bronx here in 1941. A gas station and an apartment building are pictured near the south end of the Grand Concourse. Sperr's streetscapes examine the city's buildings and infrastructure.

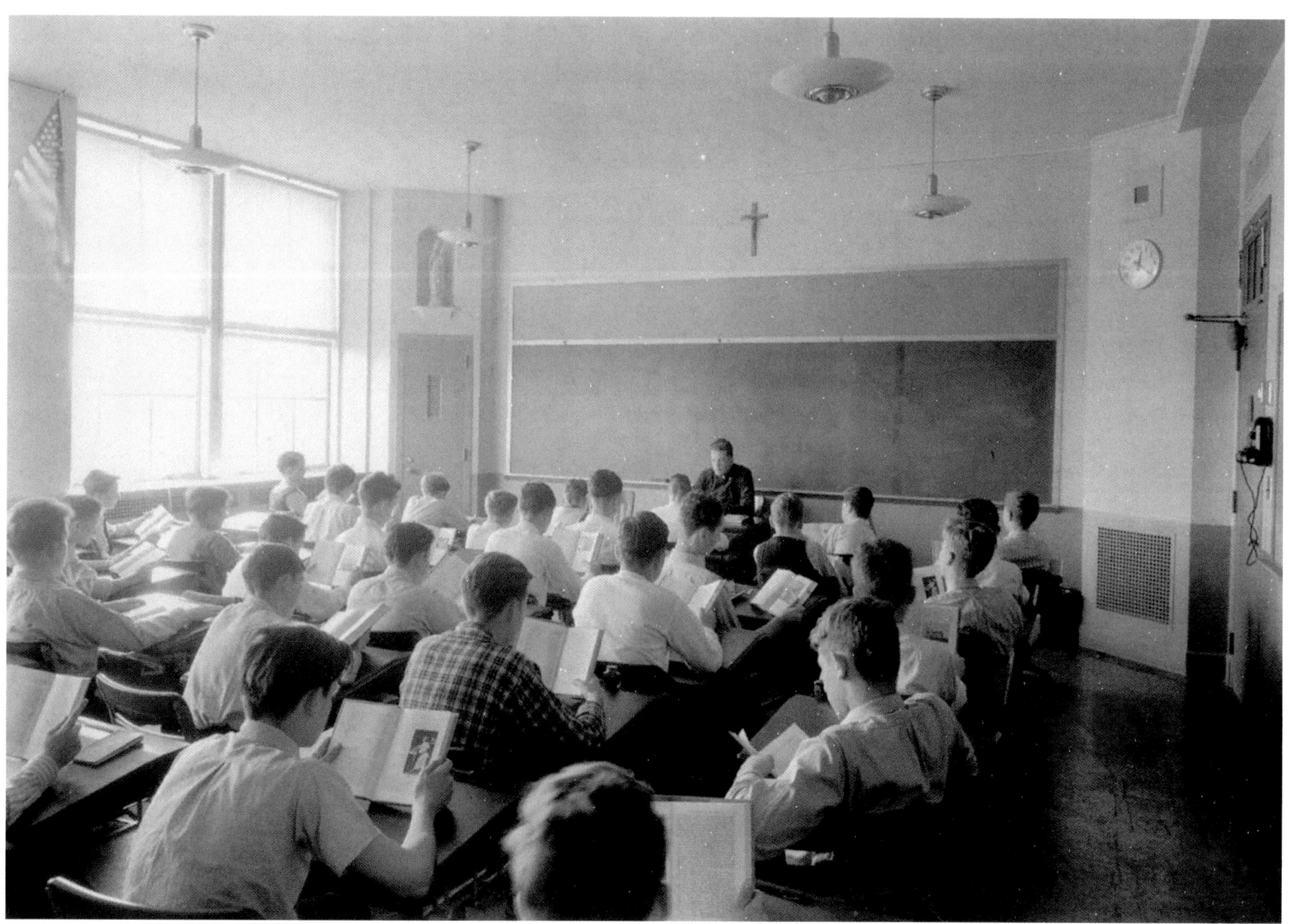

The architectural firm of Eggers and Higgins designed Cardinal Hayes Memorial High School on the Bronx's Grand Concourse. Here is a classroom in the all-boys high school, completed in 1941. Cardinal Patrick Hayes (1867–1938) was the archbishop of New York, and the school was the brainchild of his successor, Cardinal Francis Spellman (1889–1967). Before construction, its odd-shaped lot was home to a gas station and some cabins.

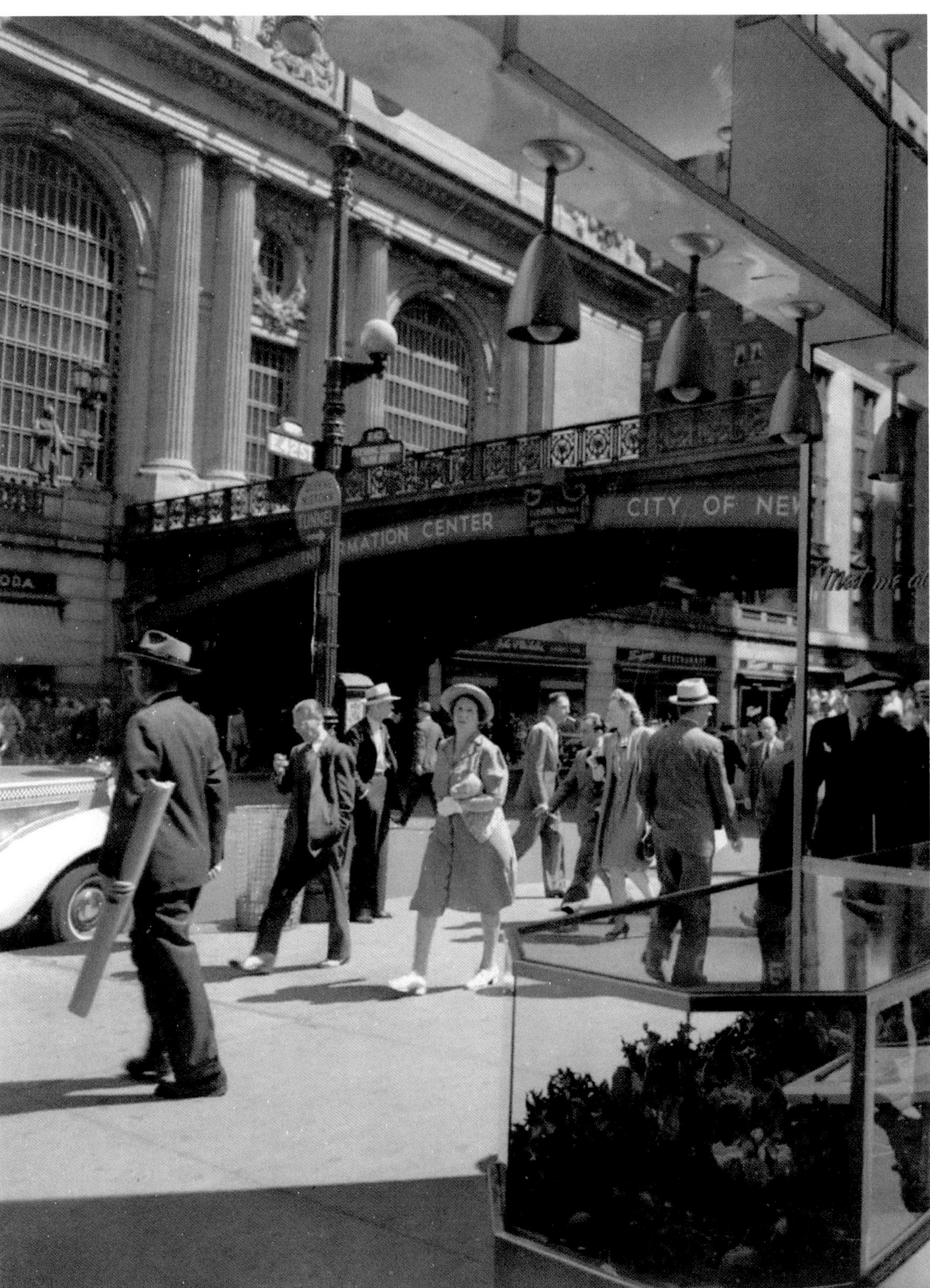

Pedestrian traffic opposite Grand Central Terminal on 42nd Street. Marjory Collins (1912–1985) took the photograph in 1942. Collins was a freelance photographer working for the Farm Security Administration alongside Arthur Rothstein, Dorothea Lange, and other well-known photographers of the era.

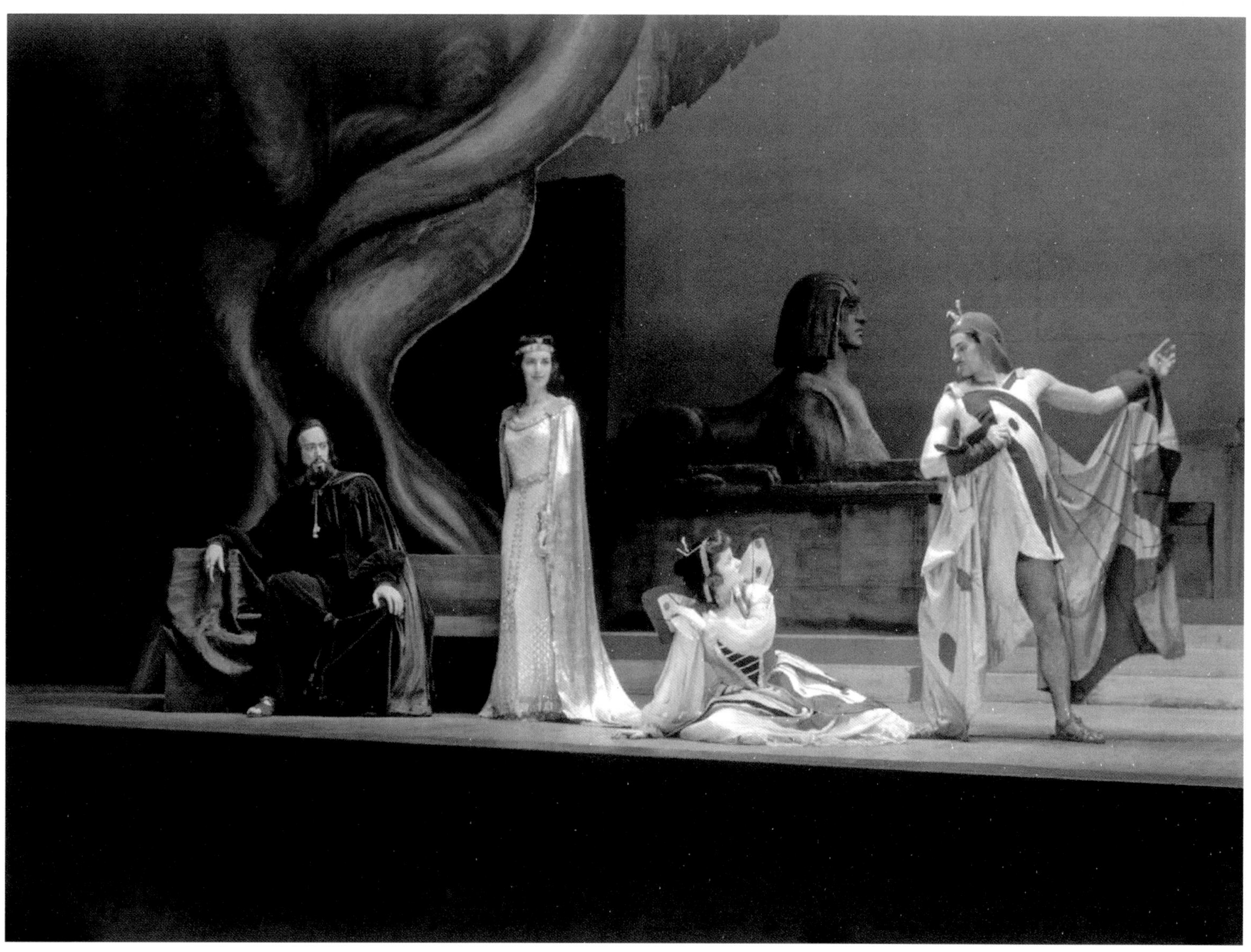

In 1931, Sergei Rachmaninoff gave a concert to celebrate the opening of the Juilliard School of Music's new home at 130 Claremont Avenue, in the Morningside Heights district of Manhattan. Eleven years later, this production of the opera *Solomon* was performed at the school. Juilliard was first located near Riverside Church and Union Theological Seminary, but would later move to Lincoln Center.

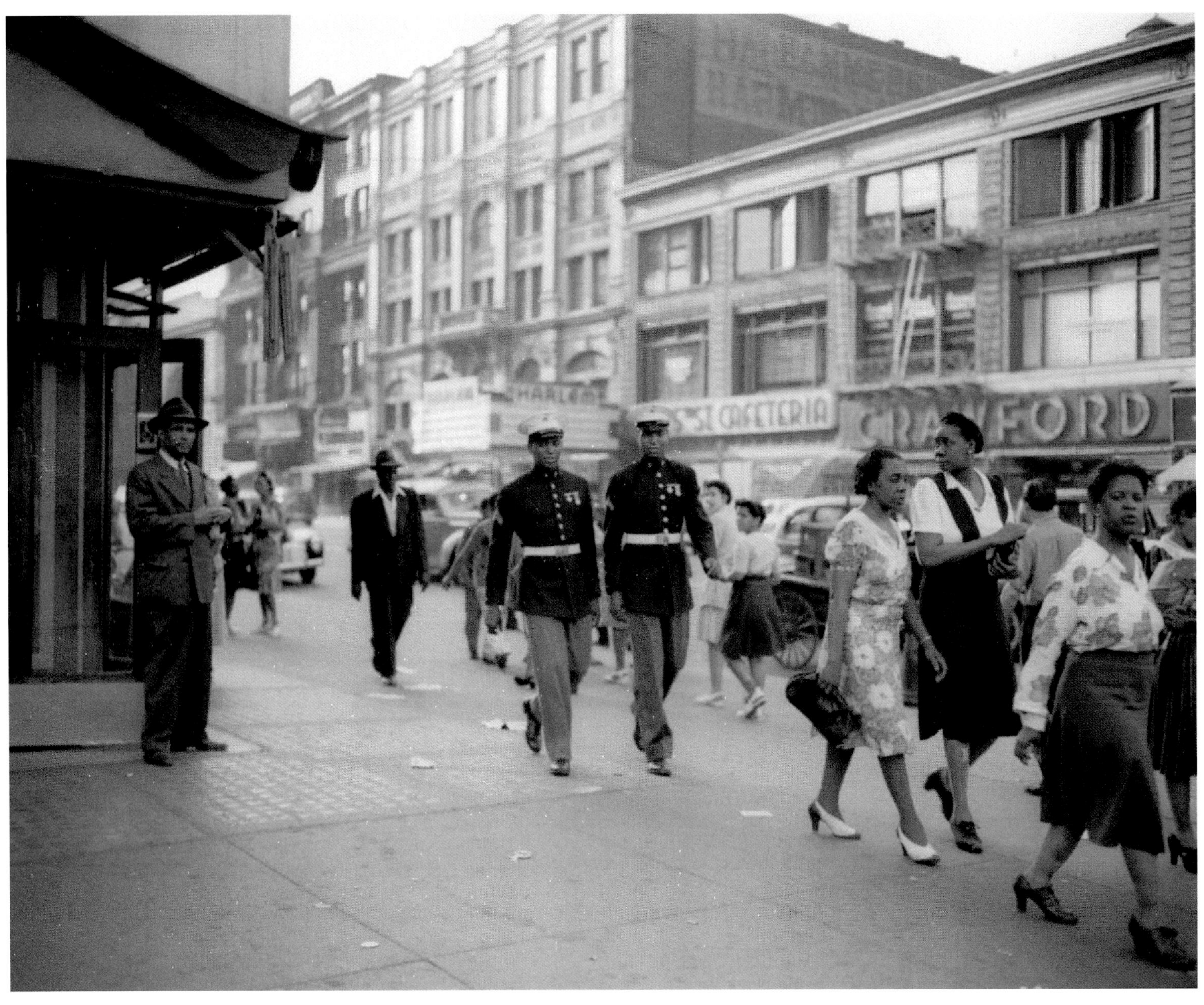

Two servicemen stroll on Harlem's 125th Street in 1943. The first waves of African-American migration to the district arrived in the first decade of the twentieth century. World War II stimulated a new wave of southern, African-American migration to New York.

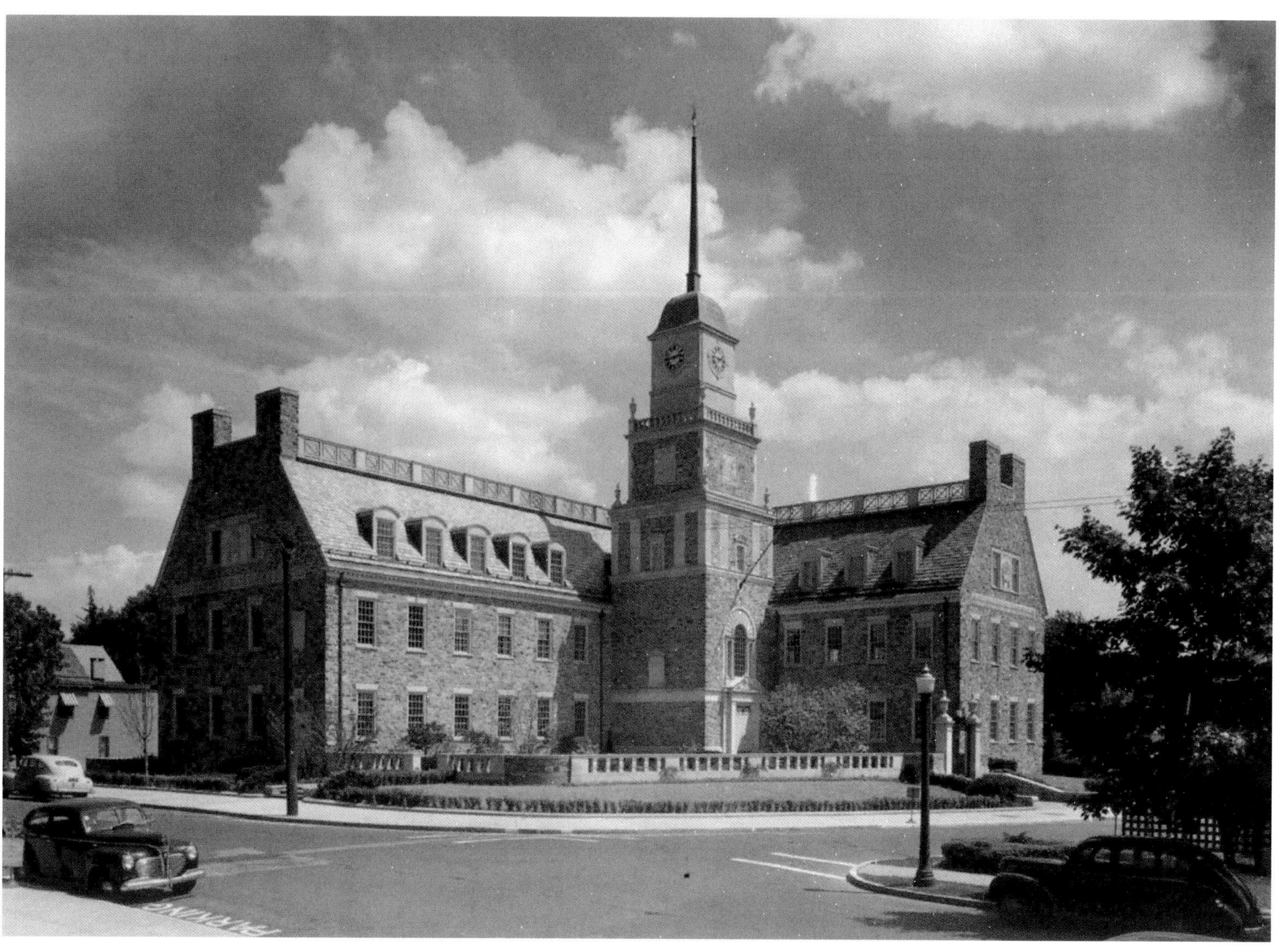

Eugene Benham designed the Poughkeepsie New Yorker Building, seen here in 1943. Now named the Poughkeepsie Journal Building, it was built of fieldstone in a style that suggested the city's Dutch colonial past. The New Yorker Building is located at Market and Mansion streets and was built opposite a post office designed under the guidance of President Franklin D. Roosevelt.

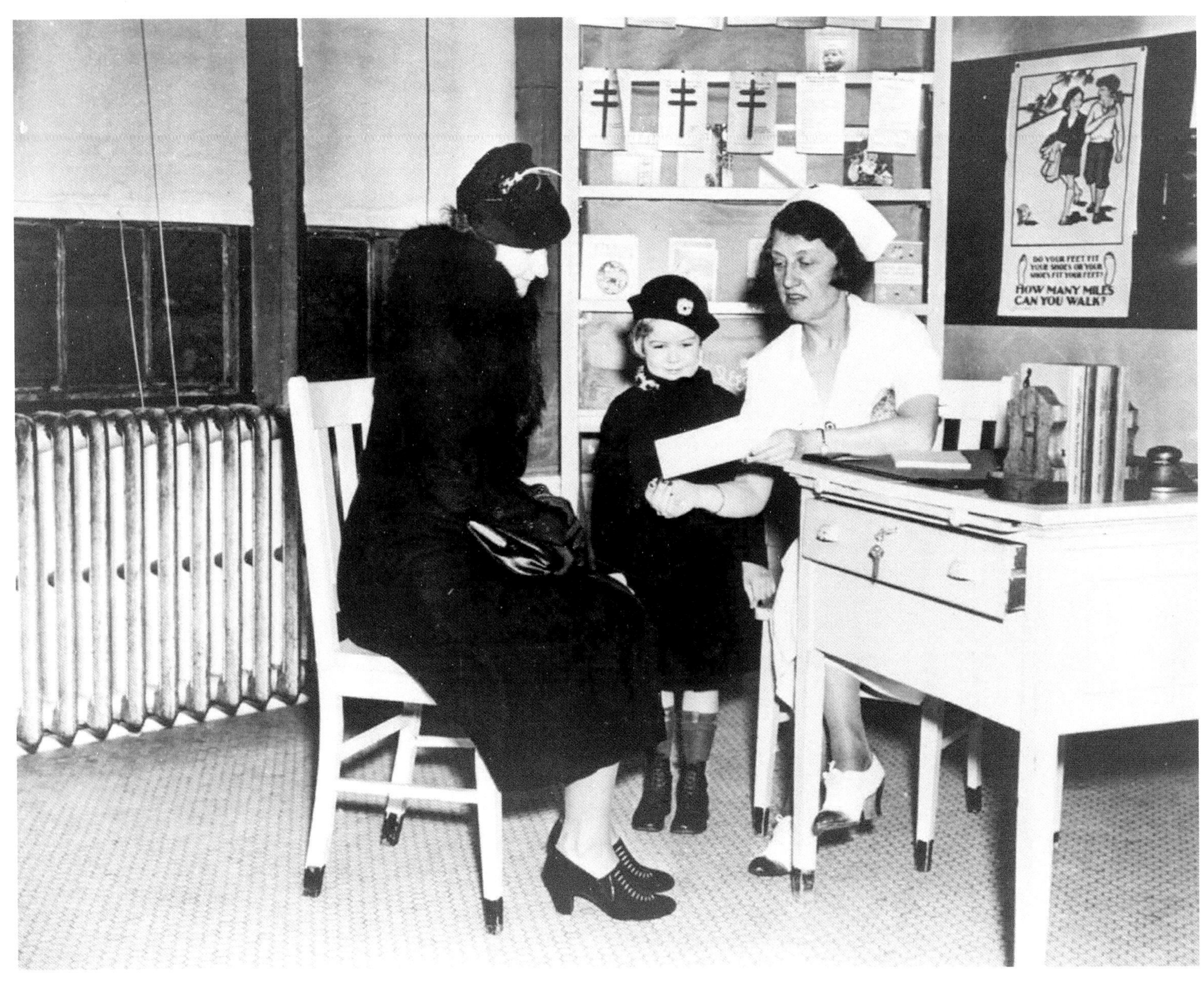

In Yonkers, around 1943, a girl and her mother are visiting the school nurse.

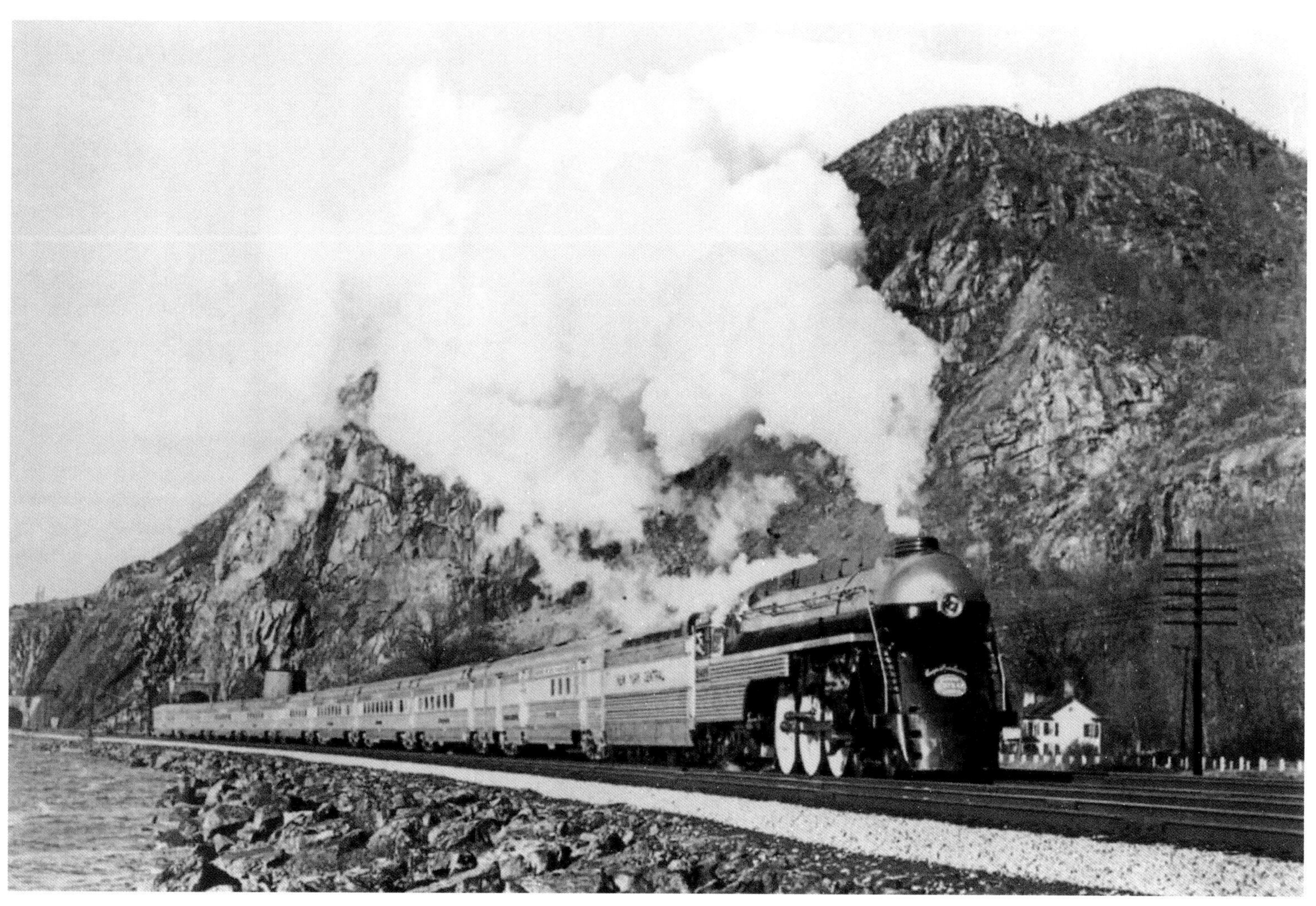

The speedy Empire State Express is seen here streaking along the banks of the Hudson River in the 1940s. In 1891, it became the world's first high-speed passenger train when it ran from New York to Buffalo averaging more than 60 miles an hour.

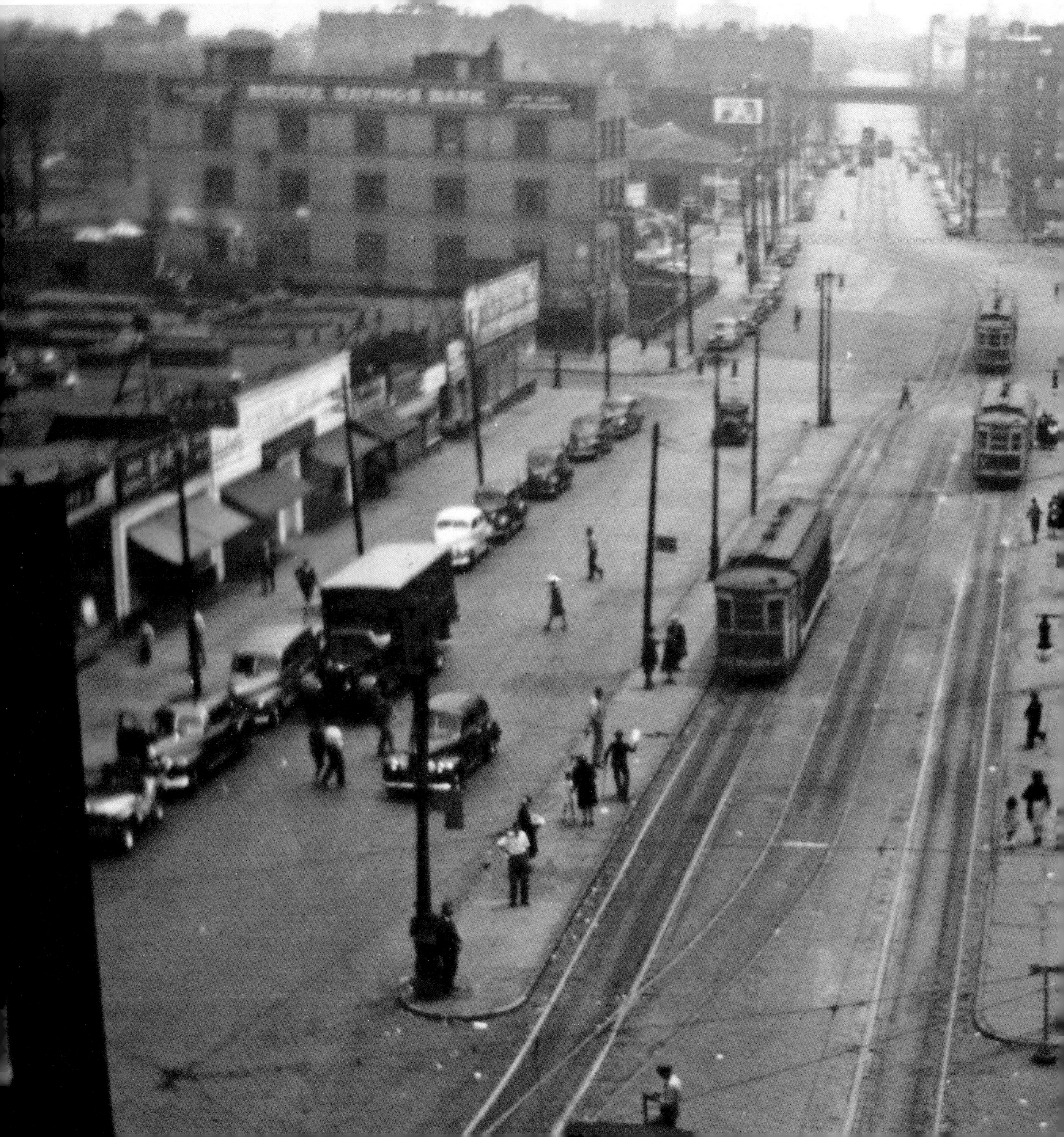
BRONX SAVINGS BANK

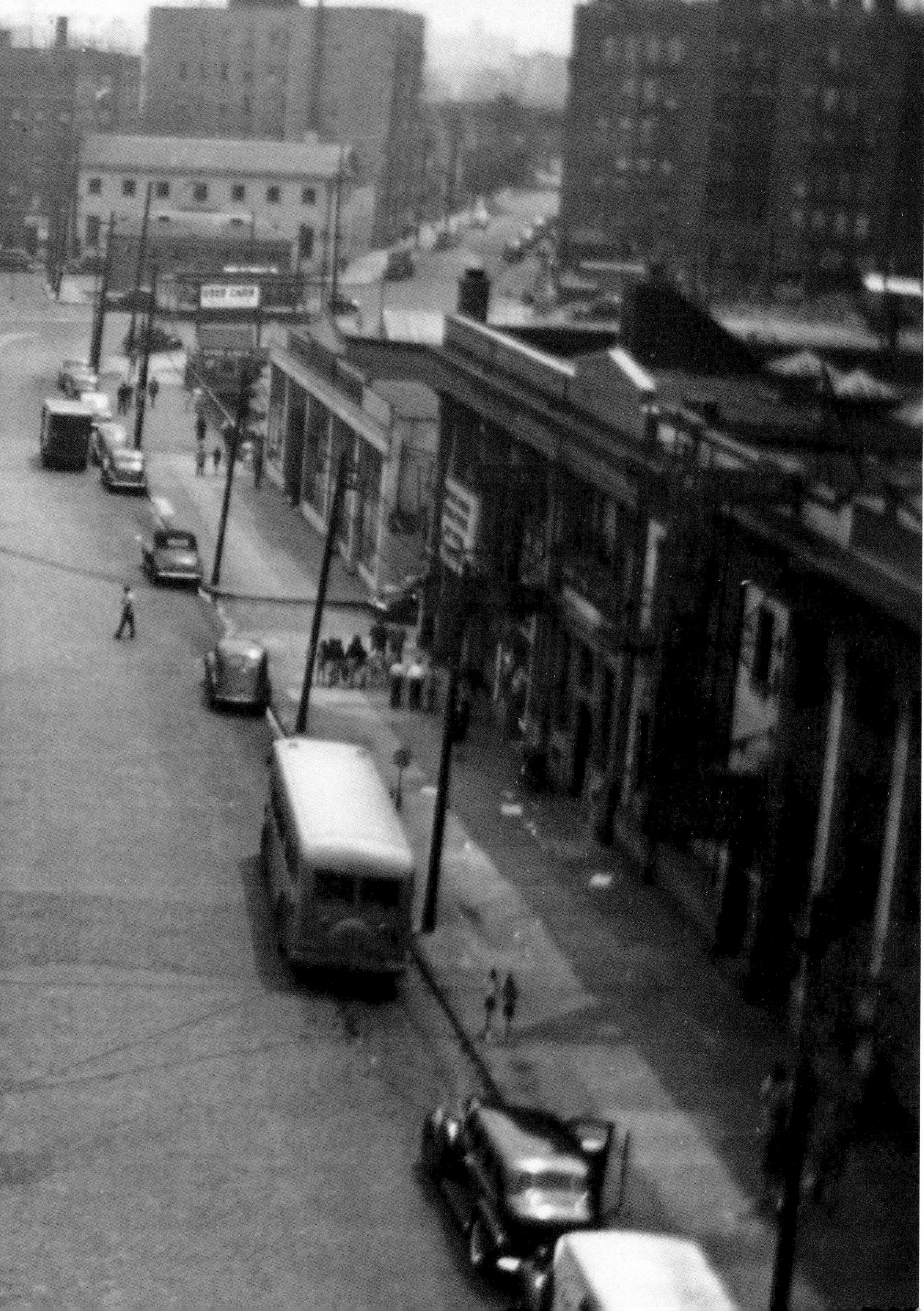

West Farms was an old colonial center that became a part of the Bronx when New York City consolidated. Situated to the east of the Harlem River, the community preserved its name as a section of the Bronx. In recent years, West Farms has been categorized as one of the poorest communities in America. This 1946 photo shows West Farms Square at 176th Street.

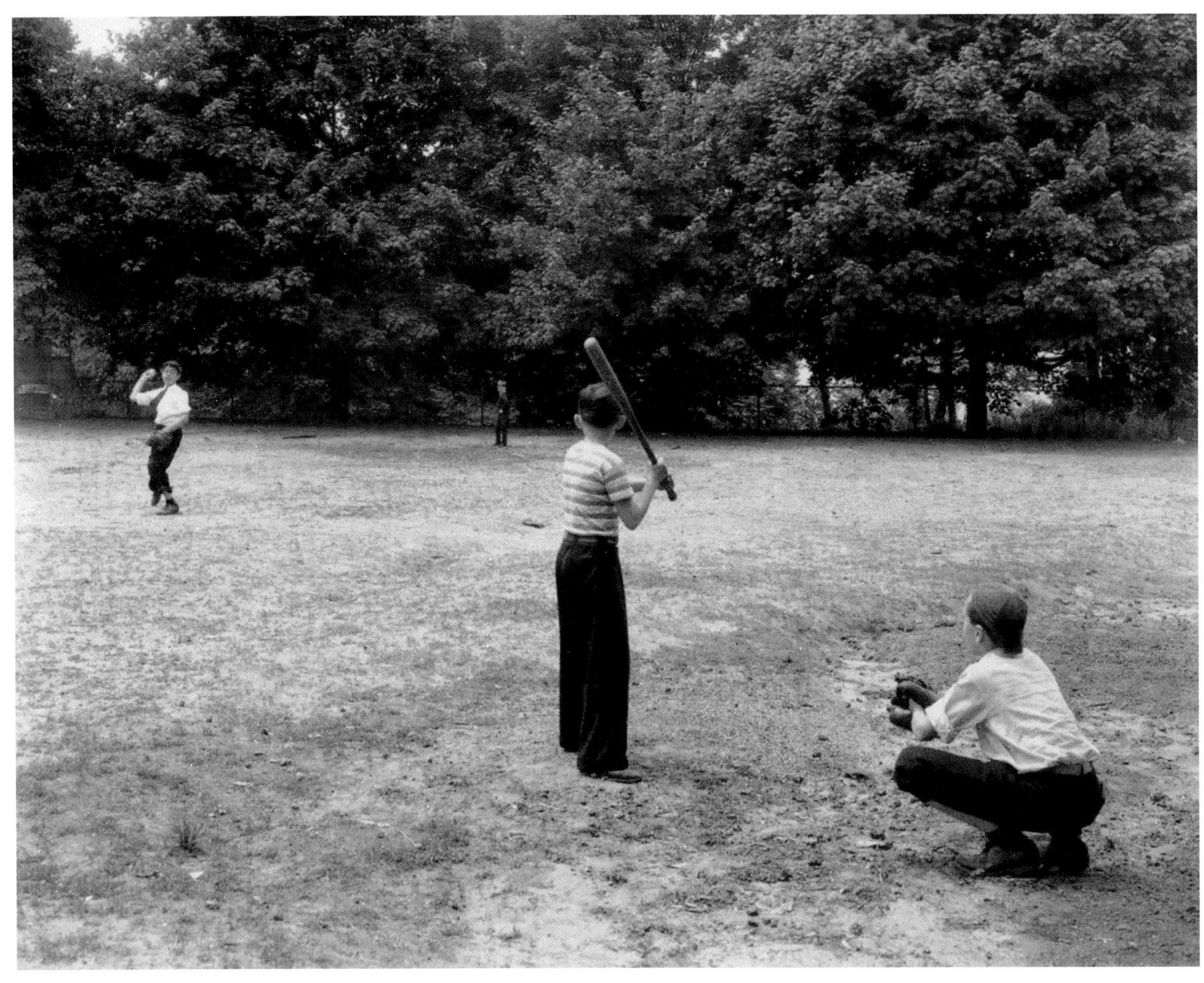

In the 1920s, Saint Vincent de Paul Institute moved to Tarrytown, assuming control of the Hudson River estate of John Archbold, following the death of the owner. Archbold was a president of the Standard Oil Company. Before Archbold, the estate belonged to William E. Dodge of the Phelps Dodge Company. Boys are seen here playing ball on the wide lawn in 1947.

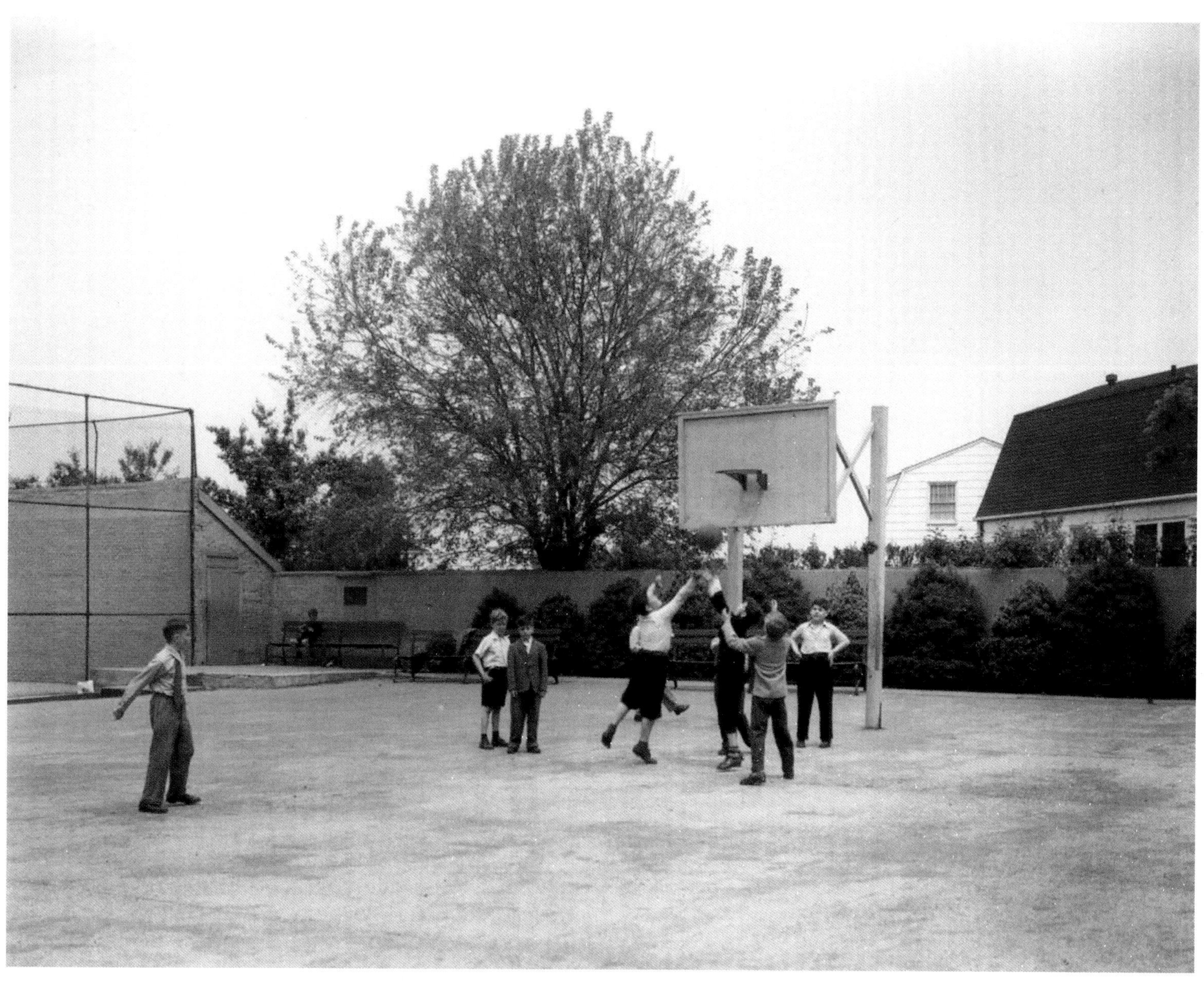

These boys are playing basketball at Saint Vincent de Paul Institute in Tarrytown in 1947. By 1980, the institute's 12 acres overlooking the Hudson had been bought by developers to build condominiums.

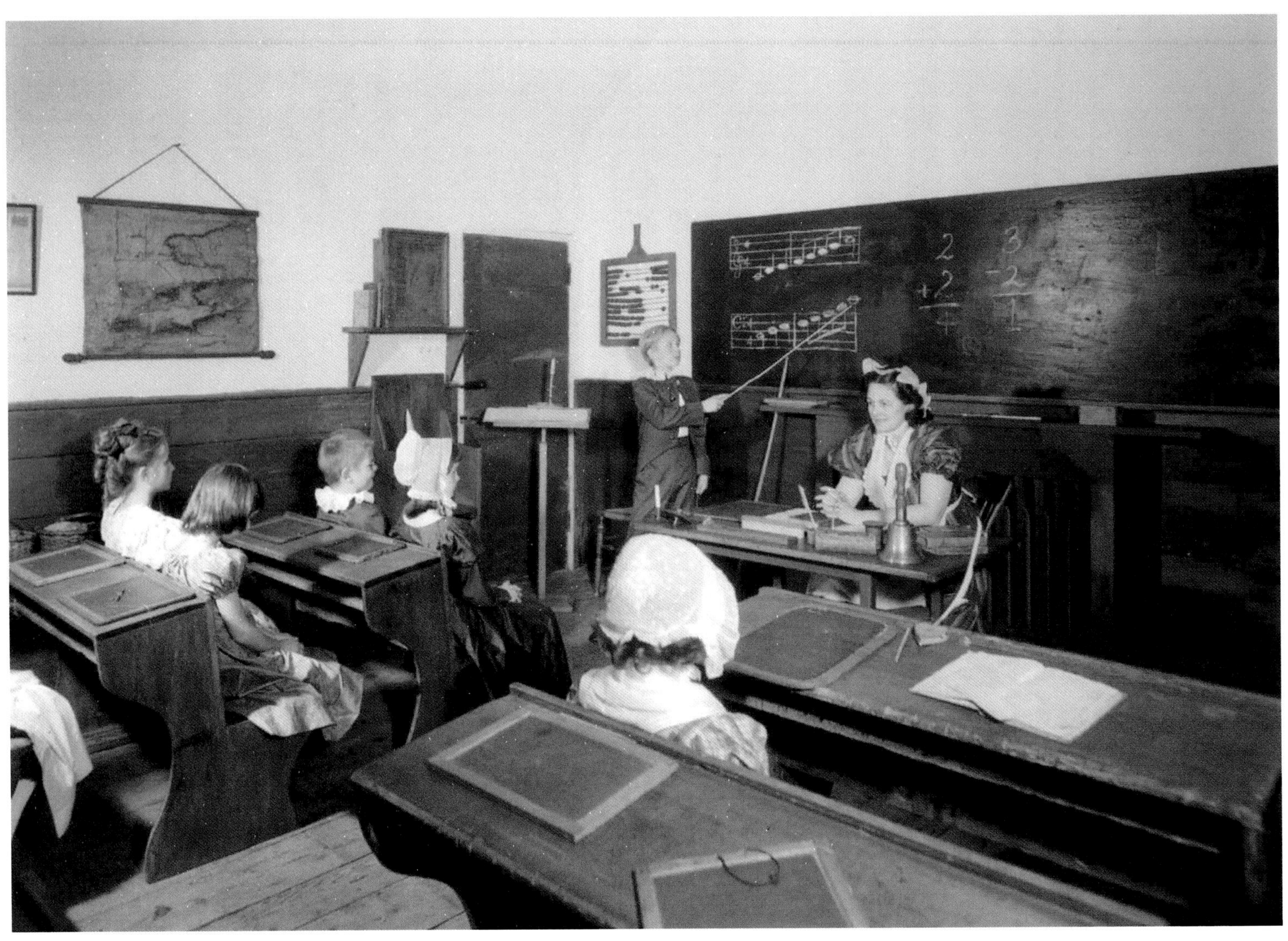

Heritage House was a Tarrytown educational site located near Prospect Avenue. This photo dates from 1947. Mrs. Lawrence J. Ullman is apparently teaching the class the musical scales, in a one-room schoolhouse that had been moved to Tarrytown from Connecticut. Period costume suggests that other subjects and events were planned for the day.

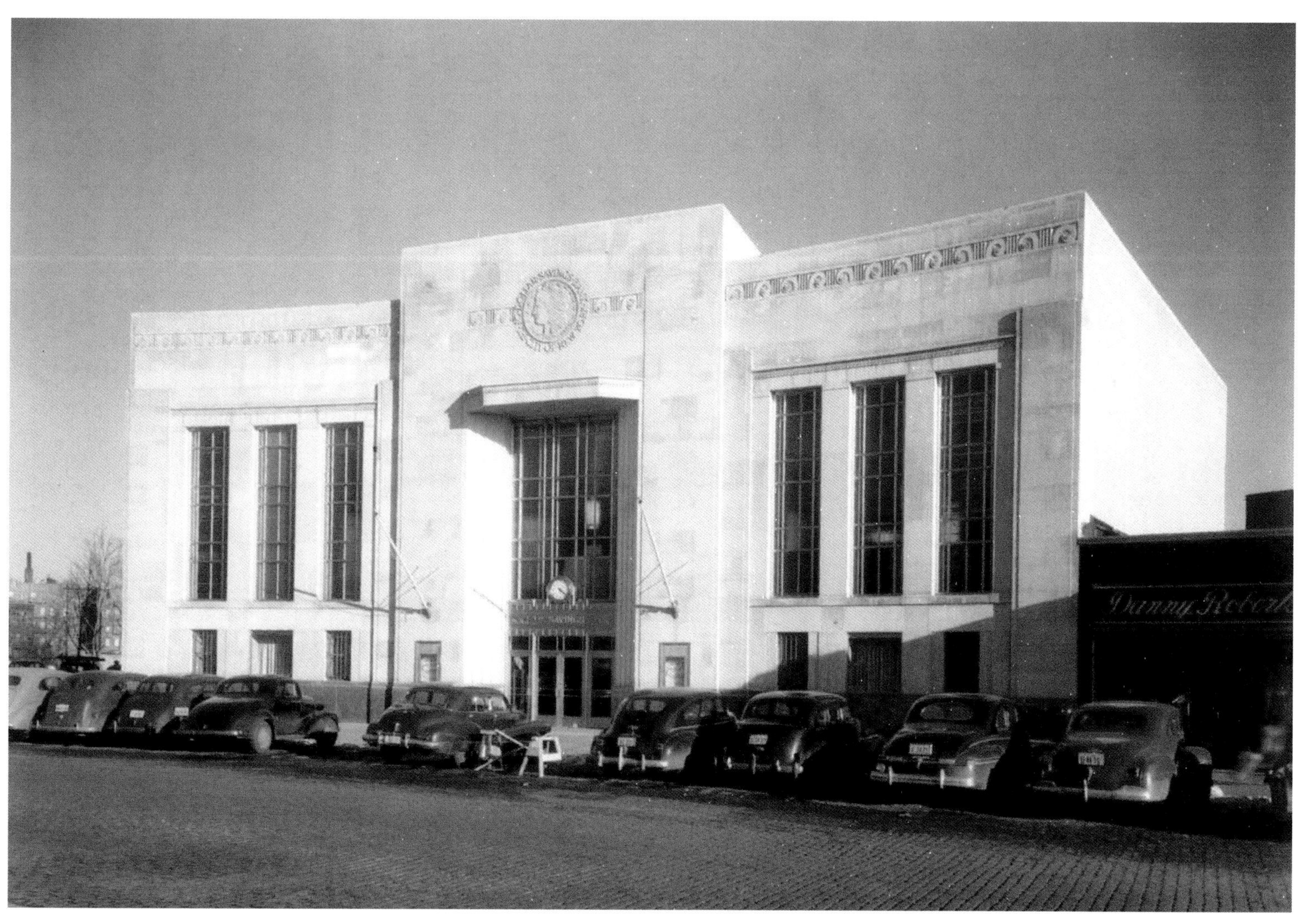

Parkchester is a residential neighborhood in the Bronx. In 1948, this photo was taken of the old Dollar Savings Bank, now a different bank. The Parkchester complex was built between 1939 and 1942 as a middle-class rental community. The area was beset with social problems in the mid to late twentieth century.

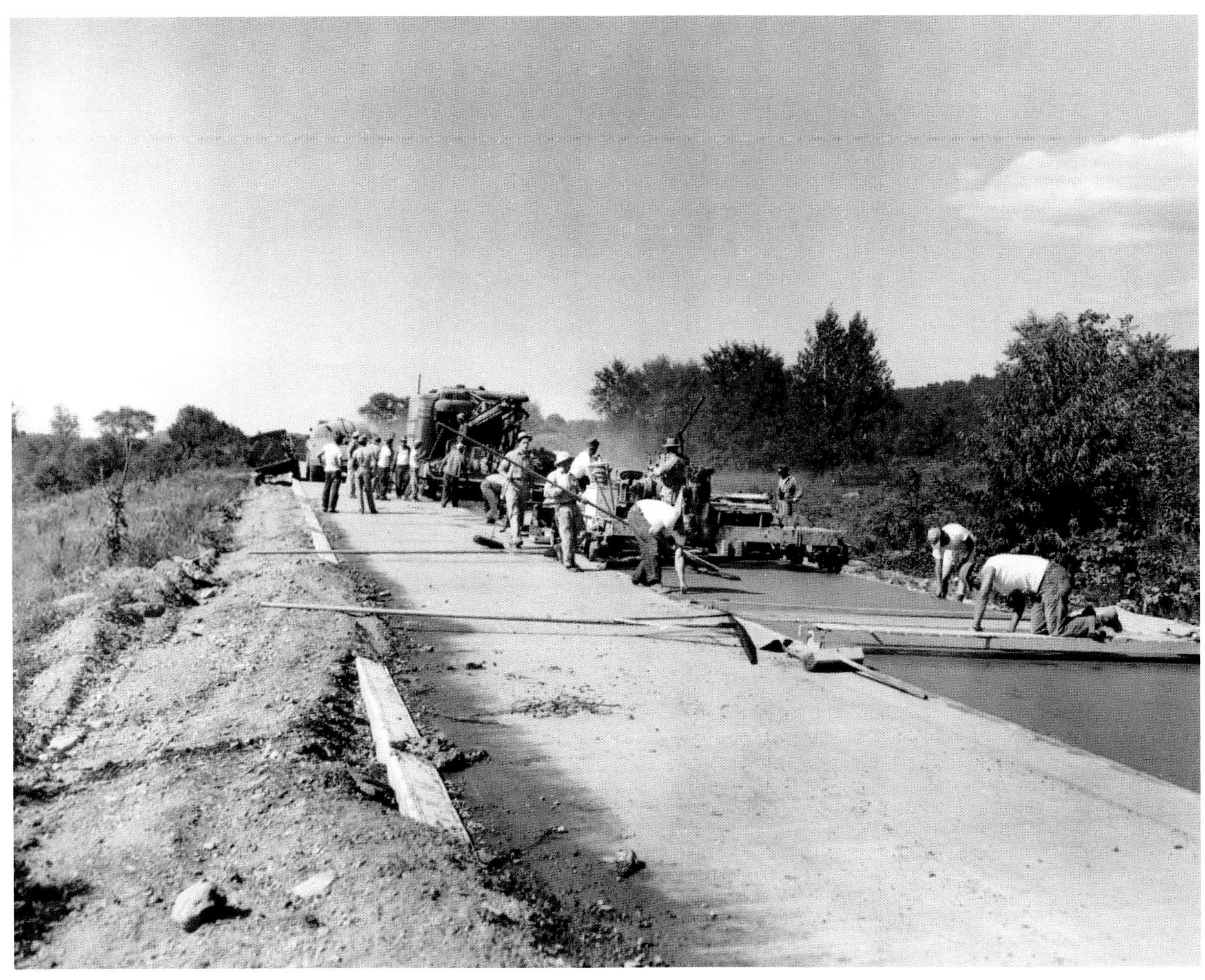

Here is a section of the Taconic State Parkway between Routes 55 and 199, as it is extended through Duchess County. The photograph is by David W. Haas. The parkway is considered to be one of the highest achievements of the parkway concept, combining sensitivity to terrain and speed.

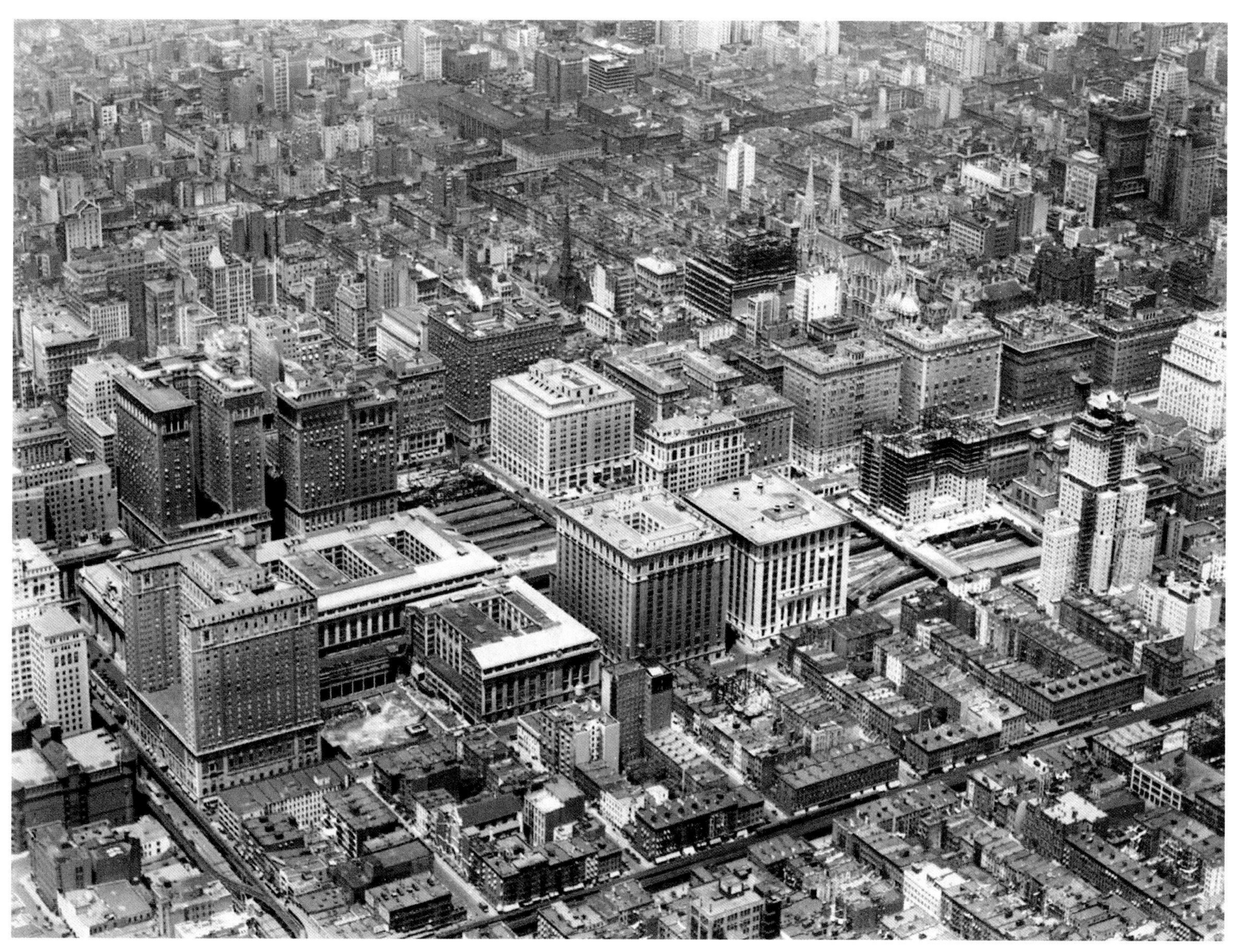

Many of these buildings are still standing, and many are not. This shot illustrates the great density of midtown Manhattan; today it is even more built-up, for many of the structures have been replaced with much larger ones. Grand Central Terminal can be seen (partially obstructed) to the lower left in this twentieth-century aerial photograph. The twin steeples of Saint Patrick's Cathedral are faintly visible at upper-right.

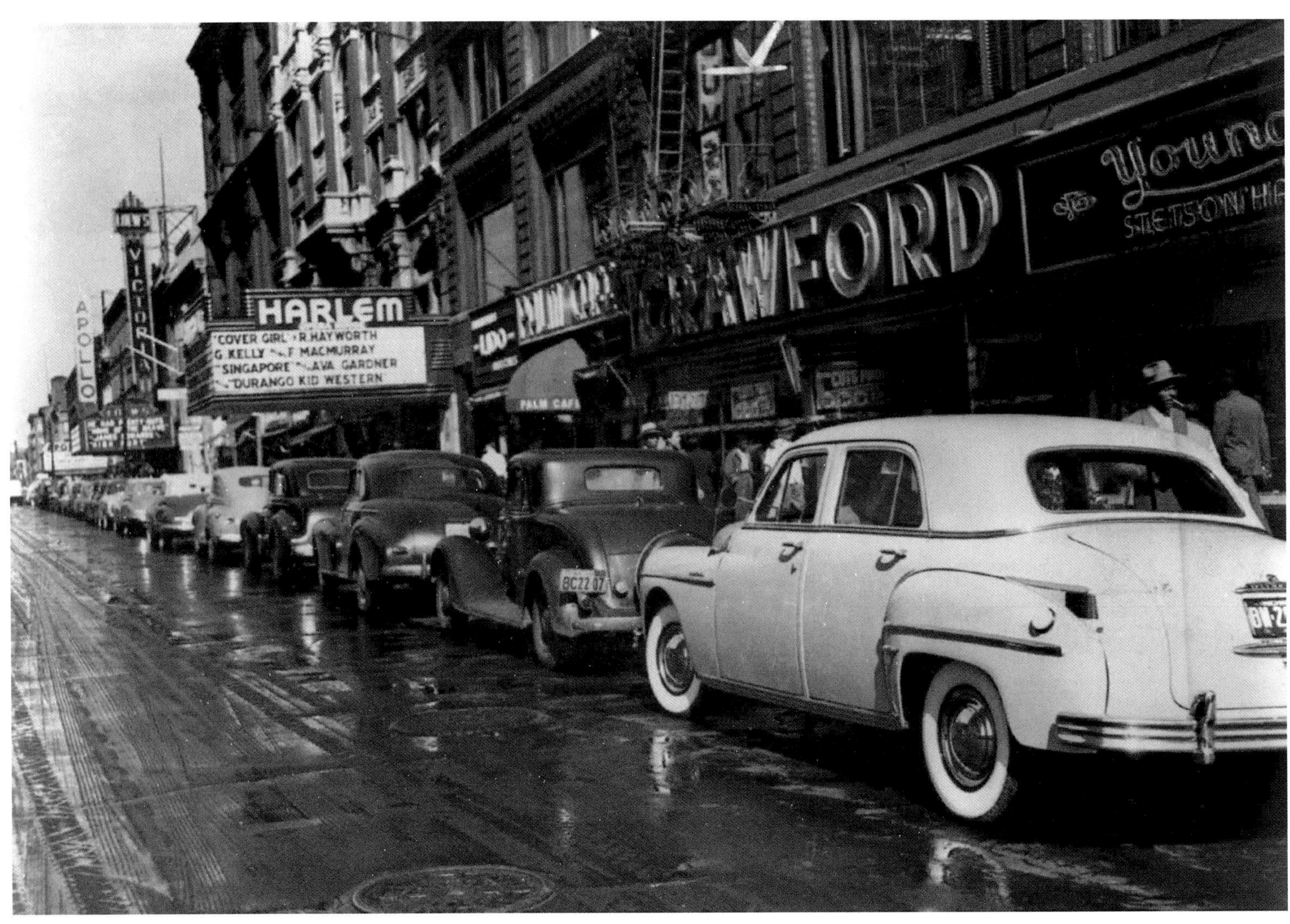

In 1889, Oscar Hammerstein I opened his first New York City opera house in Harlem. Early performers included the great Edwin Booth. The Harlem Opera House was joined by other theaters along 125th Street, including the famous Apollo, opened as a burlesque theater about 1914 and visible down the street in this 1949 photo. Harlem's economy was beset with challenges after World War II by the deindustrialization of Manhattan.

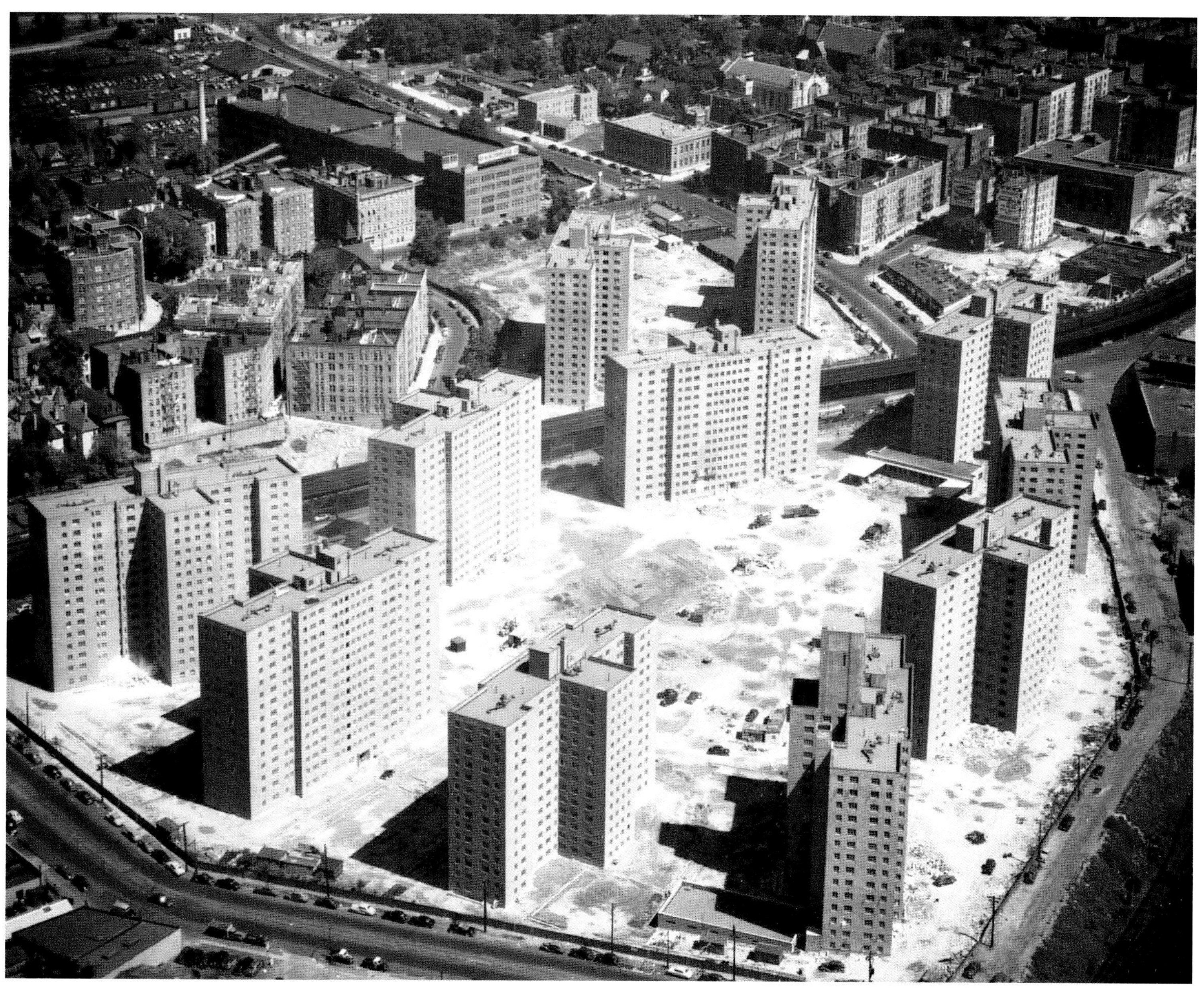

Located at Broadway and 225th Street and named for the stone that was quarried there, Marble Hill Houses was completed in 1952. The development, composed of 11 hi-rise buildings, was earmarked for public housing. Geographically and politically it is part of Manhattan, but was cut off from the island by the Harlem River Ship Canal. Spuyten Duyvil Creek was filled in during 1914, thus connecting Marble Hill with the Bronx.

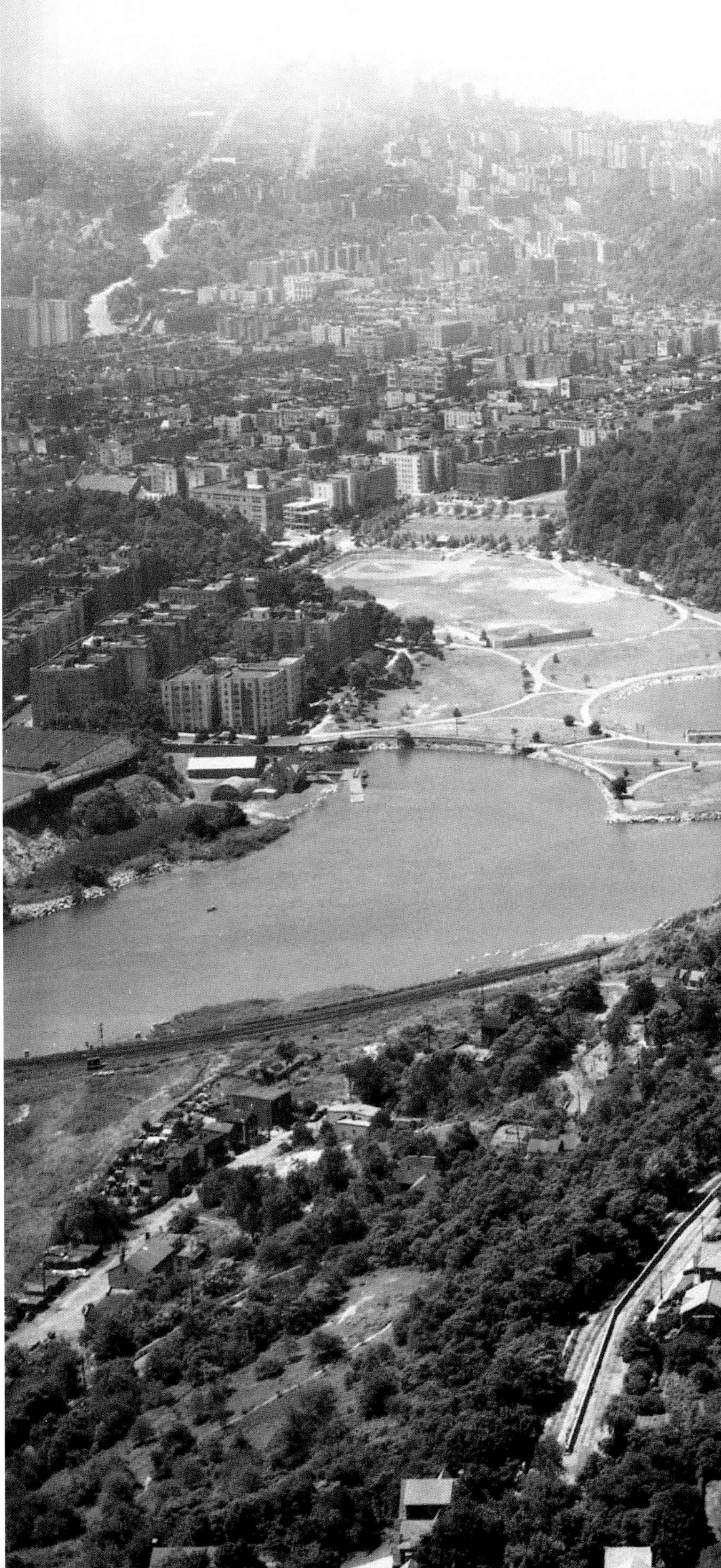

This aerial panorama shows the distant George Washington Bridge crossing the Hudson River to New Jersey. The Henry Hudson Bridge crosses the Harlem River on the right. Inwood Hill Park lies on the opposite shore in northern Manhattan. Streets of the Bronx are visible in the foreground of this 1951 photo.

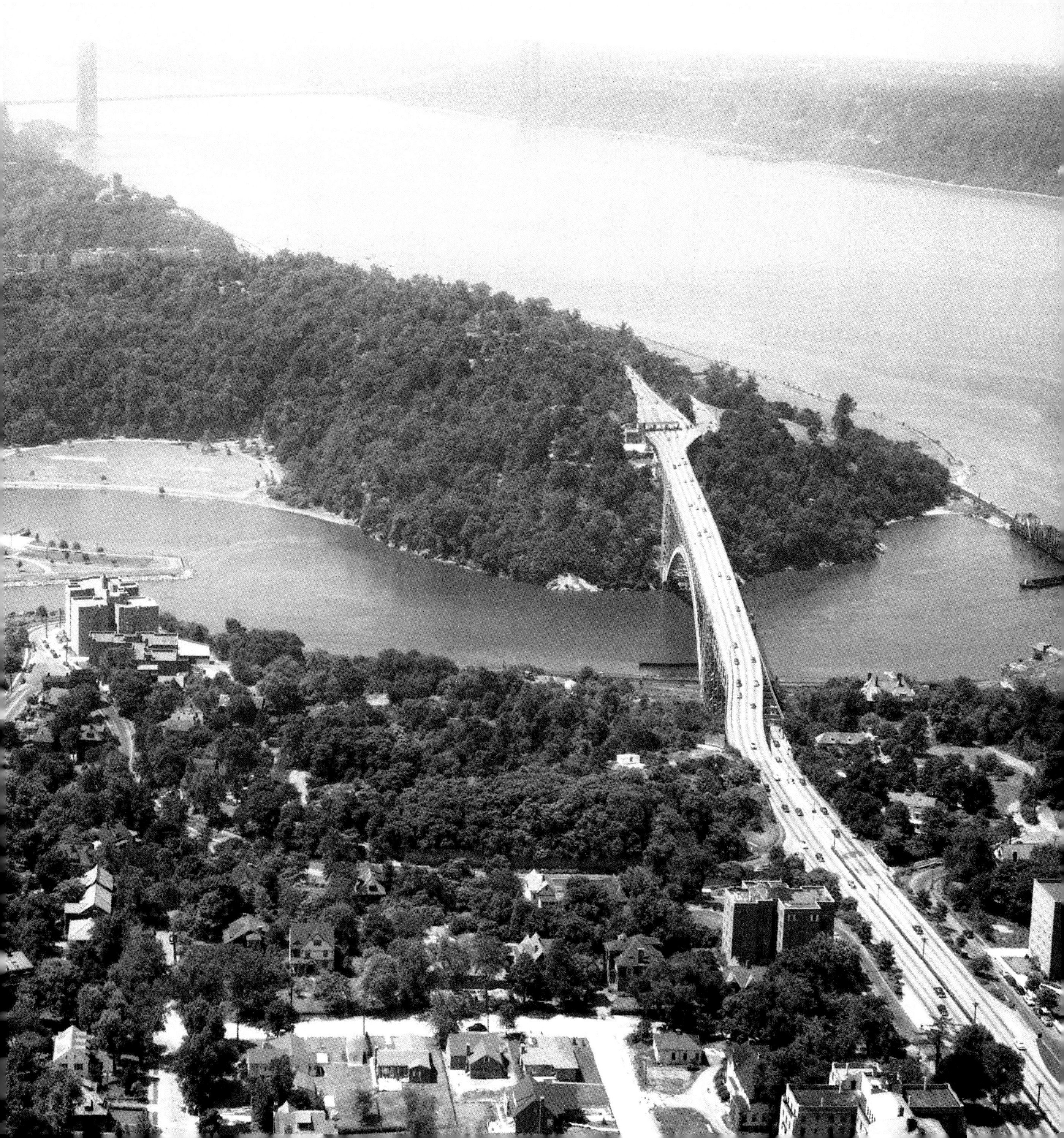

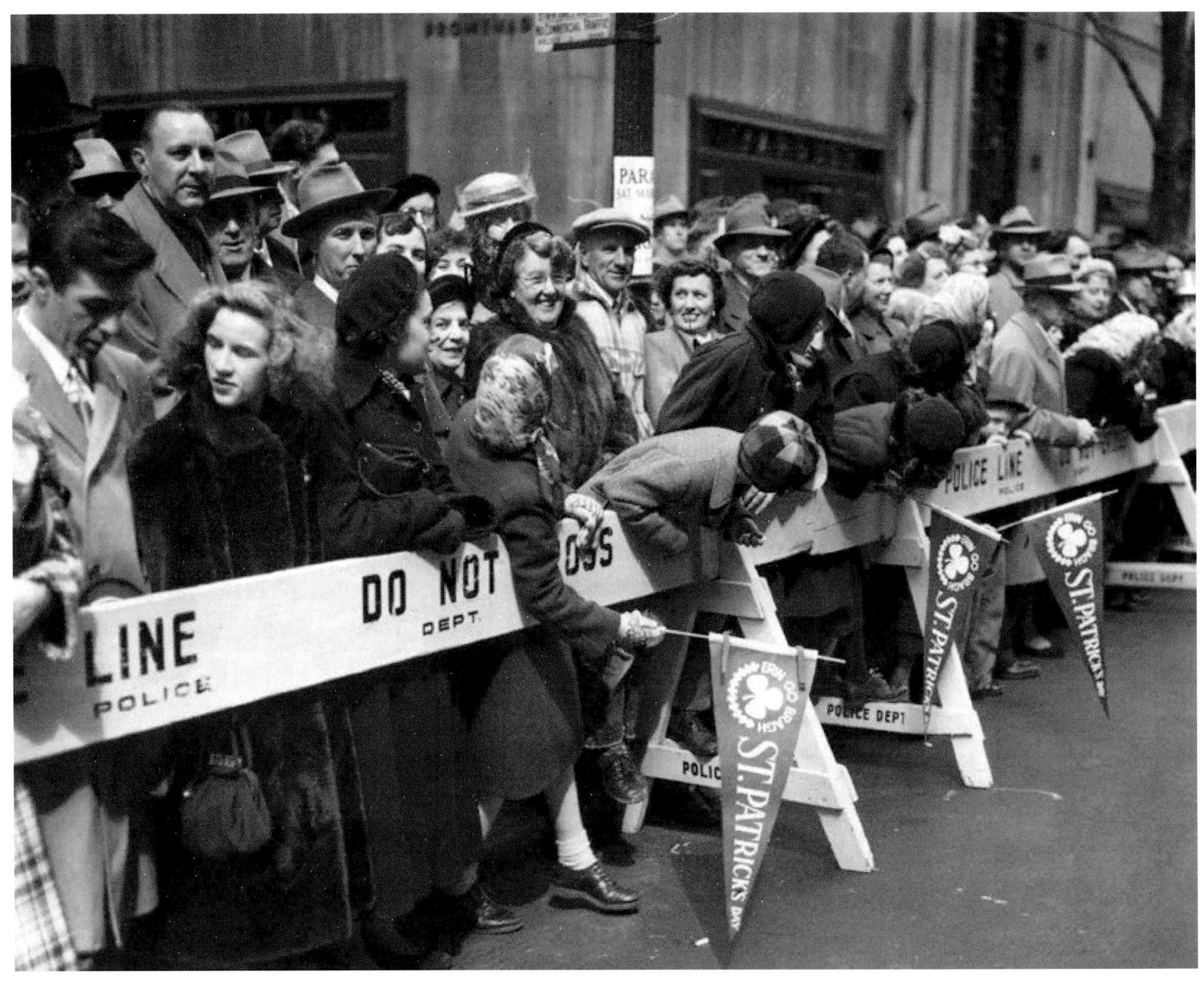

Saint Patrick's Day spectators are seen here on Fifth Avenue in Manhattan, near Rockefeller Center and Saint Patrick's Cathedral. Roger Higgins took the photo in 1951.

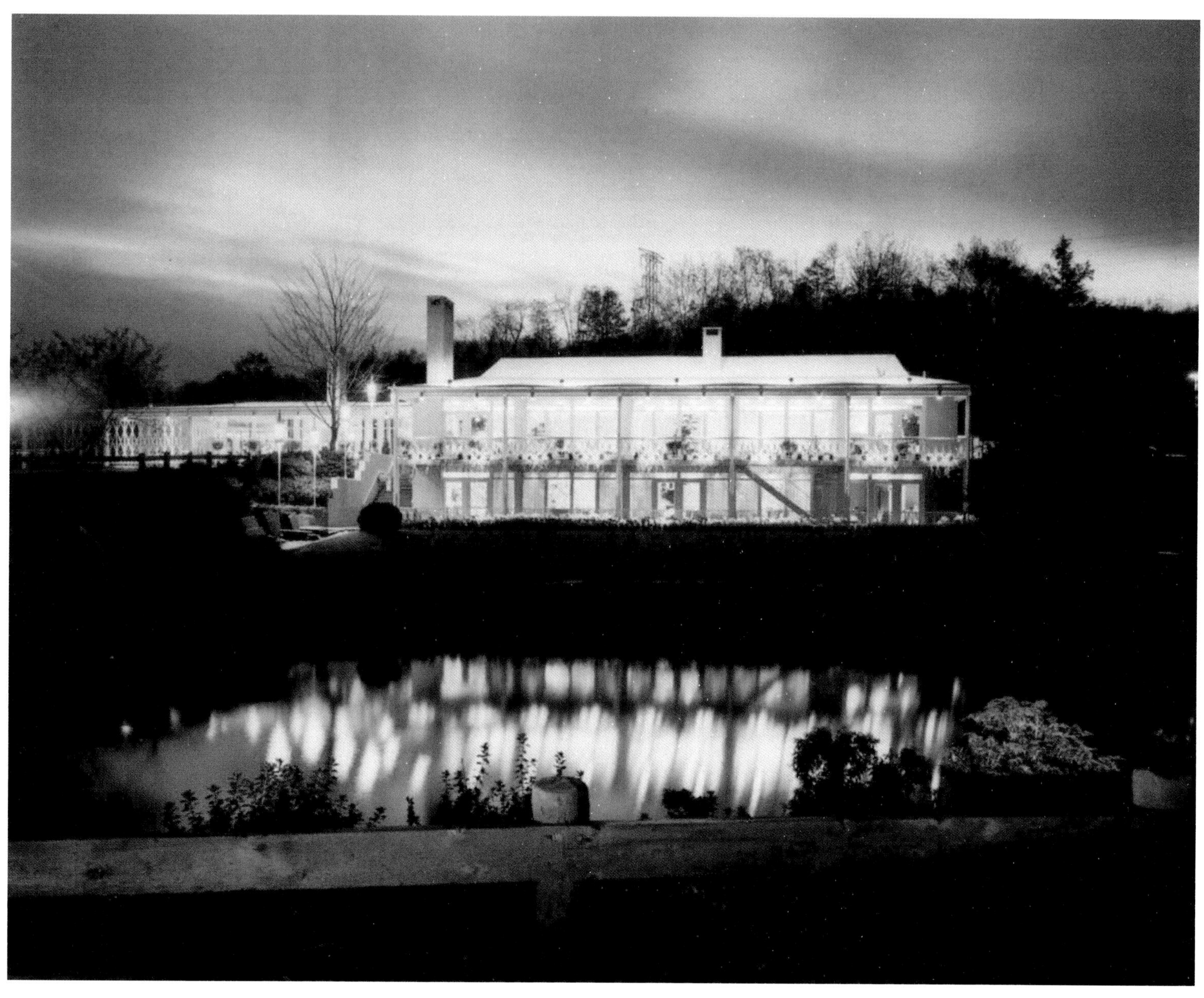

Patricia Murphy's Candlelight Restaurant on Yonker's Central Avenue was a favorite dining destination for people from Westchester County and the Bronx. The restaurant was part of a chain.

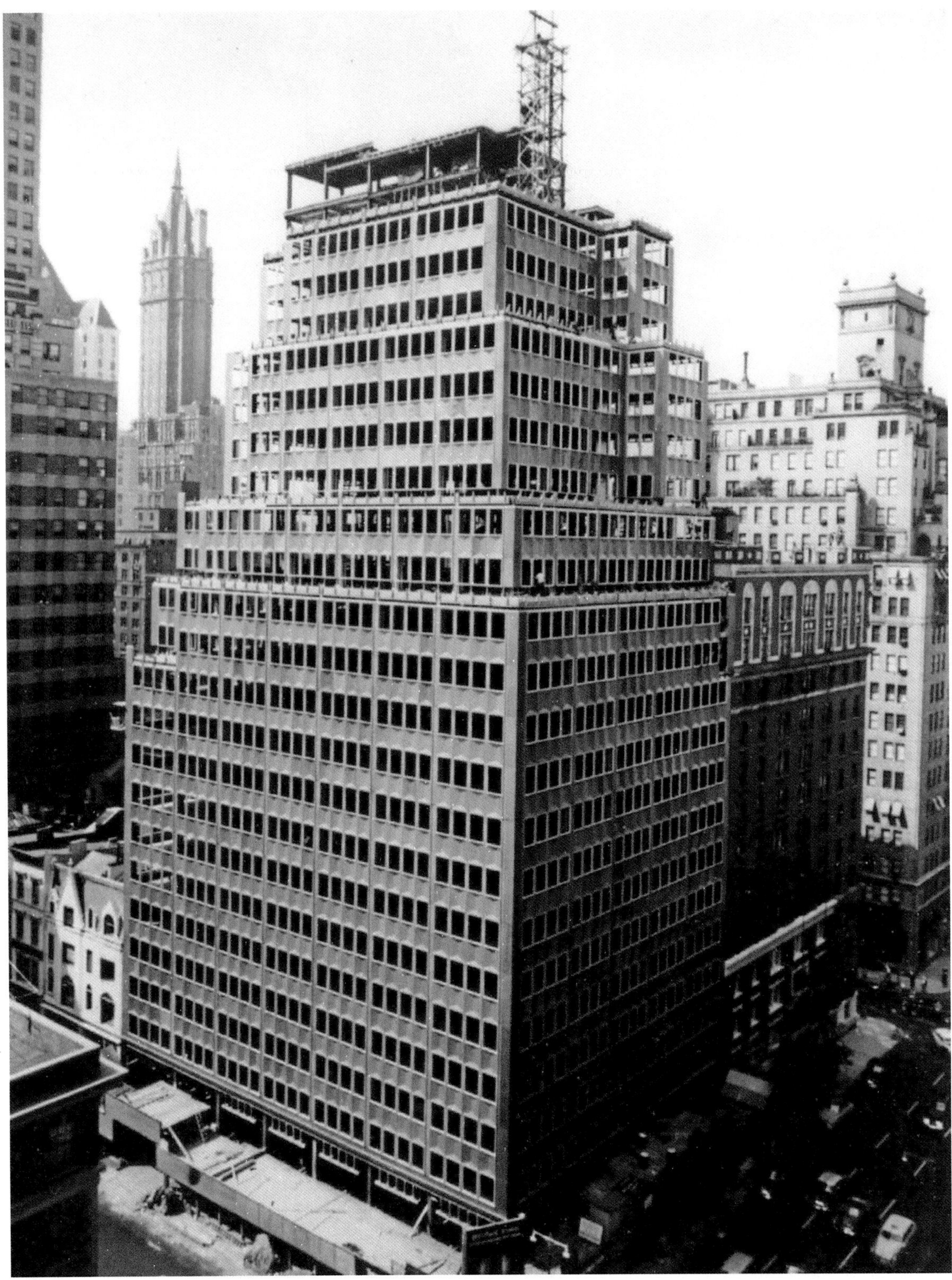

A 22-story building under construction at 57th Street in Manhattan was completed at record pace in 1954. It took 61 workers nine and a half hours to cover the entire building in prefabricated aluminum sheets.

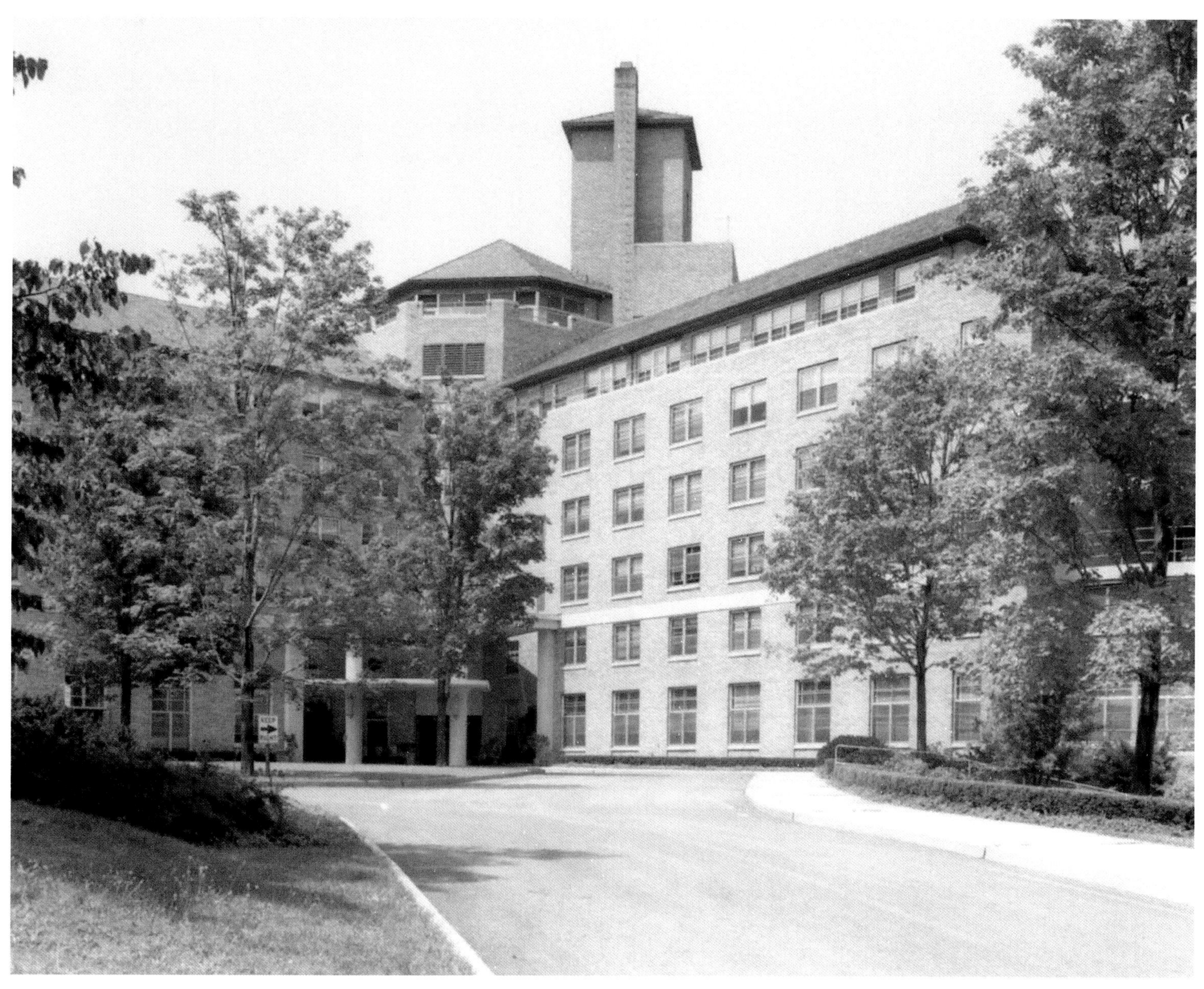

John Andrus Memorial Home in Hastings-on-Hudson is shown here in 1955, shortly after its opening. Set on 26 acres near the Hudson River, the nursing home was established by Helen Andrus Benedict (1888–1969), the youngest daughter of John E. Andrus (1841–1934). Both father and daughter were local philanthropists.

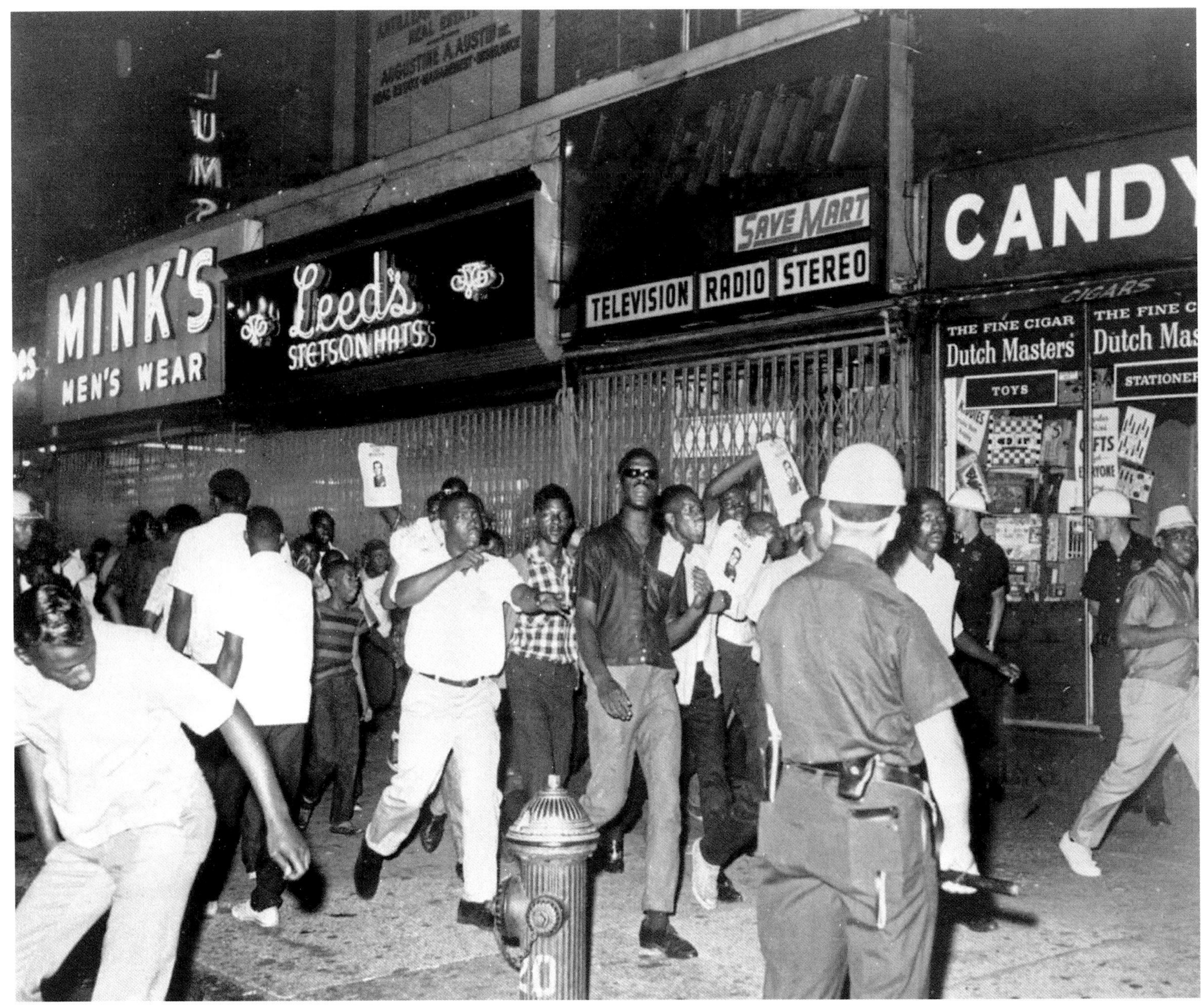

The fatal shooting of a 15-year-old African-American youth by a white police officer was followed by rioting in Harlem in July of 1964. Two days of rioting led to more than 100 injuries and hundreds of arrests. The riot foreshadowed much greater social clashes in Newark and Watts later in the decade.

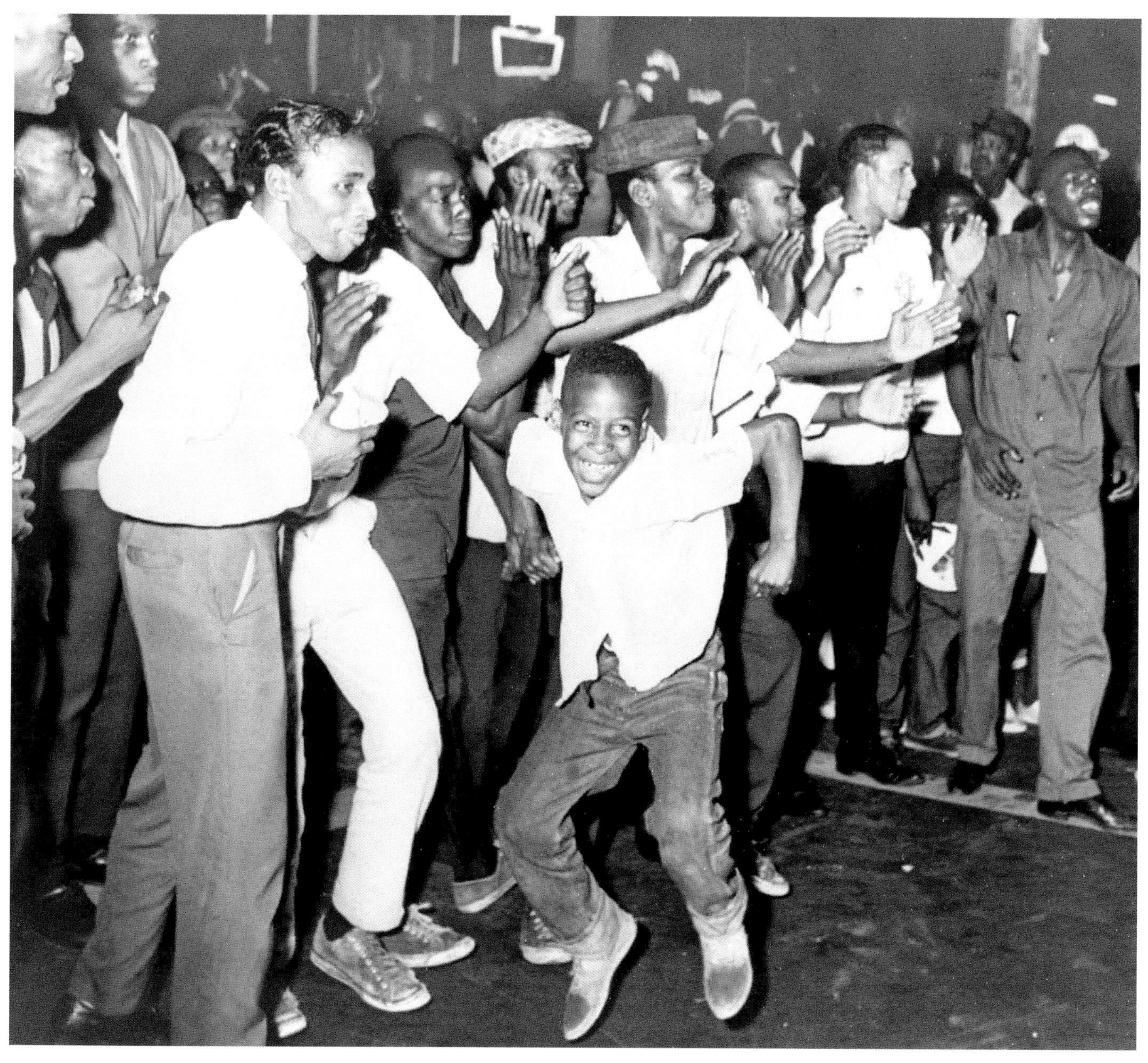

A Harlem crowd is seen here taunting police on Lenox Avenue during the summer disturbances of 1964. Stanley Wolfson captured the scene on film.

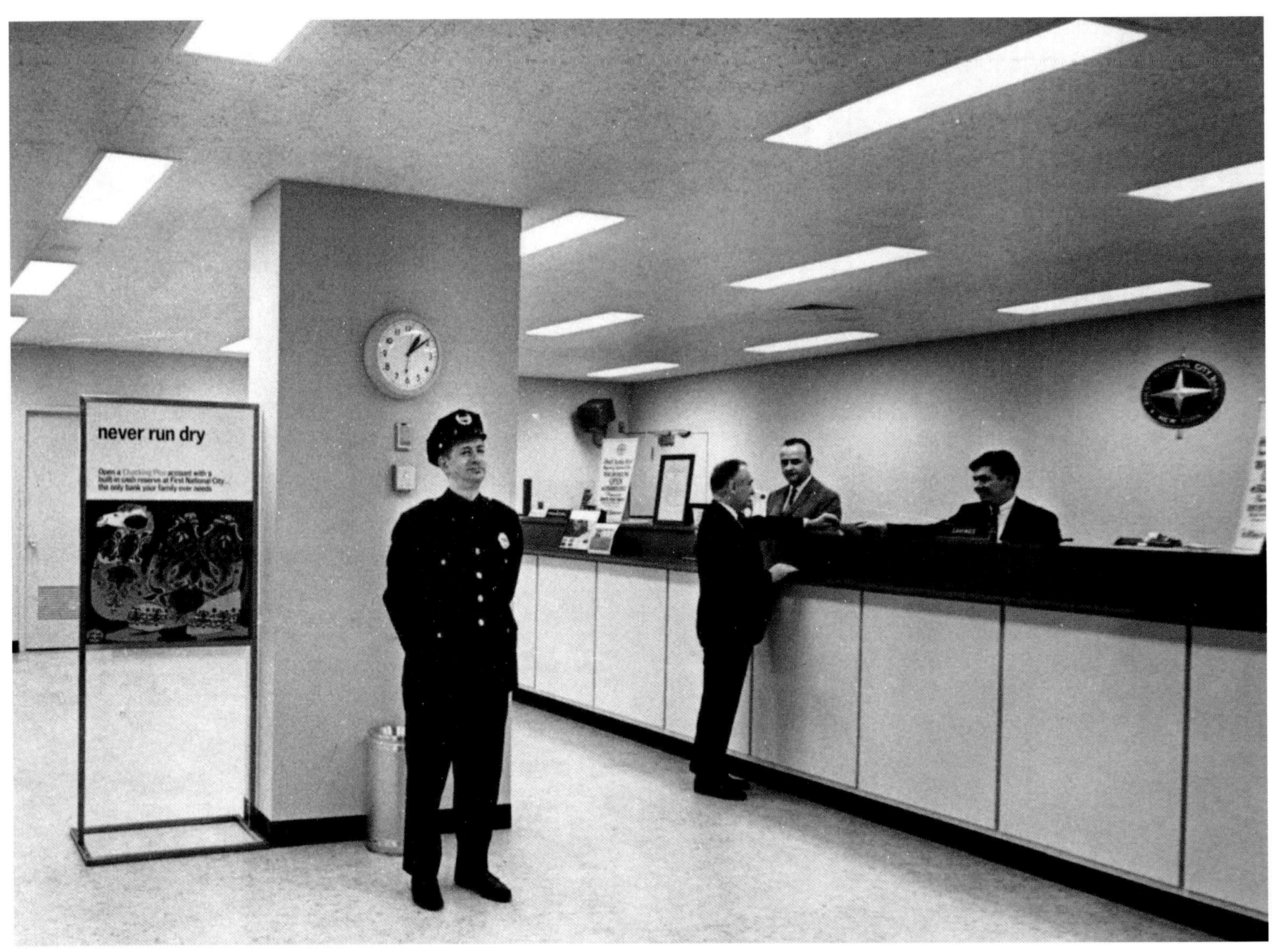

The Bronx First National Bank at Hunt's Point was photographed by Nat Fein (1914–2000) in 1967. Hunt's Point is located between the Bruckner Expressway and the Bronx River Parkway and is home to one of the largest food distribution centers in the world.

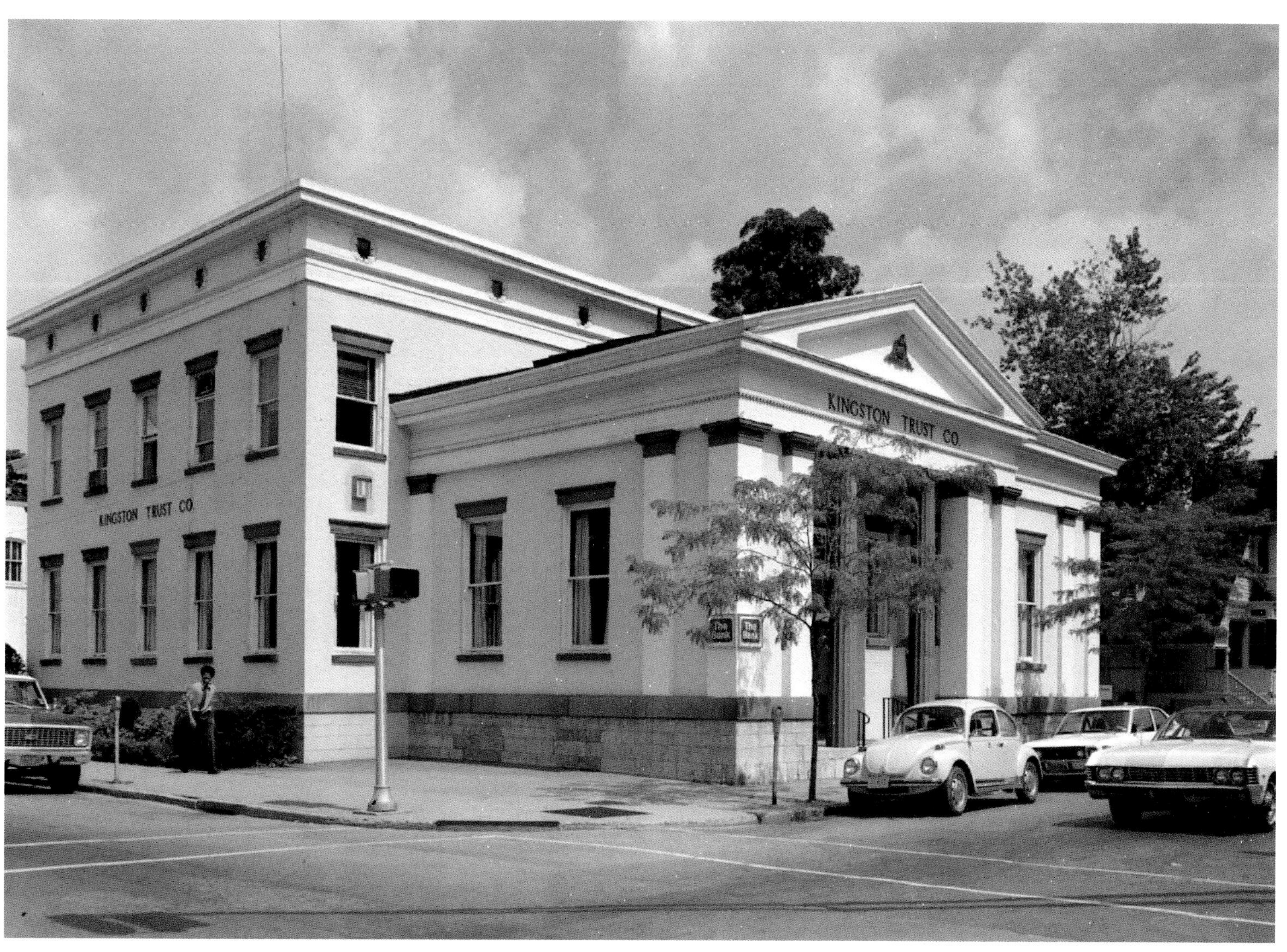

Kingston Trust Company was located at 27 Main Street in Kingston, New York. The building remains a bank today. The Greek Revival structure was constructed in 1839 and originally used as both a bank and a residence. Kingston has been known for its cement, blue stone, and brick. The town became the first capital of New York immediately after the Battle of Saratoga.

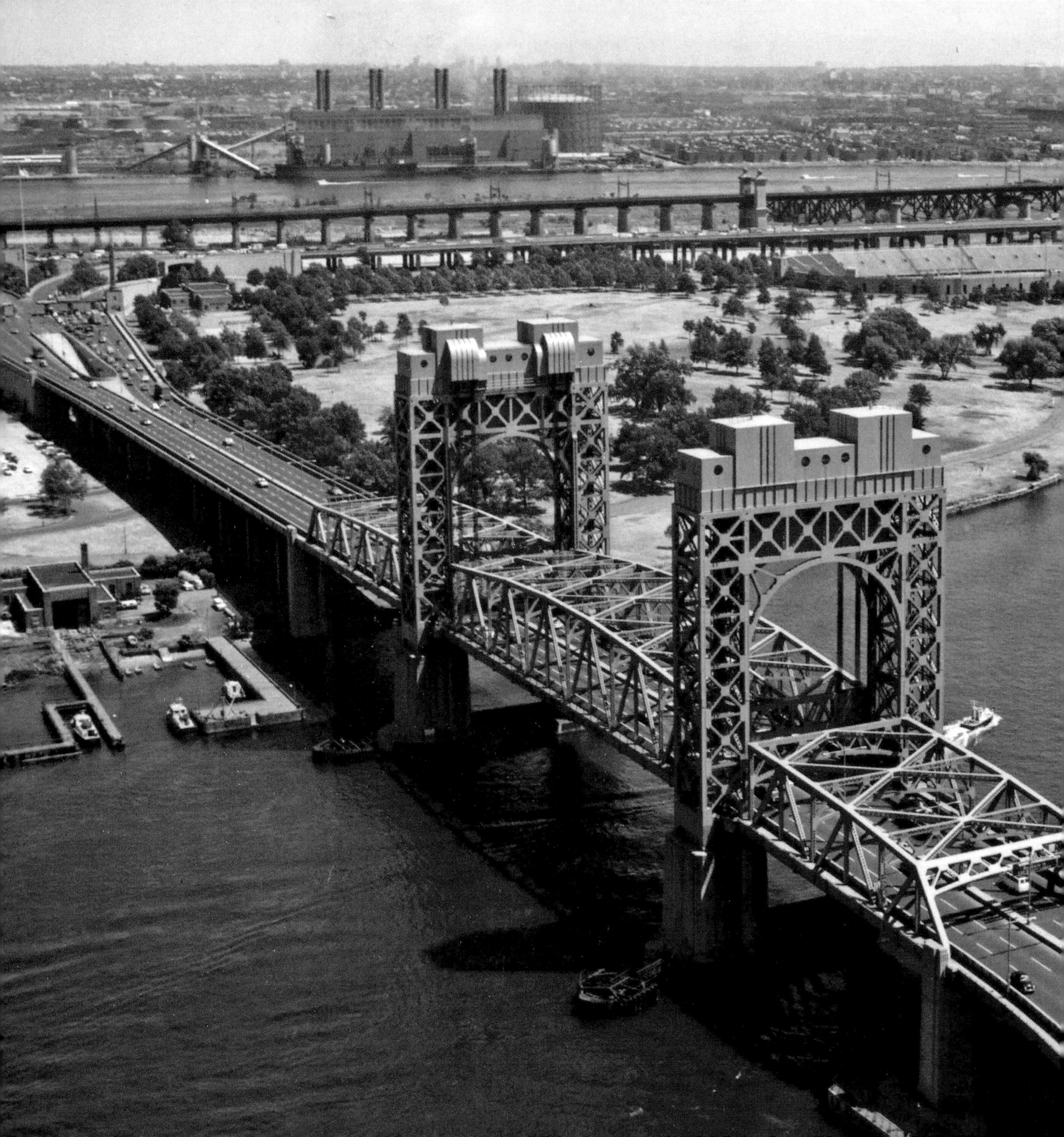

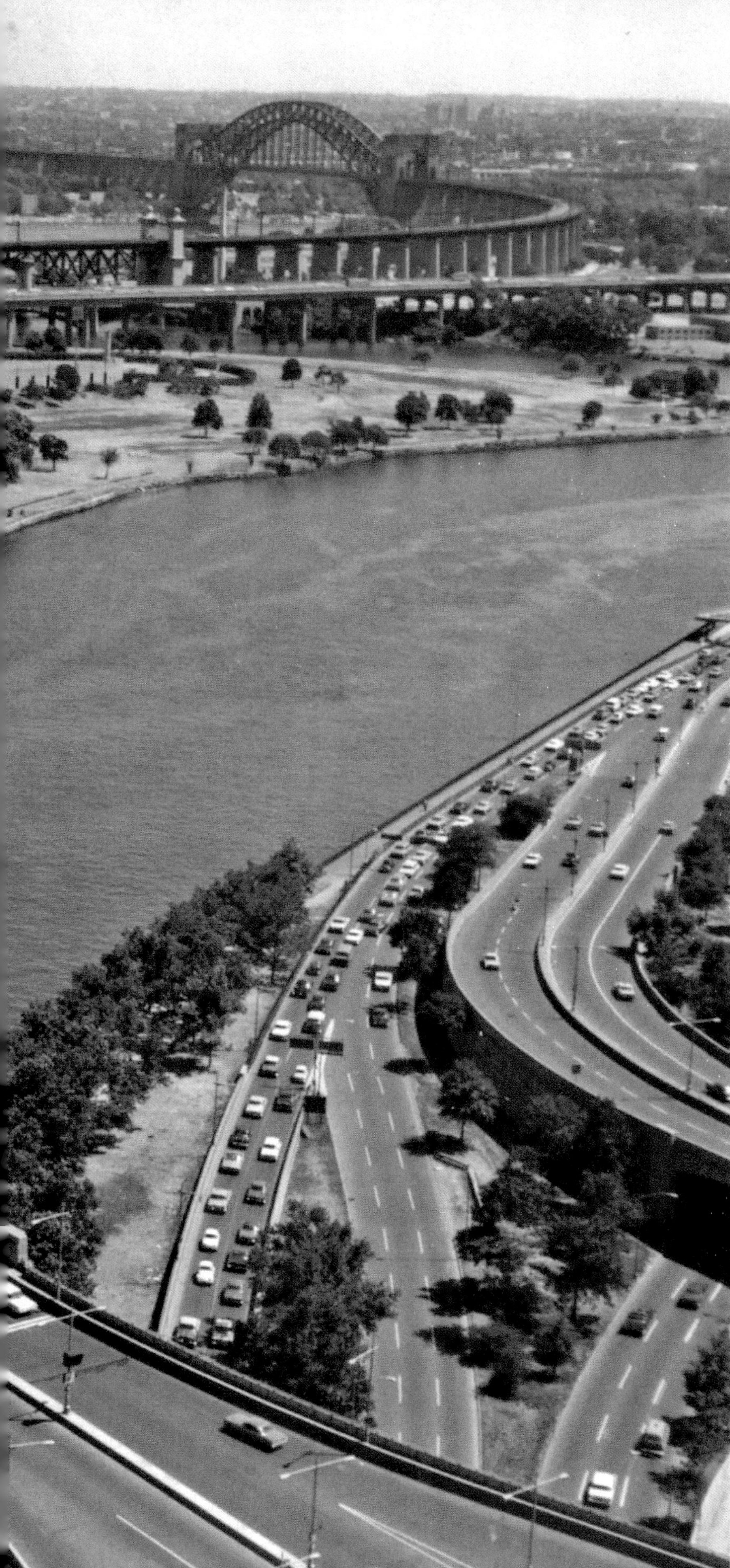

This 1965 image gives some idea of the vastness of the Triboro Bridge, which connects three of the city's boroughs, as the name suggests. In the foreground is the Harlem River lift span. The curve of the Hell Gate Bridge is visible in the distance.

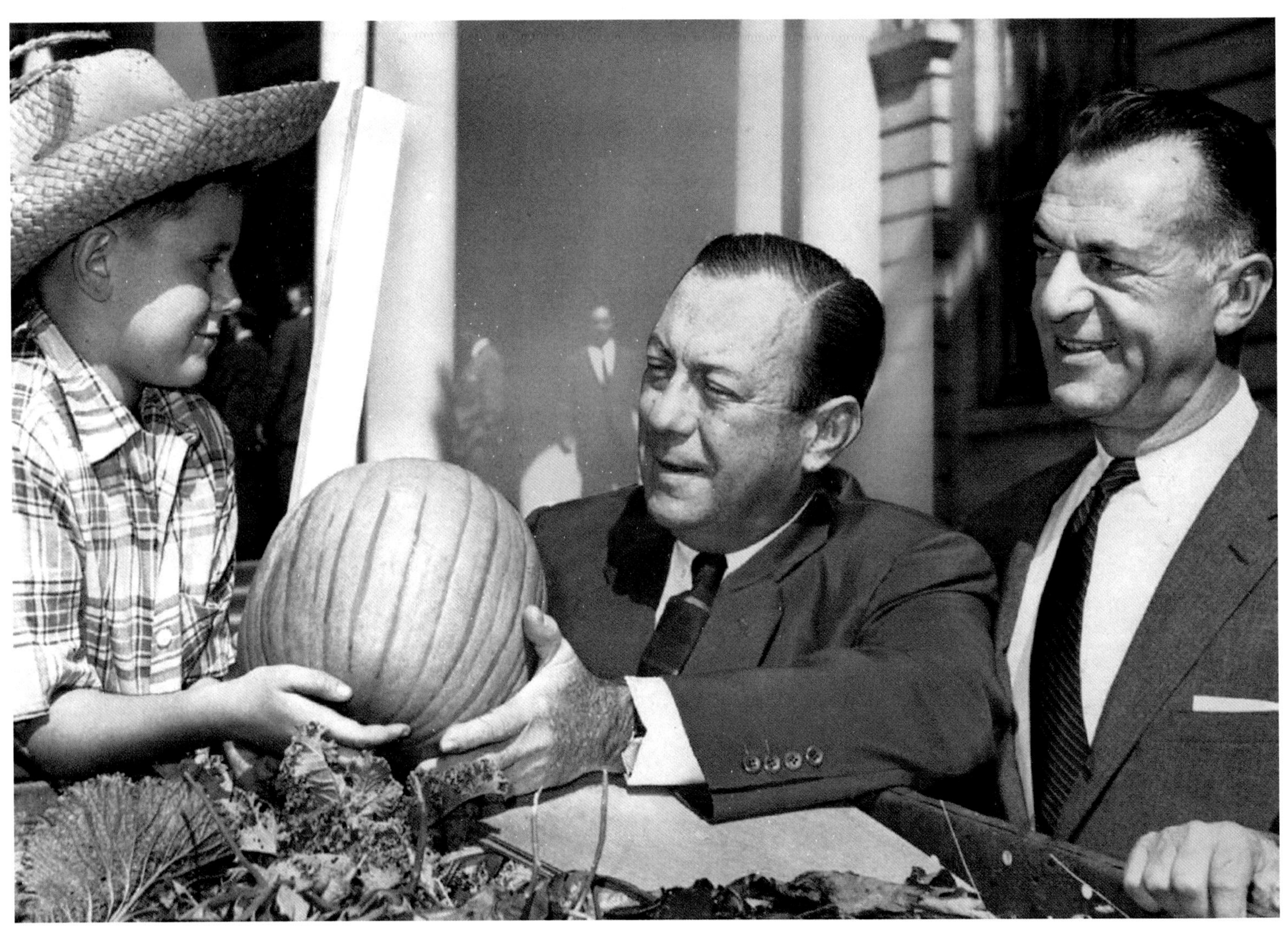

New York City mayor Robert Wagner (1910–1991) buys a pumpkin from a boy named Arthur Conklin at a farmer's market in the Bronx. Photographer Roger Higgins recorded this vignette. Wagner was the city's mayor between 1954 and 1965.

Notes on the Photographs

These notes, listed by page number, attempt to include all aspects known of the photographs. Each of the photographs is identified by the page number, photograph's title or description, photographer and collection, archive, and call or box number when applicable. Although every attempt was made to collect all data, in some cases complete data may have been unavailable due to the age and condition of some of the photographs and records.

ii **Steam Train at the Washington Bridge**
New York State Archives
NYSA_A3045-78_D47_NB944

vi **Lansing-Pemberton House**
Library of Congress
114344pv

x **Sunnyside at Tarrytown**
Library of Congress
1s01728u

2 **Apse of Second Reformed Church**
Library of Congress
HABS NY,56-KING,24-8

3 **Herrick's Castle in Tarrytown**
Library of Congress
3b32034u

4 **Harlem River Tourism, 1862**
Library of Congress
1s01468u

5 **State Street in Albany, 1865**
New York State Archives
Lincoln Funeral

6 **Albany Waterfront Panorama**
New York State Archives
Waterfront

7 **Garrison Hotel**
Library of Congress
LC-USZ62-70951

9 **Yonkers Panorama**
New York State Archives
NYSA_A3045-78_D47_YA

10 **Grand Central Train Shed**
Library of Congress
LC-DIG-stereo-1s01729

11 **Sing Sing at Ossining**
New York State Archives
NYSA_A3045-78_D47_OsP

12 **Sleepy Hollow Bridge**
New York State Archives
NYSA_A3045-78_D47_TaS2

13 **Train Wreck at Batavia**
Library of Congress
LC-USZ62-12981

14 **Hudson River at Chip Rock Reach**
New York State Archives
NYSA_A3045-78_D47_YA6

15 **Ludlow Street Workers**
Library of Congress
LC-USZ62-23305

16 **Albany's Museum Building**
New York State Archives
Museum Building

17 **Morning Tranquillity on the River**
Library of Congress
4a32413u

18 **Dobbs Ferry Crossing**
Library of Congress
LC-D43-T01-1506-L

19 **Spuyten Duyvil Junction**
Library of Congress
LC-D43-T01-1505-L

20 **Peekskill Bay Panorama**
Library of Congress
LC-D43-T01-1511

22 **An American Standard**
Library of Congress
LC-USZ62-116416

23 **Vassar College Grounds**
Library of Congress
3b43882

24 **Market Sloops and Sailboats**
New York State Archives
NYSA_A3045-78_D47_HuS3

25 **Bird's-eye View of the Harlem River**
New York State Archives
NYSA_A3045-78_D47_NB943

26 **Citizens at Garrison Station**
Library of Congress
4a03775u

27 **The New York State Capitol**
Library of Congress
97552

28 **Early View of Bronx Botanical Garden**
New York State Archives
NYSA_A3045-78_D47_NC25

29 **Bronx Zoo Chimpanzees**
Library of Congress
LC-USZ62-47701

31 **Steamboats on Albany Waterfront**
Library of Congress
LC-D34-T01-6062-L

32 **The Scene at North Pearl Street**
Library of Congress
114411pu

33 **Dobbs Ferry Hudson Line Station**
Library of Congress
4a03808u

34 **Ingersoll and Family at Walston**
Library of Congress
LC-USZ62-86626

35 **Blizzard of 1899**
Library of Congress
3c13361u

36 **Harlem River Speedway**
New York State Archives
NYSA_A3045-78_D47_NB954

37 **Harlem River Speedway no. 2**
New York State Archives
NYSA_A3045-78_D47_NB941

38 **The Hudson at Morningside Heights**
New York State Archives
NYSA_A3045-78_D47_NG818

39 **Rooftop View at 107th Street**
Library of Congress
3c07329u

40 **Site of Battle of Harlem Heights**
New York State Archives
NYSA_A3045-78_D47_NZ7

41 **Grand Central Depot at Turn of Century**
New York State Archives
NYSA_A3045-78_D47_NG72

42 **New York State Capitol Library**
Library of Congress
15347u

43 **New York State Capitol Senate Chamber**
Library of Congress
114396pu

44 **Old State House at Kingston**
New York State Archives
NYSA_A3045-78_D47_KS

45 **Peekskill Manufacturing**
New York State Archives
NYSA_A3045-78_D47_HuH2

46 **Steamer at Anthony's Nose**
New York State Archives
NYSA_A3045-78_D47_HuH21

48 **Peekskill State Camp**
New York State Archives
NYSA_A3045-78_D47_PS2

50 **Sleepy Hollow Lighthouse**
Library of Congress
4a24572u

51 **Flamingos at the Bronx Zoo**
New York State Archives
NYSA_A3045-78_378

52 **Trackside at Poughkeepsie Station**
Library of Congress
4a03782u

53 **Harlem Sports Facilities, 1901**
Library of Congress
3b44016u

54 **Albany City Hall**
Library of Congress
114373pu

55 **Harlem River Speedway no. 3**
Library of Congress
3c19117u

56 **Park Hill at Yonkers**
Library of Congress
6a15099u

57 **Downtown Yonkers from Park Hill**
Library of Congress
6a15089u

58 **Park Hill Homes**
Library of Congress
6a15094u

59 **Old Croton Aqueduct at High Bridge**
Library of Congress
3c36632u

61 **Harlem River Panorama**
Library of Congress
3c00103u

62 **The Rip Van Winkle House**
Library of Congress
4a09636u

63 Sunnyside at Tarrytown no. 2
Library of Congress
18256u

64 Morris Park Racecourse
Library of Congress
6a11231u

66 Main Street and Pleasant Square in Ossining
Library of Congress
124608pu

67 The Delaware and Hudson Railroad Building
Library of Congress
28878

68 Panorama of Albany, 1906
Library of Congress
6a11184u

69 Hudson Line Newsies
Library of Congress
03448u

70 Woody Crest Children at Lyndhurst
Library of Congress
3c08048u

71 High Bridge at Turn of the Century
New York State Archives
NYSA_A3045-78_D47_NB953

72 Vassar Lake at Poughkeepsie
New York State Archives
NYSA_A3045-78_D47_PuV6

73 Peekskill Trolley
Library of Congress
LC-USZ62-70953

74 Garrison Train Station, Early Twentieth Century
Library of Congress
LC-USZ62-91527

76 Moving the Broadway Ship Canal Bridge
Library of Congress
349948pu

77 The University Heights Bridge, 1908
Library of Congress
349950pu

78 University Heights Hudson Line Stop
Library of Congress
349952pu

79 Leisure Craft on Bronx Lake
Library of Congress
3b21696u

81 Bronx Lake Panorama
Library of Congress
3b21695u

82 Yonkers Marathon Champion James Crowley
Library of Congress
02969u

83 Rensselaer Polytechnic Class of 1911
Library of Congress
3b41717u

84 Syracuse University Freshman Rowers
Library of Congress
3b42074u

85 The Newburgh Waterfront, 1909
Library of Congress
6a11062u

86 The Henrick Hudson
Library of Congress
pan 6a11243

87 State Normal School at Albany
Library of Congress
6a11285u

88 Glenn Curtiss Airplane
Library of Congress
3b24453u

89 Curtiss Plane in Flight
Library of Congress
08242u

90 Classroom at Saunders Trade School in Yonkers
New York State Archives
NYSA_A3042-77_B7_F13_05

91 Teddy Roosevelt at Yonkers
Library of Congress
05332u

92 Bird's-eye Panorama of Albany
Library of Congress
6a11088u

94 The Albany Executive Mansion
Library of Congress
08917u

95 Ice Harvesters at Knickerbocker Ice Company
New York State Archives
NYSA_A3045-78_D47_HuZ29

96 New York Motorboat Club
Library of Congress
04031u

98 Sunset Lake at Vassar
Library of Congress
6a11133u

99 Suffragette Campaign in Yonkers
Library of Congress
3a25016u

100 Preparing for the 1912 Poughkeepsie Regatta
Library of Congress
10611u

101 The Stanford Crew Set to Race
Library of Congress
LC-DIG-ggbain-10613

102 Hastings Coach in Central Park
Library of Congress
00330u

103 Carpentry Class at Riverdale School
Library of Congress
3b35025u

104 Thompson Library at Vassar College
Library of Congress
6a11162u

105 Senior Parlor at Vassar College
Library of Congress
3c00847u

106 Harlem River Subway Construction
Library of Congress
14991u

107 Van Slyke Tobacco Factory at Kingston
New York State Archives
NYSA_A3045-78_10523

108 New York State Assembly Official Photograph 1913
Library of Congress
3b41614u

109 New York State Capitol with Staircase
Library of Congress
3b06973u

110 Old Dutch Church and Cemetery at Kingston
Library of Congress
6a11070u

111 Interior of First Reformed Church at Albany
Library of Congress
114333pu

112 Military Parade on State Street in Albany
Library of Congress
LC-USZ62-97739

114 Van Rensselaer Home Across the Hudson at Albany
Library of Congress
3b42157u

115 State Street in Albany
New York State Archives
State Street

116 Harlem at 135th Street
Photographs and Prints Division, Schomburg Center for Research in Black Culture, The New York Public Library, Astor, Lenox and Tilden Foundations
1168424u

118 The Rockland Ferry
Library of Congress
3c10683u

119 Inspection Tour at Grand Central
Milstein Division of United States History, Local History & Genealogy, The New York Public Library, Astor, Lenox and Tilden Foundations
733413fu

120 Bronx and Pelham Parkway
Milstein Division of United States History, Local History & Genealogy, The New York Public Library, Astor, Lenox and Tilden Foundations
700598fu

121 UNIA Protest
Photographs and Prints Division, Schomburg Center for Research in Black Culture, The New York Public Library, Astor, Lenox and Tilden Foundations
1228871u

122 Yankee Stadium of Yesteryear
Library of Congress
LC-USZ62-113346

123 Rockwood Country Club Ski Jump
Library of Congress
LC-USZ62-135333

125 View from the Yankee Stadium Elevated Subway, 1926
Milstein Division of United States History, Local History & Genealogy, The New York Public Library, Astor, Lenox and Tilden Foundations
700171fu

126 Traffic on the University Heights Bridge
Library of Congress
349957pu

127 Grant's Tomb and Riverside Church
Library of Congress
LC-USZ62-101739

128 Saint Peter's Episcopal Church in the Bronx
Milstein Division of United States History, Local History & Genealogy, The New York Public Library, Astor, Lenox and Tilden Foundations
702127fu

129 Claflin Avenue Residential Buildings
Milstein Division of United States History, Local History & Genealogy, The New York Public Library, Astor, Lenox and Tilden Foundations
700767fu

130 The Willis Avenue Bridge
Milstein Division of United States History, Local History & Genealogy, The New York Public Library, Astor, Lenox and Tilden Foundations
731106fu

131 The New York Central Building
Milstein Division of United States History, Local History & Genealogy, The New York Public Library, Astor, Lenox and Tilden Foundations
730278fu

132 Bird's-eye View of Manhattan
Milstein Division of United States History, Local History & Genealogy, The New York Public Library, Astor, Lenox and Tilden Foundations
730283fu

134 Grand Central Station
Library of Congress
LC-USZ62-85992

135 Hoffman Street in the Bronx
Milstein Division of United States History, Local History & Genealogy, The New York Public Library, Astor, Lenox and Tilden Foundations
701266fu

136 Park Avenue Baptist Church
Library of Congress
LC-USZ62-119067

137 Washington Bridge Traffic, 1932
Milstein Division of United States History, Local History & Genealogy, The New York Public Library, Astor, Lenox and Tilden Foundations
731076fu

139 First Avenue Elevated Railroad from Below
New York State Archives
NYSA_A3045-78_Dn_NY72

140 Southern Boulevard in the Bronx
Milstein Division of United States History, Local History & Genealogy, The New York Public Library, Astor, Lenox and Tilden Foundations
701837fu

141 Arthur Avenue in the Bronx, 1930
Milstein Division of United States History, Local History & Genealogy, The New York Public Library, Astor, Lenox and Tilden Foundations
700431fu

142 Commuters at Grand Central Turnstiles
New York State Archives
NYSA_A3045-78_Dn_NY28

143 The Park Avenue Firehouse
Photography Collection, Miriam and Ira D. Wallach Division of Art, Prints and Photographs, The New York Public Library, Astor, Lenox and Tilden Foundations
482705u

144 Triboro Bridge over the Harlem River
New York State Archives
NYSA_A3045-78_B17243

145 Approach to the Triboro Bridge
Photography Collection, Miriam and Ira D. Wallach Division of Art, Prints and Photographs, The New York Public Library, Astor, Lenox and Tilden Foundations
482574u

147 Mullaly Park Swimming Pool
Milstein Division of United States History, Local History & Genealogy, The New York Public Library, Astor, Lenox and Tilden Foundations
701516fu

148 The Grand Concourse
Milstein Division of United States History, Local History & Genealogy, The New York Public Library, Astor, Lenox and Tilden Foundations
701183fu

149 WPA Street-paving Project
Milstein Division of United States History, Local History & Genealogy, The New York Public Library, Astor, Lenox and Tilden Foundations
700607fu

151 The Park Avenue Tunnel at 96th Street
New York State Archives
NYSA_A3045-78_Dn_NY7

152 Sing Sing Prison Guard Tower
Library of Congress
LC-USZ62-119802

153 A Harlem Tapestry
Photography Collection, Miriam and Ira D. Wallach Division of Art, Prints and Photographs, The New York Public Library, Astor, Lenox and Tilden Foundations
482597

154 Depression-era Bronx Traveling Library
The New York Public Library Archives, The New York Public Library, Astor, Lenox and Tilden Foundations
434283u

155 Sidewalk Employment Applicants, 1939
Photographs and Prints Division, Schomburg Center for Research in Black Culture, The New York Public Library, Astor, Lenox and Tilden Foundations
1212152u

156 Hutton Brickworks at Kingston
Library of Congress
LC-G612-T-36128-B

158 Community Theater in Hudson
Library of Congress
LC-G612-T-36228

159 Myron J. Michael School in Kingston
Library of Congress
LC-G612-T-36242

160 Park Avenue Brick Church
Library of Congress
LC-USZ62-91575

161 The Rennselaer House (Fort Crailo), 1940
Library of Congress
122491pu

162 Arthur Avenue and Crescent Avenue
Library of Congress
12707u

164 Taconic State Parkway
Library of Congress
351751pu

166 Grand Central Station, 1941
Library of Congress
8c33198u

167 Grand Central Station War Bond Display
Library of Congress
8e04174u

168 Park Avenue and 136th Street
Milstein Division of United States History, Local History & Genealogy, The New York Public Library, Astor, Lenox and Tilden Foundations
701565fu

169 Cardinal Hayes Memorial High School Classroom
Library of Congress
LC-G612-T-41117

170 The Scene at Grand Central Station in Wartime
Library of Congress
LC-W3-9851-D

171 Performance at the Juilliard School in Morningside Heights
Library of Congress
LC-G612-T-43195

172 Servicemen on Harlem's 125th Street
Library of Congress
LC-W3-31097-C

173 The Poughkeepsie New Yorker Building
Library of Congress
LC-G612-T-43679

174 Visit to the Nurse in Yonkers
Library of Congress
3c32029u

175 Empire State Express En Route
Library of Congress
LC-USZ62-109770

177 West Farms Square at 176th Street, 1946
Milstein Division of United States History, Local History & Genealogy, The New York Public Library, Astor, Lenox and Tilden Foundations
702083fu

178 Baseball at Saint Vincent de Paul Institute in Tarrytown
Library of Congress
LC-G613-T-51065

179 Basketball at Saint Vincent de Paul Institute
Library of Congress
LC-G613-T-51062

180 Heritage House Classroom, Tarrytown
Library of Congress
LC-G612-T-51785-B

181 Dollar Savings Bank at Parkchester
Library of Congress
LC-G612-T-52555

182 Extending the Taconic State Parkway
Library of Congress
351763pu

183 Aerial View of Manhattan
New York State Archives
NYSA_B1598-99_105306

184 Harlem Theater District, 1949
Photographs and Prints Division, Schomburg Center for Research in Black Culture, The New York Public Library, Astor, Lenox and Tilden Foundations
1212153u

185 The Marble Hill Development
New York State Archives
NYSA_B1598-99_B1F64_51-1467

186 Aerial View of the Hudson and Harlem Rivers
New York State Archives
NYSA_B1598-99_B2F127_51-1874

188 St. Patrick's Day on Fifth Avenue near Rockefeller Center
Library of Congress
01203u

189 Patricia Murphy's Candlelight Restaurant
Library of Congress
LC-G613-66390

190 High-rise Construction at 57th Street
Library of Congress
LC-USZ62-96685

191 John Andrus Memorial Home at Hastings-on-Hudson
Library of Congress
LC-G613-67819

192 Harlem Rioters
Library of Congress
3c36895u

193 Harlem Taunts
Library of Congress
3c36929u

194 First National Bank at Hunt's Point
Library of Congress
12703u

195 Kingston Trust Company
Library of Congress
124086pu

197 Triboro Bridge and Hell Gate Bridge from the Air
Milstein Division of United States History, Local History & Genealogy, The New York Public Library, Astor, Lenox and Tilden Foundations
731002fu

198 Farmer's Market Commerce
Library of Congress
12706u

HISTORIC PHOTOS OF

THE HUDSON LINE

For thousands of years prior to Henry Hudson's voyage, the Hudson River was a vital commercial and strategic route for the indigenous peoples who settled near its banks. The river's importance continued for centuries afterward, linking the great trading center of Manhattan with remote places upstate and beyond. In Revolutionary times, the successful struggle for the Hudson was key to American victory over the power of the British military.

The Hudson River railroad succeeded earlier modes of transportation in the Hudson Valley—the river sloop, the Albany Post Road, the steamboat, and the Erie Canal. The Hudson Line was both an early product of America's industrial age and a catalyst for the intense and complex developments of that age.

The advent of photography coincided with the inauguration of the Hudson River railroad, and American photographers were on-hand to witness and record the progress of commerce and community in the villages, towns, and cities along the Hudson River Line.

WWW.TURNERPUBLISHING.COM

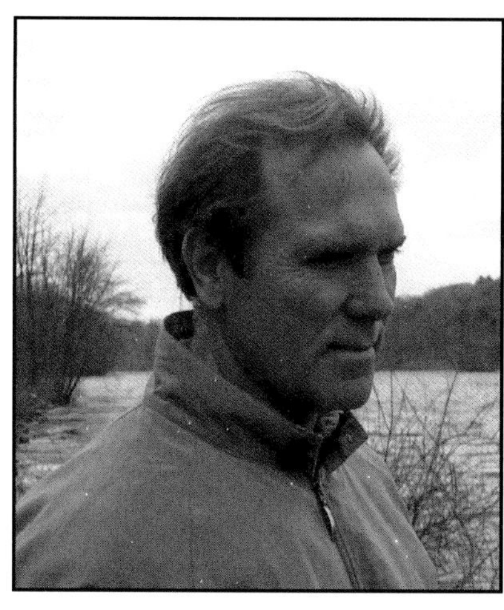

Henry John Steiner is the municipal historian of Sleepy Hollow, New York, and the author of books about the history of the Hudson Valley, including *The Place Names of Historic Sleepy Hollow and Tarrytown.* He is a regular columnist for the River Journal, published in Tarrytown, New York, and a contributor to the *Encyclopedia of New York State.* He has lectured on historical subjects at the City University of New York, the State University of New York, and various New York high schools and elementary schools. Among his favored subjects are the life and works of Washington Irving and New York State in the American Revolution. Steiner is a graduate of Pace University. He was raised in Tarrytown and has lived with his family in Sleepy Hollow for many years. He is a board member of the Historical Society Serving Sleepy Hollow and Tarrytown.